A HISTORY OF ENGLISH POETRY

A HISTORY

OF

ENGLISH POETRY

BY

W. J. COURTHOPE, C.B., M.A., D.Litt.

LATE PROFESSOR OF POETRY IN THE UNIVERSITY OF OXFORD
HONORARY FELLOW OF NEW COLLEGE, OXFORD

VOL. II

THE RENAISSANCE AND THE REFORMATION:
INFLUENCE OF THE COURT AND
THE UNIVERSITIES

NEW YORK
RUSSELL & RUSSELL · INC
1962

PUBLISHED, 1962, BY RUSSELL & RUSSELL, INC.
BY ARRANGEMENT WITH THE ESTATE OF WILLIAM JOHN COURTHOPE
L. C. CATALOG CARD NO: 61—13773
PRINTED IN THE UNITED STATES OF AMERICA

CONTENTS

ANALYSIS OF CONTENTS

CHAPTER I

Necessity of examining the progress of English Poetry by reference to the history of Europe as a whole.

Influence of Continental Poets on the English Poets of the Sixteenth Century.

The State of European Politics in the Sixteenth Century illustrated by the Diet of Augsburg in 1518.

THE RELIGIOUS AND POLITICAL SYSTEM OF EUROPE

Apparent Unity indicated by the objects of the Diet of Augsburg.

Want of real Unity shown by the international relations of the Powers.

The Papacy: Leo X. : His worldliness.

The Empire: Maximilian I. : His weakness: Corruption of the Electors to the Imperial Throne.

The Authority of the Church: Decay of the Scholastic Logic: The New Learning at the Universities: Good Works: Luther and the Legate of the Pope.

The Anarchy of Feudalism: Decay of the principle of Chivalry: Advance of Monarchical Power: Organisation of National Life.

The State of European Thought in the Sixteenth Century illustrated from European Literature.

THE RENAISSANCE AND THE REFORMATION

The Chivalric Standard of Manners and Morals modified mainly by influences from Italy.

The Catholic order of thought modified mainly by influences from Germany.

Castiglione's *Cortegiano*:

Chivalric basis of Education: Refined by Literature and Art: Standard of refinement in language : Preservation of the Standard of Manners prescribed by the *Cours d'Amour :* Influence of *Il Cortegiano.*

Machiavelli's *Principe* and *Discorsi :*

Machiavelli's philosophical principles the product of his feelings as an Italian patriot : Antagonism to the Catholic and Chivalric Standard of Morals : Influence of his opinions on Literature in the North of Europe.

Erasmus's *Colloquies :*

Conservatism of Erasmus : Endeavour to reform the existing religious and social system of Europe by means of Education : Attempt to reconcile the principles of Classical Taste with Catholic Doctrine.

Luther's *Christian Liberty :*

Luther's antagonism to the external system of the Church : Effects of his Mystical Theology : Opposition to the teaching of Aristotle's *Ethics.*

EFFECTS OF THE RENAISSANCE AND THE REFORMATION ON THE LITERATURE OF THE WESTERN NATIONS OF EUROPE

Spain :

The long struggle between the Christians and Infidels in Spain the cause of the intensity of Spanish Catholicism : Exclusion of the influence of the Reformation from Spain : Influence of the Renaissance on Spanish Literature : Characteristics of the native Spanish Genius : Its effect on English Literature.

England :

Effects of the Wars of the Roses on the Feudal System in England : Constructive political genius of the English illustrated by Sir Thomas More's *Utopia:* Mixed character of *Utopia:* More's ideas of Toleration.

France :

Deep roots of Feudalism in France : Struggle between the Feudal and Monarchical principles : The Crown aided by the Bourgeoisie. Victory of the Crown : Francis I. encourages the principles of the Renaissance. Antagonism to the principles of the Reformation : The antagonism between the Feudal tradition, on the one side, and the Crown and the Bourgeoisie, on the other, reflected through the whole course of French Literature, beginning with the *Roman de la Rose :* Coquillart : Marot : Analytic Spirit of French Literature, first revealed in Jean de Meung, developed in Rabelais : Absence of constructive ideas in the satire of Rabelais.

Résumé of the Argument in the Chapter.

CHAPTER II

Birth, Education, and Character of Sir Thomas Wyatt: Autobiographical allusions in his poetry: Wyatt's characteristics, originality of thought, and imitation of foreign models: Energy of Conception: Imperfection of Expression.

HIS SONNETS

Imitated from Petrarch: Decay of the love-poetry of the Italians: Growth of *Concetti* in Italian Poetry: Mellin de St. Gelays' attempts to naturalise the Sonnet in France: Wyatt translates his attempt into English: His harsh and metaphysical manner of poetical conception: His vigorous assertion of the principle of Justice in Love.

HIS SONGS

His best lyrical performances: His force and fervour: Examples of his love songs: Intended for musical accompaniment.

HIS EPIGRAMS

Imitated or translated from many authors: Want of Art in expression: Examples of his epigrams.

HIS SATIRES

Imitated from Alamanni and Horace: Alamanni; his satiric style; example of his allusive satire: Wyatt's own nature reflected in his satire on the Court and his Tale of the Town and Country Mouse: His sympathy with the Humanistic Reformers.

HIS DEVOTIONAL POETRY

Paraphrases of the Penitential Psalms of David suggested to him by the versions of Dante and Alamanni: His own treatment of the subject: Depth and strength of religious feeling.

Ineffectual efforts of Wyatt to harmonise the language in various kinds of metre: His Sonnets: *Ottava* and *Terza Rima:* "Poulter's" metre: Short-metred Songs with burdens.

Wyatt's place in English Poetry: Surrey's Verses to his Memory.

CHAPTER III

Birth, Education, and Character of the Earl of Surrey : Autobiographical allusions in his Poetry.

Surrey a type of the Chivalry of the Sixteenth Century : Double aspect of the Knight and Courtier : His poetry reflects the character of his order.

Examination of the fable of the Fair Geraldine : Surrey's Love Poetry merely a reflection of the manners of the time.

ANALYSIS OF SURREY'S METHODS OF COMPOSITION

His poems exercises on the set themes of love recognised by the Code of the *Cours d'Amour* : His adaptations from Petrarch and Ariosto.

Genuine feeling expressed in his Lines written in Captivity : Beauty and Nobility of this Elegy : A Mirror of Chivalric Sentiment, and an anticipation of the final downfall of the Feudal Monarchy in England.

SURREY'S REFORM OF ENGLISH VERSIFICATION

Survey of the changes in English verse from the time of Chaucer : Chaucer's scientific use of the iambic line of five accents : His use of the cæsura : Lydgate's failure to maintain Chaucer's system of metrical harmony : Continued degeneration of the system in the hands of Hawes and Barclay : Wyatt's inharmonious versification ; His misconception of the metrical structure of the Italian Sonnet : Comparison of the respective styles of Wyatt and Surrey in a translation of a sonnet by Petrarch.

Surrey's metrical reforms considered as regards—

1. The regular recurrence of the accent.
2. The limitation in the number of the syllables.
3. The incidence of the cæsura.
4. The rejection of weak rhymes.
5. The invention of blank verse.

SURREY'S STANDARD OF POETIC DICTION

Wyatt's diction based on the poetry of Chaucer : Want of refinement and harmony in his selection of words.

Surrey follows Wyatt in making Chaucer's diction the basis of his own : His occasional archaism : His aim to refine ancient literary practice by the conversational idiom of his time : New System of poetical Syntax founded on the study of Petrarch and the Latin poets : Antithesis and Zeugma : Examples of his constructive skill and facility of style.

CHAPTER IV

Distinction between the technical aim of the Court Poets and the poetical ideas of the nation at large.

Strong political tendencies in the English people reflected in poetry at an early date : *Vox Clamantis ; The Vision of Piers the Plowman ; De Regimine Principum.*

SIR DAVID LYNDSAY

Properly included by Warton in his *History of English Poetry.*

His birth, education, and character.

History of Scotland and the striking materials afforded by it for poetical moralising.

Comparison of Lyndsay's method of moralising with that of Dante, Langland, and Gower : Scholastic framework of his political poems.

His *Dream :* Analysis of the Poem : " John the Commonweal."

Complaint of the Papingo : Account of the Poem : Satire on the Court and the Clergy.

The Tragedie of the Late Cardinal : Modern political feeling ; Mediæval form.

The Monarchie : Uncouth versification.

Similar political influences at work in England.

"THE MIRROR FOR MAGISTRATES"

Suggested by Lyndsay's poetry and the tragic history of the time in England.

Increased importance assigned to History as a branch of Education : Examples from Lyndsay's poetry and Sir Thomas Elyot's *Governor.*

Revived popularity of Lydgate's *Fall of Princes :* Editions published by Tottel and Wayland.

Wayland's enterprise the originating cause of *The Mirror for Magistrates.* Warton's incorrect account of the origin of the poem : Facts of the case : William Baldwin : Design of *The Mirror for Magistrates :* Publication of the poem delayed through the action of the Privy Council : Various editions, enlargements, and alterations of the original work by Higgins, Niccols, and others : Sackville's *Induction,* and its relation to the poem as originally designed.

Influence of *The Mirror for Magistrates* on the imagination of the country.

Great mixture of styles in the different tragedies.

JOHN LYLY

His birth, education, history, and character.

Euphues: Origin of the title of the book : Analysis of the story : *Euphues and his England.*

Long surviving admiration for *Euphues:* Opinions of Webbe, Dekker, and Blount : Dryden's Euphuistic manner in the " dedications " of his plays.

Euphuism the product of the revived study of Rhetoric : Mixture of the sentiment of the *Cours d'Amour*, with the style encouraged by the New Learning : the style of *Euphues* intended to separate the language of the Court from the language of the People.

Flattery of the Queen : Influence of the royal taste in the construction of the Euphuistic style : Elizabeth's love of logical disputation.

Sidney's opposition to the Euphuistic school at Court : His Sonnet against the Euphuistic style.

Characteristics of Euphuism : Metaphors drawn from Scholastic Natural History : Antithesis : Alliteration : Cultivation of " Wit " in courtly circles.

Downfall of the Euphuistic manner with the hereditary dynasty in 1688 : Opposing influence of the *Tatler* and the *Spectator*.

Merits of Lyly : abiding influence of *Euphues* on the construction of English prose.

CHAPTER VIII

Changes in the education of the Knightly Class.

SIR PHILIP SIDNEY

His birth and education :

Travels on the Continent : His friendship with Languet : Residence in Venice : Instruction in horsemanship by Pugliano at Vienna : Returns to England : Nature of employment at Court : Embassy to the Emperor Rudolph : Subscription to Frobisher's Expedition : Anxious to serve with John Casimir in the Low Countries : Desirous to retire from Court : Languet's disapproval of the manners of the English Court : Sidney at the head of a literary party at Court : Quarrel with the Earl of Oxford : Protests against the Queen's marriage with the Duke of Anjou : Obliged to leave the Court : Retires to Wilton : Returns to Court : Takes part in the Tournament held in honour of the visit of the Duke of Anjou : Death of Languet : Sidney's acquaintance with Giordano Bruno : Anxious to take part in Sir Humphrey Gilbert's voyage to Newfoundland : Obtains a charter for the colonisation of America : Attempts to join Drake in his expedition to America : Appointed Governor of Flushing : Surprises Axel : Invests Zutphen : Wounded in a skirmish with the Spanish cavalry at Zutphen : Dies at Arnheim.

Sidney's character : New conception of Romance.

"ARCADIA"

Development of the poetical idea of Arcadia in Latin poetry and during the Middle Ages : Transformations of the Eclogue : Union between the Eclogue and the principle of the Greek pastoral Romance.

Boccaccio, *Ameto :* Sanazzaro, *Arcadia :* Montemayor, *Diana Enamorada :* Sidney combines the ideas of Sanazzaro and Montemayor.

Story of Sidney's *Arcadia.*

Defects of *Arcadia :* Its hybrid character : Its affected style.

Merits of *Arcadia :* A lyrical outlet for the expression of chivalrous sentiment : Beauty of its pastoral descriptions : Allegorical mode of expressing antipathy to Court life : Prepares the way for the Elizabethan drama : Female character : Idealisation of incident : Human interest.

"ASTROPHEL AND STELLA"

Misconceptions by modern critics of the nature of the sentiment expressed in Sidney's sonnets : Their supposed biographical value : This interpretation opposed to

1. Facts of the case.
2. The character of Sidney.
3. The character of the Sonnets.

Specimens of the Sonnets : Analogy of Pope's *Elegy on an Unfortunate Lady :* Amount of reality underlying Sidney's Sonnets.

Summary of Sidney's life, character, and genius.

CHAPTER IX

EDMUND SPENSER

Characteristics of his genius : His birth, education, history, and character.

Allegory the distinctive feature in Spenser's poetry : Opposite opinions as to the interpretation of his allegory : Opinions of Milton, Ruskin, Dowden : Opinions of Hume and Lowell.

EXAMINATION OF THE DESIGNS OF SPENSER'S POEMS

Hymns to Love and Beauty : The result of his Cambridge education.

The Shepherd's Calendar : Origin of the name : Professed design of the poem, moral and didactic : Actual design, purely literary and artistic : Spenser's purpose to expand the tradition of the Eclogue : His obligations to Bion, Mantuan, and Marot : His own inventions : Technical motives : Experiments in the formation of a new standard of Poetical Diction : And of Metrical Harmony.

The *Faery Queen:* Professed design of the Poem explained in the prefatory letter to Raleigh: Actual design literary as in *The Shepherd's Calendar.*

EXAMINATION OF THE EXECUTION OF SPENSER'S DESIGNS

The Shepherd's Calendar: Unity of the design: Propriety in the Allegory: Unreality in the characters of the speakers justified by the traditions of the Eclogue: Sidney's criticism on the rustic character of the diction: How far just: Spenser's archaism the result of deliberate experiment: Contrast with Surrey's standard of Poetical Diction: Contrast with the standards of the Classical Revivalists and the Letter-Hunters: Spenser's attention to subject matter: His misunderstanding of Chaucer's style: Rustic effects produced by his adaptation of Chaucer's style: Features and general effect of Spenser's archaism: Metrical Experiments: Lyrical passages in *The Shepherd's Calendar* the prelude to the style of the *Prothalamion* and *Epithalamion,* and to Milton's *Lycidas:* General criticism of *The Shepherd's Calendar.*

The *Faery Queen:* Great variety of matter in the poem: How far reduced to unity: Upton's and Hurd's theories as to the unity of the design not tenable: Comparison of the *Faery Queen* with the *Orlando Furioso:* Secret of the Unity of the *Furioso:* The poem not seriously romantic; Specimens of its Irony: Ariosto's character and circumstances; Character of the *Furioso:* Materials of the poem: Their treatment by Pulci and Boiardo: Ariosto's Philosophy: His feeling for Chivalry: His sense of Humour: His genius as a Painter: Harmonious fusion of all his materials in his style: Spenser's misunderstanding of Ariosto's motives: His own aim in the *Faery Queen:* How far he was able to apply his poetical principles to his subject: Propriety of the allegory in the First and Second Books: Collapse of the allegorical principle in the remaining books: Comparison of the narrative methods of Ariosto and Spenser: Fight between Orlando and the Ork: Fight between the Red-Cross Knight and the Dragon: Ariosto's superiority to Spenser as a story-teller: Superiority of Spenser to Ariosto in sublimity of Feeling: In Delicacy; In Allegorical Painting: Specimens of Allegorical Painting in Ariosto and Spenser: Comparison between Ariosto and Spenser as word-painters: Spenser a great metrical Musician as well as a great Word-Painter: His construction of the Spenser stanza; Variety and beauty of its metrical effects.

SPENSER'S PLACE IN THE HISTORY OF ENGLISH POETRY

Not to be ranked with Homer, Dante, and Shakespeare: Nor with Chaucer, Ariosto, and Cervantes: His genius in Poetry resembles that of Sidney in Romance.

Spenser, the Poet of Chivalry.

His ideas of Chivalry rendered unpractical by the nature of Court life: His picture of the perfect courtier in *Mother Hubberd's Tale:* His flattering allegories of the Queen: His own distresses as a suitor at Court: Illustrated from *Mother Hubberd's Tale.*

Spenser the Poet of Mediæval Allegory.

The successor of Dante and Langland : Contrast between the allegory of Spenser and the allegory of Dante and Langland : Effects of the Reformation on Allegorical Interpretation.

The beauty of Spenser's poetry derived, not from his subject matter, but from the beauty of his own mind : His power of harmonising opposite ideas : Illustrated from the Second Book of the *Faery Queen :* Poetry and Religion.

CHAPTER X

Reflection of the Change in Taste in the later Miscellanies of Elizabeth's reign : *The Phœnix Nest ; England's Helicon ; England's Parnassus ; The Poetical Rhapsody.*

Growth of the Critical spirit : Illustrated by the Critical Treatises published in the latter half of the sixteenth century.

Wilson's *Art of Rhetoric :* Not relating to Poetry.

Gascoigne's *Notes of Instruction concerning the Making of Verse :* Remarks on the nature of English "feet" and on the cæsura.

Treatises advocating the adoption of "Quantity" in English verse : Correspondence between Spenser and Gabriel Harvey : Campion's *Observations on the Art of English Poesy :* Webbe's *Discourse of English Poesy :* His specimen of the English hexameter : Admiration for Spenser, Lyly, Harvey, and Phaër.

Puttenham's *Art of English Poesy :* His good sense and right perception : Contents of his Treatise : Remarks on the Cæsura.

Sidney's *Defence of Poetry :* Its contents : Arguments against the Euphuists.

Various groups of Euphuistic Poets aiming at different objects.

I. THE UNIVERSITY SCHOLARS

Gabriel Harvey : His birth, education, history, and character : His attempt to introduce the principle of quantity in place of accent and rhyme : Specimens of his and Spenser's hexameters : War between him and Thomas Nash.

Abraham Fraunce : His translation of Thomas Watson's *Amyntas* into English hexameters.

2. THE SONNET-WRITERS

Thomas Watson : His birth, education, history, and character : His poetical motives : Specimen of the Sonnets in his Ἑκατομπαθία : Spenser's allusion to him in *Colin Clout's Come Home Again.*

Henry Constable : His birth, education, history, and character : His poetical aims : Specimens of his style in the sonnet.

Other writers of sonnets : Lodge, Giles Fletcher, Daniel, Drayton : Purely ideal character of their compositions : Barnabe Barnes : Character of his sonnets : Marston's satire on him and other sonnet-writers of the time.

3. THE COURT POETS

Their comparatively unaffected style.

Sidney : Specimens of his lyrical poetry.

Dyer : His birth, education, history, and character : Specimens of his lyrical poetry.

Essex : His position as favourite of Elizabeth : Specimens of his poetry.

Raleigh : Directness and absence of affectation in his style : Specimens of his poetry.

Oxford : Coxcombry of style : Early chivalric manner : His most characteristic verse epigrammatic.

4. THE PASTORAL AND MYTHOLOGICAL POETS

General influences productive of Pastoralism.

Nicholas Breton : His birth, education, history, and character : His early compositions in Gascoigne's manner : Imitation of Barclay's satirical style : Adoption of the new pastoral vein : His *Passionate Shepherd :* Specimens of his verse.

Richard Barnfield : Birth, education, history, and character : Lack of matter in his verse : Originality of style : Specimens of his poetry.

Robert Greene : His Love-tales in prose : Specimen of his lyrical poetry.

Thomas Lodge : His birth, education, history, and character : Versatility of his genius : Specimen of his Sonnets : More successful in his Songs : First to introduce the mythological tale in the manner of Ovid's *Metamorphoses :* His *Scilla's Metamorphosis :* His *Euphues' Golden Legacy :* Origin of *As you Like It :* Specimens of his lyrical poetry.

Christopher Marlowe : Vigour of his genius : Exemplified from his *Hero and Leander :* His style contrasted with that of Chapman : Nature and limits of his powers.

CHAPTER XI

The English Drama the product of a long development : Schlegel's mistaken view of Shakespeare's genius.

The development of the drama determined by changes in the taste of the audience and improvements in the tradition of the art.

CHANGES IN THE TASTE OF THE AUDIENCE IN ENGLAND

The progress of the Stage from the Miracle Play to the Morality : Declining influence of the Church : Increased influence of the popular taste :

of the "Vice": Allegorical Personages: Neglect of external Unity for the sake of the unity of Moral Idea.

CHAPTER XII

CONFLICT IN ENGLAND BETWEEN THE PRINCIPLES OF THE RENAISSANCE AND THE REFORMATION

The Puritans: Their antagonism to the stage: Political prejudice: Attacks on the stage in various pamphlets.

The "Italianate" Englishmen: Their revolt against the standard of English morals.

GEORGE GASCOIGNE

His autobiographical poems and romances: His repentance: Whetstone's account of his life.

GEORGE WHETSTONE

His criticism of the contemporary stage: His *Promos and Cassandra*: The source of *Measure for Measure*.

ROBERT GREENE

His birth, education, character, and autobiography: His professional rhetoric: His Love Pamphlets: Marlowe's Influence on his genius: Examples from his plays of his imitation of Marlowe: His natural tendency as a poet: His Pastoralism and his Female Characters: Illustrations of his genius in his plays.

GEORGE PEELE

His birth, education, character, and history: Analysis of his *Arraignment of Paris*: Extracts from the play: Characteristics of Peele's genius as a dramatist: Marlowe's influence on him: Illustrated by his *David and Bethsabe*: Examples of his style in this play.

CHRISTOPHER MARLOWE

His birth, education, character, and history: Effect of his genius on the English Romantic drama: Mr. J. A. Symonds' opinion: Consideration of its justice: Influence of Seneca on Marlowe: Influence of Machiavelli's moral principles on Marlowe: His *Tamburlaine* (first part): Embodiment of the principle of *Virtù*: Illustrations of the principle from the play: Examples of the principle in the Second Part of *Tamburlaine*: in *Faustus*: In *The Jew of Malta*: In *Edward II.*: In *The Massacre at Paris*: Marlowe's style the natural vehicle for the expression of his moral and dramatic principles: Drayton's description of his genius: His value of Eloquence as a principle of

English.	Date of Birth.	Date of Death.	French.	Date of Birth.	Date Dea
David Lyndsay . .	1490	1558	Mellin de St. Gelays .	1487	155
Thomas Wyatt . .	1503	1542	Jean Marot . . .	1463	154
George Ferrers . .	circ. 1505-1579		Pierre Ronsard . .	1524	158
Thomas Phaër . .	circ. 1510-1560		Gui Pibrac . . .	1528	158
William Baldwin . .	circ. 1510	1565	Etienne Jodelle		
Lord Vaux . . .	circ. 1512	1562	Jean Antoine Baif ⎫ Other		
Earl of Surrey . .	1516	1547	Joachim du Bellay ⎟ members		
Nicholas Grimald . .	1519	1562	Joachim de Tyard ⎬ of the	Fl. circ. 155	
Thomas Churchyard .	1520	1604	Joachim Daucrat ⎟ Pleiad.		
George Gascoigne . .	1525	1577	Remi Belleau ⎭		
Nicholas Turbervile .	1530	1594	Guillaume du Bartas .	1546	159
Jasper Heywood . .	1535	1598	Philippe Desportes . .	1546	160
Thomas Sackville . .	1536	1608	Théodore Agrippa D'Au-		
Arthur Golding . .	1536	1605	bigné	1550	163
Barnabe Googe . .	1540	1594	Francois de Malherbe .	1555	162
Edward Dyer . . .	circ. 1540	1607			
Nicholas Breton . .	circ. 1545	1626			
Earl of Oxford . .	circ. 1545	1604			
Gabriel Harvey . .	circ. 1547	1630			
Walter Raleigh . .	circ. 1552	1618			
Edmund Spenser . .	1552	1600			
Philip Sidney . . .	1554	1586			
Thomas Watson . .	1557	1592			
Thomas Lodge . .	1558	1625			
Henry Constable . .	1562	1613			
Earl of Essex . . .	1567	1601			
Richard Barnfield . .	1574	1627			
Dramatists.			*Dramatists.*		
John Bale . . .	1495	1563	Etienne Jodelle . .	1532	157
John Heywood . .	1497	1580	Robert Garnier . .	1545	160
Thomas Udall . .	1500	1557	Pierre de Larivey . .	1540	162
John Still . . .	1543	1607			
John Lyly . . .	1553	1606			
Thomas Kyd . . .	circ. 1557-1595				
Robert Greene . .	1558	1592			
George Peele . . .	1558	1597			
Christopher Marlowe .	1564	1594			

Italian.	Date of Birth.	Date of Death.	Spanish.	Date of Birth.	Date of Death.
teo Boiardo . .	1434	1494	Juan Boscan . . .	*circ.* 1490	1540
fino dell' Aquila .	1466	1500	Cristobal de Castillejo .	*circ.* 1490	1556
ovico Ariosto . .	1474	1533	Francisco de Castillas .	1500	1552
hel Angelo . .	1475	1564	Garcilaso de la Vega .	1503	1536
vanni Ruccellai . .	1475	1526	Diego de Mendoza . .	1503	1575
oria Colonna . .	1490	1547	Luis de Leon . . .	1528	1591
nardo Tasso . .	1493	1564	Fernando de Herrera .	1534	1597
cisco Berni . .	1497	1535	Luis de Gongora . .	1561	1627
vanni del Casa . .	1503	1556	Lupercio de Argensola .	1563	1610
para Stampa . .	1523	1554	Leonardo de Argensola .	1564	1631
quato Tasso . .	1544	1594			
Dramatists.			*Dramatists.*		
colo Machiavelli .	1469	1527	Juan de la Enzina . .	1468	1534
lovico Ariosto . .	*v. supra*		Gil Vicente . . .	*fl.* 1502-1557	
vani Trissino . .	1478	1550	Juan de Temoneda . .	1510-1597	
vanni Maria Cecchi .	1518	1587	Lucas Fernandez . .	*fl.* 1514	
vanni Battista Porta .	1550	1615	Torres Naharro . .	*fl.* 1517	
vanni Battista Guarini .	1537	1613	Lope de Rueda . .	*fl.* 1540-1567	
rquato Tasso . .	*v. supra*				

CHAPTER I

THE INTELLECTUAL CONFLICT IN EUROPE IN THE
SIXTEENTH CENTURY : THE PAPACY, THE EMPIRE,
AND THE NATION : CATHOLICISM AND CHIVALRY :
THE RENAISSANCE AND THE REFORMATION.

I HAVE said that the purpose of this History is to trace
the course of our Poetry rather by the stream of the
national thought and imagination than by that of the
national language, and this involves a constant reference
to the state of morals and politics in Europe at large.
However the nations of Europe may have diverged from
each other in idiom of speech, character, and institution,
there is not one of them whose genius can be judged, like
that of the states of ancient Greece, as if it were the product of an inward, self-developed, energy.   They are bound
together by instincts derived from primeval affinities of
race ; by the traditions of a common religion, which has
supplanted their original heathenism ; by their joint inheritance of more ancient civilisations.   And therefore,
though the history of English Poetry furnishes a clear
mirror of the intellectual growth of the nation, this progress
is to be regarded, not from a mere insular point of view,
exhibiting the march of the Anglo-Saxon, or any other
single element in the constitution of the people, but rather
in its European aspect, which shows us the gradual blending of many opposing spiritual forces into the organic
conscience that now directs our national life.

We have reached a point in the history of our poetry
at which it becomes necessary to dwell with emphasis on

this design. In the last volume I endeavoured to show
how the Mediæval System of European art and literature
grew by slow degrees out of the decaying elements of the
Roman Empire ; and how the influence either of the
scholastic education, or of Christian manners, or of both,
discloses itself in the work of men like Chaucer and Langland. At the same time we saw how this mainly ecclesiastical mode of conception and expression was beginning to
be modified all over Europe by the reappearance of the
civic spirit, and to what an extent powerful intellects in
other countries, such as Dante in Italy, and John de
Meung in France, influenced the thought and style of
powerful intellects in England. This later movement will
be seen through the present volume to be working with
accelerated force. The sixteenth century is the great age
of transition from mediæval to modern times ; the chief
poets of the period work from the basis of culture provided for them by the Middle Ages, but they are alive to
all the influences of their own age ; and, like their ancestor
Chaucer, they avail themselves of ideas and feelings flowing in upon them from a foreign source. Wyatt and
Surrey are imitators of Petrarch ; Sidney is inspired by
Sanazzaro, George de Montemayor, and Castiglione ;
Lyly develops the manner of Guevara ; Spenser emulates
Marot and Ariosto ; Marlowe embraces the doctrines of
Machiavelli.

It is, therefore, of the utmost importance that we should
have a conception in outline of the manner in which men's
minds were working, and of the ideas which occupied them,
at the beginning of the sixteenth century, in the still
Catholic European community. For this purpose I shall
pursue a method I have already adopted. In an earlier
chapter I endeavoured, by a concrete example, to illustrate
the beginnings of the Renaissance ; and I selected the
Diet of Coblenz, in 1339, as an external indication of the
comprehensive and far-reaching theory of order underlying the society of mediæval Europe.[1] I now propose to
illustrate the working of the ancient system in Europe on

[1] Vol. i. chap. v.

the eve of the Reformation by reference to the Diet of Augsburg held in 1518. The professed objects for which this Assembly was summoned, the various powers represented in its constitution, the rival interests which encountered in it, the passions and divergencies which it disclosed, will give us a general idea of the contemporary state of European Order. When we have formed a conception of the organic whole, I shall then turn to the parts, and seek in the most characteristic literature of the sixteenth century what I before sought in the literature of the fourteenth,—a general idea of the movement of European Liberty.

I. Looking at the external form of Catholic unity presented to the minds of those who assembled at the Diet of Augsburg, there were many circumstances in the situation which might have hidden the approaching disruption of Europe from the eyes of a superficial observer. Suppose an inhabitant of Augsburg in the eleventh century to have fallen, like the Seven Sleepers of Ephesus, into a trance at the time of the First Crusade, he might have waked in the sixteenth century in the midst of sights and sounds not altogether unfamiliar to him. The Diet assembled professedly for the purpose of forming a European league against the Infidel. It was presided over by an Emperor, it was attended by the Legate of a Pope. The Pope, to encourage his secular coadjutor in his pious labours, sent him a sword and cap blessed by himself, as though the Princes of the Empire still shared the convictions and desires of their ancestors who listened to the exhortations of Peter the Hermit. But underneath this time-honoured symbolism how vast was the inward change! Instead of a stream of knights pressing eastward for the recovery of the Holy Sepulchre, the Crescent had become the attacking power; the tide of conquest now rolled from east to west. Constantinople had been in the hands of the Turks for more than half a century. The great Sultan, Selim I., having brought under his rule all the country between the Tigris and Euphrates, having vanquished the Sultan of Egypt, destroyed the dynasty of the Mamelukes,

and occupied Syria and Palestine, had consolidated his
dominions in Asia, and threatened to descend on Europe
by land and sea.

No less significant was the change in the relations of
the Christian Powers among themselves. The tendency
to harmonious action among the states of Europe had
certainly not advanced since the taking of Constantinople,
and at that epoch the Papal Legate, Æneas Silvius, had
thus described the machinery of what he called the
Christian Republic : " It is a body without a head, a
republic without laws or magistrates. The pope and the
emperor may shine as lofty titles, as splendid images ; but
they are unable to command, and none are willing to obey,
every state has a separate prince, and every prince has a
separate interest. Could they be assembled in arms, who
would dare to assume the office of command ? What
order could be maintained ? What military discipline ?
Who could undertake to feed such an enormous multitude ?
Who would understand their various languages, or direct
their stranger and incompatible manners ? What mortal
could reconcile the English with the French, Genoa with
Arragon, the Germans with the nations of Hungary and
Bohemia ? If a small number enlisted in the Holy War,
they must be overthrown by the infidels ; if many, by
their own weight and confusion." [1]

How was the spiritual power of the Christian Republic
represented at the Diet ? It is sufficient to say that the
reigning Pope was Leo the Tenth. Not devoid of a
certain ambition, Leo, a better man than Alexander the
Sixth, a better statesman than Julius II., was capable
of taking a comprehensive view of the true interests
of the Papacy. But he was, above all things, an Epi-
curean. " God," said he, soon after his election, " has
given us the Papacy ; let us enjoy it." He had many of
the tastes of his uncle, Lorenzo de' Medici, and used his
position to minister, though with discretion and judgment,
to his sense of what was humorous, curious, and beautiful.

[1] Cited by Gibbon, *Decline and Fall of the Roman Empire,* vol. viii.
p. 184 (Smith's edition).

His thoughts were rarely elevated above the enjoyments
of the moment, so that when he appeared before the
world in the character of a Hildebrand or an Innocent, the
incongruity was startling.   Was this a fitting representative of the Conscience of Christendom, qualified to direct
the energies of the rival nations towards a common and
noble end ?

Who represented the secular principle of authority
derived from the Empire of Charlemagne ?   Maximilian I.
was a monarch of generous and romantic temper, and of
large ideas.[1]   But the actual imperial power was curtailed
by the cumbrous constitutional machinery required to
call it into exercise : and the inadequacy of Maximilian's
resources, in proportion to his duties and responsibilities,
had often caused him to appear before the world in circumstances of almost grotesque humiliation.   Throughout
the Empire, the headquarters of what remained of the mediæval system, the feudal principle presented a spectacle of
hopeless anarchy.   The power of the Emperor was opposed
alike by the power of the Pope and of the princes ; the
power of the princes by the power of the knights ; the
power of the knights by the power of the cities.   Every
interest struggled for its own end and sought to neutralise
the action of the central authority.   Maximilian's main
object in the Diet was to secure the succession to the
imperial throne for his grandson the Archduke Charles,
who by the vastness of his hereditary dominions seemed
likely to be able to restore to the Empire something of its
ancient splendour.   The dignity of the position was also
coveted by Francis I. of France, and by Henry VIII. of
England, and Augsburg during the Diet became the scene
of negotiations between the princely electors and the
various candidates for the throne.   The names and offices
of the Seven Electors seem to breathe the grandeur of
feudal antiquity.   The Archbishops of Mayence, Cologne,
and Treves, were arch-chancellors of the Empire, and
represented the kingdoms of Germany, Italy, and Arles ;

---

[1] For an account of the life of Maximilian, and the state of Germany at this
period, see Ranke's *History of the Reformation,* vol. i. Book I.

the King of Bohemia, the Duke of Saxony, the Count Palatine of Bavaria, the Margrave of Brandenburg, were respectively chief cup-bearer, high marshal, high seneschal, and high chamberlain, and represented the various German princes. But the pledges and promises given and received by these lofty potentates in the course of the electoral struggle would probably have appeared sordid even to the burgesses of Gatton and Old Sarum.[1]

The authority of the Church as a whole was symbolised in the Diet by the presence of the Papal Legate, who was supported throughout Europe by all the forces of scholastic logic and of monastic discipline. Both in their time had done good service to the Christian Church. Logic had maintained the cause of Papal Supremacy when this was indispensably necessary to the unity of Christendom, and when St. Anselm laid the foundations of the great structure of thought which was carried to completion by the hands of the schoolmen. But lapse of time and change of circumstance had greatly decayed the power of this instrument of Authority.

The stronghold of the scholastic system lay in the Universities. The encyclopædic education, passing after the fall of the Roman Empire from the Imperial to the Episcopal schools, had been carried thence into Charlemagne's schools of the Palace, and these again formed the nucleus of learned bodies which in Paris, Bologna, Louvain, and many other cities gradually formed themselves into self-governed corporations. As the study of logic prevailed over all the other arts, it was inevitable that experts in the science of disputation should acquire a vast intellectual influence ; and the University of Paris, above all others, with its great college of the Sorbonne, was renowned for its School of Theology. Any departure from the strictly formulated doctrine and discipline of the Church was promptly detected and condemned by the doctors of this University. On the other hand, the course of events had done much to expand the rigid limitations even of the

---

[1] A very good description of the intrigues of the time is given in Mignet's *Rivalité de Francois Premier et Charles Quint*, chap. 2.

Paris schools. Though the curriculum in the University had come to be practically confined to Logic, Physics, and Metaphysics, this *régime* had not produced beneficial results either as regards learning or discipline ; and in the middle of the fifteenth century there arose a strong disposition to revive the study of rhetoric, basing the study of grammar, which accompanied the former art, more systematically than hitherto on philology. This tendency received fresh impulse from the taking of Constantinople by the Turks in 1453, which naturally caused a great exodus westward of men skilled in Greek and Hebrew letters. The fathers of the Council of Basle, in 1430, having recommended the study of Hebrew in the University, effect was given to the suggestion in 1455 by the appointment of a salaried professor in that subject.[1] In 1458 Gregory of Tiferno, the pupil of the famous Chrysoloras, was permitted to teach Greek in the University, and numbered among his scholars Reuchlin, afterwards celebrated for his critical writings on Hebrew literature, and for the prosecution which they brought upon him from the scholastic party.[2] The study of Greek was not at first admitted within the regular circle of the arts, and the University of Paris incurred the reproaches of Erasmus for the facility it showed in allowing ill-qualified teachers to give instruction in the Humanities.[3]

Nevertheless the new learning having once been admitted into the ancient system of University study was not slow to enlarge its borders, and its fortunes were promoted by many external circumstances. Of these undoubtedly the most important was the invention of printing, an art which was introduced into the University of Paris by Guillaume Fichet and Jean de la Pierre in 1470, the year before Caxton set up his press in England.[4] Opinions contrary to established authority, which in the days of Abelard had to be purchased in the costly MS. or by the personal toil and danger required to bring a scholar from some far-off country to the lecture-room of a

[1] Crevier, *Histoire de l'Université de Paris*, vol. iv. p. 223.
[2] *Ibid.* vol. iv. p. 243. [3] *Ibid.* vol. iv. p. 439. [4] *Ibid.* vol. iv pp. 326-330.

famous teacher, were now scattered broadcast for the
benefit of any one who chose to possess himself of them
by the expenditure of a few small coins. While the minds
of all were still agitated by this great change, the ideas of
mankind were enlarged by Columbus' voyage to America,
nor was it long before the established conception of the
framework of the universe was revolutionised by Copernicus'
discovery of the real movements of the heavenly bodies.

Meantime, while these new ideas appealed with always
increasing power to the human mind, the study of logic, and
the whole educational system connected with it, lost their
vitality. Scholars were anxious, above all things, to learn
how to dispute and to obtain the victory in argument.
Beauty, elegance, humanity of style, all that discipline of
thought and taste which implies that the powers of the
mind have been directed to some intelligible and practic-
able aim, were sacrificed to the vanity of mere intellectual
display. Stereotyped in forms, religion itself tended to
become more and more external, and in proportion as
the essentials of faith were strictly defined, the requirements of devotion came to be identified almost completely with the due performance of what were called
Good Works. In every monastery of Europe the duty
of the inmates was supposed to be discharged if the
appointed round of service, fast, or vigil was punctually
observed. In every University of Europe the student
was taught, as the end of knowledge, to aim at a flawless
syllogism, to see that his conclusion followed without let or
hindrance from his premises. In every town of Europe the
average householder believed that if he ate fish on fast-days,
went on pilgrimage to the shrine of some eminent saint,
attended mass, and confessed his sins, he had done all that
was required of him as a good Christian. The entire tendency of the system of mediæval education was, accordingly,
to exalt Form at the expense of Reason, and even
Conscience. The abuse reached its climax in the sale of
Indulgences ; and when the Diet of Augsburg was held
this practice had just been challenged by Luther. Summoned to appear at the Diet before the Papal Legate,

the Reformer had openly refused to submit himself to the Pope's authority.

As the schools and the monasteries were the pillars of the spiritual portion of the Christian Republic, so the fabric of secular authority in the Middle Ages rested mainly on the institution of Knighthood. We have already had occasion, in considering the poetry of Langland, to notice that, in the feudal conception of society, the knights were, like the clergy, an integral element of the Commonwealth.[1] It was their duty to maintain by their swords the order of things which God had revealed to mankind through the Christian Church ; and this high spiritual conception of their functions had called into existence a code of chivalry associated at all points with the usages of religion. The elaborate symbolical ceremonies performed at the initiation of the young knight were only an index of the standard of conduct expected from every member of the order in the days when the institution was in its glory. Knights and gentlemen were recognised as such not by their external position, but by the exercise of the virtues peculiar to their order. Loyalty, the virtue that bound the vassal to his lord ; Honour, the sentiment that forbade the knight to advance or defend his own interests by a lie ; Courtesy, the principle that taught him to give to each man the consideration due to him,—all these were cultivated by practical rules of conduct, which implied a strict social discipline and a large amount of self-surrender on the part of the individual will.

The standard of knighthood was the unwritten law that had long helped to preserve the unity of European society ; but at the opening of the sixteenth century many causes had combined to weaken its authority. What had become of the Godfreys, the Tancreds, and the Bohemonds, the heroes who had given character and glory to the early Crusades ? These men were the natural offspring of the great decentralising movement which followed the partition of the Empire of Charlemagne, the

[1] Vol. i. p. 229.

representatives of the inherited rights and the local
liberties that sprang out of the decay of the imperial
power. Europe in their days presented in a real sense
the spectacle of a Christian Republic, a multitudinous
society of petty sovereigns, each of whom was almost
absolute within his own domains, yet was associated with
his neighbours by ties loose but strong on the imaginative
and spiritual side, by the sympathies of a universal faith,
and by the influence of customs derived from a common,
if barbarous, ancestry. As the struggle for existence constantly proceeded in the midst of this state of organised
anarchy, the less powerful of the feudal principalities disappeared in the ordinary course of nature, some of them
swallowed up by over-lords, some voluntarily surrendered
to superiors for the sake of protection, some passing away
by marriage into a different family, and others again
lapsing from defect of inheritance into the possessions of
the Crown.

Thus feudal society gradually separated itself into
large groups, defined with more or less precision by the
limits of race and nationality. Europe began to settle
down into a new order, composed of rival nations, with
opposing interests, and boundaries determined partly by
the laws of nature, partly by the lot of inheritance, partly
by the right of conquest. Within these national societies
the monarchical principle, consecrated by long custom,
grew always stronger by the necessities of internal order
and external self-defence. The king was enabled to exercise effectually his rights of maintaining the peace within
the domains of his vassals ; the subjects of the latter
looked for justice to the king's courts and the king's
judges ; paid standing armies, in the wars between nations,
superseded the undisciplined levies of the feudal militia.
The power of the local aristocracy, thus restricted by the
progress of the principle of self-preservation inherent in
every society, was almost annihilated by the course of
the foreign or civil wars which prevailed in every European
country during the thirteenth, fourteenth, and fifteenth
centuries. Thousands of the French leaders of chivalry

had perished in the battles of Courtrai, Crecy, Poitiers, and Agincourt, or in the expeditions of St. Louis against Egypt and Tunis ; the English nobility had been decimated by the Wars of the Roses ; the flower of the Burgundian aristocracy fell with Charles the Bold in his struggle with the Swiss ; and the feudal nobility of Spain, weakened by centuries of conflict with the Moors, sank before the united power of the Crowns of Arragon and Castile.

Out of this decaying fabric of the Christian Republic emerged, gradually but distinctly, the idea of the modern State. In almost every country in Europe, but more particularly in Italy, Germany, and England, we find philosophic writers in the first quarter of the sixteenth century deliberately busying themselves with speculations as to the manner in which communities of men should be created and organised ; and their inquiries are no longer conducted on the basis approved by the Schoolmen, as in the days of Dante and Petrarch, but leave out of account, or rather throw into the background, the old fundamental principles of the Empire and the Papacy. Each thinker, whether More, Luther, or Machiavelli, fixed his eyes on the well-being of his own country, though his ideas were coloured with associations derived from the old order in which he had been educated. It was as though the great central sun of Catholicism and Feudalism, a fiery mass of inorganic elements, had parted on all sides with huge bodies of matter, each of which had formed into a separate system with an orbit of its own. Every one of these new worlds, while sharing, by means of its constituent elements, in the life of the original source of its being, soon developed a life and character peculiar to itself, and opposed to the characteristic life of its neighbour's centre. Or, to speak without metaphor, in the sixteenth century the various kingdoms in the West of Europe, Spain, France, and England, began to display a clearly marked individuality in all matters relating to religion, art, literature, and manners. The creative impulse in each nation came from the small central region in which the Crown was supreme, but which represented the life of the whole community, and accordingly all national interests, political, spiritual, and intellectual, gravitated to the Court, as the seat of the monarchy. We have, therefore, now to consider what were the ideas that predominated in men's conceptions of the modern State, and the sources from which these ideas were derived. And having endeavoured, by reference to the Diet of Augsburg, to present the image of the old European order in a concrete form, I shall next attempt to illustrate the nature and operation of the new forces, by reference to the works of the great European writers in which these forces find their clearest and most beautiful expression.

II. In examining the rise of the existing European system, two circumstances at once strike the imagination. In the first place, the principles of thought which fundamentally disturbed the unity of Christendom proceeded from the east of Europe, but they were translated into action in the west; they originated in Italy or Germany or the Netherlands; they were applied on a large scale, as part of the machinery of government, in Spain, France, and England. The explanation of this fact is readily furnished when it is observed that, in the three Western countries, monarchy had established itself as the supreme centre of authority, while, in Italy and Germany, united national action was impossible; in the former, on account of the internecine conflict of rival principalities; in the latter, where Feudalism was more vigorous than in any other part of Europe, on account of the antagonism of equally balanced powers. In the second place, it is observable that, of the elements which compose the life of the modern State, Italy furnished the ideas that most powerfully modified the institutions of chivalry in respect of manners and art,—in other words, the movement of the Renaissance; while Germany supplied the religious, moral, and intellectual conceptions that helped to expand the ancient system of ecclesiastical discipline— in other words, Germany led the Reformation. The causes of this phenomenon require to be carefully considered.

The essence of all that is most vital in Italian thought and art lies in the principle of city life. It is manifest at first sight that the genius of the mediæval cities of Italy, in the golden age of their freedom, strongly resembles that of the free states of ancient Greece, and especially the character of Athens as described by Pericles. The citizen of every sovereign Italian city was eligible to take part in its government, his intellect was sharpened by political discussion, his sense of beauty was educated by the necessity of constructing and adorning the churches or other public buildings, which made so large a part of the life of each community. So long, therefore, as the Italian cities retained their freedom, the imagination of their inhabitants had large scope for active employment. Unfortunately, the period of their liberties was of short duration. Every free city in Italy ran through one unvarying circle of change, from elective monarchy to patrician oligarchy, and thence to democratic faction, which, ending in anarchy, prepared the way for despotism. When this final stage was reached the motives which produce great results in politics ceased to operate, and the inspiration of art did not long survive them.

Behind the image of the city loomed always, in the minds of the Italians, the ideal of a larger society—the Church, the Empire, the Feudal System, and, in later times, united Italy. While freedom flourished there was no collision between these two ideas. The doctrines and traditions of the Church lifted the imagination of the painter, the poet, and the architect into a loftier atmosphere. The power of the Emperor, too remote to interfere largely with civic liberty, linked them, however loosely, with the memories of Roman grandeur. But when, through internal faction or the jealousy of the rival cities, the principle of federal freedom, on which the Lombard League was established, lost its vitality, a sense of discord arose in the minds of the most intellectual Italians. We have already seen this expressed in the works of Dante and Petrarch ; but in the two following centuries the course of events inflamed the ancient wound with feverish intensity. One by one the free cities sank into servitude. In their place arose a group of states, all more or less despotically governed, the chief of which were the Duchy of Milan, the so-called republics of Venice and Florence, the kingdom of Naples, and the Papacy; while a subordinate group was constituted by the Duchies of Mantua, Urbino, and Ferrara. Each of the larger states was ambitious of establishing its supremacy in the whole Peninsula, and the position of affairs was complicated by the presence of the foreigner, since France and Spain both asserted their claims to the Duchy of Milan and the kingdom of Naples, while the Emperor exercised a titular supremacy over Italy at large. Between these conflicting powers the typical Italian mind was hopelessly distracted. The offspring of municipal liberty, each of its faculties had been quickened into the highest activity; and in all matters involving the exercise of wit, taste, reason, and refinement, the Italians were ages in advance of the French, Germans, and English. On the other hand, as a citizen of Pisa, Genoa, even of Florence, the Italian could only look back with hopeless yearning on the springtime of a vanished freedom. As a native of Italy he saw his country trampled under the feet of the semi-barbarians, whom he heartily despised. Hence arose in his mind a feeling of incongruity and impotence. Conscious of *virtù* —virile energy and power—he could find no practical object in pursuit of which he might exercise his rare endowments. All around him spoke of such deep corruption and decay that natures of the lower order, resigning themselves to their position, acquiesced in a life of material enjoyment without reference to the standards of honour and public spirit. Men of nobler genius either busied themselves with the positive observation of state affairs, like Guicciardini; studied the refinement of manners, like Castiglione; reasoned scientifically, like Machiavelli, on the manner in which a free state might be established by force; or, like Ariosto, engaged their sense of irony on poetic invention, bringing into fine imaginative relief the contrast between the fables

of romance and the facts of reality.   In all these directions the positive shrewdness and brilliancy of the Italian
genius produced forms of art which exercised a vast
influence on the imagination of the peoples of the north,
who, with institutions established on a feudal basis, and
with far larger scope for political action, translated the
civic ideas of the Italians into language adapted to the
circumstances of their own societies.   To illustrate what
has been said, I shall briefly refer to certain Italian
works which particularly impressed the minds of knightly
poets and scholarly dramatists in England—namely, the
Cortegiano of Castiglione and the *Discorsi* and *Principe* of
Machiavelli.   From these we may obtain a general idea
of the manner in which the civil genius of the Italians
modified the institutions of chivalry on their social, their
political, and their spiritual sides.

The *Courtier* represents the highest conception of free
social activity which the Italian imagination of the sixteenth
century was able to form.   Its author, Baldassare Castiglione,
possessed one of those sane and brilliant minds which were
not rare among his countrymen of that period, and which
made their envoys to foreign courts, like Guicciardini and
Navagero, unrivalled observers and critics of manners.   He
had been educated under conditions which enabled him to
view in the most favourable light the standards of Lombard
chivalry that still survived.   The servant of the Duke of
Milan, and afterwards of the Duke of Urbino, one of the
few respectable princes of Italy, he had been ambassador
to the sovereigns both of France and England, from the
latter of whom—Henry VII.—he had brought back to his
master the Order of the Garter.   In every region through
which his duties compelled him to pass he made himself
thoroughly acquainted with the language and manners of
the inhabitants, and observed with the closest accuracy
the forces that were transforming the constitution of
society.   He was, therefore, qualified in the highest degree
to form a comprehensive idea of the refined and chivalrous
courtier.   Nor is it wonderful that his creation should
have deeply impressed the imagination of men in every

country of Europe, serving as a model to the brilliant courts of the northern monarchs, and retaining its prestige, as a mirror of taste and manners, as late as the age of Dr. Johnson.[1]

The place which Castiglione selected as the scene of his dialogue was equally representative of Italian chivalry. As Florence was the highest example of the Guelphic city state of mediæval Italy, preserving in its constitution many of the municipal traditions of classic antiquity, so the Duchy of Urbino was a favourable type of the government which had arisen in many districts from the ranks of that Ghibelline aristocracy, which for the most part exercised its powers outside the city walls. In this principality, while the popular element was practically deprived of authority, its rulers, adopting fairly equitable methods of administration, were enabled securely to develop such a standard of princely magnificence, elegance, and refinement, as made their court, small as was its political influence, a school of art and good breeding. The Dukes of Urbino had, for several generations, been eminent in the science of arms. They were equally distinguished as patrons of art ; and the great palace erected by Duke Frederic enjoyed a reputation as one of the earliest and finest specimens of the architecture of the Renaissance. Hither, as to a recognised centre of taste, the Italians of the time most eminent in position or intellect were in the habit of resorting, and on this circumstance Castiglione bases the fictitious action of his book. The plan of the *Courtier* is modelled partly on the *Decameron* of Boccaccio, partly on the *De Oratore* of Cicero, and consists of a conversation which is sustained by a number of ladies and gentlemen, who are supposed to be enjoying the hospitality of the Court of Urbino. Among the chief male speakers are persons so well known as Frederigo Fregoso, brother of the wise Doge of Genoa ; Giulio dei Medici, afterwards Clement VII. ; Bibbiena, the facetious cardinal whose *Calandra* first popularised the plot of the *Menæchmi* of Plautus, of which Shakespeare afterwards

[1] Boswell's *Life of Johnson* (Croker's edition), p 359.

availed himself in the *Comedy of Errors ;* and Bembo, secretary of Leo X., famous for the fastidious preciseness of his literary taste. The ladies are represented by Elizabeth, Duchess of Urbino, and Donna Emilia, her principal attendant, who, in her wit and vivacity, seems to be modelled on Boccaccio's Pampinea, and to have furnished the model for Shakespeare's Beatrice. By command of the Duchess the company amuse themselves by proposing a subject for common discussion. After several suggestions have been made and rejected, one of the guests proposes " that our diversion of the night may be this, that one of the company be chosen to describe a perfect courtier, and explain all the conditions and particular qualities required of the man who deserves the character." Four nights are occupied in the discussion, which divides itself into four parts : (1) Of the Form and Manner of a Court Life ; (2) of the Qualifications of a Courtier ; (3) of the Accomplishments of a Court Lady ; (4) of the Duty of a Prince. A representative orator is appointed on each night to conduct the main line of the discourse ; the other guests criticise the chief speaker, and dispute among themselves on the points raised in the course of the argument.

The most interesting feature in the discussion of the character of the courtier is the evidence it affords of the deep roots which the institutions of chivalry had thrown into the life of the aristocracy of Europe, even in Italy. Thus, in the first place, we may observe that all the externals of knighthood, as regards prowess in arms and athletic exercises, are insisted on as the most indispensable accomplishment of the courtier. He must be " a perfect horseman in every respect " ; and under this head the speaker notices that " we Italians are peculiarly famous for riding, running at the ring, and tilting, as the French are at tournaments and the Spaniards at running at the wild bull, and throwing the dart." The courtier should also be skilled in hunting, " as having a certain resemblance to war, well becoming the dignity of a nobleman and courtier, and as much in vogue with the ancients." He must also be able to swim, leap, and cast the stone, and to play tennis.[1]

We may take it that this athletic training was as much a part of the discipline of a gentleman's education in every country of Europe in the sixteenth century as the exercises of the palæstra were in the education of the Greek youth. In the north of Europe we know that especial pains were given to the instruction of the young knights and squires in all the arts of the tilting yard, and so high was the standard of proficiency that the aspirant to knighthood was expected to be able in complete armour to mount a horse at full gallop. The system was a survival from the days of the Crusades, when chivalry reached its zenith. Then every castle was a school for knights, and knighthood itself had a practical aim. Now that authority was being centralised in the hands of sovereign princes, and life was ebbing away from the castle and flowing towards the Court, the leading features of the old chivalrous discipline were retained and carried to unexampled perfection, as the accomplishments naturally to be expected in those who were ambitious of being the companions of monarchs. Such, in fact, was the schooling to which Surrey alludes in his reflections in captivity on the happy days spent with the Duke of Richmond at Windsor.

But in the eyes of the Italians at least this merely martial discipline was inadequate for the development of the perfect courtier ; the education of arms had to be accompanied by the education of letters. And here we see the first signs of the modifying influence introduced into chivalry by the Renaissance. Castiglione blames the French for their distaste for literary refinement,[2] and at the same time looks forward with hope to the accession of the Duke of Angoulême, who, in fact, as Francis I., transplanted to the French Court all the arts with which he had become acquainted in Italy. "We would have

---

[1] *Cortegiano*, lib. i.

[2] He says that the French "not only think nothing more detestable than literature, but that even the very name of men of letters is become hateful and odious among them."—*Ibid.* lib. i.

our courtier," says Castiglione in the person of Count
Louis, "something more than passably learned, at least
in those sciences which we call 'humane,' and that not
only in the Latin, but in the Greek, for the sake of
the excellent matter which is to be found beautifully
expressed in both languages.   Let him be well read in
the poets as well as in the orators and historians, and
also let him practise himself in writing in verse and prose,
especially in the vulgar tongue.   Besides the pleasure he
will himself derive from this he will not fail to make himself hereby most agreeable to the ladies, who as a rule
take delight in these pursuits." [1]   The courtier must also
be acquainted with the theory of music, and be able to
play upon the lute ; he must even cultivate the art of
painting.[2]   In all this we note the extremely clear and
positive character of the Italian genius.   Taste is to be
cultivated not in the abstract, but as something which is
valuable to the man of action.   Letters, Castiglione says,
must be added to the pursuit of arms which is the groundwork of all education ; and in the admirable rules which
he lays down for the cultivation of style he is always guided
by practical considerations.   One of the company having
maintained that the diction of the writer must be carefully
separated from that of the speaker, and that the style of
the former is to be so rigidly determined by literary
authority that even archaic words are to be preserved,
Count Louis of Canossa, whose business it is to describe
the ideal courtier, replies :—

If a man might use in writing words which he would think
improper for speaking, there would arise, in my opinion, a very
great inconvenience, for licence would then be admissible in
matters where the greatest exactness is required, while the pains
given to this kind of writing would be rather of disservice than
of advantage to him.   It is certain, therefore, that whatever is
allowable in writing ought also to be allowable in speaking, and
that the most beautiful kind of speech is that which resembles
elegant writing ; indeed I think it even more necessary to be
understood in writing than in speaking, because those that write

---

[1] *Cortegiano*, lib. i.   [2] *Ibid.*

are not always in the presence of those that read, which is different in the case of conversation. I would accordingly recommend him (the courtier) not only to avoid all old and obsolete Tuscan words, but both in writing and speaking to make use of such words as are in vogue in Tuscany and in other parts of Italy to-day, and which have some grace and charm in themselves ; and in my judgment whoevei follows a different rule must inevitably fall into that stiffness and affectation which we have been all along condemning." [1]

This is precisely the principle *usus* which would have been approved by Cicero and Horace in the days when the Latin language attained its highest excellence.

We have seen how the qualifications of the courtier are in Castiglione's system largely determined by the ancient traditions of chivalry. The same principle is also followed in another most important particular. In the discourse on the conditions to be maintained in the inter-course between the sexes, it is interesting to note how carefully all the rules of the art of love have been pre-served according to the code of the ancient *Cours d'Amour*, while at the same time they have been toned down and chastened so as to suit the rational require-ments of a modern court. The following passage will be immediately recognised as an inheritance from the school of André le Chapelain :—

They therefore who are too precipitate, and show a pre-sumption, and as it were a mad pertinacity in their addresses, often miss their mark and that deservedly ; for it is always displeasing to a noble lady to be so little esteemed, as that any one should, without due respect, require her love before he has done her due service. In my opinion the way that a courtier should declare his love to his mistress is by signs and tokens rather than by words. For without doubt more love is shown in a sigh, or in some mark of timidity or reverence, than can be shown in a thousand words ; and the eyes may afterwards be made the faithful messengers of the heart, because they frequently declare, with more eloquence, the inward passion, than can open speech, or letter, or any other kind of message.[2]

We shall hereafter see this kind of sentimental

---

[1] *Cortegiano*, lib. i.   [2] *Ibid*. lib. iii.   Cf. vol. i. pp. 173, 174.

analysis frequently illustrated in the poems of Wyatt, Surrey, and Sidney ; and there is certainly much more of what is easy and agreeable in the manner, than in the elaborate style of romantic compliment which came into vogue in France under the *régime* of the Hôtel Rambouillet. Meantime it is to be observed that even a passion so spiritual and exalted as that of love is made the subject of analysis and rule, and this fact is symbolical of Castiglione's whole treatment of the character of the courtier. Everything in it is external and well defined, and so well adapted to its limited sphere of action, that no opportunity is found for the expansion of the nobler part of the spirit of chivalry. The author keeps his gaze fixed on the Court ; of the aspirations in man's nature, of the duties owed by the individual to the family, to the city, the country, he takes no account. No mention is made of the moral virtues which make up the character of the knight as it is treated in the *Faery Queen ;* and, for all that appears, the presence of the foreigner in Italy, which was so galling to the soul of patriotic Florentines, was a matter of perfect indifference to the polished guests of the Duke of Urbino. On the other hand, an error in manners or outward behaviour is in their eyes a deadly sin. There is, accordingly, a certain defective sense of proportion pervading the pages of *Il Cortegiano.* Nevertheless, the strict attention it devoted to form was beneficial, as far as it went, in establishing the standard of good taste and refinement essential to the conduct of a gentleman after the decay of the institution of knighthood. Carried to the north of Europe, and grafted on the still chivalrous manners of the English aristocracy, the ideal of Castiglione contributed to form the character of Sir Philip Sidney.

The element of passion and imagination, wanting in the *Courtier*, is abundantly present in the *Discourses* and the *Prince* of Machiavelli. Macaulay has forcibly expressed, in his well-known essay, the perplexity with which the English mind will probably always regard the writings of this extraordinary thinker. " The whole man seems to be an enigma, a grotesque assemblage of incongruous qualities, selfishness and generosity, cruelty and benevolence, craft and simplicity, abject villainy and romantic heroism. . . . Two characters altogether dissimilar are united in him. They are not merely joined but interwoven."[1] Since Macaulay wrote this the character of Machiavelli has been analysed with the finest skill by Professor Villari, from whose estimate it seems almost presumptuous for an Englishman to differ even in the smallest particular. While he appears to me to have established his principal contentions beyond the reach of cavil, I nevertheless venture to think that, in his patriotic desire to remove the exclusive responsibility for Machiavelli's doctrines from his own country, he has attributed to his hero an intelligence of a European order beyond what the evidence warrants.[2] Machiavelli, in my judgment, is clearly the child of the Italian Renaissance. A Florentine, endowed in the fullest measure with the wit, shrewdness, and positive intelligence of his city, he yearned passionately for the state of freedom in which alone these qualities could be freely exercised. He recognised clearly that energy

[1] Macaulay, *Critical and Historical Essays* (one vol. edition, 1850), pp. 29, 30.

[2] He says: "Certainly it might be objected that all this resulted from the decadence and moral corruption of Italy, and that it would, therefore, be better to seek elsewhere for a model of good government. But on looking beyond the Alps, Machiavelli only found new and stronger confirmation of his theories. Did not all know the cruel tricks and stratagems of Louis XI., who nevertheless succeeded by their means in initiating the unity and greatness of France? Was not Ferdinand the Catholic a master of deceit, and yet had he not, together with Queen Isabella, founded the new Monarchy of Spain? Was not England, and was not all Europe overflowing with treason and bloodshed? And if he looked back to the Middle Ages, did he not find still greater barbarity, ferocity, and iniquity of all kinds?" (*Niccolò Machiavelli*, Pasquale Villari. English translation, vol. iii. pp. 332, 333). No doubt Machiavelli saw statesmen all over Europe making use of the violent and crooked methods which he recommended on principle. But if his political view had been more extensive he would have seen that neither Louis XI. nor Ferdinand the Catholic could have succeeded in their aims solely by means of these. He takes no account of influences like the Spanish Cortes, the French Parliaments, the English House of Commons,—free institutions which the sovereigns of these countries had to deal with in managing their affairs. And though political action in the Middle Ages may often have been bloody and savage, those who were guilty of crime never ventured to be its apologists. It is only in Italy, in the pages of a great Italian writer, that the actions of a Cæsar Borgia are proposed as models.

(*virtù*), social activity, and patriotism, had passed away from his country,[1] and there were times when it seemed to him that nothing remained for the man of lofty soul but to express, in an imaginative form, the scorn he felt for the life about him. It was in such a mood that he composed his comedy, *Mandragola*.[2] But his thought was still haunted by the memory of that "sober and chaste Florence" which had filled the memory of Dante, and in general his whole mind was employed on devising means by which the life of Florence and Italy might be restored. Patriotism, at least a patriotic ideal, was in fact to Machiavelli, as to many other of the nobler Italians of the age, a substitute for religion,[3] and accordingly he declares : "Where it is an absolute question of the welfare of our country we must admit of no consideration of justice or injustice, of mercy or cruelty, of praise or ignominy, but putting all else aside we must adopt whatever cause will save its existence and preserve its liberty."[4]

Though he dreamed of the regeneration of Florence in the spirit of an enthusiast, the methods by which, in

---

[1] Virtue, in Machiavelli's opinion, is always on the move : "Hence it follows that he who is born in Greece or Italy must praise the past and blame the present times, in which there is nothing to compensate for their extreme misery, infamy, and shame ; when there is no observance of religion, or of law, or of military discipline. The thing is clearer than sunlight ; wherefore I will plainly declare the conclusion that I derive from it so that the mind of youth may flee these times, and prepare itself to copy the ancients, since it is the office of an honest man to teach to others that good which, through the malignity of time and fortune, he has not been able to carry into effect."— *Discorsi*, Proem to Book ii.

[2] Scusatelo con questo, che s' ingegna
    Con questi van pensieri
    Fare il suo tristo tempo più soave ;
    Perchè altrove non ave
    Dove voltare il viso,
    Che gli è stato interciso
    Mostrar con altre imprese altre virtue
    Non sendo premio alle fatiche sue.
                 Machiavelli, *Opere* (Milano, 1805), viii. p. 8.

[3] He greatly admired, and often repeated with enthusiasm, the encomium of Gino Capponi upon "those who loved their country better than the safety of their souls," a phrase that was highly popular at that period.—*Machiavelli and His Times* (English translation), vol. iii. p. 271.

[4] *Discorsi*, Book iii. c. 41.

his *Principe* and *Discorsi*, he proposed to accomplish his object were marked by all the cool analysis and close observation characteristic of the Italian mind. Professor Villari says of him excellently : " He has quite the aspect of a physiologist making experiments in vivisection and using his anatomical knife to dissect the different organs and ascertain their functions." He calmly reasoned to the conclusion that, in the midst of universal corruption, the free state can only be founded by force ; hence, in his logic, everything is to be left to the art and power of an absolute prince ; and to him all means are permissible for the attainment of his end. Whatever stands in the way of that end is to be removed by force or fraud. The end is liberty, and " this," says he, " always implies equality, and sovereignty inequality." Machiavelli is thus at once brought into collision with the two great institutions on which the life of mediæval Europe was based, the Catholic Church and the Feudal System ; and it is important to observe the purely local and individual grounds on which he condemns them. As to the former, " we Italians," he says, " are first indebted to the Church and the clergy for the loss of our faith, and the gain of wickedness ; but we likewise owe them another and greater obligation which is the cause of our ruin. It is that the Church has kept and keeps our country divided." [1] The Papacy was thus viewed by him mainly on its temporal side. As to the feudal aristocracy Machiavelli's words are not less bitter. " Of these nobles Naples, Rome, Romagna, and Lombardy are full ; whence it comes that these lands have never had any true republic nor any political existence ; for such races of men are entirely hostile to all civilisation, and any man who should undertake to establish order among them would find the only means to be that of constituting a kingdom, since nothing, save the weight of a royal hand and absolute and excessive power, could hold in check the excessive ambition and corruption of the nobility. In Tuscany, on the other hand, there are the Republics of Florence, Siena, and Lucca, and it is

[1] *Discorsi*, Book i. c. 12.

apparent that the other cities, even if they have it not, are all desirous of liberty. And all this is because there are no feudal chieftains in those parts, but so much equality that any sagacious man, with some knowledge of the ancient civilisations, could easily introduce free institutions among them ; but the ill luck of these provinces has been so great that down to these days no one has been able or willing to effect this." [1]

Here, then, we have for the first time the civic ideal of antiquity brought into harsh and open conflict with the ecclesiastical and feudal ideal of the Middle Ages. And it is plain that this conflict of political extremes must bring with it a further conflict in the standards of morality, since undoubtedly the existing principles of religion and conduct are derived wholly or largely from the Church, and from Feudal Institutions. Nor does Machiavelli hesitate for a moment in the application of his logic. He avowedly finds the model of his prince in Cæsar Borgia, a tribute paid to the success achieved by that blood-thirsty bandit in crushing the feudal nobility in Romagna ; and in the eighteenth chapter of the *Prince*, he formulates opinions which have ever since made his name —on the whole justly—a byword of reproach. Thus he allows that it is right for men to keep their word ; "nevertheless," says he, "experience has proved in our own times that the princes who have achieved great deeds are those who have held good faith of small account, and who have known how to bewilder men's brains by cunning, and in the end have succeeded better than those whose actions have been ruled by honour." [2] Even hypocrisy is legitimate in his system. "It is necessary to give a good colouring to your nature, and to be a great dissembler and dissimulator, because men then readily allow themselves to be deceived. Alexander VI. did nothing but deceive, and thought of nothing else during the whole of his life, nor did any other man ever vow with stronger oaths to observe promises that he afterwards broke ; nevertheless, he succeeded in everything,

[1] *Discorsi*, Proem to Book ii. [2] *Principe*, ch. xviii.

for he was well acquainted with this part of the world." [1] And again : " A prince should be very careful to let nothing escape his lips that is not pregnant with the five qualities above described, so that in his aspect, as in his words, he may seem all piety, faith, humanity, integrity, and religion. And nothing is more necessary than to appear to possess this latter quality—religion, inasmuch as the mass of mankind judge rather by sight than by touch, for all can see while few can feel. Every one sees that which you seem to be, few feel that which you are, and those few do not dare to oppose the voice of the majority who have the majesty of the State at their back." [2]

In forming a judgment on the character and opinions of Machiavelli it is just to bear two things in mind. First, as all government is founded to some extent on force, rulers and statesmen are not as strictly bound as private individuals to obey in all circumstances the universal laws of morality and religion : they may be even morally bound, in virtue of their position, in certain contingencies to depart from them. In the second place, the circumstances in which Machiavelli himself was called upon to act as a politician were, in the highest degree, exceptional. For all this, we must decide that his published opinions were not only an argument against his own character, but that, even in view of his particular object, his reasonings were scientifically unsound. In respect of the first point we cannot avoid the conclusion that only a man whose nature had been largely tainted by the corruption that surrounded him could have coldly set down on paper his approval, under any circumstances, of the use of lying and hypocrisy; and as regards the second, when his principles are considered in relation to their practical utility, we see at once how inadequate is the basis of his observation to bear the great structure of his conclusions ; how many essential factors have been omitted from the calculation of the means required for the attainment of the end. What exaggerated attention, for example, is given to the actions

[1] *Principe*, ch. xviii. [2] *Ibid.*

of Cæsar Borgia, a mere bandit, however able, contending with rival banditti! How could it be supposed that the scope of such a man's motives and actions was sufficiently comprehensive to determine the conditions required to establish the freedom and unity of a great nation? Again it is an astonishing thing that Machiavelli should not have perceived that a national militia, such as he imagined and desired, animated by patriotism and obedient to discipline, *could* not be created by force. He seems to have postulated, for the liberation of Italy, a Prince devoid of all moral scruples, under whose sway should arise a race of citizens endowed with every public virtue. The idea was not less chimerical than the reveries of Petrarch ; and indeed Machiavelli's imagination, like that of Petrarch and other eminent Italians, was led astray by his quasi-relationship to the ancient Romans of the Republic. Classical traditions are always in his mind, he seeks his precedents immediately from Livy ; he has no real historical sense of the differences between the men of his own age and the contemporaries of Scipio. The English imagination, in some respects as positive and practical as that of the Italians, perceived this defect in him even on his own ground, and Butler has given epigrammatic expression to the perception in *Hudibras :—*

> Nick Machiavel had ne'er a trick,
> Though he gave his name to our old Nick.[1]

But, in the realm of European imagination, Machia-

---

[1] This is also the judgment of Machiavelli's own countrymen. Cavour said : "This man (Guicciardini) had a real knowledge of affairs, and a far better comprehension of them than Machiavelli." Gino Capponi, Machiavelli's own contemporary, also says that Machiavelli's writings were not sufficiently practical, "not like the writings of one who had performed things himself, instead of witnessing their performance by others. . . . It has always appeared to me as though Machiavelli understood men in general better than the individual man, that he understood them as regarded what they did in common and with reference to public life ; but that he neither studied them nor understood them with reference to their individual qualities, nor to what they were at home and in the family ; the which things are obstacles disregarded by speculative minds, but well understood by men practised in government."—Villari's *Machiavelli and His Times*, vol. iii. p. 371.

velli's writings, separated from their actual object and merely local circumstances, exercised an all-powerful influence. The sixteenth century saw placed before its eyes, in all the strength of logic and the charm of eloquence, an ideal of political and moral life, at once opposed to the code of Catholicism and Chivalry, and in many respects conformable to the requirements of the world as it actually existed. Ferdinand of Spain, Francis of France, and Henry of England undoubtedly often put into practice the principles which Machiavelli recommends, and accordingly when these were systematised in an abstract form their effect was felt in the morality of society at large. Two centuries earlier the idea that a knight and a gentleman should be false to his plighted word would have been scouted by the tribunal of European opinion, which accepted as a matter of course the honourable conduct of King John of France, who returned to captivity after failing to procure from his country the sum required for his ransom. But Francis I. had no difficulty in finding philosophic reasons to excuse himself for the violation of his *parole d'honneur* when he escaped from captivity ; nor did Charles V. meet with universal sympathy when his ambassador publicly denounced the conduct of his rival as unworthy of a knight and a gentleman. Such examples of Machiavellian conduct in high places naturally led to frequent imitation in all countries, and not least in England. The " Italianate " Englishman (that is to say, an Englishman who had spent some time in Italy and had adopted Machiavelli's principles and Italian manners) became a byword among his own countrymen ; while, in the sphere of imagination, the doctrines of the *Prince* long exercised a fascination over the mind of the dramatist, partly on account of the force of character produced by the cultivation of mere *virtù*, partly on account of the interesting situations arising out of the conflict between the will and the conscience of man.

As Italy led the way in the Renaissance, so Germany was the pioneer of the Reformation ; and a somewhat striking parallel to the course respectively followed in

Italy by Castiglione and Machiavelli is furnished by the intellectual opposition between Erasmus and Luther in the north of Europe. Erasmus wished to adapt the ancient structure of tradition and authority to the reception of the new ideas generated by liberty and science. A native of a country in which civic and feudal associations were strangely blended ; bred up from early years in the discipline of a monastery ; accomplished in all the arts of classical scholarship ; of a character humorous, shrewd, and penetrating, rather than enthusiastic ; the friend equally of princes, popes, and philosophers ; everything conspired to make him in the best sense of the word a conservative. What Castiglione did to adapt the standard of chivalry to the circumstances of the Court, Erasmus did in liberalising the education of the Church. His *Familiar Colloquies* was, in the first instance, intended to improve the methods of instruction in grammar ; but, " when," says he, " I perceived it was received by students with great applause, I made use of the affection of the common people for the furtherance of studies." [1] Employing the form of the Dialogue as it had been used by Lucian, and thus seeming to lighten the labours of the student by the imaginative form in which he conveyed his instructions, he at the same time exhibited to him, in a lively and satirical spirit, the absurdities of many of the beliefs and customs of the time. A representative of almost every class and order in society figures among his *Dialogi Personæ*. Butchers and Fishmongers, Soldiers and Carthusian Monks, Abbots and Learned Ladies, Midwives, Pilgrims, Beggars, Scholars, Travellers, meet and engage in discourse on the topics in which they are interested, and with a closeness of logic imitated from the forms in use in the schools, just as Lucian's style is adapted from the dialogues of Plato. It would be difficult to exaggerate the effect which the *Colloquies* must have produced among the more reflective part of European society in the sixteenth century, by educating public opinion thus indirectly in a more rational scheme of manners and

[1] Erasmus, Preface to the *Colloquies*.

conduct. Yet it will be observed that in every essential respect Erasmus assumes the established basis of society, religious and political, as the sphere determining the limits of human action. In the *Ichthyophagia*, for example, we find a Butcher and a Fishmonger debating with each other concerning the principles of true religion. Both accept without question the supremacy of the Pope as the spiritual head of the Christian Republic, and the authority of the Emperor and his subordinate princes as the chiefs of the Temporal Power in Europe. Thus :—

Fishmonger. But there is no salvation out of the pale of the Church. *Butcher.* I confess it. *F.* Whosoever does not own the authority of the pope is out of the pale of the Church. *B.* I don't deny that either. *F.* But he that neglects his injunctions does not own him. *B.* But I hope a time will come that the pope, who is Clement by name, and most of all so by nature, will mitigate all these things which hitherto have alienated some people from the Roman Church, that he may bring all nations to the communion of it, and will rather pursue those things that are for the good of the Church than his own private interest. I hear daily complaints of yearly offerings, pardons, dispensations, and other exactions and church grievances ; but I believe he will so moderate all things, that in time to come it would be impudent to complain.[1]

So, too, with the Temporal Head of the Christian Republic :—

F. I wish all monarchs would do the like, and then I would not doubt but Christianity, which is now confined to a narrow compass, would extend itself, when the barbarous nations did perceive that they were called, not to human servitude, but to gospel liberty, and that they were not sought after to be made a prey of, but to a fellow enjoyment of happiness and holiness. If once they came to be united with us, and found in us manners truly Christian, they would of their own accord offer us more than the utmost violence can extort from them. *B.* I should soon hope to see that accomplished, if that mischievous Ate, that has engaged the two most mighty monarchs in the world in a bloody war, were sent to her place. . . . *F.* Were I Emperor I would without delay thus treat with the king of France : "My brother, some evil spirit has set this war on foot between you and

---

[1] *Colloquies of Erasmus.* Translated by N. P. Bailey (Johnson's edition), vol. ii. p. 53.

me; nor do we fight for our lives but our dominions. You,
as to your part, have behaved yourself as a stout and valiant
warrior; but fortune has been on my side, and of a king made
you a captive. What has been your lot may be mine, and your
mishap admonishes all of our human condition. We have experienced that this way of contention has been detrimental to
both of us; let us engage one another after a different manner.
I give you your life and restore you your liberty, and instead of
an enemy take you for a friend. . . . As for me, the fame of
this clemency will get me more true glory than if I had added
all France to my dominion; and in you, a grateful mind will be
more to your praise than if you had driven me quite out of
Italy." . . . How great and glorious would this act of humanity
render Charles all over the world? What nation would not
readily submit to so generous and kind a prince?[1]

With reference to the common Christian life of the
time, the following passage from *The Religious Banquet*
condenses into a nutshell the code of purely external
discipline to which Papal authority and the scholastic
education had reduced the standard of religious duty:—

Chrysoglottus. I will be plainer then. If you look into
Christians in common, don't you find they live as if the whole
sum of religion consisted in ceremonies? With how much pomp
are the ancient rites of the Church set forth in baptism? The
infant waits without the church door, the exorcism is performed,
the catechising is performed, vows are made, Satan is abjured
with all his pomps and pleasures; then the child is anointed,
signed, seasoned with salt, dipped, and charge given to its sureties
to see it well brought up; and the oblation money being
paid, they are discharged, and by this time the child passes for a
Christian, and in some sense is so. A little time after it is
anointed again, and in time learns to confess, receives the sacra-
ments, is accustomed to abstain from flesh, and if he observes all
these he passes for an absolute Christian. He marries a wife,
and then comes on another sacrament; he enters into holy
orders, is anointed again, and consecrated, his habit is changed,
and then to prayers. Now I approve of the doing of all these
well enough; but the doing of them more out of custom than
conscience, I don't approve; but to think that nothing else is
requisite for the making of a Christian, I absolutely disapprove.
For the greatest part of men in the world trust to these things,
and think they have nothing else to do but get wealth by right

---

[1] *Colloquies of Erasmus*, vol. ii. pp. 54, 55.

or wrong to gratify their passions of rage, lust, malice, ambition. And this they do till they come upon their death-bed; and then there follow more ceremonies—confession upon confession, more unction still, the eucharists are administered, if they are to be had for love or money; orders are given for a magnificent funeral; and then comes another solemn contract—when the man is in the agony of death, there is one stands by bawling in his ear, and now and then despatches him before his time, if he chance to be a little in drink, or have better lungs than ordinary. Now, although these things may be well enough, as they are done in conformity with ecclesiastical customs, yet there are some more internal impressions which have an efficacy to fortify us against the assaults of death by filling our hearts with joy, and helping us to go out of the world with a Christian assurance.[1]

Again, as regards education and taste, Erasmus takes up a middle position, the effect of which is to restore the study of Rhetoric to its right place in the Christian course, whence it had been driven by the encroachments of Logic. He by no means shared the sentiments of Bembo, who recommended a friend not to read St. Paul's Epistles lest he should spoil his style. Sophronius, one of the inter-locutors in *The Religious Banquet*, asks:

What book is that, Eulalius, you take out of your pocket? It seems to be a very neat one, it is gilded all over. *Eul.* It is more valuable for the inside than the out. It is St. Paul's Epistles, that I always carry about with me as my beloved entertainment, which I take out now upon the occasion of something you said, which minds me of a plan that I have beat my brains about a long time, and I am not come to a full satisfaction in yet.[2]

But of the higher class of the *Literæ Humaniores* he entertains an opinion very different from that held either by Tertullian or the contemporary Schoolmen:—

Eul. Whatsoever is pious and conduces to good manners ought not to be called profane. The first place must indeed be given to the authority of the Scriptures; but, nevertheless, I sometimes find some things said or written by the ancients, nay, even by the heathens, nay, by the poets themselves, so chastely, so holily, so divinely, that I cannot persuade myself but that when they wrote them they were divinely inspired; and perhaps

[1] *Colloquies of Erasmus*, vol. i. pp. 186, 187.   [2] *Ibid.* vol. i. p. 178.

the spirit of Christ diffuses itself farther than we imagine ; and there are more saints than we have in our catalogue. To confess freely among friends, I cannot read Tully on *Old Age, On Friendship,* his *Offices,* or his *Tusculan Questions,* without kissing the book and veneration for that divine soul. And, on the contrary, when I read some of our modern authors, treating of politics, economics, and ethics, good God ! how cold they are in comparison of these ! Nay, how insensible they seem of what they write themselves. So that I had rather lose Scotus and twenty more such as he, than one Cicero or Plutarch. Not that I am wholly against them neither, but because by the reading of the one I find myself become better; whereas I rise from the other I know not how coldly affected to virtue, but most violently inclined to cavil and contention.[1]

Sane and witty and admirable as all this is, we cannot but feel that a mind like that of Erasmus was mainly of the critical order. He could point out, by means of reason and ridicule, the existence of disease in the midst of European society ; he could not supply the spirit which was required to renew the life of the ancient order. The Catholic system had been the growth of centuries ; it had adapted itself step by step to many of the spiritual wants of mankind ; but, in doing this, it had paid so much attention to machinery that it had come to identify it with the very life of the soul. Hence the deeper and more passionate desires of human nature found in the sixteenth century no nourishment in the religious system of the Church about them. By a natural reaction in the contrary direction they sought to obtain for themselves outlets which were destructive of the very existence of the Church, regarded as an external society.

No one can read the treatise of Luther on *Christian Liberty* without perceiving that the doctrines it contains are practically incompatible with any system of external Christian unity, and also that they contain the germs out of which the various forms of schismatic Church government have since been developed.[2] For to Luther the one primal

---

[1] *Colloquies of Erasmus,* vol. i. p. 182.
[2] See *First Principles of the Reformation,* or *The Ninety-five Theses and the Three Primary Works of Dr. Martin Luther,* p. 95. Translated into English. Edited by Henry Wace, D.D., and C. A. Buchheim, Ph.D.

necessity of being was precisely that which had been smothered by the materialisation of the mediæval Church —the reconciliation of the individual soul to God.   In pursuit of this absorbing object he reached his great fundamental doctrine of justification by faith ; and from this again he proceeded to two conclusions, both of which were fatal to the unity of the Church, at least as then existing ; first, the unessential nature of rites and ceremonies ; and, secondly, the merely representative nature of all Church government.   It matters not that Luther modified his own logic by his strong common-sense ; that he himself had, in the first instance, no more wish than Erasmus to overturn the basis of the existing order.   A logical idea once started must run its course ; and it was inevitable that, from the new Scholasticism, the doctrine of justification by faith, and the corollaries deduced from it, would arise the democratic form of Church government as formulated by Calvin, and the anarchical individualism of the Anabaptists of Münster.

At every single point the high spiritual reasonings of Luther encountered the high logic of the Schoolmen. Three centuries before, the Mystical Theology of St. Bonaventura, which was precisely of the same character —however different in doctrine—as that of Luther, could coexist harmoniously with the philosophical theology of Thomas Aquinas.   Now, the mystical theology was endeavouring to make itself the basis for external action, and the consequence was the rupture of Christian unity. Nor was it only within the sphere of religion that the new doctrines of Luther affected the life of Europe ; they exercised a vital influence on the course of education and art.   Luther directed some of his most violent attacks against the system of philosophical education pursued in the schools, and among the books which excited his fiercest dislike was the *Ethics* of Aristotle ![1] In itself the Reformation tended to revive the teaching of Tertullian, and, except in places where it was in close alliance with the Renaissance, its tendencies were un-

[1] Luther's *Address to the Nobility* (Wace and Buchheim), pp. 78, 79.

doubtedly hostile to the study of classical literature. And beyond this, the great Teutonic religious movement represented by Luther, in turning the eye of the soul inward upon itself, and away from mere external things, enormously affected the whole movement of the imagination. The soul, the conscience, the relation of man to God, became subjects of meditation to minds which had previously been accustomed to move among the beliefs of the Church as matters settled by authority and logic ; and though it was long before the poet discarded the forms which he had evolved under the old system of education, these were modified sensibly by the new current of ideas.

Turning from the east to the west of Europe, we find three great monarchies in a state of sufficient organisation to assimilate the new ideas with the national system. Of these Spain closed her gates resolutely against all influences coming to her from the north of Europe. Catholicism was, with her, the first instinct of national life. Through the Middle Ages the larger part of her energies had been absorbed in a home struggle with the Infidel. When the victory was achieved, the question of national unity presented itself, and after this had been settled by the junction of the Crowns of Castile and Arragon, the cardinal principles of Ferdinand the Catholic were to suppress liberty of individual thought by means of the Inquisition, and to crush the power of the local nobility by methods which resembled those of Cæsar Borgia. Hence he is praised by Machiavelli as the most sagacious prince of his time, and doubtless the intense energy with which the mind of the nation followed the lead of its monarch in these directions, helped to make Spain the predominant political power in Europe for more than a century. But such conditions were unfavourable to the production of great results in the sphere of art and philosophy. A faint impulse from without was communicated to Spanish thought by the connection between Arragon and Naples, the most definite result of which— at least as far as the rest of Europe was concerned—was perhaps a tendency to make experiments in language, which stimulated similar movements in other countries, and notably in England. But the native Spanish genius was always darkened by the influence of a living fanaticism, or haunted by the memory of a vanished past. In days when the trouvères and troubadours beyond the Pyrenees were being inspired by the enthusiasm of the Crusades, the Spaniards were writing ballads about their own struggle with the Infidels ; when this struggle ended chivalry was dying in the north of Europe. It was in the Spanish peninsula, accordingly, that the sentimental ideal peculiar to the later Romances first appeared, furnishing the basis for an extravagant conception of adventure, and preparing the way alike for the immortal satire of Cervantes, and for the intricacy of plot and action which is the main characteristic of the Spanish drama. It will be seen in the sequel that the Spanish conception of romance contributed an important element to the pastoral and dramatic poetry of England.

But in the early part of the sixteenth century the imagination of Englishmen was turned rather in a political direction. The overthrow of the ancient feudal order by the Wars of the Roses had made way for the growth of a mitigated absolutism in administration, but had left untouched the national customs and laws, which are the best foundation of individual liberty. As the reflective minds in the nation gazed on the ruins around them, and observed the effects of the new principles which were at work on the Continent, they contemplated the reconstruction of order in a universal system in which the constitution of their own country should occupy its proper place. Among these thinkers stands eminent the noble mind of Sir Thomas More.

Probably the first philosophic conception of the manner in which the unity of Christendom might be expanded so as to satisfy modern requirements is to be found in More's *Utopia*. It is exceedingly important to appreciate accurately the character of this work. *Utopia* is not like the *Republic* of Plato—the picture of an ideal state ; for not only is the western commonwealth supposed to be actually in existence, but it is described as wanting in some of the arts which have been developed among the nations of Europe. Nor again is More's treatise, like the *Prince* of Machiavelli, intended to convey practical lessons as to the manner in which a state should be founded and administered ; for many of the customs prevailing among the Utopians are obviously absurd. The book (which first appeared in 1516) is a *jeu d esprit*, inspired partly by ancient classical models, and partly by the thoughts, actions, and discoveries of the age ; hence the influence it exercised on the leading intellects of Europe, and notably on Rabelais. It was evidently the author's purpose to describe an imaginary society, by contrast with which he might at choice satirise the political tendencies in the states of Europe as they presented themselves to actual observation, suggest ideas of social improvement in his own country, and at the same time amuse the reader by the whimsical character of the conception as a whole. Many of the practices of the Utopians in war, for ex- ample, are clearly unfitted for adoption in Europe[1] ; on the other hand, in their dealings with mercenary troops, More reflects on the changes which the military art was then actually undergoing ; and in the same way he finds an opportunity, in the character of his traveller Hythloday, to satirise the ambition of the Emperor and the king of France, which was involving the Continent in hopeless confusion.[2]   Again, in the matter of education, he uses the example of the Utopians, among whom Hythloday him- self introduces the study of Greek literature, as an indirect argument for encouraging the new learning in England.[3] But some of the institutions in the government of the Utopians represent More's own ideal ; and among these is the idea of Toleration. If the description in the follow- ing passage be contrasted with the ideas as to the methods of preserving religious unity prevailing in any European community at that period, we shall see how novel, as well as how just, was the conception of More :—

---

[1] *Utopia* (Lupton's edition of Ralph Robinson's Translation, 1895), ch. viii.
[2] *Ibid.* pp. 81, 83.   [3] *Ibid.* pp. 213, 214.

King Utopus, even at the first beginning, hearing that the inhabitants of the land were, before his coming thither, at continual dissension and strife among themselves for their religions, perceiving also that this common dissension (whilst every several sect took several parts in fighting for their country) was the only occasion of his conquest over them all, as soon as he had gotten the victory, first of all he made a decree that it should be lawful for every man to favour and follow what religion he would ; and that he might do the best he could to bring others to his opinion, so that he did it peaceably, gently, quietly, and soberly ; without hasty and contentious rebuking and inveighing against other. If he could not by fair and gentle speech induce them unto his opinion, yet he should use no kind of violence, and refrain from displeasant and seditious words.   To him that would vehemently and fervently in this cause strive and contend, was decreed banishment or bondage.[1]

It is one of the tragedies of history that the philosopher who was the first to present the ideal of Toleration should have been, in his latter years, forced, not to banish, but (contrary to his own principles) to *burn* the Schismatics opposing themselves to the established faith.   And as we reflect on the persecutions of the Protestants by Mary, and of the Roman Catholics by Elizabeth, we are inclined to conclude that philosophers are not very practical guides in human affairs.   Still it was plain that, in a nation whose constitution encouraged such ideal conceptions with regard to religion as those of *Utopia ;* whose government, under existing circumstances, gave large scope to the reforms of a powerful monarch ; whose Universities had not been slow to welcome the arrival of the new learning ; such teaching as that of More in his philosophical romance would necessarily hereafter bear great fruit in action.

In France the new ideas germinated on a very different soil.   There the principle of Feudalism had rooted itself far more deeply than in England, and the conflict between local liberty and the central monarchical power was proportionately severe.   It had practically ended, however, in the victory of the Crown.   The king had concentrated in his own hands most of the active powers in the nation.

1 *Utopia* (Lupton's edition of Ralph Robinson's Translation), pp. 271, 272.

By his alliance with the middle classes in the towns he had overthrown, as the futile revolt of the Constable Bourbon was soon to show, the authority of the great vassals ; by his alliance with the Papacy he was master of the liberties of the Gallican Church ; the close corporations of the local Parliaments and the Universities were no match for the resources of the Crown. Encouraged by Francis I., all the arts and learning of Italy gave a refined splendour to the life of the court. But while France thus assimilated the principles of the Renaissance, she remained almost untouched by the principles of the Reformation. In certain districts, and among certain classes, the opinions of the Reformers had firmly established themselves, but the bulk of the population remained under the sway of the old Catholicism, mixed with a large element of ancient Pagan traditions, so that between the decay of the old genius of local liberty and the stationary character of beliefs and customs, there was little opportunity for the fusion of the ancient with the modern spirit. The analytic and destructive genius which, as we saw in the last volume, displayed itself at an early stage of French society, continued to prevail ; the genius of political construction remained in abeyance.[1]

There can be no more striking proof of the continuity of spiritual force than the essential identity of character in the great works of literature which have influenced the French intellect at critical epochs in the history of the nation. I have already pointed out the double tendency in the first great literary monument of France, the *Roman de la Rose*, and the descent of this twofold tradition may be easily traced through the whole course of French literature. Crebillon the younger on the one side, and Voltaire on the other, are the offspring respectively of William de Lorris and John de Meung. The primitive pioneers of the French Renaissance are the progenitors of the apostles of the French Revolution ; the half-way stage in the journey is represented by Marot and Rabelais, the ornaments of the reign of Francis I. An unbroken line

[1] See vol. i. pp. 175-185.

of poets had carried on the opposing principles of the *Romance of the Rose* through two centuries and a half, the chivalrous and feudal ideal being maintained by Guillaume de Machault (1295-1377), Eustache Deschamps (1340-1420), Alain Chartier (1386-1449), and Charles d'Orleans (1391-1465); while the mocking analytic spirit embodied in the *fabliau* of the trouvères finds its exponent in François Villon (1431-1490), and Guillaume Coquillart (*circ.* 1440-1510).

In the reign of Francis I., Clement Marot, the first refiner of the French language, adapted, as far as was possible (and that was not very far), the sentiments of Guillaume de Lorris to the manners of the Court. He modernised the *Romance of the Rose;* imitated the chivalric side of this poem in his *Temple de Cupidon*, and developed the style of the old French rondeau. But just as Bayard was almost the last illustrious representative of the ancient chivalry, so the genuine spirit had almost died out of chivalric poetry ; and Marot was obliged to import into the style something of the bourgeois element which Coquillart [1] had made popular in the refined circles of the previous generation. On the other hand, the vast increase of energy imparted to the literary tradition of John de Meung by the alliance between the Crown and the Bourgeoisie, is indicated by the abounding force in the works of Rabelais. The spirit by which the creations of this author—like Erasmus, educated in a monastery—are animated, tends to undermine the whole basis of Catholicism and Feudalism. The Histories of Gargantua and Pantagruel are grounded on mockery of the Romances ; all the ridicule is directed against the excesses of monastic training, and the pretensions of the Scholastic Philosophy. Doubtless the germ of Rabelais' ideas is to be found in the *Utopia;* but in the French romance there is a complete absence of the serious and constructive thought which accompanies the invention of More. Whatever ideals the spirit of negative Reason may suggest to

---

[1] An interesting account of Coquillart is given in the edition of his works in 2 vols. by M. C. d'Héricault. Paris, 1857.

Rabelais are only employed by him to bring the absurdity of existing institutions into stronger relief. He shows no perception of the spiritual cravings in human nature which called the monastery into existence ; he has no sympathy with the ideal side of chivalry. Gigantic shouts of bourgeois laughter, horse-play, and obscenity, resound through his pages ; the soul of John de Meung has passed into the being of a great writer of the Renaissance. In the following description of the female sex, for example, every one will recognise the opinions of the man who completed the *Roman de la Rose :*—

> Quand je diz femme, je diz un sexe tant fragil, tant variable, tant muable, tant inconstant et imperfaict, que nature me semble . . . s'estre esguarée de ce bon sens par lequel elle avoit créé e formé toutes choses quand elle a basty la femme. . . . Certes Platon ne sçait en quel ranc il les doibve colloquer, ou des animans raisonnables, ou des bestes brutes.[1]

In such an atmosphere it would be vain to look for those ideas of rational liberty and toleration which illuminate the *Utopia.* Rabelais sympathised with many of the opinions of the Humanist Reformers, and embodied them in passages of the earlier issues of his *Histories ;* but when he found that they were unfavourably regarded by authority, he at once removed them.[2] The destructive power of his imagination was enormous, but I do not think he can be said to have furnished a single constructive idea to the edifice of modern society. A distinguished French critic admirably describes his genius as follows :—

> We must give up all thought of living in the Republic of Plato or the Utopia of More. Gargantua and Pantagruel are, indeed, princes of Utopia. We remark in them occasional features of perfect government, of patriarchal and benevolent monarchy, suitable for a young and ingenuous nation. But Rabelais, who, like all his contemporaries, was in this respect a mere *tiro*, was of too critical a disposition to enlarge and complete his picture. His design was not to build the social edifice anew from top to bottom, but to indicate what parts of the ancient structure required to be rehandled by the architect. He intends to point to the most deplorable abuses of royalty, the excesses of

---

[1] Rabelais, *Works*, Bk. III. c. 32.   [2] Rabelais (Gebhart), p. 127.

war, the vices of certain institutions, the decay of the traditions and
the discipline of the Church.   But he does not give even the echo
of opinion about contemporary events, and the last thing his
book does is to represent the passions and ideas which, growing
in force up to the end of the century, culminate in the Satire
Ménippée.[1]

I have attempted in this chapter, by the aid of the facts
of history and the concrete evidence of literature, to give
a comprehensive, though a necessarily superficial, view of
the collective forces acting on the imagination of Europe
at the beginning of the sixteenth century ; and the reader
is now in a position to appreciate the main intellectual
motives which inspired the English poets of the age in
their metrical compositions. We are entering upon a
period of transition. The great social fabric of Catholicism
and Feudalism, in which civil and ecclesiastical elements
are so strangely blended and balanced, is still standing ;
an ideal of faith and morals is still before the mind
pointing out the duty of man to God in the scholastic
theology of the Church, and the duty of man to his neighbour in the chivalric institutions of the Holy Roman
Empire. This ideal we have seen reflected in the various
types of English poetry brought under review in the first
volume of this History, in the *Vision of Piers the Plowman*, in the *Confessio Amantis*, and in the numerous streams
of Love allegory taking their rise in the *Romance of the
Rose*. The character of all such poetry was derived from
the great principle of Universal Authority, which was its
inspiring cause : it was catholic, conventional, didactic.
In the poetry of Chaucer alone we observed the predominance of the new power which, in the sixteenth
century, will become throughout Europe the determining motive of literary composition. But now in every
European country, in various forms and under different
aspects, arises the idea of liberty of thought and action,
in the constitution both of the State and the Individual.
All of these influences beat, like the waves of an advancing

[1] Translated from Rabelais (*Classiques Populaires*), pp. 179, 180. Emile
Gebhart, Professeur à la Faculté des Lettres de Paris.

sea, upon the English imagination, and begin to break up the solid structure of traditional belief and ancient chivalry.

The history of Ideas has in it something of the solemnity of tragic action. As the chant of the monks on the Capitol called up in the imagination of the historian the long drama of the Decline and Fall of the Roman Empire, so the monuments of architecture, painting, sculpture, and poetry, record the dynastic revolutions in the march of human thought. Humiliating in many respects to our pride is the scene of waste, change, and decay, that such a retrospect discloses. Conceits and affectations elevated into the chief aims of poetry ; the idols of beauty confounded with its true forms ; experiments in language conducted at the expense of thought ; vain though noble attempts made to reanimate exhausted ideals ; admiration lavished on the shadows rather than the substance of art ; such are the ruins that will encounter us in this period of our history, like the fallen temples, tombs, and aqueducts, that sadden the memories of the traveller in the Roman Campagna. Nevertheless, it is encouraging to observe that, in spite of mistakes and failures, a definite advance in poetical composition is made on clearly-marked lines. Wherever there is honest and independent effort to give expression to an imaginative conception, there, however ineffectual the execution of the design may be in itself, we shall see that ground is gained for some later and more successful labourer in the same field ; even the pursuit of technical trickery discovers the road to genuine beauties of style. Wyatt is the pioneer of the artistic reforms of Surrey; Euphuism, false and misleading in its own aims, contributes a valuable element to the structure of the Elizabethan drama and the refined wit of the eighteenth century ; the pastoralism of the *Arcadia* prepares the way for *As You Like It* and *The Winter's Tale ;* and the moral allegory in the *Faery Queen* foreshadows the religious epic in *Paradise Lost.*

CHAPTER II

SIR THOMAS WYATT: ORIGINALITY OF THOUGHT: IMITATION OF FOREIGN MODELS OF EXPRESSION

THOMAS WYATT was the elder of the two sons of Sir Henry Wyatt, a faithful adherent of the House of Lancaster, who, having suffered imprisonment in the Tower in the reign of Richard III., was, on the accession of Henry VII., advanced to posts of high honour and trust in the Court, and acquired considerable properties in the county of Kent, among others the Castle of Allington, where Thomas was born in 1503, his mother being Anne the daughter of John Skinner of Reigate, in Surrey. It may be presumed that the future poet was a boy of precocious powers, for in 1515 he was entered at St. John's College, Cambridge, being only twelve years old, an early age for study at the University even in those times. He took his Bachelor's Degree in 1518, and his Master's in 1520. While at Cambridge he formed an intimate acquaintance with Leland the Antiquary, who afterwards celebrated his genius in Latin verse.[1] Anthony Wood asserts that after finishing his course at Cambridge he went to Cardinal Wolsey's new college at Oxford, but as this college was not founded till 1524, and as Wyatt was married in 1522 or 1523, and his eldest son, Thomas, was born in the year following his marriage, the statement seems no better founded than many others advanced by that patriotic but not very scrupulous author.[2] Wood

[1] Me tibi conjunxit comitem gratissima Granta. Leland, *Næniis in mortem T. Viati*, 1542, p. 4.   [2] *Athenæ Oxonienses*, vol. i. p. 124.

also says that, on leaving Oxford, Wyatt travelled on the
Continent, and in view of the poet's wide acquaintance
with Italian literature, we may perhaps assume that he
did so on leaving *Cambridge*. It is at any rate certain
that in 1525 he was in attendance at Court, for he is
found taking part there with other gentlemen in one of
those splendid masquerades in which Henry VIII. so
much delighted.[1] Most of Wyatt's love poems were
probably written between this date and 1537, when he
was sent as ambassador to Spain, and was accordingly
removed from the sphere in which he would naturally
have employed his fancy on compositions that had procured him in England a high reputation as a graceful
poet.[2]

How far these poems were inspired by serious feeling
we have no means of knowing. The tradition is that
Wyatt was in love with Anne Boleyn, and some of the
more malignant writers on the Roman Catholic side, at
a later period in the century, did not hesitate to spread
the report that their intercourse was of an immoral
nature.[3] But the circumstantial story on which the
scandal is based is full of improbabilities. No charge
of the kind was made against Wyatt at Anne's trial,
where evidence of the flimsiest kind was brought forward
to criminate the Queen ; it is, morever, plain that, if the
King had regarded Wyatt as in any way a rival in his
wife's affections, he would never have admitted him to
his confidence, or promoted him to honour. It is true
that Wyatt in 1536 was sent to the Tower, but he
himself, in his speech before the Privy Council in 1541,
expressly ascribes his imprisonment on this occasion to

---

[1] Hall, *Chronicles*, p. 631. Edition 1809.
[2] As early as 1527 Leland, writing to him from Paris, says—

> Tu nunc fac animum, rogo, Viate,
> Nostrum, non veneres styli fluentis
> Expendas propius nitentiores,
> Quas sic Castaliæ tibi puellæ
> Consensu facili simul dederunt
> Ut vel montibus Aonis in ipsis
> Te natum chorus æstimet virorum
> Doctorum niveus fuisse plane.

[3] Nott, *Memoirs of Sir T. Wyatt*, pp. xviii. xix.

the influence of the Duke of Suffolk, and not to the
personal displeasure of the King.[1] The story of his
attachment to Anne Boleyn rests partly on tradition,
partly on inference from expressions in his own poems.
An epigram of his, in which, like Petrarch, he plays upon
his mistress's name, is addressed " To His Love called
Anna "; and in one of his sonnets he hints enigmatically
that a royal lover has made it impossible for him to
persevere in his old pursuit :—

> Whoso list to hunt? I know where is an hind.
> .   .   .   .   .   .
> Who list her hunt, I put him out of doubt,
>   As well as I may spend his time in vain.
>   Graven with diamonds in letters plain ;
> There is written her fair neck round about,
>   " Noli me tangere " : for Cæsar's I am.[2]

There is no very deep feeling here ; and it is quite
possible, as far as Anne Boleyn is concerned, that her
intercourse with Wyatt was limited to a game of gallantry,
played by both parties in strict conformity with the rules
of the Courts of Love, and not intended to have a serious
ending. There are, indeed, as we shall presently see,
many of Wyatt's love poems, in which the flame of his
ardent and enthusiastic nature seems to burn in the very
movement of the verse ; but these may well have been
inspired by some other object than the unfortunate Queen.

Anne was beheaded in 1536, and Wyatt, who received the honour of knighthood in the same year, was
in 1537 sent as ambassador to the Spanish Court, with
the object of reviving "the old amity" between the
Emperor and the King of England. The position was
one of peculiar delicacy, for not only had the Emperor
been bitterly offended with Henry on account of the
divorce of Katharine of Arragon, his aunt, but the King
was also anxious to obtain the consent of the Emperor
to removing the Princess Mary from the succession to the
throne. There was, further, the religious difficulty, the

---

[1] Wyatt's *Oration* (Nott's edition of *Works*, vol. ii. p. 300).
[2] *Works*, vol. ii. p. 143.

question of the divorce having naturally brought the
Emperor and the Pope together, while it had inclined
Henry towards an alliance with the Protestant princes of
Germany, who were opposing Charles V. It is no great
wonder if, in such a web of tangled interests, Wyatt did
not succeed in obtaining any definite promises from a
monarch so accustomed as Charles to dissemble. Henry,
however, seems to have thought that more might be done,
and he sent out two other representatives, of whom
Bonner, afterwards Bishop of London, was one, to join
Wyatt in his embassy. This arrangement proved very
unsuccessful. Bonner, a man of coarse and violent
manners, was quite unqualified to act either as a diplomatist, or as a companion to a gentleman like Wyatt.
Nothing was accomplished, and at last, in 1539, the
embassy was recalled to England. Wyatt, who had been
long hard pressed for money, expressed his joy at the
thought of seeing his country once more in the following
vigorous " epigram " :—

> Tagus, farewell ! that westward with thy streams
>   Turns up the grains of gold already tried ;
> With spur and sail for I go seek the Thames,
>   Gainward the sun that sheweth her wealthy pride ;
> And to the town which Brutus sought by dreams
>   Like bended moon doth bend her lusty side.
> My king, my country, alone for whom I live,
> Of mighty love the wings for this me give.[1]

On his return to England the King, as a reward for
his services, granted him the house of the Friars at
Ailesford in Kent. Bonner had done his best to prejudice Wyatt in Henry's opinion, but for the moment
he was unsuccessful, and Sir Thomas was shortly afterwards again sent on an embassy to treat with the
Emperor, when the latter passed through France to
Netherlands, to take possession of the Duchy of Guelders.
Wyatt's despatches give a lively picture of the diplomatic
struggle which followed, and speak to the penetration, the
readiness, and the high spirit with which he discharged
his mission.

[1] Wyatt's *Works*, vol. ii. p. 71.

Though he was as unsuccessful as before, the King expressed his appreciation of his conduct. But on his return to England his fortunes changed. Cromwell, his chief friend, fell from power in July 1540. Bonner renewed his intrigues, and in the winter of the same year Wyatt was committed to the Tower on the charge of traitorous correspondence with Pole and of disrespect to the King. He must have remained in captivity nearly six months, and it was then that he wrote to his friend Bryan the "epigram" which gives a condensed idea of his sufferings and feelings :—

> Sighs are my food ; my drink they are my tears ;
> 　Clinking of fetters such music would crave ;
> Stink and close air away my life wears ;
> 　Innocency is all the hope I have ;
> Rain, wind, or weather I judge by mine ears ;
> 　Malice assaults that [what] righteousness should have.[1]
> Sure I am, Bryan, this wound shall heal again,
> But yet alas ! the scar shall still remain.

In his trial before the Privy Council he defended himself with great manliness, energy, and humour. His innocence was plain ; he was acquitted ; and the King himself must have been quite satisfied, for on the 10th of July 1541 he made him a grant of lands in Lambeth ; in 1542 appointed him high steward of the Manor of Maidstone, and gave him lands in Dorsetshire and Somersetshire in exchange for estates of less value in Kent.

Wyatt now retired to his house at Allington to enjoy the repose he had justly earned and ardently longed for. Here he wrote his Satires and his Paraphrase of the Seven Penitential Psalms, and occupied himself with the education of his nephew and the improvement of his property. But his services were too valuable to be dispensed with. In the autumn of 1542 Henry resolved to enter into close alliance with the Emperor, who sent an ambassador into England to arrange the terms of a

---

[1] This is the reading as given by Dr. Nott (*Works*, vol. ii. p. 72). It may be conjectured that Wyatt wrote "*Save*."

treaty.   The King ordered Wyatt to conduct the envoy
to London, and as the latter seems to have arrived at
Falmouth sooner than was expected, Wyatt hastened
thither on horseback at unusual speed.   From his exer-
tions and the badness of the weather he overheated himself, and, having reached Sherborne, fell into a fever
which prevented him from continuing his journey.   A
friend who lived in the neighbourhood went to him, and
nursed him through his illness, which, however, ended
fatally in October 1542.   The nature of the fever of
which he was the victim made it impossible to remove
the body to Kent, and it was buried by his friend Horsey,
perhaps in his own family vault in the Great Church at
Sherborne, but without even an inscription to mark the
exact resting-place of so great a man.[1]

Two very marked and contrary features distinguish
Wyatt's poetry, the individual energy of his thought, and
his persistent imitation of foreign models.   The former is
what separates him sharply from the poets of the Middle
Ages.   Hitherto, with the exception of the *Canterbury
Tales*, almost every English poem of importance had been
didactic in intention, thereby denoting its clerical source ;
symbolical in form, thus revealing the influence of the
allegorical method of interpreting Nature and Scripture
encouraged in the Church schools.   Wyatt, on the other
hand, looked at Nature through his own eyes, and sought
to express directly the feelings of his own heart.   He was
a man of many moods and ideas ; his compositions include
love verses, epigrams, devotional meditations, satires ; and
in all of these the force and ardour of his thought is sensibly
felt.   But equally, in all of them, the poet shows himself
to be aware of the imperfection of his native language as
an instrument of expression, and submits himself with
humility to the superiority of the foreign masters whose
manner he seeks to reproduce   In consequence of this
his actual poetical achievements are of very unequal

---

[1] Most of the foregoing particulars of Wyatt's life were collected by Dr.
Nott, whose very careful and industrious edition of his and Surrey's works
was published in 1816.

merit ; he often aims at objects which he ought to have
avoided, or at effects to which his resources are unequal ;
he is most successful when his fiery genius can find out a
way for itself untrammelled by the precedents of art.

This is particularly the case in those of his love-poems
in which he abandons the models of Petrarch and the Italian
and French successors of that poet. The groundwork of the
style of the Petrarchists was the poetry of the Troubadours,
refined and modified by the classical tastes of the Humanists.
The genius of the Troubadours being the natural product
of the institutions of chivalry, when these decayed the
genuine motive of production ceased, and the poet, seeking
merely to preserve the outward manner, fell into a style
hard, mechanical, and affected. For example, in the
sixteenth century and long afterwards, the most quoted of
Petrarch's sonnets was the 156th, which is as follows :—

> Passa la nave mia colma d' obblio
> 　　Per aspro mar a mezza notte il verno,
> 　　Infra Scilla e Cariddi, ed al governo
> 　　Siede 'l Signor, anzi 'l nemico mio.
> A ciascun remo un pensier pronto e rio,
> 　　Che la tempesta, e 'l fin par ch' abbi a scherno.
> 　　La vela rompe un vento umido eterno
> 　　Di sospir, di speranze, e di desio.
> Pioggia di lagrimar, nebbia di sdegni,
> 　　Bagna, e rallenta le già stanche sarte ;
> 　　Che son d' error con ignoranza attorto.
> Celansi i duo miei dolci usati segni ;
> 　　Morta fra l' onde è la ragion, e l' arte.
> 　　Tal, ch' incommincio a disperar del porto.[1]

Now it must be clear to every reader of manly taste
that this sonnet deserves no higher praise than that of
ingenuity. As soon as the poet has fixed on the idea
that his soul is like a ship, of which Love is the pilot, it
is easy enough to associate with this central thought a
group of subordinate conceits, in which tears are imaged
as rain, and sighs as winds ; on the other hand, it is almost
inevitable that, in endeavouring to work out the comparison, he should use such violence as to liken his

---

[1] See Wyatt's translation on p. 52.

thoughts to oarsmen, and should represent the ropes of the
vessel as being "twisted by error and ignorance." The
passion for riddles, always a symptom of declining taste,
caused this mechanical performance to be preferred above
sonnets in which Petrarch, having selected a really
fine thought, elaborates it with simplicity and propriety.
The Petrarchists came to reckon subject as of little
importance in poetry; and every one wishing to show
his skill aimed at finding resemblances between objects
which were to all appearance the most unlike each other
in Nature. Giusto de' Conti, for instance, composed a
whole volume of sonnets on "the beautiful hand" of his
mistress; and Serafino dell' Aquila treated the subject of
Love in a series of epigrams, under the title of *Strambotti*
or Conceits, each of which consisted of an abstract
thought illustrated by a sensible image, and was expressed
within the limits of a stanza in *ottava rima*. So great was
the admiration felt for this poet by his contemporaries
that his epitaph assures the traveller that he may hold it
an honour even to have seen his tomb.[1]

It is not surprising that the French and English poets
who imitated Petrarch should have tried to reproduce
those qualities in his sonnets which they found most
appreciated by his own countrymen. Mellin de St.
Gelays, who made an attempt—ineffectual as it proved—
to transplant the sonnet into French literature some few
years before Wyatt introduced it into England, was the
author of the following lines, in which it will be seen that
the manner of Petrarch, as above exemplified, is prosaically
copied :—

> Voyant ces monts de veue ainsi lointaine,
> Je les compare à mon long déplaisir :
> Haut est leur chef, et haut est mon désir,
> Leur pied est ferme, et ma foy est certaine.
> D'eux maint ruisseau coule et mainte fontaine :

---

[1] Qui giace Serafin ! Partirti or puoi.
Sol d' aver visto il sasso che lo serva,
Assai sei debitore agli occhi tuoi.
*Vita del facundo Poeta Seraphyno Aquilano,
per Vincentio Calmeta composta*, 1505.

De mes deux yeux sortent pleurs à loisir ;
De forts souspirs ne me puis dessaissir,
Et de grands vents leur cime est toute pleine.
    Mille troupeaux s'y promènent et paissent ;
Autant d'Amours se couvent et renaissent
Dedans mon cœur, qui seul est ma pasture.
    Ils sont sans fruict, mon bien n'est qu'apparence ;
Et d'eux à moy n'a qu'une différence,
    Qu'en eux la neige, en moi la flamme dure.

Of the thirty-one sonnets composed by Wyatt ten are translated more or less closely from Petrarch,[1] one from Mellin de St. Gelays,[2] two are indebted to Petrarch,[3] one is constructed out of two of Serafino's *Strambotti*,[4] one from J. A. Romanello ;[5] and the remaining nine are apparently the product of original thought. Not one of the series shows any marks of inspiration, they are the work of a man who has been impressed with the beautiful and ingenious form of the sonnet as handled by the Italians, and who seeks to reproduce its effects in a language not yet sufficiently refined for his purpose. The following, which are renderings of the sonnets by Petrarch and Mellin de St. Gelays already cited, may be taken as average examples of his style :—

My galley, charged with forgetfulness,
    Thorough sharp seas in winter nights doth pass
    'Tween rock and rock ; and eke mine enemy alas !
    That is my lord, steereth with cruelness :
At every oar, a thought in readiness ;
    As though that death were light in such a case.
    An endless wind doth tear the sail apace
    Of forced sighs, and trusty fearfulness.
A rain of tears, a cloud of dark disdain,
    Hath done the wearied cords great hindrance,
    Wreathed with error and eke with ignorance.
The stars be hid that led me to this pain ;
    Drowned is reason that should me consort ;
    And I remain, despairing of the port.

---

[1] Compare Wyatt, Sonnets i. ii. v. ix. xi. xiii. xiv. xviii. xx. xxv. with Petrarch, Sonnets 109, 61, 136, 81, 12, 104, 156, 44, 19, 229.

[2] Sonnet xxi. ; compare Mellin de St. Gelays, *Œuvres Poetiques* (1719), p. 73, cited above.

[3] Compare Wyatt, Sonnets iv. viii., and Petrarch, 220, 188.

[4] Wyatt, Sonnet xxiii., Serafino's Strambotti *Il cor ti diedi* and *La donna di Natura.*

[5] Wyatt, Sonnet i. (Nott, p. 243), Romanello cited by Nott, p. 571.

This is the production of an energetic mind ; nevertheless the means employed are inadequate to the end, as may be specially noted in the unsuccessful attempt to render

> A ciascun remo un pensier pronto e rio,
> Che la tempesta e 'l fin par ch' abbi a scherno ;

[At each oar a thought bold and guilty, which seems to think scorn alike of the tempest and the goal]

and by the omission of any equivalent for " arte " in the thirteenth line caused by the necessity of rhyming.   On the other hand, Wyatt's strong individuality asserts itself in his alteration of Petrarch's " i duo miei dolci *usati* segni [my two sweet familiar stars]," into the vehement

> The stars be hid *that led me to this pain.*

The translation of Mellin de St. Gelays' sonnet seems to have been occasioned by a tasteless admiration for the French poet's trivial conceits, and is as follows :—

> Like to these unmeasurable mountains
> Is my painful life, the burden of ire ;
> For of great height be they, and high is my desire ;
> And I of tears, and they be full of fountains.
> Under craggy rocks they have barren plains ;
> Hard thoughts in me my woeful mind doth tire.
> Small fruit and many leaves their tops do attire ;
> Small effect with great trust in me remains.
> The boisterous winds oft their high boughs do blast ;
> Hot sighs from me continually be shed.
> Cattle in them and in me love is fed ;
> Immoveable am I, and they are full steadfast.
> Of restless birds, they have the tone and note ;
> And I alway plaints that pass through my throat.

The reader will have some difficulty in making up his mind whether more to blame Wyatt for the flat and feeble close of this sonnet, or to commend him for the glimmering of good taste he shows in rejecting the contrast between fire and snow, in which Mellin de St. Gelays' readers doubtless found a fine stroke of poetical art. Wyatt's fondness for the form of the sonnet was probably

caused by a certain metaphysical turn of thought that
made him select for imitation those compositions of
Petrarch which are most distinguished for the excruciating
ingenuity of their sentimental logic.   In one sonnet he
prays his mistress to receive the heart he proffers her ; for
if, he says, she rejects it, he will disdain to receive back
what she has refused : the heart will then no longer be
his :—

> If I then it chase, nor it in you can find
> In this exile no manner of comfort ;
> Nor live alone, nor where he is called resort,
> He may wander from his natural kind.
> So shall it be great hurt unto us twain,
> And yours the loss, and mine the deadly pain.[1]

In another place he upbraids his tongue because it
fails to express his love, his tears because they will not
flow when he wishes to " make his moan," his sighs which
are passive when they should be active ; he concludes that
his look only is left to reveal his heart.[2]   All this is in
the traditional vein of the Troubadours.   But the manliness which is, after all, Wyatt's distinguishing characteristic, is constantly revolting against the servility enjoined
on the male lover by the code of chivalry, and in several
sonnets he gives a different turn to the original he is
translating.   Thus Petrarch in his 61st sonnet says that,
though he is not tired of loving, he is tired of hating himself and weeping, and he wishes himself dead, with Laura's
name written on his tomb.   But Wyatt, while imitating
Petrarch's sonnet, says :—

> I will not yet in my grave be burièd,
> Nor on my tomb your name have fixed fast,
> As cruel cause that did the spirit soon haste
> From th' unhappy bones, by great sighs stirrèd.[3]

And at another time he protests that he will renounce
his mistress in consequence of her injustice.   The sonnet
in which he proclaims this intention is perhaps his best :—

> My love to scorn, my service to retain,
>   Therein, methought, she used cruelty,

---

[1] *Works* (Nott), vol. ii. p. 13.   [2] *Ibid.* p. 8.   [3] *Ibid.* p. 2.

> Since with good will I lost my liberty,
>   To follow her which causeth all my pain.
> Might never care cause me for to refrain,
>   But only this which is extremity,
>   Giving me nought, alas ! nor to agree
> That as I was her man, I might remain.
> But since that thus ye list to order me,
>   That would have been your servant true and fast,
>   Displease thee not, my dotting days be past ;
> And with my loss to leave I must agree.
>   For as there is a certain time to rage,
>   So is there time such madness to assuage.[1]

The idea of justice in love is not common in the poetry of the Troubadours, who enforced the principle that it was the lover's duty to prove his devotion by submitting to his mistress's will. It is, however, the predominant note in Wyatt's love poetry, who insists that long and faithful service deserves a full reward. For the expression of a feeling so ardent and elementary, the sonnet, with its elaborate structure, was not a good vehicle. Wyatt's best poems are written in simple metrical forms, which enable him to pour himself forth with a strength and energy rarely equalled in English poetry. A fine example of this simpler manner remains in the fervent lines beginning " Forget not yet the tried intent " ;[2] and in the following, which is less known, there is not a superfluous word to diminish the heat of indignation which inspires the movement of the verse :—

> What should I say !
>   Since Faith is dead,
> And Truth away
>   From you is fled ?
>   Should I be led
>   With doubleness ?
>   Nay ! nay ! mistress.
>
> I promised you,
>   And you promised me,
> To be as true
>   As I would be.
>   But since I see
>   Your double heart,
>   Farewell my part !

---

[1] *Works*, vol. ii. p. 10.   [2] They are inserted in *The Golden Treasury*.

Thought for to take
'Tis not my mind ;
But to forsake
One so unkind ;
And as I find,
So will I trust ;
Farewell, unjust !

Can ye say nay,
But that you said
That I alway
Should be obeyed ?
And thus betrayed
Or that I wist !
Farewell, unkist ! [1]

Here again is an admirable specimen of forcible feeling expressed in the fewest and best words :—

Is it possible ?
That so high debate,
So sharp, so sore, and of such rate,
Should end so soon, and was begun so late ?
Is it possible ?

Is it possible ?
So cruel intent,
So lusty heat, and so soon spent,
From love to hate, and thence for to relent ?
Is it possible ?

Is it possible ?
That any may find
Within one heart so diverse mind,
To change or turn as weather or wind ?
Is it possible ?

Is it possible ?
To spy it in an eye
That turns as oft as chance or die,
The truth whereof can any try ?
Is it possible ?

Is it possible ?
For to turn so oft ;
To bring that lowest that was most aloft ;
And to fall highest, yet to light soft ?
Is it possible ?

---

[1] *Works*, vol. ii. p. 246.

> All is possible ?
> Whoso list believe,
> Trust therefore first, and after preve ;
> As men wed ladies by license and leave ;
> All is possible ! [1]

In poems of this kind Wyatt was, no doubt, helped to his form by the circumstance that poetry was not yet divorced from music. Music, as we see from Castiglione's *Courtier*, was a necessary accomplishment for a gentleman. Henry VIII. was passionately fond of it, and almost all Wyatt's love lyrics were composed for the accompaniment of the lute. The dropping of the final *e* in the language, as spoken, enabled the poet to produce extremely musical combinations of words for the purposes of singing, as appears in that most harmonious ballad *The Nut-Brown Maid*, which is certainly a composition not later than the early part of the sixteenth century :—

> Yet take good hede, for ever I drede
> That ye shall not sustayne
> The thornie waies, the deep valleyes,
> The snow, the frost, the raine,
> The cold, the hete ; for, dry or wete,
> We must lodge on the plaine,
> None other roof us two aboof
> But a brake bushe or twayne.

The reader will have observed in all the poems of Wyatt cited above a weightiness of matter, prevailing over elegance of form, and accordingly ill adapted to modes of composition in which elaborate terseness or harmony of expression is indispensable. Want of a perfect instrument, as well as errors of imperfect taste, are very visible in Wyatt's epigrams. In these he does not aim so much at the condensed expression of a witty thought, as at the invention of an ingenious paradox. His model is Serafino, five of whose *Strambotti* he has rendered into English ; and whose form—the *ottava rima* stanza—he generally uses, whether he is expressing a thought of his own, or giving a version of ideas met with in the

[1] *Works*, vol. ii. p. 216.

course of his reading. Among the many authors to whom he is indebted for the matter of his epigrams are Josephus, Seneca, Plato, and Pandulfo Collinutio ; and the character of his style may be illustrated by his version of the following epigram ascribed to Plato :—

χρυσὸν ἀνὴρ εὑρὼν ἔλιπεν βρόχον· αὐτὰρ ὁ χρυσὸν
ὃν λίπεν οὐχ εὑρὼν ἧψεν ὃν εὗρε βρόχον.

It would be impossible to condense more thought into two lines ; indeed, the idea is so closely packed, that it would be unintelligible to any one who did not know the story on which the epigram is based. Ausonius, in his Latin version, expanded the couplet into four lines :—

> Thesauro invento qui limina mortis inibat
> Liquit ovans laqueum quo periturus erat.
> At qui quod terræ abdiderat non repperit aurum
> Quem laqueum invenit nexuit et periit.[1]

Wyatt treats the idea in Serafino's eight-line stanza :—

> For shamefast harm of great and hateful need
>   In deep despair as did a wretch go
> With ready cord out of his life to speed,
>   His stumbling foot did find an hoard, lo !
> Of gold I say, when he prepared this deed,
>   And in exchange he left the cord tho' ;
> He that had hid the gold, and found it not,
> Of that he found he shaped his neck a knot.[2]

So that while he gives Ausonius' last two lines, almost word for word in his closing couplet, he takes six lines to work up to the point, nor does he even then contrive to tell the story distinctly. On the other hand, where he expresses a sincere feeling of his own, he is often admirably energetic, as is shown by the verses I have already cited, written to Bryan from the Tower, and by his *Farewell* to the Tagus.

---

[1] Ausonius, *Epigrammata* xxii. It may be rendered into English :—

Tom meant to hang, but finding gold, found for his noose no use,
But Dick, his gold who could not find, used what he found, the noose.

[2] *Works*, vol. ii. p. 65.

The same strength of individual feeling appears in
Wyatt's Satires. These are the fruit of his retirement at
Allington, and are undoubtedly the most pleasing of all
his regular compositions. They express the ardent love
of country life natural to an English gentleman conversant
with affairs, and all the disdain and indignation proper to
a lofty mind familiar with the mean servility prevalent
among the creatures of a Court. But even when he is
dealing with matters so congenial, Wyatt gets his inspiration from foreign models. He is indebted for the form of
his Satire to Luigi Alamanni, one of the few truly noble
Italians of the sixteenth century, who were ready to suffer
all things in behalf of that ideal of liberty and patriotism
which they inherited as the late descendants of republican
Rome. After making a vain stand against the restoration
of the despotic power of the Medici in Florence, his native
city, Alamanni withdrew to France, where he was received
by Francis I. with the honour that he deserved. His Satires
breathe a fiery indignation against the corruptions of his
time, and the following very fine verses may be cited in apt
illustration of the continuous tradition cherished by the
Italian poets ; they show how readily the allusive and
metaphorical style of Dante and Petrarch lent itself to
the purposes of Satire :—

> Oggi ha d' altr' acqua Roma ed altra sete,
>   Che di Samaria, ed altri pesci prende
>   Che già il buon Pescator, con altra rete.
> Or per altro sentier nel ciel s' ascende
>   Non chi si pente, ma si monda e scarca
>   Chi la mano al pastor con l' oro stende.
> Con più ricco nocchier nuove onde varca,
>   Con le sarte di seta, e d' or la vela,
>   Lunge da Galilea la santa barca.
> D' altro Simon per te s' ordisce tela,
>   Che di chi di Cefas riporta 'l nome,
>   Per quello acceso amor ch' a te si cela.
> Oh ! chi vedesse il ver, vedrebbe come
>   Più disnor tu, che 'l tuo Luter Martino,
>   Porti a te stessa, e più gravose some.
> Non la Germania, no ! ma l' ozio, il vino,
>   Avarizia, Ambizion, Lussuria, e Gola,

Ti mena al fin, che già veggiam vicino.
Non pur questo dico io, non Francia sola,
Non pur la Spagna, tutta Italia ancora,
Che ti tien d' eresia, di vizi scola.
E chi nol crede, ne domanda ogn' ora
Urbin, Ferrara, l' Orso, e la Colonna,
La Marca, il Romagnuol, ma più chi plora,
Per te servendo, che fu d' altri Donna.[1]

In his twelfth Satire, Alamanni sets forth the various arts of the Courtier which he professes himself unequal to acquire; and Wyatt, in his second Satire, has adapted this poem with much spirit and success to his own circumstances in England. He has also borrowed Alamanni's *terza rima* as the vehicle for his first and third satires, in the former of which he imitates Horace's Fable of the Town and Country Mouse, and in the latter the Latin poet's Advice of Tiresias.[2] The opening " Of the mean and sure estate " is extremely picturesque, and shows Wyatt's satirical style at its best :—

My mother's maids, when they did sew and spin,
They sang sometimes a song of the field mouse
That, for because her livelode was but thin,
Would needs go seek her townish sister's house.
She thought herself endured to much pain ;
The stormy blasts her cave so sore did souse,
That when the furrows swimmed with the rain
She must lie cold and wet, in sorry plight ;
And worse than that, bare meat there did remain
To comfort her, when she her house had dight ;

---

[1] Alamanni, *Satire* iii. : " To-day Rome has other water and thirst for other water than that of Samaria, and takes, with other net than once did the good fisherman, other fish. Now by another path climbs to heaven, not the penitent ; but he who stretches out his hand to the shepherd with gold is purged and discharged. With a richer pilot, with shrouds of silk and sails of gold, the holy bark crosses new waves far from Galilee. By thee is woven the web of Simon, other than the one who takes his name from Cephas, smitten with that love which is hidden from thine eyes. O ! he that could see the truth would see that thou bringest upon thyself more dishonour and a more grievous burden than does that Martin Luther of thine. 'Tis not Germany, no ! but ease, wine, avarice, ambition, luxury, and gluttony, that are bringing thee to the end which we see to be so near. Nor is it I alone who say this, nor France alone, nor Spain, but all Italy to boot, which holds thee as the school of heresy and vice ; and he who does not believe this, let him ask at any time Urbino, Ferrara, Orsino, Colonna, La Marca, Romagna, but most of all her who through thee weeps in slavery, though she was once the mistress of others." I presume by the last words he means Florence.

[2] Hor. *Sat.* lib. ii. Sats. v. and vi.

> Sometimes a barley corn, sometimes a bean,
> For which she laboured hard both day and night,
> In harvest time, whilst she might go arid glean :
> And when her store was 'stroyed with the flood,
> Then well-away ! for she undone was clean.[1]

The moral of the Satire is conveyed in language full of energy, plainly coming straight from the heart of the writer, and extremely significant as the reflection of a man so widely experienced in the ways of the world :—

> Then seek no more out of thyself to find
>   The thing that thou hast sought so long before ;
> For thou shalt feel it sitting in thy mind,
> Mad if ye list to continue your sore.
>   Let present pass, and gape on time to come,
>   And deep yourself in travail more and more.
> Henceforth, my Poynz, this shall be all and sum,
>   These wretched fools shall have nought else of me :
> But to the great God, and to his high doom,
> None other pain pray I for them to be,
>   But when the rage doth lead them from the right,
>   That, looking backward, virtue they may see,[2]
> Even as she is so goodly, fair, and bright ;
>   And whilst they clasp their lusts in arms across,
>   Grant them, good Lord, as thou mayst of thy might,
> To freat inward for losing such a loss.[3]

In this passage we find a vein of sentiment which runs through the works of many of the religious Reformers, and makes a link between that party and the men of the Renaissance. As the first men of letters in mediæval Europe found a metaphysical connection between the doctrines of Christianity and the philosophy of Plato, so their successors, who opposed the corruptions of the scholastic system in the beginning of the sixteenth century, fell back on the works of those classical authors who most largely embodied the morality of the Stoics. Very many of the scholars and philosophers of that age were, in one aspect or another, favourers of the reform movement, and in this way much of the Pagan imagery employed by the Latin and Greek poets came insensibly to be associated with Christian dogma.

---

[1] *Works*, vol. ii. p. 82.
[2] Persius, *Sat.* iii. 88, "Virtutem videant intabescantque relicta."
[3] *Works*, vol. ii. p. 85.

Wyatt had early allied himself with the Lutheran party   Ardent in all his feelings, the spirit of devotion strengthened in him with advancing years, and from his Satires, which have much of the temper of Persius, he passed naturally to another line of composition, in the path which had already been opened by Dante and Alamanni, namely, a rendering of the seven penitential Psalms of David.   But here, too, he showed his originality by adopting a method different from that of his predecessors, who had contented themselves with simple translation or rather paraphrase.   Wyatt, on the other hand, presents his paraphrase of the psalms themselves in the framework of a narrative, inserting before each psalm a kind of poetical comment of his own, to explain the mood in which David composed it.   Very characteristically the idea of this framework is borrowed from the Reformer Beza's *Præfatio Poetica in Davidis Psalmos quos penitentiales vocant ;* and there is something extremely suggestive in the mixture of Pagan imagery and genuine Christian sentiment which comes from the combination.   Beza begins his preface in the following genuinely classical style :—

> Forte pererratis cælo, terraque, marique,
> Ales Amor sacras Judææ callidus urbes
> Visebat, pharetrâque minas, flammataque gestans
> Tela manu. Jamque hospitium sedemque petebat
> Venturæ nocti ; dumque acres undique versat
> Sæpe oculos, dubitatque etiam qua sede moretur,
> Tandem ad Bersabes convertit lumina formam.[1]

This is of course the manner in which Ovid would have treated the subject, but Ovid is not exactly the poet whom we should expect to be associated with a theme dealing with sin and repentance.   Still there can be no question of the depth and sincerity of religious feeling by which Wyatt's paraphrase is inspired.   It is indeed evident that each original psalm of David is only the channel into which the English poet poured the stream of his own emotion : the ten verses, for example, of which the sixth psalm consists, are expanded in the Paraphrase

---

[1] Cited in Nott's *Memoir of Wyatt,* vol. ii. p. cxxxv.

into 112 lines; and many ideas not expressed by the penitent king are developed out of his thought by the imagination of the paraphrast.   The psalm in the original says: "Have mercy upon me, O Lord; for I am weak: O Lord, heal me; for my bones are vexed.   My soul also is sore vexed: but thou, O Lord, how long?   Return, O Lord, deliver my soul: Oh save me for thy mercies' sake.   For in death there is no remembrance of thee: in the grave who shall give thee thanks?"   Wyatt's version is as follows:—

> I Lord am stray'd.   I, sick without recure,
>   Feel all my limbs, that have rebelled, for fear
>   Shake; in despair unless thou me assure.
> My flesh is troubled; my heart doth fear the spear;
>   That dread of death, of death that ever lasts,
>   Threateth of right and draweth near and near.[1]
> Much more my soul is troubled by the blasts
>   Of these assaults, that come as thick as hail,
>   Of worldly vanity, that temptation casts
> Against the weak bulwark of the flesh frail:
>   Wherein the soul in great perplexity
>   Feeleth the senses with them that assail
> Conspire, corrupt by use and vanity;
>   Whereby the wretch doth to the shadow resort
>   Of hope in thee, in this extremity.
> But thou, O Lord! how long after this sort
>   Forbearest thou to see my misery?
>   Suffer me yet, in hope of some comfort,
> Fear, and not feel that thou forgettest me.
>   Return, O Lord! O Lord! I thee beseech,
>   Unto thy old wonted benignity.
> Reduce, revive my soul; be thou the leche
>   And reconcile the great hatred and strife,
>   That it hath ta'en against the flesh, the wretch
> That stirred hath thy wrath by filthy life.
>   See! how my soul doth freat it to the bones,
>   Inward remorse, so sharp'th it like a knife.

This gives the very essence of the feeling that moved Luther, and lay at the bottom of the Teutonic revolt against the external system of Latin Christianity; the intense consciousness of sin, the "fearful looking forward to judgment and fiery indignation," the consequent fear

---

[1] Nearer and nearer.

of death, the sense of despair, and the overwhelming
need of Divine Mercy and Grace. We can understand,
from lines so charged with individual feeling, how deep
must have been the impression which these paraphrases
made on the society of the time.

Changed conditions, and the fluctuations of religious
feeling, have rendered the moral qualities of Wyatt's
paraphrase less impressive than when it first appeared;
while the inexorable hand of time has brought into cruel
relief the harshness of expression peculiar to this poet's
style, depriving his paraphrase of the popularity which it
might have secured if the loftiness and grandeur of its
spirit had found an adequate vehicle. Indeed, the fate of
most of Wyatt's poetry has been that which must overtake all compositions in which matter prevails over form.
He occupies a position in English poetry in some respects
almost as important as that of Chaucer. A statesman, a
courtier, and a scholar, he thought vigorously and felt
ardently in each position that he occupied. As he said
forcibly of himself:

> Such hammers work within my head,
> That sound nought else into my ears;

and his native energy forced him abroad in search of
moulds more suitable for his thoughts than the seven-line
Royal Stanza which had been the favourite instrument of
metrical expression in England since the time of Chaucer.
But his art was not equal to his imagination. He attempted
to naturalise the sonnet; but as I shall show, when considering the poetry of Surrey, he did not understand the
secret of its structure. Nor was he much more fortunate
in his treatment of the *ottava rima* of the Italians, which,
admirably adapted for the peculiar vein of Italian romantic
poetry, is certainly not suited to the nature of the epigram.
Of the other iambic metres introduced by Wyatt, the
most important was the *terza rima*, and as this in his hands
proved an instrument of noble compass and harmony, it
seems somewhat strange that it should never have been
naturalised in the language. It may be that the English

ear, accustomed from early times to the limitation of the
stanza, could not reconcile itself to the concatenated
harmony of this metre, and preferred, both for long narrative
poems, when the stanza was not employed, and for satire,
the heroic couplet as used by Chaucer in the Prologue to
the *Canterbury Tales.* Wyatt was also the first to combine the Alexandrine with the verse of seven accents and
fourteen syllables, a metre which was much in favour
during the sixteenth century, though it has since become
entirely obsolete. His most successful experiments were
undoubtedly his songs written for the accompaniment
of the lute, for here the laws of music kept his thought
within well-defined limits, and, at the same time, gave
sufficient scope to the energy of his genius. I have already
given specimens of his short-metred songs, the majority of
which are written to the key-note of some burden, but it
would be unjust to refrain from citing perhaps the most
beautiful and finished of his lyrical compositions, **viz.**
The Address to his Lute :—

> My lute, awake ! perform the last
> Labour that thou and I shall waste,
>   And end that I have now begun ;
> For when this song is sung and past,
>   My lute, be still, for I have done.
>
> As to be heard where ear is none,
> As lead to grave in marble stone,
>   My song may pierce her heart as soon :
> Should we then sing, or sigh, or moan ?
>   No, no, my lute ! for I have done.
>
> The rock doth not so cruelly
> Repulse the waves continually,
>   As she my suit and affectión ;
> So that I am past remedy ;
>   Whereby my lute and I have done.
>
> Proud of the spoil that thou hast got,
> Of simple hearts, thorough Love's shot,
>   By whom, unkind, thou hast them won ;
> Think not he hath his bow forgot,
>   Although my lute and I have done.

Vengeance may fall on thy disdain,
That makest but game of earnest pain :
    Trow not alone under the sun
Unquit to cause thy lover's plain,
    Although my lute and I have done.

May chance thee lie wither'd and old
The winter nights that are so cold,
    Plaining in vain unto the moon :
Thy wishes then dare not be told :
    Care then who list ! for I have done.

And then may chance thee to repent
The time that thou hast lost and spent,
    To cause thy lover's sigh and swoon :
Then shalt thou know beauty but lent,
    And wish and want as I have done.

Now cease my lute ! this is the last
Labour that thou and I shalt waste,
    And ended is that I begun ;
Now is this song both sung and past :
    My lute ! be still, for I have done.

Wyatt is a noble figure in English poetry. His strength, his ardour, his manliness, his complete freedom from affectation, make him a type of what is finest in the national character, and there is little exaggeration in the very fine epitaph written on him by his great contemporary, Surrey :—

Wyatt resteth here, that quick could never rest :
    Whose heavenly gifts increased by disdain,
    And virtue sank the deeper in his breast
    Such profit he of envy could obtain.

A head where wisdom's mysteries did frame ;
    Whose hammers still beat in that lively brain,
    As on a stithy, where some work of fame
    Was daily wrought to turn to Britain's gain.

A visage stern and mild ; where both did grow,
    Vice to contemn, in virtue to rejoice,
    Amid great storms whom grace assured so
    To live upright, and smile at fortune's choice.

A hand that taught what might be said in rhyme,
    That reft Chaucer the glory of his wit.
    A mark, the which (unperfected for time)
    Some may approach, but never none shall hit.

A tongue that served in foreign realms his king,
    Whose courteous talk to virtue did inflame
    Each noble heart : a worthy guide to bring
    Our English youth by travail unto fame.

An eye whose judgment no effect could blind,
    Friends to allure and foes to reconcile,
    Whose piercing look did represent a mind
    With virtue fraught, reposed, void of guile.

A heart where dread was never so imprest
    To hide the thought that might the truth advance,
    In neither fortune left nor yet represt,
    To swell in wealth, or yield unto mischance.

A valiant corpse where force and beauty met :
    Happy alas ! too happy but for foes,
    Livèd, and ran the race that nature set ;
    Of manhood's shape where she the mould did lose.

But to the heavens that simple soul is fled,
    Which left with such as covet Christ to know,
    Witness of faith that never shall be dead ;
    Sent for our health, but not receivèd so.

Thus for our guilt this jewel have we lost :
The earth his bones, the heavens possess his ghost.

CHAPTER III

THE EARL OF SURREY: DECAY OF CHIVALRY: REFORM OF POETICAL DICTION AND VERSIFICATION

THE work of Surrey in the reform of English poetry was of a kind altogether different from that of Wyatt. His poems have none of the vehement individuality and character which distinguish the style of his predecessor and contemporary. He is essentially the representative of a class. A member of an ancient and noble house, he received the education usually given to the baronial aristocracy, and his verse reflects the polish and accomplishment esteemed by the society to which he belonged. His love poetry preserves the chivalrous tradition on this subject which had been originated by the Troubadours and the *Cours d'Amour*, and had been popularised and refined by the genius of Petrarch. His most beautiful verses are an elegy not merely on the death of a friend but on the institutions, the manners, and the sentiment of the castled nobility of Europe. Yet in Surrey's reflection of feudalism there is nothing abstract or obsolete. His chivalrous code is based on the principles of Castiglione. He follows Wyatt in the imitation of foreign models, but he succeeds where Wyatt failed, in naturalising the ideas he borrows by the beauty of his style. Style is, in fact, Surrey's predominant poetical virtue ; and, appearing as he did when art was the one thing needful for the development of the language, it is to his style that he owes his great position in the History of English Poetry.

Henry Howard was the eldest son of Lord Thomas

Howard, and the grandson of Thomas, Earl of Surrey, the victor of Flodden. The family of Howard had long been eminent in the State. They were descended on the female side from the Mowbrays, whose line as Dukes of Norfolk became extinct in 1475. Thomas, Earl of Surrey, had attached himself to the House of York in the Wars of the Roses, and was taken prisoner at the battle of Bosworth Field, valiantly fighting to the last in behalf of Richard III. After being imprisoned in the Tower he was restored to favour by Henry VII., and for his conduct at Flodden was promoted to the Dukedom of Norfolk. His son, Thomas, was married first to Anne Plantagenet, daughter of Edward IV., and after her death in 1512 or 1513 to the Lady Elizabeth Stafford, daughter of Edward Stafford, Duke of Buckingham. By his second wife he had five children, the eldest of them being Henry who, probably born in 1516,[1] became Earl of Surrey in 1524, on his father's succession to the Dukedom of Norfolk.

Of Surrey's childhood nothing has come down to us on certain authority. It has been supposed that he was brought up with the Duke of Richmond at Windsor, an inference drawn from his own lines :—

> So cruel prison how could betide, alas !
> As proud Windsor? where I in lust and joy
> With a king's son, my childish years did pass—

but it is plain from the context in which these verses occur that they refer to youth rather than childhood ; and, as it is certain that Surrey's early years were spent almost entirely at Tendring Hall in Suffolk, and afterwards at Kenninghall in Norfolk, while the Duke of Richmond was being educated at Sheriff Hutton in Yorkshire, the word "childish" probably only signifies infancy

---

[1] The only authority by which the date of Surrey's birth can be determined is a portrait now in Arundel Castle on which the painter has placed the age of the Earl at the time—viz. 29. The motto also inserted in the picture is *Sat superest ;* and it is stated by Surrey's youngest son, the Earl of Northampton, that this was assumed by his father in consequence of "the breach of a distressed hope" (Nott's *Memoirs of Surrey*, vol. i. p. ix.). It would seem probable that this refers to Surrey's recall from Boulogne in 1546.

in the technical sense. It may be supposed, however, that Surrey received the knightly training usually given to the children of noble families, the character of which is described in his lines written in captivity at Windsor, and that he endeavoured to perfect himself in all the accomplishments recommended by Castiglione in his *Courtier*.[1]

Fitted by this preliminary education to begin the serious business of life, it appears that he was actually contracted in marriage to the Lady Francis Vere, daughter of the Earl of Oxford, in 1532, when he could not have been more than sixteen. In this year he is mentioned together with the Duke of Richmond among the nobility in attendance on the King, when the latter visited Francis I. of France at Boulogne, hoping to secure the French king's friendship on the eve of his own marriage with Anne Boleyn. The Duke of Richmond proceeded to Paris to study at the University, and it is said—with probability though on very slight authority—that Surrey accompanied him.[2] In 1533 he attended at the Coronation of Anne Boleyn, being appointed to carry the fourth sword in its scabbard upright before the king. The Duke of Richmond returned to England at the end of this year, and was contracted in marriage to Surrey's sister, the Lady Mary Howard, after which he took up his abode in Windsor Castle, where he was joined by Surrey, who speaks of this period of their companionship in the famous lines to which I have already referred. Surrey's own marriage, formally completed in 1532, was probably not consummated till 1535 ; his eldest son, Thomas, was born in March 1536. This year was, in other respects, embittered by two great misfortunes. His cousin, the Queen, was beheaded on the 19th of May, and on the 22nd of July he lost his brother-in-law and dear friend, the Duke of Richmond.

In October 1536 he received the honour of knighthood, and for the next three years his name is not prominently mentioned, but it may be supposed that his fame as an

---

[1] See *ante*, p. 17.
[2] Nott's *Life of Surrey* (*Works*), vol. i. p. xxvi.

accomplished knight rose rapidly, for in 1540, when the King, on the Feast of the Epiphany, was married to Anne of Cleves, Surrey appears as the leader of one of the bands of combatants who contended against each other in the tournament held to celebrate the occasion. Towards the end of the same year he was sent by Henry, with Lord Russell and the Earl of Southampton, to see that the defences of Guisnes were in a proper state to repel the expected attack of the French on the English Pale. He must already have had a reputation for scholarship and learning, for in the autumn of 1541 he was appointed Steward of the University of Cambridge. Yet his sense of the great position he occupied in the eyes of the country was not always sufficient to hold in check the impulses of his fiery nature. In July 1542 he was summoned before the Privy Council for having sent a challenge to one John à Legh, and, his offence having been proved, he was committed to the Fleet Prison, from which he was not released before he had bound himself by a recognisance of 10,000 marks not to offer " any bodily displeasure " to John à Legh or any of his friends.

Within a few months he accompanied his father, the Duke of Norfolk, in an expedition against Scotland, which resulted in little more than the burning of towns and villages across the Border, and among others of Kelsal, as he himself mentions in his Epitaph on Clere.[1] The army having been withdrawn into winter quarters, Surrey returned to London, where the ardour of his imagination once more involved him in serious difficulties. It appears that he shared Wyatt's convictions in religion, and was a vehement champion of the Reformation. The study of Petrarch had led him to find a close resemblance between the corruptions of Rome and London, and on one occasion he manifested his disapproval of the manners of the London citizens in so open a manner that he found himself again arraigned before the Privy Council, on the charge of eating

---

[1] Shelton for love, Surrey for lord, thou chase,
    (Aye me ! while life did last that league was tender)
Tracing whose steps thou sawest Kelsal blaze. (See p. 100.)

flesh in Lent, and breaking windows in the city with a cross-bow. As he indignantly denied that his conduct was the result of a drunken frolic, we must suppose that his motive was what he gravely avows in his Satire against the Citizens of London :—

> London ! hast thou accusèd me
> Of breach of laws, the root of s rife ?
> Within whose breast did burn to see
> So fervent hot thy dissolute life ;
> That even the hate of sins that grow
> Within thy wicked wall so rife
> For to break forth did covet so,
> That terror could it not repress :
> Therefore (by words since preachers know
> What hope is left for to redress),
> By unknown means it liked me
> My hidden burthen to express.
> Whereby it might appear to thee
> That secret sin hath secret spite ;
> (From justice' rod no fault is free)
> And that all such as work unright
> In most quiet, are next ill rest.
> In secret silence of the night,
> This made me with a reckless breast,
> To wake thy sluggards with thy bow :
> A figure of the Lord's behest ;
> Whose scourge for sin the Scriptures shew.
> That as the fearful thunder clap
> By sudden flame at hand we know ;
> Of pebble stones the soundless rap,
> The dreadful plague might make thee see
> Of God's wrath, that doth thee enwrap.

The Privy Council naturally felt themselves unable to sanction these allegorical methods of arousing the slumbering consciences of the citizens of London, and committed Surrey to the Fleet together with his two companions, Pickering and Thomas Wyatt the younger. It is not unreasonable to suppose that Surrey's paraphrase of the 73rd Psalm was composed while in prison for this offence. In the Proem to the 87th Psalm he says :—

> When reckless youth in an unquiet breast,
> Set on by wrath, revenge, and cruelty,
> After long war patience had repress'd ;
> And justice, wrought by princely equity ;

> My Denny, then mine error, deep imprest,
>   Began to work despair of liberty ;
> Had not David, the perfect warrior, taught
>   That of my fault thus pardon should be sought.

This seems rather to refer to the merely personal quarrel which caused his first imprisonment, and in the Paraphrase of that Psalm itself he says :—

> Oh Lord, thou hast me cast headlong to please my foe.

But in the Preface to the 73rd Psalm, which is addressed to his friend Blage, he says :—

> The sudden storms that heave me to and fro
>   Had well-nigh pierced Faith, my guiding sail,
> For I that on the noble voyage go
>   To succour truth, and falsehood to assail,
> Constrained am to bear my sails full low,
>   And never could attain some pleasant gale.

In this Paraphrase he expresses no penitence, but looks forward to his own justification and the punishment of his enemies.

Surrey's captivity began in April 1543. It could not have lasted more than a few months, nor could his offence have been considered very serious, for in the October of this year he was sent to join the English forces who under Sir John Wallop had orders to assist the Emperor against the French in the siege of Landrecy. Having been highly praised by Wallop for his military conduct, he returned to England in November, and occupied himself, perhaps, with building his great house on St. Leonard's Hill, near Norwich, said to have been the first specimen of the classical style of architecture erected in England. This house was occupied by Kett, at his rebellion in 1549, and so much injured that it was allowed to fall into ruins, and was never rebuilt. In the following year the war with France was renewed, and Surrey distinguished himself on many occasions, especially by his defence of Boulogne. Of his conduct, however, in these military matters it is unnecessary to speak particularly. It is sufficient to recall the passage in the Sonnet on the death of Clere which mentions the severe wound he received at the siege of Montreuil ; [1] and one incident in the siege of Boulogne may be cited as illustrating the spirit of chivalry which still animated modern warfare, and which was so congenial to the temper of Surrey. Some of the French knights having challenged any of the English to break a spear with them for their ladies' sake, Surrey directed Shelley, one of the bravest of his followers, to accept the defiance. Shelley encountered the challenger, killed him, and returned, himself unharmed, to his own friends.[2]

In April 1545 Surrey was recalled from his command. His removal seems to have been due to the intrigues of the Earl of Hertford, brother of the late Queen, Jane Seymour, who had long been working to secure the chief place of influence in the councils of the King, now falling, through accumulated diseases, into a state of infirmity. Both Surrey and his father were on bad terms with Hertford, whom they disliked and despised as the chief representative of the new nobility ; and after his return to England the former openly avowed his intention of taking his revenge on his supplanter, when a new reign should furnish him with the opportunity. This and other speeches being reported to the King with malicious additions, Surrey was arrested and committed to prison in Windsor Castle, where he wrote his beautiful elegy on the Duke of Richmond. By August in this year, however, he was released, and was once more in attendance on the King ; but at the close of the year his enemies' arts again

---

[1] See p. 100.

[2] The story is told in a quasi-classical style by Challoner, one of the Latin versifiers of the day :—

> Quisque suas gestit vires per facta referre
>   Fortia, quæ rediens narret, amica probet ;
> Quisque alacri exoptans animo meditatur in hostem
>   Irruere ; et proprior voce lacessit item.
> Hæc oculis cernens torvis Surreius heros,
>   Quem penes Anglorum tunc stetit imperium,
> Non tulit instantes nostris illudere Gallos ;
>   Notaque Schellæi pectora sic acuit ;
> "Aspicis? et patere intactos sub mœnibus hostes
>   Insolita demum laude referre pedem?
> Vah, age !" Sed multis ferventem accendere dictis
>   Quorsum opus, aut alacri subdere calcar equo?
> Qua data porta ruit.

Cited by Nott, *Memoirs of the Earl of Surrey*, vol. i. pp. lxxix.-lxxx.

prevailed, and he was sent to the Tower, charged with the offence for which he was almost immediately tried, condemned, and brought to the scaffold.

It seems clear that Surrey was completely innocent. He was accused solely of quartering on his shield the arms of Edward the Confessor ; but his right to do so was undoubted, as it had been granted by Richard II. to all the descendants of Thomas Mowbray, Duke of Norfolk, Surrey's ancestor through the female line. Other evidence entirely unconnected with this indictment was admitted against Surrey at his trial. It was said that he kept Italian servants whom " some suspected to be spies " ; that he was unfavourable to the Reformed religion ; and that he had set up an altar in a church at Boulogne. The animus of the proceedings appears in the evidence of the Duchess of Richmond, Surrey's own sister, who deposed that he had spoken evil of the Earl of Hertford, whom he regarded as the cause of his previous imprisonment, and scornfully of the new nobility. Against charges so frivolous a man of Surrey's ability could have had no difficulty in defending himself. We have no record of his speech as in Wyatt's case ; but it would appear that his ardent temper must have displayed itself without restraint, as he offered, in the most approved spirit of chivalry, to do battle with one of the witnesses in his shirt. His innocence and genius were of no avail with a court doubtless chosen by his enemies, and resolved beforehand on his destruction. He was found guilty on the 13th of January. The King is said by the chroniclers to have been " lying in the extremities of death " ; he was certainly so unwieldly that documents requiring his signature were completed with a stamp and not with his own hand,[1] so that the warrant ordering the execution can hardly be regarded as a personal act on the part of the sovereign. Surrey was beheaded on Tower Hill on the 19th or 21st of January 1547.

Surrey's character has the double aspect of the Knight

---

[1] The Duke of Norfolk lays stress on this fact in his petition for the reversal of the attainder. See Nott's *Memoirs of the Earl of Surrey*, vol. i. Appendix no. l. p. cxxxi.

and the Courtier, which is peculiar to the sixteenth century: he is one of the greatest representatives of that line of chivalry which includes Bayard, and closes, perhaps, with Sir Philip Sidney. As a member of an old baronial house, he shared all the sympathies and instincts of the mediæval nobility, and took little pains to conceal his contempt for the men of the newer families who owed their advancement to the favour of the Court. On the other hand, from the favour of the King, from his close association with the King's son, and from his consequent employment in State affairs, his chivalrous temper was largely leavened with the growing feeling of patriotism which was beginning to form the chief support of the central institution of Monarchy. In spite of the accusations brought against him at his trial, he seems, like Wyatt, to have been a favourer of the Reformation, and the character of his devotional poems leads us to suppose that he would have adapted himself to the stream of national opinion, which was disposed to reconcile some, at least, of the opinions of Luther with the traditions of the Established Church. Had the opportunity been allowed him, his enthusiastic spirit, chastened by experience, would have given him a high place among the great band of statesmen who upheld the throne of Elizabeth.

As far as regards the subject matter of his poetry, Surrey must be regarded as the follower of Wyatt. Almost all his poems deal with the subject of Love, and the age of the lady who is celebrated in them makes it certain that they cannot have been written earlier than 1540. The legend of Surrey's devotion to the Fair Geraldine is one of those traditions which take deep root in literature, and which survive vaguely in the mind of a nation, long after criticism has destroyed the grounds on which they rest. Anthony Wood in his *Athenæ Oxonienses*,[1] Horace Walpole in his *Royal and Noble Authors*,[2] and Thomas Warton in his *History of English Poetry*,[3] have all contributed to confirm the popular belief that Surrey nourished a

---

[1] Vol i. pp. 153, 154. [2] Vol. i. p. 263 (Park's edition).
[3] Vol. iii. p. 23 (edition 1840).

romantic attachment to a mistress, whose peerless beauty he proclaimed in foreign parts, and maintained in the lists against all knightly challengers ; that in his travels on the Continent he met with Cornelius Agrippa, who conjured up for him in a magic mirror the apparition of the Fair Geraldine bewailing his absence ; and that at Florence he went to visit the chamber where his lady was born, which inspired him with a sonnet, not preserved among the poems published in Tottel's *Miscellany.* It is probable that this story, decorated in popular fiction, still conveys to the larger part of the English people the only ideas that survive as to the character of the first refiner of the language they use.

The source of the fable was a kind of romance written in 1594 by Thomas Nash, the antagonist of Spenser's friend, Gabriel Harvey, in which one Jack Wilton is supposed to record his adventures autobiographically.[1] As for the authenticity of the narrative, it is enough to say that this person, who represents himself as having been at the taking of Münster, relates how he met with Surrey at Middleborough, and was persuaded to accompany him into Italy. The incident could not have happened before 1536 ; nevertheless it appears that the travellers at Rotterdam fell in with Erasmus (who died that year at Basle), and with Sir Thomas More (who had been beheaded in 1535); and that, as a result of the interview, the former resolved to write *Encomium Moriæ* (which was published in 1509), and the latter *Utopia* (which was published in 1516). The incidents of the magic mirror exhibited by Cornelius Agrippa (who died in 1535) and of the tournament at Florence, in which Surrey defeated all his opponents, are related by this veracious person, with the fullest detail ; and as a further proof of the truth of the story, it is said that a shield, preserved among the relics of the Norfolk family, was given to the victor by the Duke of Florence at the close of the tournament, though this is known to have been painted by Giovanni Stradano, who was born in 1535 !

[1] *The Unfortunate Traveller:* or, *The Life of Jack Wilton,* 1594.

Turning from a fiction which has been the foundation of so much grave history and criticism, the following appear to be the facts relating to the Fair Geraldine. Lady Elizabeth Fitz-Gerald was the daughter of Gerald Fitz-Gerald, ninth Earl of Kildare, her mother being the daughter of Thomas Grey, Marquis of Dorset. She was born in Ireland in 1528,[1] and when she was only six years old her father died, in the Tower, of a broken heart, caused by the rebellion of his son Lord Thomas Fitz-Gerald, who was executed at Tyburn in the following year. Her mother, being in great distress, appealed to the King's clemency, and the Lady Elizabeth was brought up in the household of the Princess Mary, where she became one of the ladies of the chamber, and after Mary's accession continued her attendance on the Queen. In 1543, when she was only fifteen, she married Sir Anthony Brown, a man of sixty, and, after his death in 1549, became the third wife of Edward de Clinton, then Baron, afterwards Earl of Lincoln, who died in 1584. She herself died in 1589.[2]

That Elizabeth Fitz-Gerald is the subject of many, if not of all, Surrey's love poems is certain. In one sonnet beginning " From Tuscane came my lady's worthy race," he dwells on her family, her physical and moral qualities, and the beginning of his own love [3]; in another, beginning " The golden gift that Nature did thee give," he addresses her as " Garret," the name by which the family signed themselves, and by which she herself is styled in Mary's household accounts.[4] We may conclude also, with little doubt, that Surrey had professed himself her " man," and that she had accepted his service after

[1] The date of her birth is ascertained by a detail in her funeral in 1589, when sixty-one old women were appointed to walk in the procession as representing the number of her years.

[2] On the marriage of the Lady Elizabeth to Sir Anthony Brown, the Princess made a present to "Mrs. Garrett" of "a broach of gold with one Balace of the History of Susanne" (Nott's *Memoirs of the Earl of Surrey*, p. cxx., Note A). Her husband is called by Nott and other writers *Henry* Clinton. Henry *Brandon*, 11th Earl of Lincoln, died during the lifetime of Sir Anthony Brown, and the title became for the time extinct. See Nicolas and Courthope's *Historic Peerage* (1857), p. 289.

[3] *Works* (Nott), vol. i. p. 3.   [4] *Ibid.* p. 17, and *Memoirs*, p. 120.

the manner prescribed by the laws of courtesy.[1] The
tender age of the Lady Elizabeth is no objection to the
literal interpretation of the expressions used by Surrey,
as far as regards the ceremonious aspect of the matter,
for we know from the code of André le Chapelain and
numerous poetical examples, that twelve years was the
age when the female sex became amenable to the service of
love, fourteen being that prescribed for the male sex.[2] Nor
need we doubt that both the lady and her knight enacted
their parts with all the earnestness required by the laws
of chivalry ; that the Fair Geraldine, for example, after
exhibiting the necessary amount of " strangeness," banished
Danger—to use the phrase of Lydgate—and let in Mercy;[3]
or that the Earl on his side cultivated all those feelings of devotion, obedience, and single-hearted patience
which became the character of the *preux chevalier.* But
to infer from Surrey's language that either party carried
their attachment beyond the limits of sport and fancy,
would be to misinterpret the genius of the age in which
they lived, and the literary motives by which all the poetical compositions of Surrey seem to have been inspired.

Surrey's love poems consist of thirty-one pieces, of
which some are sonnets ; others *canzoni,* composed either
in *terza rima,* or in that mixture of twelve and fourteen
syllable verse which had been introduced by Wyatt ; and
others again, lyrics in the shorter metres that Wyatt
used for an accompaniment on the lute. They represent,
in various forms, the different moods of the lover, reproduced with all the skilful analysis which the art of
Petrarch had introduced into the subject, and on which
his successors had ever since continued to ring the
changes.

Wyatt, as we have seen, had taught his companions
at court to look to Italy and Petrarch for the models
of expression in subjects relating to the art of love.
But for the proper treatment of such themes terseness,

---

[1] Describing his mistress's image as it appears in his mind, he speaks of—
    Her strangeness when I said, " her servant for to be,"
And what she said, and how she smiled, when that she pitied me.—*Works,* p. 11.
[2] André le Chapelain, *De Amore,* lib. i. cap. 5.   [3] See vol. i. p. 385.

sweetness, purity and facility of style, were absolutely
necessary, and Wyatt had not skill enough so to refine
the genius of the English language as to make it an
instrument for the expression of these qualities. Surrey
possessed the necessary gifts. What has already been
said will be sufficient to show that his love poetry is not
likely to have been the result of an ardent passion ; an
examination of his methods of composition will prove
conclusively that, in all his love poetry, he is merely working out his own conception of a social convention and an
artistic theme.

His poems are invariably composed upon the principle
approved by the example of Petrarch, namely, the selection
of a central thought which is to be surrounded with a
variety of analogous ideas and images leading up to an
artistic climax. These central or fundamental conceptions
are simple and elementary, and they are constantly repeated
under different forms. For example, one of his axioms
is, that the power of love produces effects in the heart contrary to the general course of nature. In the first of his
songs this idea is set forth in the following lines, which
are afterwards illustrated by a number of images :—

> Alas ! I see no-thing hath hurt so sore
> But time sometime reduceth a return ;
> Yet time my hurt reduceth more and more.

In the song beginning, " If care do cause men cry,"
the thought recurs with a variation :

> For all things having life sometime have quiet rest,
> The bearing ass, the drawing ox, and every other beast ;
> The peasant and the post that serves at all assays,
> The ship-boy and the galley-slave have time to take their ease ;
> Save I alone whom care of force doth so constrain
> To wail the day, and wake the night continually in pain.

And in the very beautiful sonnet beginning, " The
Soote Season," he works up to the closing couplet :—

> And thus I see among these pleasant things
> Each care decays, and yet my sorrow springs.

Another favourite topic is the inconsistency and con-

tradictoriness of the moods of love.   In one of his songs
he says :—

> But wilful will did prick me forth ;
> Blind Cupid did me whip and guide ;
> Force made me take my grief in worth ;
> My fruitless hope my harm did hide.

> Wherein is hid the cruel bit,
> Whose sharp repulse none can resist,
> And eke the spur that strains each wit,
> To run the race against his list.

In another song he illustrates, by a great number of
instances, the text :—

> Such wayward ways hath Love, that most part in discord,
> Our wills do stand, whereby our hearts but seldom do accord.

One of the received statutes of Love in André le
Chapelain's code was, as we have seen, *Verus amans
assidua sine intermissione coamantis imagine detinetur.*[1]
This theme of course is handled by Petrarch in a variety
of forms, and Surrey is not behind his master in dwelling
on the image of his mistress.   Here is one of several
examples :—

> Methink within my thought I see right plain appear
> My heart's delight, my sorrow's leech, mine earthly goddess here,
>   With every sundry grace that I have seen her have :
> Thus I within my woful breast her picture paint and grave.
>   And in my thought I roll her beauties to and fro,
> Her laughing chere, her lively look, my heart that pierced so.

Again it is ruled, *Qui non celat amare non potest,*[2] and
Surrey says :—

> But all too late Love learneth me,
>   To paint all kind of colours new ;
> To blind their eyes that else should see,
>   My sparkled cheeks with Cupid's hue.

> And now the covert breast I claim,
>   That worships Cupid secretly ;
> And nourisheth his sacred flame,
>   From whence no blazing sparks do fly.

---

[1] See vol. i. p. 175.   [2] *Ibid.*

And once again, *Nemo duplici potest amore ligari*[1] :—

> The fire it cannot freeze,
> For it is not his kind ;
> Nor true love cannot lese
> The constance of the mind.

> Yet as soon shall the fire,
> Want heat to blaze and burn ;
> As I in such desire,
> Have once a thought to turn.

Such are the ideas which Surrey, like all lyric poets inspired by the genius of mediæval chivalry, is constantly reproducing in various forms. Wyatt follows the beaten track up to this point ; but he generally seeks to impart an air of originality to his thought by the extremely metaphysical character of the conceits which he expresses. Surrey's aim is different. He gives distinction to his commonplaces by the grace and elegance of the form in which he presents them, and with this object he borrows beauties from all sides, but particularly from the Italian poets ; above all from Petrarch and Ariosto. The following sonnets are taken directly from Petrarch: " Set me whereas the son doth parch the green,"[2] " Love that liveth and reigneth in my thought,"[3] " Alas! so all things now do hold their peace,"[4] " I never saw my Lady lay aside."[5] The main thought in the sonnet beginning, " The golden gift that Nature did thee give," comes from Petrarch,[6] who also seems to have furnished the suggestion for " The soote

---

[1] See vol. i. p. 175.

[2] *Works* (Nott), vol. i. p. 15. Compare Petrarch, Sonnet 113 : " Pommi ove 'l Sol occide i fiori e l' erba."

[3] *Ibid.* p. 16 ; Petrarch, Sonnet 109 : " Amor, che nel pensier mio vive e regne."

[4] *Ibid.* p. 20 ; Petrarch, Sonnet 131 : " Or che 'l ciel, e la terra, e 'l vento tace."

[5] *Ibid.* p. 17 ; Petrarch, Canzone 1 : " Lassare il velo o per sole, o per ombra."

[6] *Ibid.* p. 17 ; Petrarch, Sonnet 126 :—

> In qual parte de ciel, in qual Idea
> Era l' esempio onde Natura tolse
> Quel bel viso leggiadro in ch' ella volse
> Mostrar quaggiù, quanto lassù potea.

season that bud and bloom forth bring ";[1] while Ariosto (himself a borrower) provides the conception of the two fountains whose waters inspire respectively love and hate.[2]

But it is not only in his translations, where he has simply attempted to reproduce the thoughts of a foreign author in an English dress, that Surrey shows the profit he has derived from other men's genius. It is most curious and instructive as a lesson in art to observe how, when this poet has settled on a general line of thought of his own, his execution in detail is so coloured by his recollection of what he has read and admired, that the composition as a whole seems almost like a mosaic of phrases collected out of the works of Petrarch and Ariosto. In their new context these remembered expressions are often given a new and original turn ; and this is particularly the case in the first song. In his Third Canzone Petrarch says : " To every animal that makes its inn in the earth, save those that hold the sun in hate, the time to labour is while it is day ; but after that the heaven kindles its stars, one turns to his house, another to its nest, to find repose there at least until the dawn." Surrey separates the particular images in this passage to combine them into a new form of thought :—

> All thing alive, that seeth the heavens with eye,
> With cloak of night may cover and excuse
>> Itself from travail of the day's unrest,
>> Save I alas ! against all other's use,
> That then stir up the torments of my breast,
>> And curse each star as causer of my fate.
> And when the sun hath eke the dark opprest
> And brought the day, it nothing doth abate
>> The travail of mine endless smart and pain ;
>> For then, *as one that hath the light in hate,*
> I wish for night more covertly to plain.

Soon afterwards we find that he has levied contributions on two separate sonnets of Petrarch for the composition of a single thought of his own :—

---

[1] *Works* (Nott), vol. i. p. 19. Compare Petrarch, Sonnet 269 : "Zefiro torna e 'l bel tempo rimena."

[2] See Ariosto, *Orlando Furioso*, c. I, st. 78 : " E questo hanno causato due fontane."

> And in my mind I measure pace by pace
> To seek the place where I myself was lost,
> That day that I was tangled in the lace,
> In seeming slack that ever knitteth most.

Petrarch says in his 28th Sonnet : " Alone and pensive I go measuring the most deserted fields with tardy steps and slow " ; and his 142nd Sonnet contains the following expressions : " There came before my mind the time and place where I lost myself ; and the beloved noose wherein Love with his own hand bound me in such manner that he made bitter sweet for me, and sorrow sport."

We conclude then that it was Chivalry on its decaying side, its mixed social and literary tradition, which inspired the love-poetry of Surrey. But Chivalry also elevated his spirit to greater things ; and where he is really speaking the language of the heart few English poets have surpassed Surrey in dignity and pathos of style ; witness his truly noble lines written in captivity :—

> So cruel prison how could betide, alas !
> As proud Windsor? where I in lust and joy
> With a king's son, my childish years did pass
> In greater feast than Priam's son of Troy.
> Where each sweet place returns a taste full sour,
> The large green courts where we were wont to hove
> With eyes cast up unto the Maiden's tower,
> And easy sighs, such as folk draw in love.
> The stately seats, the ladies bright of hue,
> The dances short, long tales of great delight ;
> With words and looks that tigers could but rue,
> Where each of us did plead the other's right ;
> The palme-play where despoiled for the game
> With dazed eyes oft we by gleams of love,
> Have missed the ball and got sight of our dame,
> To bait her eyes which kept the leads above.
> The gravelled ground, with sleeves tied on the helm,
> On foaming horse with swords and friendly hearts,
> With chere as though one should another whelm,
> Where we have fought, and chased oft with darts :
> With silver drops the meads yet spread for ruth,
> In active games of nimbleness and strength
> Where we did strain, trained with swarms of youth
> Our tender limbs, that yet shot up in length ;

The secret groves, which oft we made resound
  Of pleasant plaint, and of our ladies' praise ;
  Recording soft what grace each one had found,
  What hope of speed, what dread of long delays.
The wild forest, the clothed holts with green ;
  With reins availed, and swiftly-breathed horse,
  With cry of hounds, and merry blasts between,
  Where we did chase the fearful hart of force.
The void walls eke that harboured us each night :
  Wherewith alas ! revive within my breast
  The sweet accord, such sleeps as yet delight ;
  The pleasant dreams, the quiet bed of rest ;
The secret thoughts imparted with such trust ;
  The wanton talk, the divers change of play ;
  The friendship sworn, each promise kept so just,
  Wherewith we past the winter nights away.
And with this thought the blood forsakes the face ;
  The tears berain my cheeks of deadly hue :
  The which as soon as sobbing sighs alas !
  Up-supped have, thus I my plaint renew :
" Oh place of bliss, renewer of my woes !
  Give me account where is my noble fere ?
  Whom in thy walls thou didst each night enclose,
  To other lief, but unto me most dear."
Echo alas ! that doth my sorrow rue,
  Returns thereto a hollow sound of plaint.
  Thus I alone, where all my freedom grew,
  In prison pine with bondage and restraint :
And with remembrance of the greater grief
To banish the less, I find my chief relief.

I have cited this poem at length for several reasons
First for its beauty and nobility. I know of few verses in
the whole range of human poetry in which the voice of
nature utters the accents of grief with more simplicity and
truth ; it seems to me to be the most pathetic *personal*
elegy in English poetry.. But it is something more. In
Surrey's verses we seem to be listening to a lament over
the chivalry that is passing out of the order of the modern
world. They contain the concentrated essence of the
traditions of knighthood, taught for generations in the
school of every castle in Europe, and accepted in their
purged and perfected form as the code of courtly manners.
The splendour of noble apparel is before our eyes ; the
sound of knightly gaiety is in the air. We hear the

baying of the hounds with the royal chase in the woods ; the splintering of lances in the tilting-yard ; the crash of swords on helmets decorated with the pledges granted by feminine beauty to manly valour ; the laughter of the brightly-clad ladies in the gallery of the tennis-court. Mingled with this brilliancy of external action, is an under-note of moral sentiment, that gives the poem character and elevation ; the principle of inviolable honour and loyalty, forming the strongest bond in the society of gentlemen ; the idea of a lofty courtesy investing with all the atmo-sphere of poetry the common intercourse of everyday life. These memories group themselves in the mind of the poet, about the image of a lost companion, round the grave of a royal prince. The poet himself is the representative of an ancient and warlike nobility, almost annihilated by a generation of civil conflict, and now giving way before a new race of men ambitious, intriguing, the creatures of court favour, rising to power by the arts of statecraft and diplomacy. The prison in which he is confined, and the scaffold which awaits him, seem to be emblems of the fate which has fallen upon the unity of the Catholic Church, and of the ruin which, within a hundred years, would over-throw in England the ancient fabric of feudal monarchy. As we dwell on this noble and unfortunate figure, a certain sense of reality is imparted even to the artifice of Surrey's love-poetry, and historic sympathy enables us to appreciate the nature of the refining influence which he exercised on the genius of the English language.

How deep and lasting this influence was can only be understood by a careful survey of the various stages through which the art of metrical composition in England had previously passed. We have already seen how Chaucer re-fined the mixed language rising out of Saxon and Norman elements by the introduction of the more elaborate French metres, and by the scientific use of the iambic movement in his verses of ten or eleven syllables. The opening of the Prologue to the *Canterbury Tales* furnishes as good a specimen as can be desired of his finished style :—

1. Whánne that | Apríǀle ‖ wíth | his shóurǀes sóte |
2. The dróught | of Március ‖ had pércǀed to | the róte, |
3. And báthǀed évǀery veíne ‖ in swíche | licóur, |
4. Of which | vertú ‖ engéndǀred ís | the flóur ; |
5. When Zéǀfirús ‖ eke with | his sóǀte bréath |
6. Enspíǀred hád ‖ in évǀery hólt | and heáth |
7. The ténǀder crópǀpes, ‖ ánd | the yónǀge súnne |
8. Háth in | the Rám ‖ his hálǀfe course | y-rúnne ; |
9. And smálǀe fóuǀles ‖ mákǀen méǀlodý, |
10. That slépǀen áll | the níght ‖ with ópǀen éye ; |
11. So prikǀeth hém | Natúre ‖ in hér | coráges ; |
12. Then lóngǀen fólk ‖ to gón | on píǀǀgrimáges, |
13. And pálǀmeres ‖ fór | to sékǀen ‖ stránge stróndes, |
14. To sérvǀe hályǀes ‖ coúth | in súndǀry lóndes ; |
15. And spécǀiallý ‖ from évǀery shírǀes énd |
16. Of Éngǀelónd ‖ to Cánǀterburý | they wénd. |

It is plain that every line in this passage is constructed regularly on the iambic principle ; but it is equally plain that many of the feet are formed by the aid of syllables which in later English have ceased to be sounded. We see, moreover, that if some of the words *licóur* (liquor), *natúre*, were pronounced in the modern manner, the regular iambic movement of the verse in which they occur would be destroyed. Lastly—and this point is of the greatest importance —we perceive by the ear that there is a cæsura or pause in the middle of every line, as well as at the end, and that this pause may be made after any syllable between the third and the seventh, though it is most frequently made after the fourth. In lines 2, 4, 5, 6, 8, 12, 15, 16, the cæsura is after the fourth syllable ; in lines 1, 7, 9, 14, after the fifth ; in lines 3, 10, 11, after the sixth ; while in line 13 there is a double cæsura after the third and the seventh. In the last-named case the effect of the cæsura is to lighten the stress of the iambus, so that the voice passes rapidly over the unimportant word " for." [1]

Now if this extremely harmonious and scientific versification be compared with the opening of Lydgate's *Book of Thebes*, we shall at once perceive how the natural development of the language tended to undermine the foundations of Chaucer's metrical system.

[1] Compare vol. i. p. 74.

> When bright Phœbus ‖ passed was the Ram
> Mid of April, ‖ and unto the Bull cam,
> And Saturn olde, ‖ with his frosty face,
> In Virgine ‖ taken had his place,
> Melancholick ‖ and slow of motion,
> And was also ‖ in opposition
> Of Lucina, ‖ the mone moist and pale,
> That many shoures ‖ from heaven made availe ;
> When Aurora ‖ was in the morwe red,
> And Jupiter ‖ in the crabbes head
> Hath take his place ‖ and his mansion,
> The lusty time ‖ and joly fresh season,
> When that Flora ‖ the noble and mighty queen
> The soil had clad ‖ in new and tender green,
> With her flowres ‖ craftily y-ment.

This is the work of a disciple and imitator of Chaucer, but of one who—as has been already urged—did not understand either the grammatical or the rhythmical principle on which his master wrote, and who, in dealing with a language that was rapidly undergoing transformation, was guided by no inborn sense of harmony.[1] The lines frequently want the number of syllables required to maintain the iambic movement ; the metrical accent is thrown on syllables which have no tonic accent ; the cæsura is always monotonously made after the fourth syllable.

When we pass on to Barclay or Hawes, the ruin wrought by time in Chaucer's metrical system becomes still more apparent. For example, in the extract from Barclay's Eclogue, cited in the first volume in illustration of a different point :—

> Alas ! Amynt(as), ‖ nought bideth that is good,
> No, not my cok(ers) ‖ my tabert, nor my hood ;
> All is consum(ed) ‖ all spent and worne be ;
> So is all good(nesse) ‖ and welth of the cyté.
> The temples pyll(ed) ‖ doth bytterly complaine,
> Poore people wayl(eth) ‖ and cal for helpe in vayne ;
> Poore wydows sor(owe), ‖ and chyldren fatherles
> In vayne bewayl(eth), ‖ whan wolves them oppresse.
> Syn hath no scourge ‖ and vertu no rewarde ;
> Who lov(eth) wisdome ‖ his fortune is but harde !

[1] Compare vol. i. pp. 326-333.

Counceyll and cunn(yng) ‖ now tumbles in the dust :
But what (is) the cause ? ‖ lawe turned is to lust :
Lust stand(eth) in stede ‖ of lawe and of justyce :
Whereby good lyv(ynge) ‖ subdued is by vyce.[1]

In order to compress these lines within the iambic
movement it is clear that many syllables have to be
swallowed up, especially before the cæsura, while the
cæsura itself is invariably placed, in Lydgate's mechanical
manner, after the fourth syllable.

Such was the metrical instrument which Wyatt had
to use, when he endeavoured to reproduce in English the
sweet and complicated harmony of the Italian sonnet.
The final *e*, of which Chaucer had so judiciously availed
himself, was no longer at his disposal ; on the other hand
the chaotic modes of accentuation, with which Wyatt's predecessors were content, had almost buried out of his sight
the regularity of the principle on which the father of
English verse had proceeded.   A comparison of Petrarch's
work with the first crude attempts of Wyatt to render the
refinements of Italian thought into English will enable us
to measure intelligibly the greatness of Surrey's achievement.
The following is one of Petrarch's most ingenious sonnets
in his worst manner :—

> Amor, che nel pensier mio vive e regna,
> E 'l suo seggio maggior nel mio cor tene,
> Talor' armato nella fronte viene :
> Ivi si loca, ed ivi pon sua insegna.
> Quella ch' amare, e sofferir ne 'nsegna,
> E vuol che 'l gran desio, l' accesa spene
> Ragion, vergogna, e reverenza affrene,
> Di nostro ardir fra sè stessa si sdegna.
> Onde Amor paventoso fugge al core,
> Lassando ogni sua impresa ; e piange e trema :
> Ivi s' asconde, e non appar più fore.
> Che poss' io far, temendo il mio signore.
> Se non star seco infin all' ora estrema ?
> Che bel fin fa chi ben amando more.[2]

We have to exercise a considerable amount of thought
here in order to understand the nature of the poet's

---

[1] Compare vol. i. p. 390.   [2] Petrarch, part i. sonnet 109.

metaphysical machinery. Three distinct persons have to be conceived, the Lover, his Mistress, and Love who is presented under the figure of the lover's liege lord, and who, as a rule, occupies his vassal's heart as his chief residence. The lady has taught her lover to keep in check all that tumultuary army of hopes and desires, together with looks, sighs, and the like, which give outward manifestations of the power of Love ; but Love, says the poet, sometimes leaves his retired castle and encamps in the face and the forehead, where he displays his banner. This is displeasing to the lady, who exhibits her displeasure, and Love, being a coward, flees back to his fortress. The lover is left exposed to his mistress's anger, and asks what he is to do under the circumstances. His answer is framed in perfect accordance with the scholastic logic of the times ; he must, as a loyal vassal, stand by his lord ; that is to say, he must henceforth conceal his love, even though the effort to do so should cause his death. A conceit of such extreme subtlety could only be rendered tolerable by the beauty of the form in which it is embodied. Wyatt's translation is as follows :—

> The long love that in my thought doth harboúr,
>   And in my heart doth keep his residence,
>   Into my face presseth with bold pretence,
>   And therein campeth, spreading his bannér.
> She that me learns to love and suffér,
>   And wills that my trust, and love's negligence
>   Be reined by reason, shame, and reverence,
>   With his hardiness takes displeasúre.
> Wherewithal unto the heart's forest he fleéth,
>   Leaving his enterprise with pain and cry,
>   And there him hideth, and not appearéth.
> What may I do, when my master fearéth ?
>   But in the field with him to live and die :
>   For good is the life ending faithfully.

This can only be called a barbarous piece of poetical architecture. The thought itself is not clearly presented, only a slight attempt being made to express the feudal relation between Love and the lover ; there is neither selection nor arrangement in the language. The number of syllables in each line is not equal, so that the movement of the whole is almost as halting as in Barclay's verse ; the tonic accent is constantly thrown on weak syllables; the rhymes are harsh and imperfect ; the marking of the cæsura is indistinct.

But beyond this, Wyatt, familiar only with the different types of stanza introduced by Chaucer, does not understand the structure of the Italian sonnet. For it will be observed that the form he employs is neither that sanctioned by Italian usage nor that adopted by Surrey. The Italian sonnet consists of two portions, one containing eight and the other six lines. The first portion is linked together by two sets of rhymes invariably disposed as follows—*a b b a a b b a ;* the second containing six lines is harmonised by sequences of two, or more often three, sets of rhymes, variously distributed, but always in such a manner as to avoid the formation of a rhyming couplet in the last two lines.

Now the reason for the avoidance of the couplet in the second portion of the sonnet is, I think, plain. In the first eight lines the thought ascends to a climax ; this part of the sonnet may be said to contain the premises of the poetical syllogism. In the last six lines the idea descends to a conclusion, and as the two divisions are of unequal length it is necessary that the lesser should be the more individualised. Hence while, in the first part, the expression of the thought is massed and condensed by reduplications of sound, and the general movement is limited by quatrains ; in the second part the clauses are separated by the alternation of the rhymes, the movement is measured by tercets, and the whole weight of the rhetorical emphasis is thrown into the last line.

Wyatt was evidently unaware of the secret principle underlying the extremely complex structure of the Italian sonnet, which distinguished it as a metrical instrument from such a strophe, for example, as the stanza of *ottava rima ;* and being unfortunately misled by his admiration for the *Strambotti* of Serafino, which sum up the conclusion in a couplet, he endeavoured to construct his sonnets on the same principle, thereby leading all English sonnet writers

before Milton on a wrong path.[1] Surrey, however, avoided
the difficulty by ignoring altogether the elaborate structure of the Italian sonnet, for which he substituted three
quatrains with alternate rhymes, closed by a rhyming
couplet.   This has a beauty of its own ; at any rate the
advance beyond Wyatt is remarkable :—

> Love that liveth and reigneth in my thought,
>   That built his seat within my captive breast ;
>   Clad in the arms wherein with me he fought,
>   Oft in my face he doth his banner rest.
> She, that me taught to love and suffer pain,
>   My doubtful hope, and eke my hot desire
>   With shamefac'd cloak to shadow and restrain,
>   Her smiling grace converteth straight to ire.
> And coward Love then to the heart apace
>   Taketh his flight ; whereas he lurks, and plains
>   His purpose lost, and dare not show his face.
> For my Lord's guilt thus faultless bide I pains.
>   Yet from my Lord shall not my foot remove :
>   Sweet is his death that takes his end by love.

The reforms of Surrey may be considered under
several heads.   1. With regard to the iambic movement
of the decasyllabic verse ; he perceived that Chaucer's
principle of harmony had been rendered obsolete, partly
by the change in the accentuation of imported words,
partly by the disappearance of the final *e*, the chief
symbol of the synthetic character of the primitive language.
Observing the essential requirements of the iambic
rhythm, he took care, therefore, to make the tonic accent
fall, as a rule, on the even syllables, so that generally he
only uses the trochee in the first two syllables of the verse.[2]

---

[1] A few of Sidney's sonnets in *Astrophel and Stella* are regularly constructed.

[2] The only exception is in the sonnet on Sardanapalus—

> Did yield, vánquisht for want of martial art.

Surrey seems purposely to have made the rhythm in this sonnet of a
rugged character.

In the sonnet on the Psalms of Wyatt he uses an anapæst in the first
line and a tribrach in the second—

> The great Măcĕdōn, that out of Persia chased
> Dărĭŭs, of whose huge power all Asia rang—

following Chaucer, who in his *Wife of Bath* writes :—

> As was the sepulchre of him, Darĭus.

The lines in which he throws the accent 'on a weak syllable, or uses a trochee before the cæsura, are so few that they can be cited :—

> Love, that livéth and reigneth in my thought.

> The soote seasón, that bud and bloom forth brings.

> The swift swallów, pursúeth the fliës smale.

> To Wyatt's Psalms should Christians then purcháse.

> Of just Davíd, by perfect penitence.

> As proud Windsór, where I in lust and joy.

2. His verses as a rule contain ten syllables, or at least five perfect iambic feet. There are two exceptions, one in the sonnet on Wyatt's death—

> Some, | that watched with the murd'rer's knife—

where we must suppose that he intended a strong emphasis to be thrown on the first syllable ; the other in the epitaph on Clere—

> Norfolk sprung thee, Lambeth holds thee dead,

where the first syllable may perhaps be expanded into a disyllable, " No-r," as in " fire," fier.

3. Besides marking clearly the movement of the iambus Surrey also defined harmoniously the place of the rhythmical pause, both in the middle of the verse and at its rhyming close. It will be observed that in the specimen of Chaucer's verse cited above, the cæsura is clearly marked and beautifully varied ; but that in the verse of Lydgate and Barclay the cæsura either often falls after a weak syllable, or is followed by a redundant syllable ; while, though Wyatt usually pauses after the fourth syllable, he seems to have had no difficulty in reconciling his ear to such an unrhythmical line as

> Wherewithal unto the heart's forest he fleéth,

which is probably meant to have the distributed cæsura after the words " wherewithal " and " forest," but cannot be read so as to sound musically. Surrey, on the con-

trary, in the great majority of his verses, pauses after the
fourth syllable, having marked emphatically the iambic
accentuation in the second foot. Occasionally, but comparatively seldom, the cæsura is after the fifth syllable,
as in the lines—

Itself from travail | of the day's ᴜnrest.

With form and favour | taught me to believe
How thou art made | to show her greatest skill.
Whose hidden virtues | are not so unknown.

So doth this cornet | govern me alas !

Whose chilling venom | of repugnant kind.

And sawst thy cousin | crowned in thy sight.

The infrequency of this movement, which is common in
Pope, points to the slow but steady persistence with which
the Teutonic element in the language asserted its supremacy ;
for it will be observed that, in all the examples adduced, the
words immediately preceding the cæsura are derived from
the French, and in Chaucer's time would have been accented
on the last syllable, *e.g.* travaíl, favoúr (faveur), virtúes
(vertu), cornét (cornette, or Latin, corneta), venom (venín,
venenum), cousín (cousin). The number of trochaic feet
in the language was, therefore, much less than at present.
On the other hand, Surrey often places the cæsura after
the sixth syllable, and this movement is combined most
musically with the ordinary pause, as may be seen from
the following beautiful sonnet :—

The soote seasón, | that bud and bloom forth brings,
  With green hath clad the hill, | and eke the vale ;
The nightingale | with feathers new she sings ;
  The turtle to her mate | hath told her tale.
Summer is come, | for every spray now springs,
  The hart hath hung | his old head on the pale ;
The buck in brake | his winter coat he flings,
  The fishes flete | with new repaired scale ;
The adder all her slough | away she flings ;
  The swift swallów | pursúeth the fliës smale ⁚
The busy bee | her honey now she mings ;
  Winter is worn | that was the flowers' bale.
And thus I see | among these pleasant things
Each care decays, | and yet my sorrow springs.

4. Not the least important of Surrey's improvements was his rejection of weak syllables for the purposes of rhyme. All his predecessors had been accustomed to the cheap device of making their consonances either out of the final syllable of words retaining the ancient inflections of verbs, expressing an abstract quality, or derived from the French, and so preserving the accent on the last syllable against the genius of the English language. Thus Wyatt rhymes—(1) "fleéth," "appeareth," "feareth"; [1] (2) "forgetfulness," "cruelness," "readiness," "fearfulness"; [2] (3) "reasón," "seasón," "condition," "fashión." [3] Another serious blot in Wyatt's versification is his practice of employing words that make a double rhyme, where only a single rhyme is intended, such as "reasón—seasón," "mountaíns—fountaíns." [4] These defects are carefully avoided by Surrey. He scarcely ever ends a verse with a trisyllabic word in which the tonic accent naturally falls on the first syllable; [5] he never rhymes on the syllable "eth," representing the ancient inflection of verbs, or on the "ing" of the present participle, or on the "on" of words derived from the French; he never uses a double-rhyming word at the close of a line. The words which, as a rule, he selects for his rhymes are either full-sounding monosyllables or disyllabic words forming a regular iambus, such as "restrain," "delight," "embrace," "restore," "return."

1 See sonnet beginning, "The long love that in my thought doth harbour," cited above, p. 90.

2 Sonnet beginning, "My galley, charged with forgetfulness." See above, p. 52.

3 See sonnet beginning, "Each man tells me I change of my devise" (*Works*, Nott, vol. ii. p. 7).

4 In the sonnet beginning, "Each man tells me," etc., and "Like to these unmeasurable mountains" (p. 53), it is plain that the double rhyme is not intended, as the corresponding rhyming words in the second quartet are, in the former instance, "condition, fashion"; in the latter, "plains" and "remains."

5 Curiously enough, the second, fourth, and sixth verses in the first of his poems present examples of this kind of rhyme. "Lustiness," "cruelness," "healthfulness," are made to rhyme together (*Works*, vol. i. p. 1). I believe the only other rhymes of the kind are in his elegant little lyric, "Of the Happy Life," in which "governance" and "continuance" are made to rhyme, and in the next stanza the second verse ends with the word "simpleness" (*Works*, p. 43).

5. To his other merits as a poetical inventor Surrey adds the distinction of having been the first to make use in English of decasyllabic blank verse. Warton supposes him to have obtained the suggestion of this novelty from Trissino's *Italia Liberata*, but Dr. Nott has shown that this poem was not published till after Surrey's death, and infers with probability that if the English poet was indebted to a foreign original, this was Molza's translation of Virgil, published in Venice in 1541.[1] I am strongly of opinion that Surrey was led to make the experiment in imitation of Molza, nor do I think that there is any probability in Nott's conjecture that the translation was, in the first instance, made in blank Alexandrine verse. But whether Surrey's idea was original or derived, he is entitled to the highest praise for the skill with which he applied the new principle, the effect of which was to protract the rhythmical period, and to diversify the harmony of the verse by the constant variation of the place assigned to the cæsura. Of the merits of the translation as a whole I shall speak in a subsequent chapter, but in the meantime the following passage will show the extent to which the art of metrical composition was advanced by the genius of this fine poet :—

> Then from the seas the dawning 'gan arise.
> The sun once up, the chosen youth 'gan throng
> Out of the gates : the hayes [2] so rarely knit,
> The hunting staves with their broad heads of steel ;
> And of Masile the horsemen forth they brake ;
> Of scenting hounds a kennel huge likewise.
> And at the threshold of her chamber door
> The Carthage lords did on the queen attend.
> The trampling steed with gold and purple trapp'd,
> Chewing the foamy bit, there fiercely stood.
> Then issued she, awaited with great train,
> Clad in a cloke of Tyre embroidred rich.
> Her quiver hung behind her back ; her tress
> Knotted in gold ; her purple vesture eke
> Button'd with gold.   The Trojans of her train
> Before her go, with gladsome Iulus.

---

[1] Surrey's *Works*, vol. i. p. cc.   [2] Nets.

Æneas eke, the goodliest of the rout,
Makes one of them, and joineth close the throngs.
Like when Apollo leaveth Lycia,
His wint'ring place, and Xanthus floods likewise,
To visit Delos, his mother's mansion,
Repairing eft ; and furnishing her choir
The Candians, and folks of Dryope,
With painted Agathyrsi shout and cry,
Environing the altars round about ;
While that he walks upon mount Cynthus' top,
His sparkled tress repress'd with garlands soft
Of tender leaves, and trussed up in gold ;
His quiver'd darts clatt'ring behind his back.
So fresh and lusty did Æneas seem ;
Such lordly port in present countenance.

6. Surrey was not only the first to harmonise English
verse in conformity with the requirements of the now fully
developed language ; he was also the first to refine the
system of poetical diction so as to adapt it to the reformed
versification. The truth of his intuition and the soundness
of his judgment are shown by his constant reference to
the practice of Chaucer, whose verse, and particularly his
Troilus and Criseyde, both Wyatt and he honoured with
the closest study. Wyatt's obligations to his predecessor
may be noted in every page. In his imitation of Horace's
Tiresias he makes a direct allusion to the character of
Pandarus ; and he never hesitates to draw whole phrases
and idioms from "the well of English undefiled." [1] But
he borrows without attempting to select and to refine.

---

[1] Compare Wyatt, *Works*, vol. ii. p. 93, with Chaucer, *Troilus and Criseyde*, iii. 261. Here are a few examples of Wyatt's obligations to Chaucer : —

> Do away your sluggardy,
> Arise, I say ! Do May some observance.—Wyatt, *Works*, p. 5.

Compare Chaucer, *Troilus and Criseyde*, bk. ii. 110 :—

> Do way your boke ! rise up and let us dance
> And let us don to May some observance.

Wyatt speaks of " Brunet that set my wealth in such a roar " (*Works*, p. 6), following Chaucer (*T. and C.* bk. v. 43), " Why n'ile I bring all Troy upon a roar." Again, he changes Chaucer's phrase of " teary face " (*T. and C.* iv. 820) into " teary eyen " (*Works*, p. 8), and borrows the expression, " That of my health is very *crop and root* " from Chaucer's " Ye that ben of beauty crop and root " (*T. and C.* bk. ii. 299).

He constantly makes use of such archaic idioms and harsh-sounding contractions as :—

> I not ne-wot = (know not) how to begin.[1]

> Where shall I *fet* (fetch)
> Such sighs that I may sigh my fill ?[2]

> Yet are ye ne'er the narre (never the nearer).[3]

> But all too rathe alas, the while! (too soon, alas!)
> She built on such a ground.[4]

> I would my lips and tongue also
> Had then been dumb, no deal to go (so as not to move at all).[5]

> They did me (made me) to depart.[6]

Surrey studied Chaucer with no less attention than Wyatt. He composed a whole song on the basis of an image suggested to him by *The Book of the Duchess ;*[7] he drew on the treasury of the old master for numberless picturesque metaphors.[8]   Occasionally he follows Chaucer in practices contrary to the genius of the language, as in coining verbs out of nouns as in the line,

---

[1] Sonnet beginning, "Such vain thoughts" (*Works*, p. 4, l. 14).

[2] Ode beginning, "Where shall I have at mine own will" (*Works*, p. 26, l. 2).

[3] Ode beginning, "Your look, so often cast" (*Works*, p. 34, l. 27).

[4] Ode beginning, "If ever man might him avaunt" (*Works*, p. 38, l. 21).

[5] Ode beginning, "When first mine eyes did view and mark" (*Works*, p. 43, l. 11).

[6] Complaint beginning, "So feeble is the thread," l. 5.

[7] Compare song beginning, "Although I had a check" (*Works*, p. 32), with *Book of the Duchess*, vv. 648-684.

[8] For example : Sonnet on the Death of Wyatt, "And kiss the ground whereas thy corpse doth rest" (*Works*, p. 47).   So Chaucer, *T. and C.* v. 1788 :—

> And kiss the steps whereas thou seest pace
> Of Virgil, Ovid, Homer, Lucan, Stace.

Surrey : Lines written in Windsor Castle, "And easy sighs such as folks draw in love" (*Works*, p. 49).   So Chaucer, *T. and C.* iii. 1366 :—

> Or elles when that folk be sike
> Easy sighes such as ben to like.

Surrey : song beginning, "O happy dames" (*Works*, p. 13, l. 33),

> Alas, now drencheth (is drowned) my sweet foe!

Compare Chaucer, *T. and C.* v. 228 :

> O herte mine! Criseyde, my swete foe!

But *mercy* him thy friend that doth thee serve.[1]

Here and there also he preserves, for the sake of rhyme, the archaic spelling of a word, as "durre" for "door."[2] In his sonnet beginning, "The soote season," he would appear to be deliberately reviving Chaucer's old-fashioned style and rhythm, while in the line of the same sonnet,

> The swift swallow pursueth the fliës smale,

he adopts the image employed in the *Parliament of Foules,*

> The swallow, murderer of the beës smale.[3]

But while Surrey, with sound artistic instinct, thus grounded himself on Chaucer, he was careful at every point to polish and refine the character of the language. And in view of this object no theme could have been more fortunately chosen than the one on which he concentrated his imagination. For it had always been the poetical aim of Petrarch and his followers to present the inconsistent and anomalous state of the human heart when subject to the power of love, and they sought to express this truth to the mind, partly by the refinement of their analysis, and partly by the union of contrary images. Surrey, in working out this principle in an artistic form, was led to introduce a new system of poetical syntax into the still rude versification of the English language. Perhaps the simplest and most obvious of his improvements was the more regular combination of substantives and adjectives as in the opening of his well-known sonnet :—

> From Tuscane came my Lady's worthy race ;
> Fair Florence was sometime her ancient seat.
> The western isle, whose pleasant shore doth face
> Wild Camber's cliffs, first gave her lively heat.

This regularity of structure enabled him to protract the metrical sentence through several clauses, as—

---

[1] Sonnet beginning, "The golden gift" (*Works*, p. 17). Chaucer uses as verbs "To *night*" (*T. and C.* v. 515); "To *cold*" (*Ibid.* v. 535).

[2] Song beginning, "When Summer took in hand" (*Works*, p. 21, l. 6).

[3] *Parliament of Foules*, 353.

> The great Macedón, that out of Persia chased
> Darïus, of whose huge power all Asia rung ;
> In the rich ark Dan Homer's rhymes he placed,
> Who feigned gests of heathen princes sung.

Again, the habit of yoking contrary thoughts led Surrey
to the antithetical balance of words, lines, and periods :—

> An eye, whose judgment no effect could blind
> Friends to allure, and foes to reconcile :
> Whose piercing look did represent a mind
> With virtue fraught, reposed, void of guile.
>
> A heart where dread was never so imprest
> To hide the thought that might the truth advance ;
> In neither fortune loft, nor yet represt,
> To swell in wealth, or yield unto mischance.

The fine effect of the constant use of the *zeugma*
may be noted in the sonnet containing the epitaph on
Clere :—

> Norfolk sprung thee, Lambeth holds thee dead,
> Clere, of the county of De Cleremont hight,
> Within the womb of Ormond's race thou'rt bred,
> And sawst thy cousin crowned in thy sight.
> Shelton for love, Surrey for lord, thou chase,
> (Aye me ! while life did last that league was tender) ;
> Tracing whose steps thou sawest Kelsal blaze,
> Landrecy burnt, and batter'd Boulogne render.
> At Montreuil gates, hopeless of all recure,
> Thine Earl, half dead, gave in thy hand his will ;
> Which cause did thee this pining death procure
> Ere summers four times seven thou didst fulfil.
> Ah, Clere ! if love had booted, care, or cost,
> Heaven had not won, nor earth so timely lost.

When we observe the comparatively rude conditions
of the language out of which Surrey constructed a sonnet
so condensed in thought, and at the same time so elegant
in expression, it seems difficult to speak with exaggeration
of the genius of this truly admirable poet.

In his songs, composed on a less elaborate principle
of harmony, Surrey's style is lucid, pure, and fluent, and
formed as it is out of sound literary tradition, corrected
and refined by the best conversational idiom of the time,

anticipates the manner afterwards brought to perfection in
the art of Milton, Dryden, and Pope. I conclude the
extracts I have already given with a passage describing
the operations of Nature at sunrise, which seems to have
inspired some of the images in the *Allegro* :—

> The hunter then sounds out his horn,
> And rangeth straight through wood and corn.
> On hills then shew the ewe and lamb,
> And every young one with his dam.
> *Then lovers walk and tell their tale,*
> Both of their bliss and of their bale ;
> And how they serve and how they do,
> And how their lady loves them too.
> Then tune the birds their harmony ;
> Then flock the fowl in company ;
> Then every thing doth pleasure find
> In that, that comforts all their kind.
> No dreams do drench them of the night
> Of foes, that would them slay or bite,
> As hounds to hunt them at the tail ;
> Or men force them through hill and dale.
> The sheep then dreams not of the wolf ;
> The shipman forces not the gulph ;
> The lamb thinks not the butcher's knife
> Should then bereave him of his life.
> For when the Sun doth once run in,
> Then all their gladness doth begin ;
> And then their skips, and then their play ;
> So falls their sadness all away

CHAPTER IV

DEVELOPMENT OF THE IDEA OF THE STATE IN POETRY:
SIR DAVID LYNDSAY: *THE MIRROR FOR MAGIS-
TRATES*: THOMAS SACKVILLE.

THE most brilliant representatives of the noble society
immediately connected with the Court were thus seeking
to refine the English language into an instrument of
metrical expression. But their skill was, as a rule, devoted
to giving the warmth and colour of words to fictitious
emotions and artificial sentiments, which lingered like the
afterglow of the sunset of chivalry. Meantime a deeper
sense of poetry was stirring in the soul of the nation at
large. The philosopher, the moralist, and the statesman,
were alive to the conflict of tragic forces in the life about
them, and strove, however imperfectly, to represent them
in verse. Hence, in much of the poetry conceived in
England and Scotland during the latter part of the reign
of Henry VIII. and in the reigns of Edward VI. and Mary,
an increased prominence was given to the idea of the State.

We have seen in the course of our history that the
development of the political element in English poetry
had been long foreshadowed. The equal balance of rival
races and antagonistic powers in England, and the deeply-
rooted attachment to Saxon laws and customs, had caused
the universal European conflict to present itself in this
country in a much clearer form than in any other of the
Western monarchies. From the reign of King John the
quarrels arising from time to time between the Court and
the baronial party, the nation and the pope, the civil and

ecclesiastical courts, furnished the poets with subjects for treatment in verse. Politics had formed the staple of such poems as the *Vox Clamantis* of Gower, the *Vision of Piers the Plowman* of Langland, the *De Regimine Principum* of Occleve. But in all these the political disorder of the times is regarded as proceeding from the disarrangement of the Catholic and Feudal Order of Europe at large ; and the subject is treated from an ecclesiastical point of view, and in that allegorical form which presupposes an acceptance of the principles of the scholastic philosophy. The examples by means of which the poet enforces his moral, are taken from universal history, just as his moral itself is taken from the Schoolmen's interpretation of the Scriptures. It is in this respect that we find the chief difference between the poems just mentioned and such political compositions as those of Sir David Lyndsay and *The Mirror for Magistrates* which we have now to consider. The latter, indeed, preserve in their design much of the mediæval framework ; but we meet less frequently with the scholastic citation of Scripture, and the attention of the poet is concentrated almost entirely on the affairs of his own nation.

Sir David Lyndsay possessed a genius racy of the soil of Scotland while it was still a separate kingdom, and he might therefore be regarded as falling outside the roll of English poets with which we are concerned. He has, however, been included by Warton in his *History of English Poetry*, and even if it were otherwise, there would be good reasons for assigning him a place in this volume. The last Scottish poet sprung of the lineage of Chaucer, he belongs to an age when the theory of the Christian Republic still survived, and the outlines of international law were yet indistinct ; and he accordingly exhibits in his poetry many of those universal features of the mediæval style which were described in the preceding volume. I think it is also probable that his poems suggested the composition of *The Mirror for Magistrates*, so that a comparison of his work with that of his English followers will throw an instructive light, by means both of likeness and contrast, on the advance of the art of poetry in England.

David Lyndsay, eldest son of William Lyndsay of Garmylton, was born about 1490, and was educated at the University of St. Andrews between 1507-1509. In 1512 he became page to the heir-apparent to the throne, then just born, and he describes, in an extremely pleasing and natural vein, the manner in which he amused the young prince who, in 1513, in consequence of the fatal battle of Flodden, became his sovereign under the title of James V.

> How as ane chapman beris his pack
> I bare thy Grace upon my back,
> And sometymes stridlingis on my neck,
> Dansand with mony bend and beck ;
> The first syllabis that thou didst mute
> Was pa, da, lyn upon the lute ;
> Then playit I twenty springs, perquier,[1]
> Quilk was great plesour for to heir ;[2]
> Fra play thou leit me never rest
> But Gynkertoun[3] thou luffit ay best ;
> And ay quhen thou come from the scule
> Then I behuffit to play the fule.[4]

He continued in attendance on the King till 1524, when the latter, by Act of Parliament, was put into possession of his power, and was allowed to choose his councillors, one of whom, the Earl of Angus, kept him in close constraint, and caused Lyndsay to be dismissed from the royal service with a pension. In 1528, however, James escaped from his tyrants, and in that year Lyndsay composed his *Dreme*, which he dedicated to the King. This was followed in the next year by his *Complaynt*, a poem in which he appeals directly to the King for advancement on the strength of old association ; and it was perhaps in answer to this prayer that in 1530 he was knighted and made Lyon King of Arms. Relying on the royal favour, he wrote in that year his satirical *Complaint of the Papingo*, and in 1535 his interlude called *The Pleasant Satire of the Three Estates*. In his capacity of herald he helped

---

[1] Par cœur.
[2] To hear.
[3] The tune of that name.
[4] Lyndsay's *Complaynt*.

to negotiate his master's successive marriages with two
French princesses ; but after the King's death in 1542 his
influence naturally sank, and he joined himself more or
less closely in opposition with the party of John Knox.
A bitter enemy of Cardinal Beaton, he wrote, after the
murder of the latter in 1546, *The Tragedie of the
Late Cardinall.*   His *Squire Meldrum*, a poem which
would appear like Chaucer's *Sir Thopas* to have been
written in ridicule of the romances, was published in
1550, and in 1553 appeared his longest poem, entitled
Monarchie or *A Dialogue of this World's Miserie Between
Ane Courtier and Experience.*   Lyndsay died about 1558.
He married in 1532 Janet Douglas, but left no children.

The history of Scotland, from the accession of James I.
down to the period when Lyndsay began to write, presented
striking materials to the imagination of a moralising poet.
The genius of feudalism seemed to have chosen that
country as the scene of its most capricious experiments.
A series of well-intentioned kings, aided by the estates of
the realm, had endeavoured, with fluctuating success, to
establish a system of law and civilisation in the midst of
a half-secular hierarchy, a turbulent nobility, a host of
marauding tribal chieftains.   Of these kings not one had
died a natural death.   James I., a true lover of justice
and letters, was murdered by his lawless Highland subjects.
James II., who attempted, but more capriciously, to follow
in his father's footsteps, was killed by the accidental burst-
ing of a cannon.   James III., with a character resembling,
in its gentle weakness, that of Henry VI. of England,
was assassinated after the second battle of Bannockburn.
The country, nevertheless, remained free from dynastic
disputes, and when James IV. became king it seemed as
if the monarchy had gained a brilliant opportunity of
establishing its authority on an enduring basis.   James
himself was a gallant knight and an accomplished scholar.
He was anxious for the prosperity and good government
of his realm.   His court, a centre for the new ideas of
refinement flowing in from France and Italy, maintained
a crowd of poets of whom the chief were the brilliant

William Dunbar and the scholarly Gavin Douglas. But a curse, like those recorded in the Greek legends, seemed to attend the family of Stuart, and in a moment of infatuation James entered on the fatal expedition which cost him his own life, and Scotland, in a single day, as much of her best blood as had been wasted in England by a whole generation of civil war. This catastrophe was followed by a long minority with all its attendant evils. Perpetual factions among the nobility naturally led to the interference of foreign powers, the party of the Regent Albany leaning on the aid of France, the party of the Douglases turning for protection to England, while a third party, prosecuting the interests of the Church, invoked the authority of the Papacy.

To the mind of Lyndsay these misfortunes appeared primarily in the light in which the disasters of their times had presented themselves to all the poetical moralists of the Middle Ages,—to Dante, to Langland, to Gower— namely, as the fruits of original sin. Whenever he makes them the subject of his verse he founds his reasoning about them on Scholastic Theology, and conveys his ideas to the reader in the established forms of allegory. In the *Dream*, the earliest of his compositions, he treads closely in the steps of his master, Chaucer. After a dedicatory "Epistle" to the King's Grace, in which he reminds James of his old attendance on him, and makes the inevitable apology for lack of art in his poem, he relates how in the Calends of January, being unable to sleep, he went out to gaze upon Dame Flora in the sad weeds of the season. By a really beautiful and original image he describes how

> The tender flouris I saw
> *Under Dame Nature's mantill lurkyng law,*

and how, going on to the sea-shore, he walked up and down the sand, and then climbed into a cave where the sound of the wind and the waves put him to sleep. In the dream which, of course, followed, he encountered Dame Remembrance, under whose guidance he passed into Hell, where he saw many popes and other ecclesiastics, emperors,

and kings, and out of this experience he makes a kind
of *précis* of Dante's Inferno.   Leaving Hell, by way of
Limbo and Purgatory, he relates how he passed through
the elements to the Planets, and onward to the Crystalline
Heaven, where is the throne of God surrounded by the
Nine Orders of the Celestial Hierarchy.   Then once more
turning on a downward course, he was shown the Divisions
of the Earth and the Earthly Paradise.

Up to this point there has been nothing to distinguish
the *Dream* from the numerous commonplace allegories of
the Middle Ages ; but the motive of the poem at last
discloses itself, and we perceive that all this elaborate
machinery has been adopted to enable the poet to discourse poetically on the state of Scotland.   For he now
tells us how he descried this kingdom among the other
regions of the earth, and dwells with fulness on the
wretched spectacle presented by his native land :—

> Quhen that I had oversene this regioun,
> The quilk of Nature is baith gude and faire,
> I did propone ane little questioun,
> Beseikand hir the same for till declare ;
> Quhat is the cause our boundis ben so bare,
> Quod I, or quhat dois move our miserie,
> Or quareof dois proceed our povertie ?

He then sees a vision of a miserable-looking man,
who announces himself to be " John the Commonweal,"
and who describes how everything is wrong in every part
of Scotland.   When this person has discoursed for some
time, a large ship of war, appearing off the coast where
Lyndsay is sleeping, and firing a broadside, effectually
awakes him out of his dream.

From this we may see that the allegorists, who, in
Gower's time, were content to moralise on the sins of
Christendom in general, have now come to fix their
attention on national matters.   The idea of the morality
of the State, which may dimly be discerned in the *Dream*,
is distinctly developed with abundance of sharp satire in
The Complaint of the Papingo.[1]   In this allegory, the poet

---

[1] The same word as Popinjay or Parrot.

relates that as he was carrying his papingo in the park, the foolish bird—an emblem of the superficial brilliancy and ambition of court life—flew from his hand on to the top of a tree, whence, the wind having snapped the twig on which she was sitting, she was dashed to the ground, and mortally hurt. Before her death, however, she found time to indite two warning epistles. One contained an exhortation to the King :—

> Amang ale uther pastyme and plesour,
> Now in thy adolescent yeris ying,[1]
> Wald thou ilk day studie but half an hour
> The regiment of princely governing,
> To thy pepile it war a pleasand thing :
> Thare micht thou fynd thy awin vocatioun,
> How thou suld use thy sceptre, sword, and croun.

The other, written to her " brother at court," recites for his instruction the whole tragic course of Scottish history from the date of the murder of the Duke of Rothesay, heir-apparent to Robert III., down to the defeat at Flodden. This epistle closes with an apostrophe which is not without a picturesque pathos expressive of the poet's love for his native country :—

> Adew, fair Snawdoun, with thy touris hie,
> Thy chapel royale, park, and tabill round !
> May, June, and July, would I dwell in thee,
> War I ane man, to heir the birdis sound,
> Quilk doth againe thy royale rocks redound.
> Adew, Lythquo, quhose palace of pleasance
> Micht be ane patrone [2] in Portugall or France.
>
> Farewele, Falkland, the forteresse of Fyfe,
> Thy polite park, under the Lowmound law ;
> Sumtyme in the I led a lustie lyfe,
> The fallow deir, to see tham raik on raw.[3]

The conclusion of the poem is a bitter satire on the

---

[1] Young.   [2] Pattern.

[3] To see the fallow deer walk in a row. As a proof of the influence exercised by Lyndsay on the authors of *The Mirror for Magistrates*, the following stanza by Ferrers may be cited :—

> Farewell, Greenwich, my palace of delight,
> Where I was wont to see the crystal streams
> Of royal Thames, most pleasant to my sight ;
> And farewell Kent, right famous in all realms,
> A thousand times I mind you in my dreams ;
> And when I wake, most grief it is to me
> That never more again I shall you see.
> Haslewood, *Mirror for Magistrates*, vol. ii. part i. p. 123.

ecclesiastical orders.   The dying Papingo must be shriven by her " Holy Executioners," the Pie (" ane chanon regulare "); the Raven (" ane blak monk "); the Glede, or Kite (" ane haly freir "). These birds, after hearing her confession, give her absolution : she then makes her bequest, distributing different parts of herself to her friends among the birds, after which she dies ; but the breath has hardly left her body when the confessors fly upon it, tear it in pieces, and then fight over the spoils.

The Tragedie of the Late Cardinall is a curious rendering of modern political feeling in venerable mediæval forms.   It was inspired by Boccaccio's *De Casibus Illustrium Virorum*, and the opening, in which the poet represents himself reading " John Boccace " in his oratory, is striking :—

> I sitting so upon my buke reading,
> Richt suddandlie afore me did appeir
> Ane woundit man aboundantlie bleeding,
> With visage pale and with ane deadlie cheir,
> Siemand ane man of twa and fiftie yeir,
> In rayment reid clothid full curtiouslie
> Of velvet and of satyn crammosie.

This tragic figure relates the story of his crimes and murder, over which the poet moralises with the grim satisfaction of a Scottish Reformer.   Something of the same grotesque mixture of styles, though in quite a different vein, appears in the *Monarchie*, an exceedingly long and dull dialogue between Experience and " Ane Courtier," in which the speakers contrive to review the whole course of the world, and anticipate its dissolution at the day of judgment.   Before setting out on this tedious voyage, the poet considers the propriety of appealing to some Muse :—

> Raveand Rhamnusia, goddis of dispyte,
> Micht be to me ane Muse richt convenabill,
> Gif I desynt sic help for to indyte
> This murning mater, mad and miserabill,
> I mon ga seik ane muse mair confortabill,
> And sic vane superstitioun to refuse.
> Beseikand the greit God to be my muse

·   ·   ·   ·   ·

> Quharefor insteid of the Mont Parnaso,
> Swiftlier I sall ga seik my soverane.
> To Mont Calvarie the straucht way mon I go,
> To get ane taist of that maist fresch fontane ;
> That sours to seik my hart may not refrane
> Of Helicon, quilk was baith deip and wyde,
> That Longinus did grave intill his syde.

In this union of Lutheran piety, political philosophy, and classical imagery, we have a vivid reflection of the mind of the more patriotic portion of the Scottish aristocracy on the eve of the Reformation in their country. The "Envoy" of the poem is also noticeable. Lyndsay laments with feeling that he can no longer despatch his book to a king ; and, with suppressed satire, bids it make its way to the Regent Arran and his brother James Hamilton, whom he well knew to be hostile to the cause of Reform. Not less significant, as a measure of national refinement, is the uncouth dialect and harsh versification of the *Monarchie*, indicating the insensibility of the author to the value of those civil arts which appealed so powerfully to the imagination of men like Wyatt and Surrey.

Something of this rudeness of style is visible also in parts of the English *Mirror for Magistrates*, a work which, published six years later than Lyndsay's *Monarchie*, seems to have been inspired by very similar political conditions and nearly identical poetical motives. For though the state of the English kingdom was less turbulent and anarchical than that of Scotland, the uncertainty as to the succession to the throne and the unsettlement of religion, together with the tragic downfall of so many eminent men, brought about by both these circumstances, had turned the minds of Englishmen in Mary's reign to the favourite mediæval theme of the instability of fortune. The poets were accordingly in a mood to moralise, and Lyndsay in Scotland had recently furnished them with a precedent. He bids his book containing the history of the world go

> To faithfull prudent pastours spirituall,
> To noble erlis and lordis temporall,

Obediently till thame thou thee addresse ;
Declaryng thame this schort memoriall
How mankynd bene to miserie made thrall ;
At lenth to thame the caus planelie confesse,
Beseikand thame all lawis to suppresse,
Inventit be mennis traditioun
Contrair to Christis institutioun.

And caus thame cleirlye for till understand,
That for the breking of the Lordis command,
His threfald wande of flagellatioun
Hes purgit this pure realm of Scotland,
Be mortall weris baith by sea and land,
With mony terrabill tribulatioun ;
Therefor mak to them true narratioun,
That all their weris, this derth, hunger, and pest,
Was nocht but for our sinnis manifest.[1]

Sir Thomas Elyot in his *Governor* (published in 1553) highly approves of this method of historical instruction. The boy, he says, must be taught history after geography ; "but fyrst to set him in a fervent courage, the master in the most pleasant and elegant wise expressing what incomparable delectacion, utilitee, and commoditee shall happen to emperors, kings, princes, and all other gentylmen by redyng of histories."[2] There was, therefore, a widespread demand for historical text-books, a circumstance which accounts for the contemporary popularity of one of the dullest poems of the Middle Ages, Lydgate's *Fall of Princes*. This work was first printed by Pynson in 1494, and no further edition was called for till 1527. The supply then furnished seems to have been sufficient till 1554, after which year it is evident that the circulation of the book became more rapid, for not only was it then reprinted by Tottel, but a fresh edition was issued in 1555 by Wayland. The commercial zeal of Wayland in the promotion of his enterprise was the main cause of the production of *The Mirror for Magistrates*, and it is desirable to record the exact circumstances under which the latter poem came into existence, since a different account has been given of its origin.

---

[1] *Epistle Nuncupatorie*, Lyndsay's *Poetical Works* (Chalmers), vol. iii. pp. 176, 177.

[2] *The Boke named the Governour* (Croft's edition), vol. i. p. 81.

Warton, with a natural predilection for the one man of genius who was associated with the undertaking, has given his sanction to a statement, repeated by more modern writers, that the designer of *The Mirror for Magistrates* was Thomas Sackville, afterwards Earl of Dorset.[1] This is an error into which the historian was led by relying too implicitly on the authority of Richard Niccols, one of the later editors of the poem, who placed the *Induction* at the beginning of the collection, and asserted confidently that Sackville was the originator of the whole work. Had Warton attended to what was said in the preface to the first edition of *The Mirror for Magistrates*, rather than to the statements of an editor who, writing sixty years after the first appearance of the work, could have had no personal knowledge of the facts, he would have seen that the account of the matter to which he gave currency was entirely mythical. " Whan the *printer*," says Baldwin in his address to the reader, " had purposed with himself to print Lidgate's book of the fall of princes, and had made privye thereto many both honourable and worshipfull, he was counsailed by dyvers of them to procure to have the story contynued from where as Bochas left unto this present tyme, chiefly of such as Fortune had dalyed with here in this ylande: which might be as a myrrour for al men, as well nobles as others."[2] Beyond the assertion of Niccols there is no proof whatever that this suggestion was first made by Sackville, or that, having made it, he then proceeded to plan the lines of the work. The natural inference from the evidence rather is that the printer, listening to the advice of his distinguished friends, applied to William Baldwin, who, as corrector of the press to one of Wayland's brothers in the craft, may have been already known to him. Baldwin is supposed to have been a graduate of the University of Oxford : he was certainly the author of *A Treatise of Moral Philosophie* published in 1547, and of a metrical version of the *Canticles* of Solo-

---

[1] *History of English Poetry* (1840), vol. iii. p. 183.
[2] Haslewood's edition of *The Mirror for Magistrates*, vol. ii. p. 7.

mon, published in 1549. During the reigns of Edward
VI. and Mary he was engaged in preparing theatrical
exhibitions for the Court ; and varied experience had
doubtless made of him one of those practised literary
craftsmen from whom a businesslike printer would have
naturally sought advice when about to undertake an
extensive poetical enterprise. Baldwin took counsel with
other writers, of whom Sackville was one ; and a partner-
ship was formed, the first-fruits of which appeared as
early as 1555 in a folio copy of *The Mirror for Magistrates*. There is nothing to show that Sackville had written
his *Induction* at this date, though he may very well have
furnished his *Complaint of the Duke of Buckingham* as a
contribution to the common stock of tragedies.

But at this point the poetical associates met with a
check. The government of the country had long viewed
with suspicion the increasing activity of the press. When
printing first superseded writing, the authorities seem not
to have foreseen the consequences of the invention, nor were
they careful to protect the property of the printer from
enterprising rivals. But in the reigns of Edward VI. and
Mary the Council began to perceive how vast an influence
the new art was exercising on public opinion, and the
Charter of the Stationers' Company recites : " That
certain seditious and heretical books, both in rhymes and
tracts, are daily printed, renewing and spreading great
and detestable heresies against the catholic doctrine of
the holy Mother Church." The Government accordingly
began to consider by what means the press might be
controlled, and, in the very same year as the preparation
of the first draft of *The Mirror for Magistrates*, a charter
was granted to the Ancient Company of Stationers,
investing the ninety-seven members included in it with
the sole power of printing, and also of seizing and burning all prohibited books, and of imprisoning any persons
who should print without their authority.[1] This measure,
identifying as it did the commercial greed of the monopo-

---

[1] Arber's reprint of the *Register of the Stationers' Company*, Introduction,
vol. i. p. xxix.

list with the duties of a State police, was doubtless regarded at the time as a masterpiece of statecraft. It was the starting-point of the long struggle which, on the one hand, was only terminated by the lapse of the Licensing Laws in 1684, and, on the other, by the consolidation of the Copyright Acts in 1870. But the Company was not yet in possession of its power, and *The Mirror for Magistrates* was subjected to the searching examination of the Chancellor, Stephen Gardiner, Bishop of Winchester, who—though he could scarcely have found in it anything " against the catholic doctrine of the holy Mother Church "—seems to have scented some dangerous tendency in its historical examples, and prohibited its publication.

In consequence of this check the work stood still till 1559, the first year of Queen Elizabeth's reign, when *The Mirror for Magistrates* appeared in the form of nineteen legends contributed, as it appears, by six poets, Baldwin, Ferrers, Cavyll, Chaloner, Phaer, and Skelton. All of these related to tragedies which had occurred in or after the reign of Richard II. In 1563 this collection was reprinted with an addition of eight legends from the hands of Baldwin, Dolman, Sackville, Segar, Churchyard, and Cavyll, and the part taken by Sackville in the work is very clearly indicated by Baldwin in the preface to his *Induction :—*

I have here the Duke of Buckingham, king Richard's chief instrument, written by maister Thomas Sackvill. " Read it, we pray you," sayd they. " With a good will," quoth I, " but first you shall hear his Preface or Induction." " Hath he made a preface ? " sayd one, " *what needeth he thereby seeing none other hath used the like order !* " " I will tell you the cause thereof," sayd I, " which is this : after that he understode that some of the counsayl would not suffer the booke to be printed in such order as wee had agreed and determined, hee purposed to have gotten at my hands all the tragedies that were before the Duke of Buckingham's, which hee would have preserved in one volume. And from that time backwards even to the time of William the Conqueror, hee determined to continue and perfect all the story himselfe in such order as Lydgate (following Bochas) had already used. And therefore to make a meete induction into the matter, hee devised this poesie, which in my judgment is so well penned that I would not have any verse thereof left out our volume.[1]

From this it may be reasonably inferred that Sackville was one of the partners in the plan originally formed, but that when the Council prohibited the publication of the book, probably on account of its modern instances, he resolved to begin with ancient history, and —by making the work more evidently a continuation of Lydgate's *Fall of Princes*—to remove the features that had raised objections in the mind of the Government. Baldwin and his companions on the other hand let their original plan drop for the moment, but revived it under the genial influence of Elizabeth's accession.

In 1571 the edition of 1563 was reprinted with a few minor alterations ; but in 1574 John Higgins, an Oxford scholar—previously known as a writer on rhetoric —enlarged the scope of the work by a new series of sixteen legends which he took from the mythological period of British history beginning with the conquest of Brutus. To these he prefixed an induction after Sackville's manner, describing how in the halls of Morpheus the complaining ghosts of the various tragedies appeared to him and related their melancholy tales. Baldwin's and Higgins's versions were in 1587 united and enlarged with additional matter, and *The Mirror for Magistrates* thus assumed its final form, though in 1610 Richard Niccols ventured arbitrarily to recast the order, to tamper with the text, and to give a misleading account of the nature and origin of the poem.

The Mirror for Magistrates survives among the classic monuments of English poetry only by virtue of the genius of Sackville. Yet history would not be discharging her functions rightly if she neglected to notice those obscure fellow-labourers with a great statesman, who, in an age of struggle and transition did much to raise the spirit of the nation by recalling the memorable deeds of its past, and

---

[1] Haslewood's edition of *The Mirror for Magistrates*, vol. ii. part i. p. 307.

not less to develop the art of English poetry by revealing new sources of poetical inspiration and promoting the improved methods of metrical harmony. Alike in its design, its subject matter, and its form, *The Mirror for Magistrates* declares itself the offspring of serious and high-minded authors. I have already said that the main purpose of the poem is didactic; but there is a melancholy solemnity in the tone in which Baldwin announces "to the Nobilitee and all other in office" the nature of the lesson that he and his colleagues intend to convey.

The goodnes or badnes of any realme lieth in the goodnes or badnes of the rulers. . . . I neede not go eyther to the Romans or Greekes for the prof hereof, neither yet to the Jewes, or other nations, whose common weales have always flourished whyle their magistrates were good, and decayed and ran to ruyne when vicious men had the government. Our countrey stories (if we reade them and marke them) will show us examples enow, would God we had not sene mo than enow.[1]

Nor was the structure of the poem wanting in a certain artistic unity. It was first intended to make the book a mere continuation of Boccaccio. But objections to this plan soon arose. Boccaccio had not conducted his history, *De Casibus Illustrium Virorum*, on any regular system, though he had here and there represented the ghosts of his illustrious men addressing himself directly; and while he had thus furnished his successors with a suggestion, their naïve imaginations felt a difficulty in linking their scheme to his.

Yet would it not conveniently serve (says Baldwin, in his address to the reader), seeing that both Bochas and Lidgate were dead, neyther were there any alive that meddled with like argument, to whom the unfortunate might make their mone. To make, therefore, a State meete for the matter they all agreed that I shoulde usurpe Bochas' roome, and the wretched princes complayne unto mee: and tooke upon themselves every man for his part to be sundry personages, and in theyr behalfes to bewail unto mee theyr greevous chances, heavy destenies, and woefull misfortunes.[2]

---

[1] Haslewood's edition of *The Mirror for Magistrates*, vol. ii. part i. p. 4.
[2] *Ibid.* vol. ii. part ii. p. 8.

The different complaints are linked together by Baldwin's narrative, in which he records the comments of the company on each tragedy as it is finished, and the circumstances under which the next speaker began his complaint. In this way the entire series of examples is connected as regularly as the *Decameron* or the *Canterbury Tales*.

There is very little poetical merit in the conception of the tragedies themselves. As the chief object of the writers was to instruct by means of historical examples, no attempt is made to observe the boundaries which separate poetry from versified history. Historical accuracy on the other hand is aimed at. The sources from which the poets derive their materials are the chronicles of Hall and of Fabian ; and when these authorities are at variance, Baldwin, as the *rex cœnæ*, is careful to call attention to the discrepancy. In the supplement to the poem dealing with the legendary period of British history, Higgins of course drew his materials from Geoffrey of Monmouth. By the union of the two parts a large number of readers obtained an extensive survey of the history and mythology of their country, while the quasi-dramatic form of the complaint paved the way for those regular historical tragedies which are among the earliest productions of the Elizabethan stage. It is worthy of note that *The Mirror for Magistrates* contains the germinal matter of Marlowe's *Edward II.*, produced in 1590 ; as well as of Shakespeare's *Henry VI.*, produced in 1592 ; of *Richard III.*, produced a little later ; and of *Richard II.*, produced about 1595.

The language and versification of *The Mirror for Magistrates* is full of instruction for the student who seeks to trace systematically the growth of the art of English poetry. Composed as it was by the co-operation of many poets varying widely in age and genius, the book offers examples of the successive experiments in poetical diction that mark the transition from the rude archaic style prevailing in the early part of the sixteenth century to the comparatively finished manner aimed at by the writers in the middle of the reign of Elizabeth. George Ferrers, who

after Baldwin was the chief contributor to the edition of
1559, was probably born before 1510; Thomas Churchyard, a follower and imitator of the Earl of Surrey,
was born about 1520, and Thomas Sackville, who also
modelled himself on the style of Surrey, was some sixteen
years younger than Churchyard. The first named, the
son of Thomas Ferrers of St. Albans, became Bachelor of
Canon Law at Cambridge in 1531, and in 1534 published
an English translation of *Magna Carta*. A member of
Lincoln's Inn, enjoying a high reputation for eloquence
at the Bar, he was elected to the Parliaments of 1542,
1545, and 1553, where he sat as member for Plymouth; in
those of 1554, 1555 as member for Brackley; and in that
of 1571 as member for St. Albans. Like Baldwin he
appears to have been skilled in the superintendence of
dramatic shows, for in Edward VI.'s reign he was made
Master of the King's Pastimes, and produced a masque
entitled *The Triumph of Venus and Mars;* while in the
time of Mary he was "Lord of Misrule." He is supposed
to have intrigued on behalf of the succession of Mary
Queen of Scots, shortly before his death, which happened
in 1579.

Ferrers' contributions to *The Mirror for Magistrates*
are characterised by the didactic spirit that pervades the
allegorical masques of the Court of Henry VII. and
Henry VIII., and which is illustrated in the poetry of
Sir Thomas More. His first thought is to instruct by
means of his historical example. When he has conceived
of himself in the situation of the Prince whose tragedy he
is relating, he cares for little beyond presenting biographical facts to the mind of the reader. Yet is he not without
a sense of dramatic effect, an experience he had doubtless
gained in his management of Court plays; witness his
Prologue to the tragedy of King Richard II. : "Therefore,
imagine, Baldwine, that you are the corps of this prince all
to be mangled with blew woundes, lying cold and wan all
naked upon the cold stones in Paul's Church, the people
standing round about him, and making his complaynt as
followeth."

But what is particularly noticeable in this poet is his
harsh and rude versification, which, though he is posterior
to Surrey, is scarcely more harmonious than the diction of
Lydgate, and resembles the metrical style of Sir Thomas
More. The following specimen from the *Complaynt of
Humphrey, Duke of Glocester*, will suffice :—

> Of King Henry the fourth fourth son I was,
> Brother to Henry, the fift of that name,
> And uncle to Henry the sixt, but alas,
> What cause had I to presume on the same?
> Or for vayne glory advancing my fame,
>   My selfe to call, in recordes and writinges,
>   The sonne, brother, and uncle unto kinges.[1]

A striking contrast to the style of Ferrers is furnished
in the style of Thomas Churchyard, a poet of whom I
shall have to say more in the next chapter, and who contributed for the edition of *The Mirror* published in 1563
a tragedy called *Shore's Wife*. While Ferrers concerns
himself with nothing but his moral, Churchyard is almost
entirely occupied with the business of versification. It is true
that his theme was well chosen as an instructive example of
the instability of Fortune. Sir Thomas More had moral-
ised on the history of Jane Shore in his *Life of King
Richard III.;* and Hall, from whom Churchyard derived his
materials, had expatiated upon it in his Chronicle, observing: "I doubt not some men will think this woman to be too
slight to be written of among grave and weighty matters,
which they shall especialy think that saw her in her age
and adversity, but me seemeth the chance so much more
worthy to be remembered in how much after welth she
fell to poverty, and from riches to beggary, unfriended,
out of acquaintance, after great substance, after so great
favour with her prince, etc." [2] This is the gist of Churchyard's "Complaint," but though the moral could best have
been drawn by a brief and sententious recital of the facts,
he has made his tragedy one of the longest in *The Mirror
for Magistrates*. This prolixity is the result of reproducing

---

[1] Haslewood's *Mirror for Magistrates*, vol. ii. part ii. p. 130.
[2] *Chronicle* (edition of 1809), p. 364.

one or two leading commonplaces in a great variety of forms, as for example :—

> The settled mynde is free from fortune's power;
> They need not feare who look not up aloft;
> But they that clyme are careful every hower,
> For when they fall they light not very soft:
> Examples hath the wisest warned oft,
>   That where the trees the smallest branches bere,
>   The storms do blowe and have most vigour there.
>
> Where is it strong but nere the ground and roote?
> Where is it weake but on the highest sprayes?
> Where may a man so surely set his foote,
> But on those bowes that groweth lowe alwayes.
> The little twygs are but unsteadfast stayes;
>   Yf they breake not they bend with every blast;
>   Who trusts to them shall never stand full fast.
>
> The wynde is great upon the highest hylles,
> The quiet lyfe is in the dale belowe,
> Who treads on yse shall slide against their wylles,
> They want not cares that curious artes would knowe.
> Who lives at ease and can content him so,
>   Is perfect wyse, and sets us all to schoole,
>   Who hates this lore may well bee calde a foole.[1]

If these lines be regarded as a mere metrical exercise, and apart from the poverty of their thought, it is strange indeed to think of them as contemporary with the hobbling verses of Baldwin and Ferrers. The poet, up to a certain point, has thoroughly understood the nature of the improvements introduced into versification by his master Surrey, both in respect of the disposition of the accent and the marking of the cæsura. But more than this he is himself, on his own poor level, something of an inventor, and in his careful balance of thoughts, words, and lines, as well as in his excessive fondness for alliteration, anticipates the coming of the Euphuists. Stanzas like these will illustrate what has been said :—

> Compell the hauke to sit that is unmande,
> Or make the hounde untaught to drive the dere,
> Or bring the free against his will in hande,

---

[1] Haslewood's edition of *The Mirror for Magistrates*, vol. ii. part ii. p. 472.

Or move the sad a pleasant tale to heare,
Your time is lost, and you no whit the nere ;
  So love me learnes of force the knot to knit ;
  She serves but those that feel sweet fancy's wit.

.   .   .

Yf I did frowne who then did looke awrye ?
Yf I did smile who would not laugh outright ?
Yf I but spake who durst my words denye ?
Yf I pursude who would forsake the flight ?
I meane my power was knowne to every wight :
  On such a height good hap had built my bowre,
  As though my sweete should nere have turnde to sowre.

.   .   .

My want was welthe, my woe was ease at will ;
My robes were rich and braver than the sunne ;
My fortune then was far above my skill ;
My state was great, my glasse did ever run ;
My fatale thriede so happely was spunne,
  That then I sate in earthly pleasures clad,
  And for the tyme a goddess' place I had.[1]

The just mean between Ferrers' excessive attention to
matter and Churchyard's excessive attention to form is
attained in the style of Thomas Sackville, who, by the
nobility of conception as well as by the skill in execution
shown in his *Induction*, towers a head and shoulders over all
the other contributors to *The Mirror for Magistrates*. He
was born in 1536, being the eldest son of Sir Richard
Sackville, the friend of Roger Ascham. According to
Anthony Wood he was a student in Hart Hall, Oxford ;[2]
he did not, however, graduate in that University, but
became M.A. at Cambridge, whence he proceeded to the
Inner Temple. When he was only nineteen he was
married to Cicely, daughter of Sir John Baker of Sissing-
hurst in Kent. In 1557-58 he was elected M.P. for
Westmoreland, and also for East Grinstead, and seems to
have been active in introducing bills. His reputation was
quickly made, for in 1567 he was knighted and raised to
the peerage as Lord Buckhurst. The Queen sent him, in
1571, as Ambassador to congratulate Charles IX. on his
marriage with Elizabeth of Austria. He was one of the
Peers who sat in trial on Thomas Howard, fourth Duke

---

[1] Haslewood's edition of *The Mirror for Magistrates*, vol. ii. part ii. pp.
466, 470, 471.   [2] *Athenæ Oxonienses* (1813), vol. ii. p. 30.

of Norfolk, in 1572 ; and in 1586, being a member of the
Commission appointed to try Mary Queen of Scots, he
was directed to convey to her the sentence of death, a
painful duty which he discharged with so much respect
and feeling as to earn the thanks of that unhappy sovereign.
Shortly afterwards (1587) he was sent as Ambassador to
the Low Countries to negotiate matters in dispute in consequence of the conduct of the Earl of Leicester, who was
acting there as the Lieutenant-Governor for the Queen ;
but as Buckhurst was too upright and honourable to
approve of all the favourite's actions he unfortunately incurred the displeasure of Elizabeth, who confined him to
his house for a year. He was, however, soon restored to
favour, and in 1591 received the Order of the Garter, while
in the same year the University of Oxford made him its
Chancellor. In 1599 he became High Treasurer, and in
the following year presided at the trial of Essex. Created
Earl of Dorset in 1604, he died in 1608, while sitting at
the Council Table, and was buried at Withyham in Sussex.

Looking to the series of State Trials in which Sackville
took part, and the air of judicial gravity which seems to
surround his character, the reader will find in his *Induction*
and *Complaint of the Duke of Buckingham*—the poetical
works of his youth—something strangely prophetic of his
political career. Sombre, solemn, austere, the conception
of these poems naturally provokes a comparison with the
settled gloom of the *Inferno*, and it was probably this
circumstance which led Pope—and afterwards Gray—to
regard Sackville as a poet of the school of Dante. His
actual poetical progenitors, however, were Virgil and
Gavin Douglas. From the former he derived most of the
details of his ideal scenery ; he imitated the latter in
associating the phenomena of Nature with the mournful
events which made the subject of his poem, and with his
own mood as their narrator ; his manner of reproducing
his borrowed materials is entirely his own. Douglas's
impressive description of Winter prefixed to his translation
of the Seventh *Æneid*, evidently inspired Sackville with
the fine opening of the *Induction* :—

The wrathful Winter, 'proaching on apace,
With blustering blasts had all ybared the treen,
And old Saturnus, with his frosty face,
With chilling cold had pierced the tender green ;
The mantles rent wherein enwrapped been
    The gladsome groves that now lay overthrown,
    The tapets torn and every bloom down blown ;

The soil, that erst so seemly was to seen,
Was all despoiled of her beauty's hue,
And soote fresh flowers, wherewith the summer's queen
Had clad the earth, now Boreas' blasts down blew ;
And small fowls flocking in their song did rue
    The winter's wrath, wherewith each thing defast
    In woeful wise bewailed the summer past.

Hawthorn had lost his motley livery ;
The naked twigs were shivering all for cold,
And dropping down the tears abundantly ;
Each thing methought with weeping eye me told
The cruel season, bidding me withhold
    Myself within ; for I was gotten out
    Into the fields whereas I walked about.[1]

The melancholy aspect of the time causes the poet to moralise :—

And sorrowing I to see the summer flowers
The lively green, the lusty leas forlorn,
The sturdy trees so shattered with the showers,
The fields so fade that flourished so beforne.
It taught me well all earthly things be born
    To die the death, for nought long time may last ;
    The summer's beauty yields to winter's blast.[2]

While the feeling of this stanza is identical with that which has been already noticed in Gavin Douglas, the course of the poem thus far resembles that which is employed by Lyndsay in his *Dreme*. But at this point the vast superiority of Sackville's imagination reveals itself. Instead of having recourse to the usual dream machinery, the sorrowful appearance of things and his own sorrowful mind conjure up the impersonation of

[1] Sackville's *Works*.   Edited by Hon. and Rev. Reginald Sackville-West, p. 97.   [2] *Ibid.* p. 99.

Sorrow, and the poet exerts all the powers of his fine
invention to paint for the reader the figure he beheld :—

> Her body small, forewithered, and forespent,
> As is the stalk that summers drought oppressed ;
> Her welked face with woeful tears besprent,
> Her colour fade ; and, as it seemed her best,
> In woe and plaint reposed was her rest,
>   And as the stone that drops of water wears,
>   So dinted were her cheeks with fall of tears.[1]

Sorrow, after some conversation with him, offers to guide
him to a region where he may behold in outward form
things hitherto merely imaged in his mind, and, taking
the place of the Sibyl in Virgil, she conducts him, amid
scenery like that described in the *Æneid*, to Avernus,
through which they pass on till "first within the porch
and jaws of hell" they encounter a group of Abstractions,
some of whom have been enumerated by the Latin poet,
but are now joined with others whom we recognise as the
offspring of Catholic theology.   Their names are, Remorse
of Conscience, Dread, Revenge, Misery, Care, Sleep, Old
Age, Malady, Famine, Death, War.   All of these are
portrayed by means of their attributes in a style which
often reaches the sublime ; but it will be sufficient to cite
the description of Old Age :—

> Crook-backed he was, tooth-shaken, and blear-eyed,
> Went on three feet and sometimes crept on four,
> With old lame bones that rattled by his side,
> His scalp all pilled, and he with age for-lore :
> His withered fist still knocking at death's door ;
>   Fumbling and drivelling as he draws his breath ;
>   For brief, the shape and messenger of death.[2]

When all these Abstractions have been described, the
travellers pass on, like Æneas and the Sibyl, in Charon's
ferry-boat into the region of departed spirits, where they
encounter the shade of the Duke of Buckingham, who
makes his complaint to Sackville in the same manner as
the actors in the other tragedies address themselves to
Baldwin.

[1] Sackville's *Works*, p. 101.   [2] *Ibid.* p. 113.

Compared with Lyndsay's *Dream* and *Complaint of the Papingo*, the *Induction* of Sackville shows clearly the beneficial effects produced on English poetry by the genius of Surrey. Lyndsay's own poems are in some respects an advance on the art of his predecessors. While they are modelled on the allegorical forms peculiar to the Middle Ages, the poet is not content, like Dunbar in *The Golden Targe*, and Douglas in *The Palace of Honour*, with the treatment of a mere scholastic theme ; his moral is intended to suggest a remedy for actual evils ; the cast of his thought, practical, and satirical, is occupied with the fortunes of " John Commonweal," or the *State*. But he has no conception of conveying his instruction in a poetical form. The old conventional machinery of allegory is good enough for his purpose. He is satisfied with showing the reader the bare fact that bad popes, emperors, and kings are in Hell ; when his *Itinerarium Mentis* has brought him within view of the realm of Scotland, he thinks only of classifying the evils he sees there ; he is quite careless whether the speeches he puts into the mouth of his dying Papingo are appropriate to a bird, so long as he can deliver a shrewd stroke of satire at the abuses which move his indignation. Something of the same kind of rudeness is visible in Baldwin's and Ferrers' scheme for presenting the different tragedies in *The Mirror for Magistrates*. It is not so with the work of Sackville. He, too, makes use of the forms of allegory for the purposes of instruction. But with him the conception of the allegory is adapted to the ends of poetry. Everything in his action—the time, the place, the abstract character of the person—is made to conform to the ideal nature of the subject ; the *Induction* is the work of a man who has moulded his materials according to the laws of art. Of the epic poets of England if Chaucer is the first to exhibit the genuinely classic spirit, Sackville is the first to write in the genuinely classic manner.

A still more striking measure of the advance of English poetry since the improvements introduced by

Surrey, is furnished by the diction and versification of
Sackville in contrast with that of his predecessors. The
English of Lyndsay is not a language, it is a dialect.
The English of Baldwin and Ferrers, poets whose style
had been formed under the old system, may be called a
language in respect of vocabulary and syntax, but it is
language which, never having been subjected to the rules
of harmony and proportion, is rude, unbalanced, unrhythmical. In Sackville we find the art that is able
to conceive alike effects of harmony as a whole, and that
relation of the component parts to each other by which
such effects are produced. The sustained music in the
structure of the following stanza from *The Complaint of
the Duke of Buckingham*, proceeds from a mind which is
moved by a sense equally of the dignity of the subject
matter, and of the metrical form in which this must
necessarily clothe itself :—

> And, Sackville, sith in purpose now thou hast
> The woeful fall of princes to descrive,
> Whom Fortune both uplift and eke downcast,
> To show thereby the unsurety in this live ;
> Mark well my fall, which I shall show bilive,
>   And paint it forth that all estates may know :
>   Have they the warning, and be mine the woe.

What an interval between this and the *versus inopes
rerum* of Churchyard !

CHAPTER V

TRANSLATIONS OF THE CLASSICS: VIRGIL, SENECA, OVID

THE accession of Elizabeth marks a distinct epoch in the history of English poetry, because it was this which first helped to blend the study of the classics and the scholarship of the Universities with the taste and imagination of the Court. The new learning had established itself without much opposition in Oxford and Cambridge. In Erasmus and his fellow-workers there was no desire to tamper with the foundations of the Catholic religion; their aim was to revive the earnestness and simplicity of faith, and at the same time to reconcile it with whatever was valuable and beautiful in the genius of Paganism. The study of Rhetoric on these lines was encouraged by the best spirits of the age, and was only opposed by ignorance and fanaticism. An attempt was made by the Scotist party at Oxford to discredit the new learning, but their stupidity was ridiculed by Sir Thomas More.[1] Wolsey promoted the study of Greek by the foundation of Christ Church. Colet and Grocyn lectured on the Greek orators and poets in the same University; and Cheke and Ascham familiarised their scholars at Cambridge with the dialogues of Plato, the philosophy most highly approved by the reformers of the Continent.

But the study of the classics had not yet been definitely made part of the education of the courtier. Henry VIII. favoured scholarship, but his temper was largely leavened with scholasticism; he prided himself on

[1] Froude, *Erasmus*, p. 131.

his knowledge of theology, and he loved disputation. Moreover, his taste for all the externals of chivalry made the chase and the tournament the chief amusements of his Court.   In his cultivation of music he approached the ideal of Castiglione, but his passion for masques and pageants had in it the colour of mediævalism.   The times of Edward VI. and of Mary were too tragic to encourage social forms of gaiety, though dramatic exhibitions were still in favour at Court.   Under the former monarch the spirit of the Renaissance continued to accompany the spirit of the Reformation.   Under Mary, however, a returning wave of pure mediævalism overwhelmed for the moment all that had been gained for the cause of the Reformation and learning, so that when Elizabeth came to the throne the task of reorganising society had to be undertaken from the beginning.

The new sovereign united in her own nature all the conflicting principles of the time.   She was born of a mother whose marriage had occasioned the separation of the English Church from the Roman Communion, but of a father who was strongly attached to all the prescriptions of the Catholic faith.   She herself adhered firmly to the usages in which she had been trained, and while she saw the necessity of yielding to the current of reform in doctrinal matters, she restrained the zeal of the Puritans when it was directed against rites and ceremonies.   In this respect she truly represented the temper of her people at large, who had no desire to separate themselves from the life of the past.   When she made her first entry into London the citizens welcomed her with a great show of those mediæval pageants which they loved: it was only in the sense of the allegory conveyed by these emblems that the spirit of change discovered itself: Time and Truth presented to the Queen a copy of the English Bible.

The same double spirit shows itself in Elizabeth's attitude towards the institution of chivalry.   She was delighted with the spectacles of joustings ·and exhibitions of arms ; she loved the reading of romances, and the

action of masquerades. But she looked on knighthood
with the eyes of a woman, and used her royal influence
to encourage the feminine element, always inclined to
predominate in romance. Hence, as her reign advanced,
the worship of the female sex, initiated by the Troubadours, was converted by flattery into the worship of the
Virgin Queen ; while the spirit of adventurous knight
errantry, reflected in the *Mort d'Arthur*, was blended with
the softer genius of pastoralism, introduced by Sidney's
Arcadia.

But the strongest influence that helped to modify
taste in its transition from the chivalrous Court of
Henry VIII. to the romantic Court of Elizabeth, was the
Queen's love of learning. The following description of
her accomplishments from the pen of Roger Ascham—
whatever deduction may be made from it in consideration
of partiality or flattery—must be accepted as the testimony
of the highest possible authority :—

Among the learned daughters of Sir Thomas More the princess
Elizabeth shines like a star of distinguished lustre ; deriving
greater glory from her virtuous disposition and literary accomplishments than from the dignity of her exalted birth. I was her
preceptor in Latin and Greek for two years. She was but little
more than sixteen when she could speak French and Italian with
as much fluency and propriety as her native English. She speaks
Latin readily, justly, and even critically. She has often con-
versed with me in Greek, and with tolerable facility. When she
transcribes Greek or Latin nothing can be more beautiful than
her handwriting. She is excellently skilled in music, though not
very fond of it. She has read with me all Cicero and a great
part of Livy, It is chiefly from these two authors alone that she
has acquired her knowledge of the Latin language. She begins
the day with reading a portion of the Greek Testament, and then
studies some select orations of Isocrates and the tragedies of
Sophocles. . . . In every composition she is very quick in
pointing out a far-fetched word or an affected phrase. She
cannot endure those absurd imitators of Erasmus who mince the
whole Latin language into proverbial maxims. She is much
pleased with a Latin oration naturally arising from its subject,
and written both chastely and perspicuously. She is most fond
of translations not too free, and with that agreeable clash of

sentiment which results from a judicious comparison of opposite or contradictory passages. By a diligent attention to these things her taste has become so refined, and her judgment so penetrating, that there is nothing in Greek, Latin, and English composition which she does not, in the course of reading, accurately discern ; immediately rejecting the one with disgust, and receiving the other with the highest degree of pleasure.[1]

A sovereign so favourably disposed to the advancement of the new learning naturally communicated her tastes to all those in attendance on her person. Nor was the influence of her taste confined within the limits of a stationary Court. Elizabeth loved change and excitement. She was constantly moving from one place to another, and wherever she went she expected to be amused by some kind of artistic display. Masques, pageants, speeches, and addresses welcomed the arrival of the Queen in every part of her dominions. The invention of the Court poets was racked to vary the entertainment provided as she passed from seat to seat belonging to her chief nobles and councillors, Kenilworth, Hunsdon, Chartley, Theobalds. The great provincial cities of Bristol and Norwich vied with each other in the splendour of the dramatic exhibitions by which they showed their sense of the honour done them by her visits.[2] Above all, the Universities and the Inns of Court, as being the chief seats of English learning, exerted themselves to make a display worthy of their monarch's erudition as well as of their own. In 1564 the Queen visited Cambridge, and listened for hours with apparent delight to the disputations of the Doctors in the Senate House ; the strain on her attention was relieved by the performance of a Latin play.[3] Two years afterwards she proceeded to Oxford, where classical diversions, resembling those of the sister University, were varied by the representation of an English play, founded on the story of Palamon and Arcite, which seems to have given the Queen much pleasure.[4] The members of Gray's Inn, Lincoln's Inn,

---

[1] Nichol's *Progresses of Queen Elizabeth*, vol. i. p. 19.
[2] *Ibid.* vol. i. pp. 393-407, and vol. ii. pp. 134-178.
[3] *Ibid.* pp. 183-189.   [4] *Ibid.* pp. 206-247.

and the Temple constantly amused her Majesty in their own Halls or at her palace at Greenwich with the various kinds of stage inventions for which their societies were becoming renowned.

The English imagination was thus in a state eminently favourable for acclimatising new poetical ideas. A period had arrived in which the genius of the nation, apt like the Roman for the assimilation of foreign elements, turned instinctively to translation. This was no new thing in our history. At a very early stage of the language Alfred had sought to enlarge the bounds of culture by his translations of Bede, Orosius, and Gregory the Great. In the reign of Edward III. Chaucer brought a new standard of refinement into the newly-formed Middle English by his translation of the *Roman de la Rose* and his adaptation of Boccaccio's *Filostrato*. The early portion of Elizabeth's reign is notable for translations of Virgil, Seneca, and Ovid, three authors whose matter and form exerted a powerful influence on the literature of the country in the latter half of the sixteenth century.

From very early days in the history of the Church Virgil had been regarded with reverence by Christian society. His reputation was in the Middle Ages partly due to his unrivalled style, the beauty of which was perceived even in the ages of decline, partly to the religious feeling which pervades his verse and which endeared him to St. Augustine, but most of all perhaps to the belief that in his fourth Eclogue he had foretold the coming of the Messiah. The English poets, beginning with their founder, had unanimously done homage to his genius. Chaucer, in his *House of Fame*, makes a short abstract of the entire *Æneid*, and in the *Legend of Good Women* reproduces, with fuller detail, the story of Dido and Æneas. Caxton gave a *résumé* of the *Æneid* in English prose, but the looseness and inaccuracy with which this version was executed aroused the wrath of Gavin Douglas, who, in his enthusiasm for the poet, resolved, by rendering his great epic into English verse, to rescue him from the indignity with which Caxton

had treated him.   Douglas completed his task in 1513.
He sets forth the nature of his design in a poetical prologue
in which his honest and scholarly spirit shines through the
barbarous archaism of the diction.   Exalting his original
above all who had practised the art, he proportionately
disparaged his own powers as a translator :—

> Quhy suld I than, with dull forehede and wane,
> With ruide engine, and barrand emptive brane,
> With bad harsk speche, and lewit barbour tong,
> Presume to write quhar thi sueit bell is rong,
> Or contirfait sa precious wourdis deir ?
> Na, na, nocht sua, bot knele quhan I thame heir.
> For quhat compare, betuix murkness and lycht,
> Or quhat compare is betuix blak and quhyte,
> Far gretar difference betuix my blunt endyte
> And thi scharp sugarat sang Virgiliane,
> Sa wyslie wrocht with nevir ane word in vane.[1]

Nevertheless he will make an attempt to repair the
wrong done to Virgil by Caxton.   His own aim, he
says, is to reproduce the spirit and sense of Virgil, whose
poem is to be read for the heroic examples it offers to
princes and governors, and which is not to be studied by
unlearned and ignorant men.[2]   A glimpse of the religious
prejudices with which the early translators had to contend
is given in Douglas's reference to the descent of Æneas
into Hell, a point to which he reverts in his Prologue to
the Sixth Book :—

> " All is but gaistis and elriche fantasies
> Of brownies, and of bogillis full this buke ;
> Out on their wanderand spiritis, wow !" thou cryis.[3]

He apologises for his translation of this book by
representing it as a mysterious foreshadowing of Christian
truth.   Unreadable though it is, on account of the dialect
in which it is written, no capable critic can examine
Douglas's translation without a profound admiration for
the truly poetical spirit in which it is executed.   Surrey
had a just appreciation of its worth, and when he

---

[1] Gavin Douglas (Small's edition), *Works*, vol. ii. pp. 3, 4.
[2] *Ibid.* vol. ii. p. 13.   [3] *Ibid.* vol. iii. p. 2.

undertook the same task, constantly consulted the Scottish poet, and frequently adopted his renderings. To judge from his style he must have begun his own version after he had fully formed his poetical manner, that is to say, in the last five years of his life. Two books, the second and the fourth, were all that he was able to translate, but these are in themselves a lasting monument to his fine taste and poetical skill. I have already spoken of the metre in which his translation is composed. While Surrey's blank verse gives no indication of the harmonies which the genius of the Elizabethan dramatists and Milton afterwards evoked from the measure, it succeeds in reproducing Virgil's meaning with a purity and dignity of form not attained by any other of the Roman poet's translators till the time of Dryden.

The *Æneid* as a whole, however, remained untranslated into modern English until 1555, when the enterprise was again undertaken by Thomas Phaër, a native of Pembrokeshire. Phaër had been educated at Oxford, but, like many men of his period, he left the University without taking a degree, to proceed to Lincoln's Inn, where, as at the other Inns of Court at that time, general instruction was given in the arts of Law and Medicine. He seems to have been called to the Bar, but to have afterwards practised as a physician; in both capacities he kept up the love of letters which he had doubtless first acquired at his University. As a lawyer he had been an acquaintance of George Ferrers, who took a leading part in the composition of *The Mirror for Magistrates ;* and to that work Phaër himself contributed the tragedy of *Owen Glendower*, a poem which does not rise above the level aimed at by most of his fellow-labourers. He began his translation of Virgil in 1555 ; printed the first seven books in 1558 ; and had carried it as far as the beginning of the ninth book in 1560, when he died. His unfinished work was taken up and completed in 1562 by Thomas Twine, another physician, who had no difficulty in reproducing Virgil's sense in the bald diction and halting verse which he found in Phaër's translation. The following

passages, describing the opening episode in the death of
Priam, will serve to show in an interesting manner the
spirit in which each of these successive translators of Virgil
entered on his task. Here is Gavin Douglas's :—

> Quhen he the ciete saw takin and doun bet,
> And of his palice broken every yet,
> Amyd the secret closettis eke his fais,
> The ald gray all for nocht to him tais
> His hawberk, quhilk was lang furth of usage,
> Set on his schulderis tremblying than for age ;
> A swerd but [1] help about him beltes he,
> And ran towart his fais reddy to de.
>
>   Amid the clois, undar the hevin all bare,
> Stude there that time a mekle fair altair ;
> Nere quham there grew a richt auld laurer tree,
> Bowand toward the altair ane litel wee,
> That with his schaddow the goddis did ourheild [2]
> Hecuba thidder with her childir for beild [3]
> Ran all in vane, and about the altair swarmis,
> Brasand [4] the god-like ymage in thair armis ;
> As for the storm doves flockis togidder ilk ane :
> But quhen scho saw how Priamus has tane
> His armour, so as thoch he had been ying,
> " Quhat fulich thocht, my wrechit spous and king,
> Movis ye now sic wapnis for to weild ?
> Quhidder haistis thou ? " quod scho ; " of na sic beild
> Have we now mister,[5] nor yet defendouris as ye,
> The tyme is nocht ganand [6] thairto, we see ;
> In case Hector war present heir, my sone,
> He micht not succour Troy, for it is wone.
> Quhairfor, I pray ye, sit doun and come hiddir,
> And lat this altair salf us all togiddir,
> Or than at anis all heir let us de."
> Thus said scho, and with sic sembland as micht be,
> Him toward hir has brocht, bot ony threte,
> And set the aüld doun in the haly sete.[7]

There is true pathos and nobility in this, and the careful
reader will observe in Surrey's version of the same passage
how much the younger poet, while altering, selecting, and
refining, owes to the translation of his predecessor :—

> Percase you would ask what was Priam's fate ?
> When of his taken toun he saw the chance,

---

[1] Without.   [2] Spread.   [3] Shelter.   [4] Clasping.
[5] Need.   [6] Advantageous.   [7] Gavin Douglas, *Works*, vol. i. p. 98.

And the gates of his palace beaten down,
His foes amid his secret chambers eke,
Th' old man in vain did on his shoulders then,
Trembling for age, his cuirass long disused ;
His bootless sword he girded him about,
And ran amid his foes, ready to die.
    Amid the court, under the heaven all bare,
A great altar there stood, by which there grew
An old laurel tree, bowing thereunto,
Which with his shadow did embrace the gods.
Here Hecuba, with her young daughters all,
About the altar swarmed were in vain ;
Like doves that flock together in the storm;
The statues of the gods embracing fast.
But when she saw Priam had taken there
His armour, like as though he had been young ;
" What furious thought, my wretched spouse," quoth she,
" Did move thee now such weapons for to wield !
Why hastest thou ?   The time doth not require
Such succour, ne yet such defenders now.
No, though Hector, my son, were here again.
Come hither ; this altar shall save us all,
Or we shall die together."   Thus she said.
Wherewith she drew him back to her, and set
The aged man down in the holy seat.[1]

Phaër's translation is as follows :—

The fatall end of Priam now perhaps you will requier :
Whan he the citie taken saw and houses' tops on fire,
And buildings broke and rounde about so thick his foes to rage ;
His harneis on his shoulders (long onworn tyle now), for age
All quaking, on (good man) he putts, to purpose small, and than
His sword him gyrt, and into death and enmies thick he ran.
    Amid the court, right underneath the naked skyes in sight,
An altare huge of size there stood, and by the same upright
An ancient laurel tree did grow, that wyde abroad was shed,
And it and all the carvyd gods with broad shade overspred,
There Hecuba and her daughters all (poore soules) at the altares'
    side
In heapes together affrayed them drew, like doves whan doth betide
Some storm them headlong drive, and clipping fast their gods thei
    hold.
But whan she Priam then beclad in armes of youth so bold
Espied : " What minde, alas (quoth she) o wofull husband yow
In harneis dight : and whither away with wepons run ye now ?
Not men nor wepons us can save : this time doth axe to bere
No such defence, no not if Hector myne now present were.

---

[1] Surrey's *Works* (Nott), vol. i. p. 112.

Stand here by me ; this altare us from slaughters all shall shelde,
Or dye together at ones we shall." So said she, and gan to welde
Him aged man, and in the sacred seat hym set, and helde.[1]

The above example, not an unfavourable one, is quite
sufficient to give the measure of Phaër's merits as a translator. It is evident that for him Surrey had written in
vain. Very possibly he may never have seen Surrey's
own translation, and may therefore have had no opportunity of judging how much more adequately Virgil's
manner could be reproduced in English blank verse than
in the ambling ballad metre. But he can hardly have
been ignorant of the manner in which the latter measure
had been used by Wyatt and Surrey: nevertheless his
ear does not seem to have told him that the fourteen
syllable line must necessarily divide after the eighth
syllable. Like Ferrers he seems to have been ignorant
of the use of the cæsura, so that his lines are often broken-
backed,

No such defence, no not if Hector myne now present were ;

or make the pause after the sixth syllable,

Some storm them headlong drive, and clipping fast their gods
    thei hold.

Phaër did not see, as Gavin Douglas did, that Virgil
wrote " never a word in vain " ; all that he aimed at was
to reproduce, by hook or crook, his author's sense in the
metre he had himself chosen. Yet even so something
was gained. The *Æneid* had been translated as a whole,
and many English readers, whose imaginations had been
previously starved on allegories and metrical homilies, were
now introduced to a new ideal world. Phaër's translation
is one of the earliest monuments of the influence of
patronage on English letters. Twine, who completed it,
dedicated it to Sir Nicholas Bacon, the Lord-Keeper, who
doubtless recommended the book to a wide circle of
acquaintance.

[1] *The Thirteene Bookes of Æneidos*, translated into English Verse to the
first third Part of the Tenth Book, by Thomas Phaër, Esquire ; the residue
finished by Thomas Twyne, Doctor in Physic (1600).

The flattering arts of the dedicator were also practised by Jasper Heywood, who, in 1559, began to translate Seneca, and inscribed his first attempt to the Earl of Pembroke. He was a man of considerable ability, a younger son of John Heywood—Pope's " eldest Heywood " —famous for his Interludes. Jasper was born in 1535, and entered as a student at Oxford in 1547. In 1554 he became a Fellow of Merton, but resigned that position —in order to avoid expulsion—in consequence of some irregularity. Cardinal Pole recommended him in 1558 for a Fellowship in the newly founded Trinity College; but without success. He was elected to a Fellowship of All Souls in this year; from which, however, he was expelled after the accession of Elizabeth for non-compliance with the new religious requirements of the College. Being ordained priest, he became a Jesuit in 1562, and was for seventeen years Professor of Moral Theology in the college of that order at Dillingen in Bavaria. In 1581 he returned to England, where, in 1583, he was arrested on suspicion of being a priest, and was arraigned in 1585 in Westminster Hall, together with five other priests, all of whom were condemned and executed. Though he himself escaped this extreme fate, he was sent to the Tower and kept in captivity for seventeen months, at the end of which time he was banished, and died at Naples in 1598.

These biographical details have some significance when we remember that the man, who endured suffering with steadfast courage in behalf of his religious convictions, was in his youth the translator of some of the works of the great Roman professor of Stoicism. Seneca is an author now little read, but in the Middle Ages his supposed leanings towards Christianity, and the tradition of his correspondence with St. Paul, gave him a distinguished place among the few ancient writers still studied in the schools. His plays, consisting as they did almost exclusively of representations of the revolutions of fortune, largely contributed to sanction the meaning attached to the word " tragedy " in the *Canterbury Tales*, the *De*

Casibus Illustrium Virorum, and *The Mirror for Magistrates;* and as we shall see hereafter, exercised a weighty influence on the development of the drama under Elizabeth.   There was even something in his style attractive to an age which had lost the true tradition of classical form. Seneca exaggerated all the features of the sophistical manner which Euripides had introduced into the Greek drama.   Instead of leaving the moral to be deduced from the action, he concentrated his powers upon the dialogue ; and his tragedies are, therefore, no more than brilliant exercises in rhetoric ; but inexperienced tastes are apt to admire the pompous declamation of his actors, and the sparkle of epigrams, antitheses, and paradoxes, profusely scattered through his plays.   Jasper Heywood translated three of Seneca's tragedies—the *Troas* in 1559, the *Thyestes* in 1560, and the *Hercules Furens* in 1561.   For the rendering of dialogue he employed the ballad metre, apparently not perceiving how little suited this measure was either for the general purposes of the drama, or for the reflection of the peculiarities of Seneca's style ; the lyrical parts he translated into stanzas of decasyllabic verse variously combined.   As Seneca's text is almost unknown to the modern reader, it will be needless to give specimens of Heywood's translation, but the following passages, showing the different spirit in which he set about his task on different occasions, are of interest, because they illustrate the growth of the critical faculty in the atmosphere of the Renaissance.   In his first translation—the *Troas*— Heywood allowed himself much latitude.   After speaking of the difficulty of translating Seneca, he says :—

Now as concernyng sundry places augmented and since altered in thys translation.   Fyrst, forasmuch as thys worke seemed unto me in some places unperfytte (whether left so of the authour or part of it lost, as tyme devoureth all thynges, I wotte not), I have (where I thought good) with addicyon of mine owne pen supplied the want of some thynges, as the fyrst chorus, after the fyrst act, beginning thus: "O ye to whom, etc."   Also in the second acte I have added the spectre of Achilles spright rising from hell to require the sacrifice of Polyxena, beginning in this wise, "Forsaking now, etc." Againe the three last staves of the chorus after the same acte, and as for the third chorus, which in Seneca beginneth thus, *Quæ vocat sedes*, forasmuch as nothing is therein but a heaped nombre of farre and strange contreyes, considering with myself the names of so many unknown countreyes, mountains, desertes, and woodes, should have no grace in the English tonge, this being a strange and unpleasant thing to the reader (except I should expounde the history of eche, which would be far too tedious) I have in the place thereof made another beginning in thys manner ; "O Jove that leadst, etc." which alteracyon may be borne with seeing that the chorus is no part of the substance of the matter.[1]

But in the translation of the *Hercules Furens* he followed a very different way.

Neither could I satisfie myself till I had throughout thys whole tragedye of Seneca, a grave and wise writer, so travailed that I had in English given verse for verse (as far as the English tonge permits) and word for word with the Latyn : whereby I might both make some tryal of myself, and as it were teche the little children to goe that yet can but crepe.[2]

This close attention to nicety of phrase is indicative of a growing eagerness in English writers to refine their native language, which was presently to culminate in the Euphuistic movement. But on the whole it did not prevail to any great extent among the translators of the Classics, who were mainly desirous to introduce to their readers the substance of the works which they themselves admired. This, certainly, is the predominant motive in the next translation which calls for our notice, namely that of Ovid's *Metamorphoses*. In the Middle Ages Ovid was, I imagine, an even greater favourite than Virgil. His poems touched at numerous points the peculiar tastes and sympathies of those times. His *Art of Love* helped the Troubadours and their allegorical successors to construct the metaphysics of their poetical creed; his *Heroides* furnished the same school with most of the examples of

---

[1] Sixt Tragedie of the most grave and prudent author, Lucius Annæus Seneca, set forth in English by Jasper Heywood, student in Oxenford, 1559.

[2] Address to Lord Pembroke prefixed to the translation of *Hercules Furens*, 1561.

amorous martyrology; and his *Metamorphoses* discovered a rich mine of fable to the exhausted invention of the Trouvère.   Nevertheless his works presented certain difficulties to the Christian imagination, on account both of the Paganism of the subject matter, and the immorality of much of the sentiment.

It is therefore remarkable that the first English translator of the *Metamorphoses* should have been a man strongly imbued with the rising spirit of Puritanism. Arthur Golding, son of John Golding, one of the auditors of the Exchequer, was born about 1536.   He is said to have been educated at Queen's College, Cambridge, but there is no record of his having taken a degree at that University.   Indeed, it seems improbable that he should have been at any University, for as early as 1549 he is found in the service of the Protector Somerset.   He was well connected, being uncle through his sister of Edward, 17th Earl of Oxford, to whom in later years he acted as receiver.   He printed the first four books of his translation of the *Metamorphoses* in 1565, and completed the work in 1567.   He also translated, in 1565, Cæsar's *Commentaries;* in 1575, Beza's *Tragedy of Abraham's Sacrifice;* in 1577, Seneca, *De Beneficiis;* while in 1587 he completed the translation of Du Mornay's *Treatise on the Truth of Christianity* which had been begun by Sir Philip Sidney.   Sharing the views of the Calvinistic Reformers, he denounced the violation of the Sabbath by the performance of stage plays; and in 1580 he wrote on the subject of the earthquake which was at that time, as we see from the correspondence of Gabriel Harvey, exciting the imagination of the English people. Golding regards the earthquake as a punishment sent by God on the wickedness of the times.   He died in 1606.

Such a man must necessarily have found some difficulty in reconciling his admiration of Ovid's style with his disapprobation of Ovid's opinions.   And indeed the part of his work most interesting to the modern reader is the metrical preface, in which he explains the motive and plan of his translation.   This is contained in an epistle to the

Earl of Leicester, to whom the book is dedicated, and an Address to the Reader. The simple sort, he says in the latter, may be offended by seeing the names of heathen gods ; but this is unreasonable in view of certain considerations on which he dwells with fulness in his epistle to the Earl. According to him, Ovid was a disciple of Pythagoras, and intended in the *Metamorphoses* to illustrate the constant process of human change. But here he was met by one of the many difficulties which led the early Church to prohibit the study of heathen authors. Pythagoras believed in the transmigration of souls, and Golding is therefore at pains to inform the reader that this doctrine is not to be understood of the individual soul of man, which is immortal, but merely of the triple soul, vegetable, animal, and rational, which is born of union with the body. He goes industriously through several books of the *Metamorphoses*, and explains the moral object of the particular tales ; and then sets forth his own purpose in the translation :—

These fables out of every book I have interpreted,
To show how they and all the rest may stand a man in stead :
Not adding over curiously the meaning of them all,
For that were labour infinite and tediousness not small,
Both unto your good Lordship, and the rest that should them read,
Who well might think I did the bounds of modesty exceed,
If I this one Epistle should with matters overcharge
Which scarce a book of many quires can well contain at large.
And whereas in interpreting these few I attribute
The things to one which heathen men to many gods impute,
Concerning mercy, wrath for sin, and other gifts of grace,
Described, for example's sake, in proper time and place ;
Let no man marvel at the same. For though that they were blind
Through unbelief, and, led astray through error even of kind,
Knew not the true eternal God, or if they did him know,
Yet did not well acknowledge him, but vainly did bestow
The honour of the Maker on the creature ; yet it doth
Behove us all, who rightly are instructed in the sooth,
To think and say that God alone is he that rules all things,
And worketh all in all, a lord of lords and king of kings.
With whom there are none other gods that any sway may bear,
No fatal law to bind him by, no fortune for to fear ;
For God and Fate and Fortune are the terms of heathenness,
If men usurp them in the sense that Paynims do express ;

But if we will reduce their sense to right of Christian law,
To signify three other things these terms we well may draw.
By gods we understand all such as God hath placed in chief
Estate to punish sin, and for the godly folks relief :
By Fate the order which is set and 'stablished in things,
By God's eternal will and word, which in due season brings
All matters to their falling out, which falling out or end
(Because our curious reason is too weak to comprehend
The cause and order of the same, and doth behold it fall
Unwares to us) by name of Chance or Fortune we do call.[1]

This curious and obviously sincere sermon on the *Metamorphoses* then proceeds to adapt an argument which Eusebius had first used for the purpose of discrediting ancient culture. "If any man," says the translator, "thinks that these things may be better learned from Scripture, I agree ; but, nevertheless, some are of opinion that the Pagan poets had a knowledge of the Mosaic writings" ; and in illustration of his point he shows how Ovid's description of the beginning of things agrees with the Mosaic account of creation, except that it makes no mention of separate days.[2]

A work conceived in such a spirit was well fitted to conciliate religious prejudice, and Ovid, introduced in English, and with very little alteration of his sense, became the channel through which the knowledge of Greek mythology was diffused widely through educated society in the reign of Elizabeth. Shakespeare was evidently well acquainted with Golding's translation, and the frequency of his mythological allusions is largely due to this source. The translation itself aims simply at telling Ovid's story in a rendering of his own words, but without the slightest effort to reproduce the polish of his style. A fair example of Golding's manner, which is indeed infinitely superior to Phaër's, will be found in the story of Pyramus and Thisbe, familiar to all readers of the *Midsummer Night's Dream* :—

Within the town, of whose huge walls so monstrous high and thick
The fame is given Semiramis for making them of brick,

---

[1] Golding's Translation of Ovid's *Metamorphoses* (1612), Prefatory Epistle.
[2] *Ibid.* (paraphrased).

Dwelt hard together two young folk in houses joined so near,
That under all one roof well-nigh both twain conveyed were.
The name of him was Pyramus, and Thisbe called was she ;
So fair a man was none alive in all the East as he,
Nor ne'er a woman, maid, nor wife, in beauty like to her.
This neighbrod bred acquaintance first, this neighbrod first did stir
The secret sparks, this neighbrod first an entrance in did show,
For love to come to that to which it afterward did grow.
And if that right had taken place they had been maa and wife ;
But still their parents went about to let which for their life
They could not let.   For both their hearts with equal flame did burn ;
No man was privy to their thoughts.   And for to serve their turn,
Instead of talk they used signs.   The closelier they suppressed
The fire of love, the fiercer still it raged in their breast.
The wall that parted house from house had riven therein a cranny,
Which shrank at making of the wall.   This fault, not marked of any,
Of many hundred years before (what doth not love espy ?)
These lovers first of all found out and made a way whereby
To talk together secretly, and through the same did go
Their loving whispering, very light and safely to and fro.
Now, as at one side Pyramus and Thisbe on the other
Stood, often drawing one of them the pleasant breath from other,
" O spiteful wall " (said they), " why dost thou part us lovers thus ?
What matter were it if that thou permitted both of us
In arms each other to embrace ?   Or if thou think that this
Were overmuch yet mightest thou at least make room to kiss.
And yet thou shalt not find us churls.   We think ourselves in debt
For the same piece of courtesy in working safe to let
Our sayings to our friendly ears thus freely come and go."
Thus having where they stood in vain complained of their woe,
When night drew near they bade adieu, and each gave kisses sweet,
Unto the parget at their side, the which did never meet.[1]

[1] Golding's Translation of Ovid's *Metamorphoses*, Book iv. pp. 43, 44.

CHAPTER VI

THE PROGRESS OF THE SCHOOL OF SURREY: LORD VAUX, NICHOLAS GRIMALD, BARNABE GOOGE, GEORGE TURBERVILE, THOMAS CHURCHYARD, GEORGE GASCOIGNE.

THE first twenty years of the reign of Elizabeth are, both in a political and literary sense, perhaps the most barren period in the literature of the sixteenth century. The old chivalrous ideal of life was passing away, no longer finding a home in the imagination of the new aristocracy or the rising middle class. In the prospect of the succession to the throne, as in the policy of the sovereign, all was uncertainty. A wide interval separated the manners of the Court which educated the knightly generation of Surrey and Wyatt from the manners of the Court of Elizabeth : the school of learned courtliness represented by Sidney, Raleigh, and Oxford was not yet formed. There was a similar ambiguity in the mind of the nation. Perplexed by the suddenness of the rupture with Rome, the full meaning of which was only made apparent to it by the subsequent Spanish invasion, the imagination of the people wavered between conflicting forms of belief, though the quickening of the individual conscience is shown by the marked tendency of the Universities to adopt the extreme forms of opinion advocated by the religious reformers of the Continent.

While the mind of the nation remained in this doubtful condition, the poets necessarily lacked clear motives of composition. They had passed out of the sphere of the mediæval imagination, but they had not yet become accustomed to the atmosphere of the new region of thought, and, like the infant described by Wordsworth, they were filled with

> Blank misgivings of a creature,
> Moving about in worlds not realised.

Hence, though Surrey had put them in possession of a well-tuned instrument, his successors made no attempt to use it for the expression of any elevated scheme of art. They contented themselves with timid variations of the old Provençal themes, with religious moralising, or with metrical experiments intended to enlarge the resources of poetical diction.

At the same time we observe at this period the first indications of a force destined hereafter to exercise an important influence on the course of English poetry, the beginnings of a definite public taste. The age of minstrelsy had departed ; the jongleur, who had sung in castle halls before lords and ladies, had declined into the needy ballad singer, whose instrument was only listened to by rustic audiences on village greens and ale-house benches. Though the poetical courtier still tuned his lute for the ear of his mistress, his songs and sonnets, when committed to writing, were submitted to the eyes of only a few select and aristocratic judges. But the curiosity of the general reader soon overleaped this exclusive barrier, and an opportunity was thus given for the appearance of the man whom Johnson afterwards described as the Mæcenas of the times, the modern publisher.

One of the most noticeable features in the literature of the latter half of the sixteenth century is its numerous *Miscellanies* : collections of poems due to the enterprise of different printers who, reckoning on the public taste as a source of gain, employed some accomplished editor to unite in a single volume the productions of many ingenious minds. Between 1557 and 1602 we find the following publications : Tottel's *Miscellany ; The Paradise of Dainty Devices ; The Gorgeous Gallery of Gallant Inventions ; The Phœnix Nest ; England's Helicon ; Eng-*

land's Parnassus; and *The Poetical Rhapsody.* All of these mark very distinct stages in the progress of public taste, and are deserving of notice, not only on account of the individual names they contain, but also from the light they throw on the general forces, which, after the advent of Wyatt and Surrey, conspired to bring about those changes of imagination that prepared the way for the work of Spenser and Shakespeare.

The first of these Miscellanies was published in June 1557 by Tottel, a well-known printer. It contained almost all the poems that survive of Sir T. Wyatt the elder, and of the Earl of Surrey; a variety of compositions by Nicholas Grimald; and a collection of verses by " Uncertain Authors," among whom were included Lord Vaux, and Sir Thomas Bryan, the friend of Wyatt. The editing of the Miscellany showed how largely the reforms of Surrey had influenced the taste and ear of the general English reader. We have already seen that Wyatt had in his versification made but a small advance on his predecessors. But a comparison of the text of Tottel's *Miscellany* with the Harrington MS. of Wyatt's poems proves that the halting verses and harsh collisions of accent, which gave no offence to Wyatt's early readers, were found intolerable by the next generation. The following are examples of the changes made by the editor in the text of his original :—

{ And therein camp(e)th, spreading his banner.—Wyatt, Harrington
MS.
{ And therein camp(e)th, displaying his banner.—Tottel.[1]

{ May content you without doing grief.—Harrington MS.
{ Content your mind withouten doing grief.—Tottel.[2]

{ Blinded with the stroke, erring here and there.—Harrington MS.
{ Blind with the stroke, and erring here and there.—Tottel.[3]

{ But daily yet the ill doth change into the worse.—Harrington MS.
{ And daily doth mine ill change to the worse.—Tottel.[4]

---

[1] Wyatt's *Works* (Nott), vol. ii. p. 537.
[2] *Ibid.*   [3] *Ibid.* p. 538.
[4] *Ibid.* p. 542. Sometimes the editor seems to have been puzzled by Wyatt's expressions, and to have made rather absurd emendations. For example,

Speaking generally, the influence both of Wyatt and Surrey is plainly visible in the style of the older contributors to the Miscellany. Of these, by far the best poet is Thomas, Lord Vaux, the son of Nicholas, the first lord, a distinguished courtier in the reign of Henry VIII. We know few details of his life beyond the fact that he attended Cardinal Wolsey in his embassy to the Emperor in 1527; took his seat in Parliament as baron in 1530; accompanied the king to Calais and Boulogne in 1532; was made Knight of the Bath in 1533, and died early in the reign of Queen Mary. His verses reflect the chivalrous spirit prevailing in the Court of Henry VIII.; and I imagine that in one of his best poems, "The assault of Cupid upon the fort where the lover's heart lay wounded, and how he was taken," the imagery is suggested by Dunbar's "Golden Targe" and "Beauty and her Prisoner."

> There might you hear the cannon's roar;
>   Each piece discharged a lover's look,
> Which had the power to rend, and tore
>   In any place where as they took.
>
> And even with the trumpet's sowne
>   The scaling ladders were up set,
> And Beauty walken up and downe,
>   With bow in hand and arrows whet.
>
> Then first Desire began to scale,
>   And shrowded him under his targe,
> As one the worthiest of them all,
>   And aptest for to give the charge.[1]

Like Wyatt, Lord Vaux was profoundly influenced by the spirit of the Reformation, and perhaps his finest poem is that published in *The Paradise of Dainty Devices*, and entitled "The Instability of Youth."

Wyatt, wishing to describe the effect of his mistress's refusal on his mind writes (certainly very harshly): "Of deadly 'nay' hear I the fearful thunder." The editor alters this into sheer nonsense by printing: "Of deadly *noise* hear I, etc." (*Works*, vol. ii. p. 538).

[1] Collier's *Seven English Poetical Miscellanies*, vol. i. p. 227.

When I look back and in myself behold
The wandering ways that youth could not descry,
And mark the fearful course that youth did hold,
And mette [1] in mind each step youth strayed a-wry;
My knees I bow, and from my heart I call;
O Lord, forget these faults and follies all.

For now I see how void youth is of skill;
I see also his prime time and his end;
I do confess my faults and all my ill,
And sorrow sore for that I did offend;
And with a mind repentant of all crimes,
Pardon I ask for youth ten thousand times.

The humble heart hath daunted the proud mind
Eke wisdom hath given ignorance a fall;
And wit hath taught that [2] folly could not find;
And age hath youth her subject and her thrall
Therefore I pray, O Lord of life and truth,
Pardon the faults committed in my youth.

Thou that didst grant the wise King his request,
Thou that in the whale thy Prophet didst preserve,
Thou that forgavest the wounding of thy breast,
Thou that didst save the thief in state to sterve, [3]
Thou only God, the giver of all grace,
Wipe out of mind the path of youth's vain race.

Thou that by power to life didst raise the dead,
Thou that restoredst the blind man to sight,
Thou that for love thy life and love out-bled,
Thou that of favour mad'st the lame go right,
Thou that canst heal and help in all assays,
Forgive the guilt that grew in youth's vain ways.

And now, since I, with faith and doubtless mind,
Do fly to thee with prayer to appease thy ire,
And since that thee I only seek to find,
And hope by faith to attain my just desire;
Lord, mind no more youth's error and unskill,
And able Age to do thy holy will. [4]

A variation of the same theme is found in " A Dittye
or Sonet made by the Lord Vaux in the time of the
noble Queen Mary, representing the Image of Death."

---

[1] Put.   [2] What.   [3] Die.
[4] Collier's *Seven English Poetical Miscellanies*, vol. ii. p. 27.

Every one will recognise in the three following stanzas extracted from this poem, the original of the gravedigger's song in Hamlet :—

THE AGED LOVER RENOUNCETH LOVE

I lothe that I did love,
In youth that I thought swete ;
As time requires for my behove,
Me thinkes they are not mete.

.   •   •

For age with his stelying steppes
Hath clawed me with his cowche,
And lusty life away she leapes
As ·there had been none such.

.   •   •

A pikeax and a spade,
And eke a shrowding shete ;
A house of claye for to be made
For such a gest most mete.[1]

Vaux, it will be seen, like his immediate predecessors, Wyatt and Surrey, writes with simplicity, because, whether he selects chivalrous or religious themes, he feels in himself a certain stimulus from the life about him. A different spirit manifests itself in Nicholas Grimald, the most considerable of the remaining contributors to Tottel's *Miscellany*. This poet derived his inspiration mainly from books. In him the genius of the epigrammatist predominates, and all his poetical efforts are devoted to make the freshly-tuned language an instrument for producing terse and pregnant effects of expression. Grimald, who was born in 1519 in Huntingdonshire, was educated

---

[1] Collier's *Seven English Poetical Miscellanies*, vol. ii. p. 27. Compare *Hamlet*, Act v. Sc. 1 :—

In youth, when I did love, did love,
  Methought it was very sweet,
To contract, O, the time, for, ah, my behove,
  O, methought, there was nothing meet.

But age, with his stealing steps,
  Hath claw'd me in his clutch,
And hath shipped me intil the land,
  As if I had never been such.

A pick-axe, and a spade, a spade,
  For and a shrouding sheet :
O, a pit of clay for to be made
  For such a guest is meet.

first at Christ's College, Cambridge, where he graduated as B.A. in 1539, but afterwards, removing to Oxford, he became B.A. in that University in 1542, and M.A. in 1543. From being Senior or Theologist at Christ's Church, he was appointed chaplain to Bishop Ridley, who, valuing his scholarship, urged him to translate Laurentius Valla's book against Constantine's donation and Æneas Silvius's *De Gestis Basiliensis Concilii*. In the first year of Mary's reign he was sent to the Marshalsea, under suspicion of heresy, and his constancy not proving equal to the trial, he recanted his Protestantism. He is said afterwards to have acted as a spy on Protestant prisoners during the Marian persecutions. He died some time before May 1562, when his epitaph was written by Barnabe Googe, whose works will presently have to be noticed. He translated Cicero, *De Officiis* (1553), besides writing treatises on many classical works, and the effects of his reading are plainly visible in his style, of which the most characteristic features are the use of the heroic couplet for the purposes of epigram, and frequent imitations of Greek and Latin *concetti*. His "Description of Virtue" will illustrate what has been said :—

> What one art thou thus in true weed y-clad?
> Virtue in price whom ancient sages had.
> Why poorly rayd?   For fading goods past care.
> Why double-faced?   I mark each fortune's fare.
> This bridle what?   Mind's rages to restrain.
> Tools why bear you?   I love to take great pain.
> Why wings?   I teach above the stars to fly.
> Why tread you Death?   I only cannot die.[1]

In the following curiously conceited lines we observe

[1] Collier's *Seven English Poetical Miscellanies*, vol. i. p. 141. I have little doubt that the form of this epigram was suggested by Ausonius, Ep. xii. *In Simulacrum Occasionis et Pœnitentiæ*—

> Cujus opus? Phidiæ ; qui signum Pallados ejus,
>   Quique Jovem fecit ; tertia palma ego sum.
> Sum Dea quæ rara et paucis Occasio nota.
>   Quid rotulæ insistis?   Stare loco nequeo.
> Quid talaria habes? Volucris sum, Mercurius quæ
>   Fortunare solet, tardo ego, cum volui.
> Crine teges faciem. Cognosci nolo. Sed heu tu
>   Occipiti calvo es. Ne tenear fugiens.
> Quæ tibi juncta comes? Dicat tibi. Dic rogo quæ sis.
>   Sum De.i cui nomen non Cicero ipse dedit.

the first symptoms of a new treatment of the subject of love. The pedantry and learned allusion which characterise them are perhaps the earliest notes in English poetry of that manner which culminated in the "metaphysical" style of Cowley and his contemporaries :—

THE LOVER ASKETH PARDON OF HIS DEAR FOR FLEEING FROM HER

Lovers warn men the corpse beloved to flee,
From the blind fire in case they would live free.
Aye me, how oft have I fled thee, my Day ;
I flee, but Love bides in my breast alway.
Lo, yet again I grant I can remove :
But both I could and can say still, I love.
If woods I seek, comes to my thought Adone :
And well the woods do know my heavy moan.
In gardens if I walk, Narcissus there
I spy, and Hyacints with weeping cheer.
If meads I tread, O what a fire I feel !
In flames of love I burn from head to heel.
Here I behold dame Ceres' imp in flight,
Here see, methinks, black Pluto's steeds in sight.
Strands if I look upon, the Nymphs I mind,
And in mid sea oft fervent powers I find.
The higher that I climb in mountains wild,
The nearer me approacheth Venus child.
Towns if I haunt—in short I all [will] say—
There sundry forms I view, none to my pay.[1]
Her favour now I note, and now her eyes,
Her head amiss, her foot, her cheek, her guise
In fine, where matter wants, defaults I feign ;
Whom other fair, I deem she hath some stain.
What boots it then to flee, sith in night-tide
And day-time too, my Day is at my side ?
A shade therefore thou mayst be called by right
But shadows dark, thou, Day, art ever bright
Nay, rather worldly name is not for thee,
Since thou at once canst in two places be.
Forgive me, goddess, and become my shield ;
Ev'n Venus to Anchises self did yield.
Lo ! I confess my flight ; be good therefore ;
Jove oftentimes hath pardoned me for more.
Next day, my Day, to you I come by way,
And, if you suffer me, due pains will pay.[2]

---

[1] Pleasure.
[2] Collier, *Seven English Poetical Miscellanies*, vol. i. p. 127.

Grimald, however, was something more than an epi-grammatist.   Like Cowley, Marvell, and other scholars, he shows a cultivated feeling for the beauties of external nature, and he wrote on the pleasures of the Garden in a vein of quaint simplicity which often reappears in the English poetry of the seventeenth century :—

Here pleasance wanteth not to make a man full fain ;
Here marvellous the mixture is of solace and of gain.
To water sundry seeds, the furrow by the way
A running river, trilling down with liquor, can convey.
Behold with lively hue fair flowers that shine so bright ;
With riches, like the Orient gems, they paint the mould in sight.
Bees humming with soft sound (their murmur is so small),
Of blooms and blossoms suck the tops, on dewéd leaves they fall.
Birds chatter and some chirp, and some sweet tunes do yield ;
All mirthful with her songs so blithe they make both air and field.[1]

" A Funeral Song upon decease of his Mother," in spite of superficial marks of pedantry, has the same true tenderness of feeling which gives an undying charm to Cowper's lines on his mother's portrait :—

You me embraced ; in bosom soft you me
Cherished, as I your only child had be.
Of issue fair with numbers were you blest ;
Yet I the best-beloved of all the rest.
Good luck, certain, fore-reading mothers have ;
And you of me a special judgment gave,
Then when firm pace I fixéd on the ground,
And tongue gan cease to break the lisping sound.
You me straightway did to the muses send,
Ne suffered long a loitering life to spend.
What gain the wool, what gain the web had brought,
It was his meed that me then daily taught.
When with Minerve I had acquaintance won,
And Phœbus seemed to love me as his son,
Brownshold I bade at parent's hest farewell,
And gladly then in schools I 'gan to dwell,
Where Granta gives the ladies nine such place,
That they rejoice to see their blissful case.
With joys at heart in this Parnasse I bode,
While through his signs five time great Titan glode ;
And twice as long by that fair flood whereas
Swan-feeder Thames no further course can pass.

> O what desire had you therewhile of me !
> 'Mid doubtful dreads what joys were won't to be !
> Now linen clothes wrought with your fingers fine,
> Now other things of yours did you make mine ;
> Till your last threads 'gan Clotho to untwine,
> And of your days the date extreme assign.[1]

Besides these compositions in the heroic couplet, and in what Gascoigne called "Poulter's" metre, Grimald made experiments with the blank verse introduced by Surrey, in two narrative poems called "The Death of Zoroas" and "The Death of M. Tulius Cicero." While, as a poet, he stands on a much lower level than either Wyatt or Surrey, he must be reckoned a pioneer in the development of his art, for he was the first writer who sought to assimilate in an English style the terseness and distinctness of thought, which is the chief characteristic of Latin verse. His contemporaries were aware of his merit ; and when he died recorded their sense of his loss.

> A thousand doltish geese we might have spared,
> A thousand witless heads death might have found,
> And taken them for whom no man had cared,
> And laid them low in deep oblivious ground.
> But Fortune favours fools, as old men say,
> And lets them live, and takes the wise away.

Barnabe Googe, the writer of these lines, was the son of Robert Googe, Recorder of Lincoln. He must have been born about 1540, and was educated at Christ's College, Cambridge, which University, however, he left without taking a degree, and like many of his contemporaries migrated to Oxford, where he became a member of New College. On leaving Oxford he travelled in France and Spain, and when he returned to England entered the service of his kinsman, Sir William Cecil, as Secretary. He figures among the numerous translators of the period, and selected for his labours the Latin poem of Marcellus Palingenius on "The Zodiac of Life." His rendering of this dull mediæval allegory gave such satisfaction to his contemporaries, that while he was on his travels

---

[1] Collier's *Seven English Poetical Miscellanies.* vol. i. p. 153.

some of his compositions were put into the hands of the
printer by one of his friends, of course without the knowledge, and to the very great surprise, of the author.   As
the only way to remedy the mischief, Googe himself
issued an edition of his " Eglogues " in 1563, with a
preface in which he depreciated his own merits more
justly than he perhaps suspected.   As a writer of poetical
pastorals in English, he had had his predecessors.   We have
seen how Barclay adapted the matter of Mantuan and
Æneas Silvius to English surroundings, and Tottel's
Miscellany contains a very charming pastoral, in an archaic
manner, on the subject of love, from which the reader may
not be displeased to have the following extracts :—

> Phyllida was a fayer maid
>   And fresh as any flowre,
> Whom Harpalus the herdman prayed
>   To be his paramour.
>   Harpalus and eke Corin
> Were herdmen both yfere,
> And Phyllida could twist and spin
> And thereto sing full clere.
>
> .   .   .   .
>
>   My beastes a while your fode refrayne,
> And herken your herdman's sounde,
> Whom spiteful love, alas ! hath slaine,
> Through girt with many a wounde.
>   Oh happy be ye beastës wilde,
> That here your pasture takes ;
> I se that ye be not begylde
> Of them your faithful makes.[1]
>   The Hart he fedeth by the Hynde,
> The Bucke hard by the Doe ;
> The Turtle Dove is not unkind
> To him that loves her so.
>
> .   .   .   .
>
>   What Reason is that Cruelty
> With Beauty should have part,
> Or else that such great tyranny
> Should dwell in woman's heart ?[2]

Googe combined the treatment of Love, common to

---

[1] *i.e.* Mates.   Collier and others print, doubtless correctly from the MS.,
" faythful face," which is nonsense, besides bad rhyme.

[2] Collier's *Seven English Poetical Miscellanies*, vol. i. pp. 182-184.

this poem and to the pagan idyllists, with the moral and allegorical vein of Barclay, adapting the latter, however,— for he was a strong Protestant,—to his own religious and political purposes. His book contained eight eclogues. In the first, Amyntas describes to Daphnis the pains of sensual Love ; in the second, the spirit of the Renaissance for a moment prevails over that of the Reformation, and we hear the death-song of Damætas, a shepherd who has fallen a victim to the universal passion, and who varies his burden in the classical fashion, " Damætas for to die ; " " Damætas now must die ; " " Damætas here doth die." The third eclogue is the most interesting of the series, because it reflects something of the life and feeling of the times. Corydon describes in it to Menalcas, after the manner of Mantuan and Barclay, the evils of the town ; and his picture of the decay of the old feudal customs of the country and the rise of the new monied aristocracy is not wanting in character—

> Menalcas, I have known myself,
> Within this thirty year,
> Of lords and ancient gentlemen
> A hundred dwelling there,
> Of whom we shepherds had relief ;
> Such gentleness of mind
> Was placëd in their noble hearts
> As none is now to find ;
> But haughtiness and proud disdain
> Hath now the chief estate,
> For Sir John Straw and Sir John Cur
> Will not degenerate.
> And yet they dare account themselves
> To be of noble blood,
> But fish bred up in dirty pools
> Will ever stink of mud.[1]

In the same eclogue he looks back with horror on the days of Bonner and the Marian persecutions—

> The simple sheep constraynëd he
> Their pasture sweet to leave,
> And to their old corrupted grass
> Enforceth them to cleave.

---

[1] Google's *Eglogues, Epytaphes, and Sonettes* (Arber), p. 40.

> Such sheep as would them not obey
>   But in their pasture bide,
> With cruel flames they did consume,
>   And vex on every side.
> And with the sheep, the shepherds good
>   (O hateful hounds of hell !)
> They did torment, and drive them out
>   In places far to dwell.
> There diëd Daphnis for his sheep,
>   The chiefest of them all,
> And fair Alexis flamed in fire,
>   Who never perish shall.[1]

This eclogue, however, is a digression from the main subject. The pastoral moralists soon return to discourse, with redoubled zest, on the pains and penalties of love. The ghost of Damætas, presumably the same shepherd who in the second eclogue killed himself for love, appears in the fourth, and declares to Meliboeus his punishment in Hell ; while Egon, in the fifth, relates to Mopsus the melancholy fate of Claudia, who fell in love with Valerius, page of Faustus, and emissary, like Viola in *Twelfth Night*, of his love-sick master. Faustus, in the sixth eclogue, bewails to Felix his unrequited passion. Felix advises him, from his own experience, to cure himself by occupation and sport. Then comes Sirenus, a discarded lover, conversing with Sylvanus on woman's inconstancy : they are joined by Selvaggia, a jilted shepherdess, who makes the same complaint of man. These unfortunate experiences of earthly passion prepare the way, not inartistically, for the concluding discourse between Cornix and Corydon, which sings the Praises of Heavenly Love. There is some charm in the opening of this eclogue :—

CORYDON

> Loe how the beasts lies under trees
>   How all things seek the shade ;
> O blessed God that some defence
>   For every hurt hath made !

---

[1] Googe's *Eglogues* (Arber), p. 41.

Behold this pleasant broad-leaved beech,
And springing fountain clear,
Here shade enough, here water cold;
Come, Cornix, rest we here.

CORNIX

Both place and time, my Corydon,
Exhorteth me to sing
Not of the wretched lovers' lives,
But of the immortal King,
Who gives us pasture for our beasts,
And blesseth our increase,
By whom, while others cark and toil,
We live at home at ease,
Who keeps us down from climbing high,
Where honour breeds debate,
And here hath granted us to live,
In simple shepherd state,
A life that sure doth far exceed
Each other kind of life.
O happy state that doth content,
How far be we from strife![1]

Though Googe lived till 1594, he did not again attempt original composition. His imagination was slender, and was mastered by the genius of the writers he admired. The matter of his fifth and sixth eclogues is borrowed from the *Diana Enamorada* of Montemayor, which he had doubtless read during his travels in Spain; and, as far as I know, this is the first trace of the influence of Spanish romance on English poetry. The shallowness of his taste is proved by his preferring Phaër's translation of the *Æneid* to the versions of Gavin Douglas and Surrey.[2]   Nevertheless, like Grimald, he

[1] Googe's *Eglogues* (Arber), pp. 62, 63.

[2] The noble Henry Howard once,
That raught eternal fame,
With mighty style did bring a piece
Of Virgil's work in frame;
And Grimald gave the like attempt,
And Douglas wan the ball,
Whose famous wit in Scottish ryme
Had made an end of all.
But all these same did Phayre excel,
I dare presume to write,
As much as doth Apollo's beams
The dimmest star in light.

Googe, *Eglogues*, etc., p. 72.

explored new regions of poetical thought, and opened a mine of invention much worked by later poets. Wyatt and Surrey had recommended by their practice the study of Italian models; Grimald and Googe led the way to the imitation of the ancient classics, and the latter in his Eclogues anticipates the Pastoralism of Spenser.

In both these directions the first impulse of inspiration soon flagged, as may be seen from the poetry of George Turbervile, who was born about 1530, being the son of Nicholas Turbervile of Whitchurch, in Dorsetshire. He was educated first at Winchester and afterwards at New College, Oxford, of which he became a Fellow in 1561. Leaving Oxford, he studied at the Inns of Court, and was afterwards appointed secretary to Randolph, Elizabeth's ambassador in Russia. His *Songs, Epitaphs, and Epigrams* were published in 1567, after which he seems to have abandoned original composition, though he made in the same year a translation of his favourite Ovid's *Heroical Epistles* and of the Eclogues of Mantuan. He died in 1594.

Turbervile's chief characteristic is his deliberate attempt to polish and harmonise the language : his poems may be aptly described, in Horace's phrase, as "verses devoid of matter, tuneful trifles"; still he always tries to improve on the tune of his predecessors, and the bent of his taste is illustrated by his "Verse in praise of Lord Henry Howard, Earl of Surrey":—

> What should I speak in praise of Surrey's skill,
> Unless I had a thousand tongues at will?
> No one is able to depaint at full
> The flowing fountain of his sacred skull;
> Whose pen approved what wit he had in mew,
> Where such a skill in making sonnets grew,
> Each word in place with such a sleight is couched,
> Each thing whereof he treats so firmly touched,
> As Pallas seemed within his noble breast
> To have sojourned, and been in daily quest.
> Our mother tongue by him hath got such light
> As ruder speech thereby is banished quite.[1]

From this we may see that in the management of the

---

[1] Chalmers's *English Poets*, vol. ii. p. 588.

heroic couplet Turbervile made a considerable advance on
Grimald ; his verse has something of the ease and movement of Dryden. But as far as his matter goes, he was
quite content to look for his themes in the phrases of
older poets, and to amplify them in accordance with his
own sense of musical rhetoric. For example, Wyatt
happens to use an expression borrowed from Chaucer :
" Arise, I say, do May some observance." Turbervile
makes this the subject of a whole song beginning—

> You that in May have bathed in bliss,
>   And found a salve to ease your sore,
> Do May observance ; Reason is
>   That May should honoured be therefore.[1]

Having thus expanded and exhausted Wyatt's phrase, he
next proceeds to borrow images from Surrey's beautiful
sonnet on Spring :—

> Since snakes do cast their shrivelled skins,
>   And bucks hang up their heads on pale,
> Since frisking fishes lose their fins,
>   And glide with new repairèd scale, etc.[2]

Wyatt writes upon the external signs of love :—

> If waker care ; if sudden pale colour,
> If many sighs with little speech to plain,
> Now joy, now woe, if they my heart disdain,
> For hope of small, if much to fear therefore,
> To haste to slack my pace less or more,
> Be sign of love—then do I love again.[3]

Turbervile, resolved to reduce this archaic harshness
into smooth and flowing modern numbers, writes :—

> If banished sleep and watchful care,
>   If mind affright with dreadful dreams,
> If torments rife and pleasures rare,
>   If face besmeared with often streams ;
> If change of cheer from joy to smart,
>   If altered hue from pale to red,
> If faltering tongue with trembling heart,
>   If sobbing sighs with fury fed ;

---

[1] Compare Wyatt's *Works* (Nott), vol. ii. p. 5 ; Chalmers's *English Poets*
(1810), vol. ii. p. 634.
[2] *Ibid.* vol. ii. p. 635.   Compare Surrey's *Sonnet*, p. 94.
[3] Wyatt's *Works* (Nott), vol. ii. p. 6.

> If sudden hope by fear opprest,
>   If fear by hope supprest again,
> Be prooves that love within the breast
>   Hath bound the heart with fancy's chain :
> Then I of force no longer may
>   In covert keep my piercing flame,
> Which ever doth itself bewray,
>   But yield myself to fancy's frame.[1]

The same diffuseness is found in his paraphrase of Ausonius's epigram on the "Treasure and the Noose" (previously imitated by Wyatt), which he reproduces in twelve lines ; while for his rendering of Serafino's conceit, " Se una bombarda é dal gran foco mossa," which Wyatt had given in eight lines, he takes eighteen.[2] It is interesting, however, to watch the critical process to which he subjects the work of his predecessor where he thinks it may be amended. For example, Wyatt writes, with his usual violence of metaphor, concerning the effects of a glance from his mistress :—

> So unwarely was never no man caught
>   With steadfast look upon a goodly face,
> As I of late, for suddenly methought
>   My heart was torn out of his place ;
> Thorough mine eye the stroke from hers did glide ;
>   Directly down into my heart it ran ;
> In help whereof the blood thereto did glide,
>   And left my face both pale and wan.[3]

Turbervile, seeing that the excess of the last two lines weakened the force of the whole image, altered the passage tastefully though somewhat tamely :—

> Unwarely so was none in such a snare before ;
> The more I gazed upon her face, I liked my love the more.
> Forthwith I thought my heart out of its room was rapt,
> And wits that wonted were to wait on Reason were entrapt.
> Down by my eyes the stroke descended to the heart,
> Which Cupid never crazed before by force of golden dart.[4]

---

[1] Wyatt's *Works* (Nott), vol. ii. p. 601.
[2] *Ibid.* vol. ii. pp. 65, 70, and Chalmers's *English Poets*, vol. ii. pp. 602, 647.
[3] Wyatt's *Works* (Nott), vol. ii. p. 39.
[4] Chalmers's *English Poets*, vol. ii. p. 586.

The following is one of his most graceful poems :—

TO A GENTLEWOMAN THAT ALWAYS WILLED HIM TO WEAR ROSEMARY FOR HER SAKE, IN TOKEN OF GOOD WILL TO HER.

> The green that you would wish me wear
>   Aye for your love,
> And on my helm a branch to bear
>   Not to remove,
> Was ever you to have in mind,
> Whom Cupid hath my fere assigned.
>
> As I in this have done your will,
>   And mind to do ;
> So I request you to fulfil
>   My fancy too ;
> A green and loving heart to have,
> And this is all that I do crave.
>
> For if your flowering heart should change
>   His colour green,
> Or you at length a lady strange
>   Of me be seen ;
> Then will your branch against his use
> His colour change for your refuse.
>
> As winter's force can not deface
>   This branch his hue,
> So let no change of love disgrace
>   Your friendship true :
> You were my own, and be so still,
> So shall we live and love our fill.
>
> Then may I think my self to be
>   Well recompensed,
> For wearing of the tree that is
>   So well defenced
> Against all weather that doth fall
> When wayward winter spits his gall.
>
> And when we meet to try me true,
>   Look on my head,
> And I will crave an oath of you,
>   Where faith be fled ?
> So shall we both assured be,
> Both I of you, and you of me ?[1]

Taking the poems collected in Tottel's *Miscellany* in

[1] Chalmers's *English Poets*, vol. ii. p. 621.

combination with the work of Googe and Turbervile, we get a very clear view of the first stage of English poetry in its transition from mediæval to modern times. Wyatt, Surrey, and Lord Vaux embody the chivalrous element in its quintessence, refined on the one hand by the manners of the Court, on the other by the literary elegance of Italy. Surrey's reforms fix the standard of poetical diction henceforth assumed as a starting-point by all metrical composers. All these three are men of action, who aim at translating the ideas of chivalry into language suitable to the society about them. But the themes they choose belonging, like the men themselves, to a decaying order of things, are soon abandoned to the imagination of mere scholars such as Grimald, Googe, and Turbervile, who view them through a learned medium and in an artificial light. The mediæval tradition of the Troubadours is blended with the classical traditions of pastoral poetry or with the enigmas and conceits of the Greek Anthology, and the product of the union is a literary hybrid, in no way reflecting the social life of the period.

Nature, however, works her own way; and the two Miscellanies succeeding Tottel's, which make their appearance after an interval of nineteen and twenty-one years respectively, show that new forces are secretly effecting a revolution in the English imagination. *The Paradise of Dainty Devices*, published in 1576, presents in almost every respect a strong contrast to Tottel's *Miscellany*. It was collected by Disle, a printer, and is made up for the most part of serious and reflective poems, deeply imbued with the spirit of the Reformation. Scarcely any of the contributors strike the note of Love or Honour; their inclination is rather to fall into the religious vein characterising the verses of Lord Vaux, which have been already cited, and which were first printed in this Miscellany. The collection opens with a translation of a poem by St. Bernard, and the nature of the contents in general may be inferred from the proverbial or hortatory titles of many of the poems, such as, "Our Pleasures are Vanities," "Fair Words make Fools fain," "Promise is Debt," "No Words

but Deeds," " Think to Die."   There are also verses appropriate to various holy days.   The chief contributor to the
Miscellany was Richard Edwards, an Oxford scholar of
Corpus Christi College, appointed in 1561 Master of the
Children of the Queen's Chapel.   He seems to have been a
favourite with Elizabeth, who, when she visited Oxford in
1566, was greatly delighted with a drama on the subject of
Palamon and Arcite, which Edwards caused to be represented for her amusement in Christ Church Hall.   In his
own day he enjoyed a great reputation, scarcely explained
by the merits of his surviving verse, most of which, composed in the fashionable Poulter's metre, has no marked
character.

The Paradise of Dainty Devices resembles Tottel's
Miscellany in one important respect, namely its freedom
from literary affectation.   *The Gorgeous Gallery of Gallant
Inventions*, on the contrary, as the title shows, is mainly
inspired by technical motives.   The growing taste for
alliteration is manifest in every page.   This collection was
made by Thomas Proctor, a member of the Stationers'
Company ; and at the door of the *Gorgeous Gallery* the
editor welcomed the reader with the following poetical
address :—

> See, Gallants, see the Gallery of Delights,
>   With buildings brave, imbost with various hue,
> With dainties decked devised of various wights,
>   Which as time served unto proportion grew.
> By studies toiled with phrases fine they fraught
>   This peerless piece filled full of pretty pith ;
> And trimmed it with what skill and learning taught
>   In hope to please your longing minds therewith ;
> Which workmanship, by worthy workmen wrought,
>   Perused, lest in oblivion it should be,
> A willing mind each part together brought,
>   And termed the whole A Gorgeous Gallery :
> Wherein you may to recreate the mind
>   Such fine inventions find for your delight,
> That for desert their doings will you bind
>   To do them praise so well a work to write.[1]

Throughout the volume the reader may observe a

[1] Collier's *Seven English Miscellanies*, vol. iii. p. 3.

constant attempt "to hunt the letter." We meet with such titles as "In praise of a beautiful and virtuous virgin whose name begins with M."; and such lines as

> A mirror make of M, whose mould dame Nature in disdain,
> To please herself and spite her foes, in beauty raised to reign.[1]

or

> For Mercy is in M her breast, and modest is her life.[2]

This Miscellany contains the "Willow Song," afterwards made famous by its introduction in *Othello*. It opens thus :—

> Willow, willow, willow, sing all of green willow,
> Sing all of green willow shall be my garland.
> My love what misliking in me do you find,
>   Sing all of green willow,
> That on such a sudden you alter your mind ?
>   Sing all of green willow.[3]

The special features of these two Miscellanies are reproduced in the work of the two most popular poets of the period who resembled each other in many important respects—Thomas Churchyard and George Gascoigne. Both were men of action as well as letters ; Churchyard, in particular, having taken part in almost every campaign fought in France, the Low Countries, or Scotland, from the latter part of the reign of Henry VIII. till midway in the reign of Elizabeth ; while Gascoigne chose for his poetical motto, *Tam Marti quam Mercurio*. Both sought for employment at Court, and were employed to devise shows and pageants for the Queen's amusement. Both record their martial experiences in metrical autobiographies. Both deal largely in the proverbial philosophy of the time as reflected in *The Paradise of Dainty Devices*, and are moved by the passion for alliteration which produced *The Gorgeous Gallery of Gallant Inventions*. Neither of them is a great poet, though Gascoigne is of a class far superior to Churchyard ; each, however, in a characteristic way, represents the confused uncertain spirit of the age, and, as a soldier of fortune, forms a link between the

---

[1] Collier's *Seven English Miscellanies*, iii. p. 71.
[2] *Ibid.* p. 72.   [3] *Ibid.* p. 105.

chivalrous poets of Henry VIII.'s latter days and the learned courtiers who grouped themselves round the person of Elizabeth.

Thomas Churchyard, the son of a farmer,[1] was born at Shrewsbury in 1520. Anthony Wood, of course, ascribes his education to Oxford ;[2] but, in fact, we know from himself that from 1537 to 1541 he served in the household of the Earl of Surrey,[3] who taught him something of the art of poetry ; and as from 1541 till 1570 he was engaged, almost without an interval, in warlike adventures, little time seems to have been left him for study. During these years he served under such captains as the Emperor, Lord Grey, Sir Henry Sidney, and the Prince of Orange, and has left an account of his adventures in his autobiographical and historical poems—*A Storie translated out of French, The Siege of Leith, The Siege of Edinburgh Castle, A Tragical Discourse of the Unhappy Man's Life.* He shared in the opinions of the religious Reformers, as Wyatt, and probably Surrey, had done before him, and when in England in 1550, during an interval of rest from campaigning, got himself into difficulties through the poetical advocacy of his convictions. *Piers Plowman's Vision* had been recently republished—a fact which largely accounts for the revival of alliteration—and Churchyard imitated a striking passage from it in a short poem called *Davy Dycar's Dream*, which contained the following lines :—

When faith in friends bears fruit, and foolish fancies fade,
And crafty catchers come to naught, and hate great love hath made ;
When fraud flieth far from town, and loiterers leave the field,
And rude shall run a rightful race, and all men be well willed ;
When gropers after gain shall carp for common wealth,
And wily workers shall disdain to fig and live by stealth ;

.   .   .   .

---

[1] A wife he had, a house he held, as farmers used to do.—*Churchyard's Charge* (Collier), p. 7.   [2] *Athenæ Oxonienses* (1813), vol. i. p. 727.
[3] As I have told this young man served his master twice two year,
And learned therein such fruitful skill as long he held full dear,
And used the pen as he was taught, and other gifts also
Which made him hold the cap on head where some do crouch full low.
Churchyard s Charge (Collier), p. 11.

When riches wrongs no right, nor power prove put back,
Nor covetous creeps not into court, nor learned living lack ;
When slipper sleights are seen, and far fetches to found,
And private profit and self-love shall both be put in pound ;
When debt no serjeant dreads, and courtiers credit keep,
And might melts not with merchandise, nor lords shall sell no sheep ;
When lucre lasts not long, and hoard great heaps doth hate,
And every wight is well content to walk in his estate ;
When truth doth tread the streets, and liars lurk in den,
And *Rex* doth reign and rule the roast, and weeds out wicked men ;
Then baleful bairns be blithe, that here in England wone,
Your strip shall stint, I undertake, your dreadful days are done.[1]

It seems that these reflections gave offence, and Church-yard was brought before the Privy Council, but escaped punishment through the favour of the Protector Somerset.

When he was not fighting Churchyard supported him-self partly by Court patronage, partly by his literary skill. In 1563, as we have already seen, he contributed a " Tragedy " to *The Mirror for Magistrates ;* and he was employed to arrange pageants for the entertainment of the Queen at Bristol and Lichfield in 1574, and at Norwich in 1578. He outlived his poetical reputation, and by the Euphuistic poets at the close of the century was considered old-fashioned. Spenser refers to him in *Colin Clout's Come Home Again*, making a sly allusion to his poetical pertinacity in the character of " old Palæmon," who

Sung so long until quite hoarse he grew.

His poetical resources were, indeed, but slender. He never advanced beyond the point he reached in *Jane Shore*, which, considering the date at which it was composed, is remarkable for the smoothness of its versification. I have already given a specimen of this poem which may serve also to illustrate the style of " Thomas Wolsey," another tale contributed to an edition of the *Mirror*, issued in 1587.[2] In later years Churchyard's invention carried him no farther than the idea of presenting his own experience as a moral example of the tragedies of Fortune. His *Tragical Discourse of the Unhappy Man's Life* opens just like a " Tragedy " in *The Mirror for Magistrates :*—

[1] Compare vol. i. pp. 215, 216.   [2] See p. 120.

Come, courtiers, all draw near my mourning hearse,
Come hear my knell ere corps to church shall go,
Or, at the least, come read this woful verse
And last farewell the hapless penneth so ;
And such as doth his life and manners know,
Come shed some tears, and see him painted out,
That restless here did wander world about.

O pilgrims poor press near my pageant now,
And note full well the part that I have played,
And wisely weigh my thriftless fortune's throw,
And point in breast each word that here is said :
Shrink not, my friends, step forth, stand not afraid,
Though monstrous hap I daily here possest,
Some sweeter chance may bring your hearts to rest.[1]

In the *Siege of Edinburgh Castle* he has recourse to
the same tricks of style that he employs in *Jane Shore*,
namely, frequent alliteration and the accumulation of a
number of images in illustration of some common truth.
The flux of proverbial imagery in the second of the
following stanzas, describing the effects produced by a
lucky shot, fired during the siege, is quite in the vein of
Sancho Panza :—

That cut the combs of many a bragging cock,
That broke the gall, or galled the horse too sore,
That was the key or knack that picked the lock,
That made some muse that triumphed much before :
Yea, that was it that marred their market quite,
And daunted had their hearts in great despite ;
For after this they 'gan to step aback,
And saw at hand come on their ruin and rack.

A little harm doth breed a great mistrust ;
A simple storm makes some on seas full sick ;
A feeble puff of wind does rise up dust ;
A little salve full soon can touch the quick ;
A small attempt makes mighty matters shake ;
A silly spark a sudden fire doth make ;
An easy proof brings hard mishaps to pass
As this declares where all these mischiefs was.[2]

George Gascoigne is a poet of a very different order ;
being, indeed, the most fertile, though not the most
poetical, writer in the English language, since the appearance of Wyatt. Besides following the same auto-

---

[1] *Churchyard's Chips* (Collier), p. 125.   [2] *Ibid.* p. 206.

biographical line as Churchyard, he wrote sonnets like Surrey; flowing lyrics like Turbervile; translated a comedy from the Italian, and adapted a tragedy from the Greek; amused the Queen with elaborated masques and improvised addresses; explored in blank verse the road of moral satire which Wyatt had attempted in *terza rima ;* and gave also the first critical account of the art of English poetry. His character in its great versatility presents some of the features of the "Italianate Englishman," the object of Roger Ascham's invective; and the men of the next generation compared him, not unnaturally, with Robert Greene, whom he also resembles in the edifying tone with which, in his latter years, he speaks of the riot of his youth.

He was the eldest son of Sir John Gascoigne of Cardington in Bedfordshire, and was born about 1525. Educated at Trinity College, Cambridge, he left the University without taking a degree, and proceeded, as was then frequently the custom with young men, to complete his education at the Inns of Court. His autobiographical poem, *Dan Bartholomew of Bath,* records the love adventures through which he passed probably at this period of his life ; these have certainly nothing of the chivalrous character, nor is it very surprising, considering the manner in which he seems to have spent the early part of his time at the Middle Temple and Gray's Inn, that he should have been disinherited by his father. As he grew older he became steadier. A series of his poems, entitled "Memories," was written in earnest, as he tells us himself, of his intended reformation. He had (in midst of his youth) determined to abandon all vain delights and to return to Gray's Inn, there to undertake again the study of the Common Laws. And being required by five sundry gentlemen to write in verse somewhat worthy to be remembered, before he entered into their fellowship, he compiled these five sundry sorts of metre upon five sundry themes, which they delivered unto him, and the first was at the request of Francis Kinwelmarshe, who delivered him this theme, *Audaces fortuna juvat."* The other gentlemen were Antony Kinwelmarshe, giving him *Satis Sufficit ;* John

Vaughan, *Magnum vectigal parsimonia ;* Alexander Nevile, *Sat cito si sat bene ;* and Richard Courthope,[1] *Durum, æneum et miserabile ævum.* On these themes he wrote poems, he says, " amounting to the number of CCLVIII verses devised riding by the way, writing none of them till he came to the end of his journey, the which was no longer than one day in riding, one day in tarrying with his friend, and the third in returning to Gray's Inn, and therefore called ' Gascoigne's Memories.' "[2] The poet was proud of his powers of rapid production and improvisation ; and he afterwards displayed them during Queen Elizabeth's visit to Kenilworth, by attending her Majesty as she rode on horseback, in the character of the god of the woods, and discoursing with her in a strain of classical allegory. But as may be supposed from the circumstances of their composition his " Memories " contain nothing worthy of remembrance. While he was at Gray's Inn he wrote, in 1566, for dramatic representation, his *Supposes*—a translation of Ariosto's *I Suppositi*—and his *Jocasta*—an adaptation of the *Phœnissæ* of Euripides—both of which will be mentioned again in another chapter.

Two years later he married Elizabeth Breton, widow of William Breton, citizen of London. It may be suspected that this was a *mariage de convenance*, which perhaps proved irksome to one so unaccustomed as Gascoigne to the quiet of domestic life ; at any rate in 1572 we find him campaigning in Flanders, Zeeland, and Holland, and encountering under William of Orange the fortunes which he afterwards made the subject of his autobiographical poem *Dulce Bellum Inexpertis.* During his absence from England one of his friends, no doubt with his connivance, printed some of his earlier poems, and thus gave him an opening on his return for republishing the volume, in 1575, with a kind of apology for the nature of its contents. The title of the book is very interesting as marking the approach of Euphuism : " A Hundred sundry Flowers bound up in one small Posy, gathered partly by

---

[1] Or as the name was then frequently spelt Courtop. The theme was doubtless *aëneum ævum.*   [2] Gascoigne's *Poems* (Hazlitt), vol. i. pp. 63-72.

translation in the fine Outlandish Gardens of Euripides,
Ovid, Petrarch, Ariosto, and others : and partly by Inventions out of our fruitful Orchards in England, Yielding
sundry sweet Savours of Tragical, Comical, and Moral
Discourses, both pleasant and profitable, to the well-
swelling noses of learned readers." A very characteristic
" Epistle to the Reverend Divines " gave five reasons for
the publication of the poems, which were as follows : (1)
Poetry is an excellent quality; (2)"I have," he says, "always
been of opinion that it is not impossible, either in poems
or in prose, to write both compendiously and perfectly in
our English tongue. And, therefore, although I challenge not unto myself the name of an English poet, yet
may the reader find out in my writings that I have more
faulted in keeping the old English words (*quamvis jam
obsoleta*) than in borrowing of other languages such
epithets and adjectives as smell of the inkhorn " ; (3) he
seeks advancement by virtue, and desires that his poetry
may remain on record in token of the gifts with which it
had pleased God to endow him ; (4) there is more good
than bad mingled with his writing ; (5) his writing may
serve as a mirror to unbridled youth.[1]

The poems, though comprised under the single name
of posies are subdivided into " Flowers," " Herbs," and
" Weeds " ; flowers to comfort, herbs to cure, weeds to
be avoided. Under the first head are included several
lyric poems of considerable beauty, which show a fluency
and sweetness beyond what is found in any previous
English poet. Such, for example, are Gascoigne's " Good-
Morrow," and " The Lullaby of a Lover." The former
has the following stanzas :—

> You that have spent the silent night
>   In sleep and quiet rest,
> And joy to see the cheerful light
>   That riseth in the East :
> Now clear your voice, now clear your heart,
>   Come help me now to sing ;
> Each willing wight come bear a part
>   To praise the Heavenly King.

---

[1] Gascoigne's *Complete Poems* (Hazlitt), vol. i. pp. 2-4.

And you whom care in prison keeps,
  Or sickness doth suppress,
Or secret sorrow breaks your sleeps,
  Or dolours do distress :
Yet bear a part in doleful wise,
  Yea think it good accord
And acceptable sacrifice,
  Each sprite, to praise the Lord.

      .   .   .   .   .

And if such haps and heavenly joys
  As these we hope to hold,
All earthly sights and worldly toys
  Are tokens to behold.
The day is like the day of doom,
  The sun the Son of Man,
The skies the heavens, the earth the tomb,
  Wherein we rest till than.

The rainbow bending in the sky,
  Bedeckt with sundry hues,
Is like the seat of God on high,
  And seems to tell these news :
That as thereby he promiséd
  To drown the world no more,
So by the blood which Christ hath shed
  He will our health restore.

      .   .   .   .   .

The little birds, which sing so sweet,
  Are like the angels' voice,
Which render God his praises meet,
  And teach us to rejoice.
And as they more esteem that mirth,
  Than dread the night's annoy,
So must we deem our days on earth
  But hell to heavenly joy.

Unto which joys for to attain,
  God grant us all his grace !
And send us after worldly pain
  In heaven to have a place.
Where we may still enjoy that light
  Which never shall decay,
Lord for thy mercy lend us might
  To see that joyful day.[1]

---

[1] Gascoigne's *Complete Poems*, vol. i. pp. 56-58.

" The Lullaby of a Lover " may be taken as the companion picture of the above :—

> Sing lullaby as women do,
>   Wherewith they bring their babes to rest,
> And lullaby can I sing too,
>   As womanly as can the rest.
> With lullaby they still the child,
> And if I be not much beguiled,
> Full many wanton babes have I,
> Which must be stilled with lullaby.
>
> First lullaby my youthful years ;
>   It is now time to go to bed ;
> For crooked age and hoary hairs
>   Have won the haven within my head :
> With lullaby then youth be still,
> With lullaby content thy will,
> Since courage quails and comes behind,
> Go sleep ! and so beguile thy mind.
>
> Next lullaby my gazing eyes,
>   Which wonted were to glance apace,
> For every glass may now suffice
>   To show the furrows in my face :
> With lullaby then wink awhile,
> With lullaby your looks beguile :
> Let no fair face nor beauty bright
> Entice you eft with vain delight.
>
> And lullaby my wanton will,
>   Let Reason's rule now reign thy thought,
> Since all too late I find by skill
>   How dear I have thy fancies bought :
> With lullaby now take thyne ease,
> With lullaby thy doubts appease :
> For trust to this, if thou be still,
> Thy body shall obey the will.
>
> Eke lullaby, my loving boy,
>   My little Robin, take thy rest,
> Since age is cold and nothing coy,
>   Keep close thy coin for so is best :
> With lullaby be thou content,
> With lullaby thy lusts relent,
> Let others pay which have mo pence ;
> Thou art too poor for such expense.
>
> Thus lullaby my youth, my eyes,
>   My will, my ware, and all that was,

> I can no more delays devise,
>   But welcome pain, let pleasures pass :
> With lullaby now take your leave,
> With lullaby your dreams deceive,
> And when you rise with waking eye,
> Remember this your lullaby.[1]

In both these poems the presence of the mediæval spirit of allegory is strongly felt ; in the latter it allies itself with that awakened conscience which, in so much of the poetry of the period, marks the advent of the Reformation. It deserves to live not only on account of the eloquence of its form, but also as a genuine expression of personal emotion from the heart of a man who had sounded the depths of much human experience.

Gascoigne's *Posies* brought him deservedly a high reputation, and in the same year he was chosen to prepare the poetical entertainment for Elizabeth on her reception at the Castle of the Earl of Leicester. His compositions on this occasion are included in his works under the title of *The Princely Pleasures of Kenilworth.* They do not appear, however, to have procured him much profit or advancement at Court, and his sense of the vanity of human things is marked in all his later works. In April 1576 he published the poem by which he is best known, namely, *The Steel Glass*, a moral satire, conceived in the spirit of Wyatt, but largely inspired by Langland's *Vision of Piers the Plowman.*[2]

After an elaborate allegory, showing the relationship of Satire to Poetry, he proceeds to the subject of his poem, which is a contrast between the old-fashioned steel mirrors, typifying the plain manners and morals of feudal England, and the crystal glass of Venice, then coming everywhere into use, and used by Gascoigne as a symbol of the corruptions of the times. Of the former he says :—

> That age is dead and vanished long ago,
> Which thought that steel both trusty was and true,
> And needed not a foil of contraries,
> But showed all things even as they were in deed.

---

[1] Gascoigne's *Complete Poems*, vol. i. pp. 43, 44.   [2] *Ibid.* vol. ii. pp. 180-215.

Videri quam esse is now the rule, like the crystal glass

> Which glimseth brave and bright,
> And shows the thing much better than it is,
> Beguiled with foils of sundry subtil sights,
> So that they seem and covet not to be.

Hence all things are thrown out of their proper order, and the whole principle of the Feudal System is inverted :—

> Again I see within my glass of steel
> But four estates to serve each country soil,
> The king, the knight, the peasant, and the priest.
> The king should care for all the subjects still,
> The knight should fight for to defend the same,
> The peasant he should labour for their ease,
> And priests should pray for them and for themselves.

Kings have almost everywhere neglected their duties ; but, says he,

> I speak not this by any English king,
> Nor by our Queen whose high foresight provides
> That dire debate is fled to foreign realms,
> While we enjoy the Golden fleece of peace.

Describing the tastes and amusements of contemporary society he exclaims :—

> O crystal glass, thou settest things to show
> Which are, God knoweth, of little worth indeed.
> All eyes behold with eager deep desire
> The falcon fly, the greyhound run his course,
> The baited bull and bear at stately stake,
> These interludes, these new Italian sports,
> And every gaud that glads the mind of man.
> But few regard their needy neighbours lack
> And few behold by contemplation
> The joys of heaven, ne yet the pains of hell ;
> Few look to law, but all men gaze on lust.

He complains of Absentee Landlords :—

> O knights, O squires, O gentle bloods y-borne,
> You were not born all onely for yourselves.
> Your country claims some part of all your pains.
> There should you live and therein should you toil
> To hold up right and banish cruel wrong :

To help the poor to bridal back the rich ;
To banish vice and virtue to advance ;
To see God served and Belzebub supprest.
You should not trust lieutenants in your room,
And let them sway the sceptre of their charge,
Whiles you meanwhile know scarcely what is done,
Nor yet can yield accompt if you were called.

The stately lord, which wonted was to keep
A court at home, is now come up to court,
And leaves the country for a common prey,
To pilling, polling, bribing, and deceit,
(All which his presence might have qualified
Or else have made offenders smell the smoke) ;
And now the youth which might have served him
In comely wise, with country clothes y-clad,
And yet thereby been able to prefer
Unto the prince, and there to seek advance,
Is fain to sell his lands for courtly clouts,
Or else sits still, and liveth like a lout ;
(Yet of these two the last fault is the less.)
And so those imps which might in time have sprung
Aloft, good lord, and serve to shield the state,.
Are either nipped with such untimely frosts,
Or else grow crookt becaused they are not proyned.

He next reviews the state of the Clergy, and then,
passing on to the Commons, he summons up the spirit of
Piers the Ploughman :—

Therefore I say, stand forth Peerce Plowman first,
Thou winst the room by very worthiness.

Behold him, priest, and though he stink of sweat,
Disdain him not : for, shall I tell you what ?
Such climb to heaven before the shaven crowns.

But how ? he asks ; showing by his answer that he
does not mean to flatter the Commons at the expense of
the other orders :—

Forsooth with true humility :—
Not that they hoard their grain when it is cheap ;
Nor that they kill the calf to have the milk ;
Nor that they set debate between their lords ;
By earing up the balks that part their bounds ;
Nor for because they can both crouch and creep,

The guilefullest men that ever God yet made,
When as they mean most mischief and deceit;
Nor that they can cry out on landlords land,
And say they rank their rents an ace too high,
When they themselves do sell their landlord's lamb
For greater price than ewe was wont be worth,
I see you, Peerce, my glass was lately scoured.
But for they feed with fruits of their great pains
Both king, and knights, and priests in cloister pent;
Therefore I say that sooner some of them
Shall scale the walls that lead us up to heaven,
Than corn-fed beasts, whose belly is their God,
Although they preach of more perfection.

All this, prosaic as it is, shows how firmly established
in the English imagination was that Feudal Ideal which
two centuries before had been exalted in the verse of
Langland and Gower. Purge the corruption of the times
by this standard, and Gascoigne, like Langland, thinks the
Golden Age may yet return :—

I tell thee, priest, when shoe-makers make shoes
That are well sewed, with never a stitch amiss,
And use no craft in uttering of the same;
When tailors steal no stuff from gentlemen,
When tanners are with curriers well agreed,
And both go dress their hides that we go dry;
When cutlers have to sell old rusty blades,
And hide no cracks with solder nor deceit :
When tinkers make no more holes than they found,
When thatchers think their wages worth their work,
When colliers put no dust into their sacks,
When maltmen make as drink no fermenty,
When Davie Dyker[1] digs and dallies not,
When smiths shoe horses as they would be shod,
When millers toil not with a golden thumb,
When bakers make not barm bear price of wheat,
When brewers put no baggage in their beer,
When butchers blow not over all their flesh,
When horse corsers beguile no friends with jades,
When weavers weight is found in housewives web,

.   .   .   .

Even then, my priests, may you make holiday,
And pray no more but ordinary prayers.

---

[1] This allusion shows that Gascoigne had read Churchyard's verses on
Davy Dycar's Dream. See before, p. 165.

Nevertheless he concludes :—

> And yet therein I pray you, my good priests,
> Pray still for me, and for my glass of steel,
> That it nor I do anything offend,
> Because we show all colours in their kind ;
> And pray for me that, since my hap is such
> To see men so, I may perceive myself.
> O worthy words to end my worthless verse ;
> Pray for me, priests, I pray you pray for me.

The Steel Glass reflects in the most vivid manner both the continuity of the reforming movement in religion, which had been supported by Wycliffe and Langland in the fourteenth century, and the active operation of the individual conscience in men, which was the great agent in the Reformation of the sixteenth century. This influence shows itself in an even more marked manner in two prose tracts by Gascoigne published in the same year as *The Steel Glass*, and entitled *The Doome of Domesday* and *Delicate Diet for Dainty Mouthed Droonkards*. It also reappears in his last poem *The Grief of Joy*, a satire on the vanity of man's life divided into four songs : " The Greeves or Discommodities of Lusty Youth," " The Vanities of Beauty," " The Faults of Force and Strength," " The Vanities of Activities." Ten months after the appearance of this work the poet died on the 7th October 1577.

Without being a great poet Gascoigne is a representative English writer. He originated no fresh movement in metrical composition, but his active and robust intelligence enabled him to express clearly in verse the thoughts and feelings that were interesting his age. He called himself " Chaucer's boy and Petrarch's journeyman," but he was himself a master of the English language ; and his metrical style is singularly free from those learned affectations and conceits to the fascinations of which many of his contemporaries fell easy victims. In his prose-writings he aimed at a different object, and we shall see in the next chapter how far he prepared the way for the extension of the literary movement which received its final impulse from the hand of John Lyly.

CHAPTER VII

COURT DIALECT : JOHN LYLY

As the civic structure of the State emerged from the half-feudal, half-ecclesiastical system of mediæval Europe, and the idea of a community of nations, with rival aims and interests, began to take the place of the theory of a Universal Christian Republic, two predominant questions presented themselves in the sphere of imagination.   One related to the ideal of conduct and manners which the knight, the inheritor of the old code of Catholic chivalry, should adopt in his capacity of courtier.   The other was the refinement of the vulgar tongue into a fitting instrument for the various requirements of courtly conversation and literature.   As we have already seen, Castiglione in Italy had dealt with the problem on both sides in the *Cortegiano*.   In England it was treated under separate aspects both in poetry and fiction, in the *Faery Queen*, in the *Countess of Pembroke's Arcadia*, and in *Euphues*.   The two latter works form the starting-point of the modern novel.   Both are written in prose, but prose of a kind, so closely associated with metrical composition and with the progress of English taste that it would be unphilosophical to regard them as beyond the limits of a history of English poetry.   Pastoral Romance and Euphuism ought to be separately considered, and as the latter has the priority in point of time, I shall make it the subject of this chapter.

Euphuism was the form assumed in England by a linguistic movement which, at some particular stage of development, affected every literature in modern Europe. The process in all countries was the same, namely, to refine the vocabulary and syntax of the language by adapting the practice of early writers to the usage of modern conversation. But the difficulty of the task in each case varied according to the period at which the experiment was first made. In Italy, for example, the first country to employ the language in general use for the purposes of literature, the work was comparatively simple. Fortunate in the artistic instinct of her children, Italy, even in the thirteenth century, had been able to construct out of her numerous dialects what Dante calls " The Illustrious Vulgar Tongue." " The Vulgar Tongue," says he, " of which we have been speaking has not only been exalted by culture and authority, but it also exalts its followers with honour and glory. Now it appears to have been exalted by culture, inasmuch as we have seen it purified from so many rude Italian words, involved constructions, faulty expressions, and rustic accents, and brought to such a degree of excellence, clearness, completeness, and polish, as is displayed by Cino of Pistoia and his friend in their *Canzoni.*" [1] Starting from the vantage ground reached by Cino, it was easy for great writers like Dante, Petrarch, and Boccaccio to establish the standard of the Italian language on clear and definite principles.

Other countries, however, which were later in developing native genius, had to contend with greater difficulties. Spain resembled Italy in the number of her dialects : the close of the fifteenth century arrived before the government of the whole Peninsula, brought under a single crown, caused the Castilian dialect to be accepted as the standard of the Spanish tongue. Perpetual struggles between rival races and religions, between Latinised Goth and Arab, between Christian and Moslem, retarded the promotion of the arts of civil life. Many forms of Spanish popular poetry existed ; romances embodied in the favourite *redondillas*

[1] Dante, *De Vulgari Eloquentia*, chap. xvii. (Howell's Translation) p. 39.

(trochaic measures) ; *canciones* or songs ; *villancicos*, or rustic songs with refrains ; but Spain had produced no great writers like Dante and Petrarch to invent, out of these primitive indigenous compositions, harmonious forms of art such as the sonnet or the canzone. Accordingly, when Naples became an appanage of the crown of Arragon, and intercourse with Italy was frequent, Spanish literature succumbed to the influence of foreign models. Not only did the first literary poets of United Spain seek to acclimatise Italian forms, but, as they naturally shared the Italian enthusiasm for the classics, they attempted at an early date to copy the style of the Latin poets, without consulting the characteristics of the ancient Spanish genius, which thus delayed to assert itself till the declining days of the monarchy, when it found its true form in the fiction of Cervantes and the dramas of Lope de Vega.

France also was long in finding out the bent of her literary capacity. Though like Spain she had produced instinctively many native forms of poetry, the songs of the Troubadours, the *romans* and *fabliaux* of the Trouvères, she too waited in vain for a great original genius to lay in these materials the foundations of a national literature. The long struggle between the Crown and its great vassals hindered the establishment of any ideal of patriotic unity, nor was it till the accession of Francis I. that the French Court became a centre for the encouragement of art and literature. Thus tardy in the refinement of their language the French yielded to the distracting influences, exerted simultaneously by the superior civilisation of their neighbours in Italy, and by the prestige of the Classical Renaissance. The first improvers of the national language made many mistakes as to the right road. Attempts were made in the reign of Louis XII. to Latinise the vocabulary, a task in which the Universities had of course not been backward ; these reached a climax of monstrosity in the dialect we find ridiculed by Rabelais. When the Limousin scholar meets Pantagruel the latter asks him ; " Mon amy dond

viens tu a ceste heure ?   Lescholier lui respondist : De
lalme, inclyte, et celebre Academye, que lon vocite Lutece.
Quest ce a dire ? dist Pantagruel a ung de ses gens.   Cest
(respondist il) de Paris.   Tu viens doncques de Paris,
dist il, et a quoy passez vous le temps. vous aultres
messieurs estudians, ondict Paris ?   Respondist lescholier :
Nous transfretons le Sequane on dilucule et crepuscule :
nous deambulons par les compites et quadrivyes de
lurbe, nous despumons la verbocination latiale, et comme
verisimiles amorabondz, captons la benevolence de lomni-
juge, omniforme, et omnigene sexe feminin." [1]

Clement Marot, revolting against this pedantry, turned
with a right instinct to the old vernacular types of composition, and sought to frame from them a language suitable
to the Court of Francis I.   Marot's style is not wanting in
grace and polish, but his was a genius without dignity ; and
dignity was the element that, in the reign of Henry II. Pierre
Ronsard endeavoured to impart to the French tongue by
naturalising in it the spirit of the ancient Greek poetry,
then exciting the admiration of every scholar in Europe.
Genius and enthusiasm enabled Ronsard occasionally to
secure a measure of success in proportion to the nobility
of his aims ; but as a whole the movement he began was
too purely literary to blend with the life of the nation ; the
scholar alone could derive pleasure from learned allusions to
Greek gods and goddesses, or from Odes which, constructed
like those of Pindar, were intended to be sung by the
musicians of the Court.   Nor, though Ronsard's aims
were much more simple and rational than is often
supposed, were he and " the Pleiad " very successful in
their efforts to enrich the national vocabulary ; the
pedantry of his successors, and especially Du Bartas,
caused a reaction against his methods ; so that though he
really did much to refine the system of French versification, the poetical standard of the " Illustrious Vulgar
Language " was not definitely determined till the time of
Malherbe.

It will be seen that in France and Spain, countries

---

[1] Rabelais, Book ii. chap. vi.

which derived their vulgar tongue from a fusion of the rustic Latin with Teutonic words, the difficulties in the way of forming a standard of literary composition, whether in prose or verse, were caused mainly by the absence of good writers in the early stages of the language. In England, where the mixture of races and languages had been greater, the problem presented itself in a still more complex form. There the genius of Chaucer had imposed on what remained of the Anglo-Saxon language—now deprived of most of its inflections, and prepared by the rude efforts of early poets to assimilate new rhythmical movements—the laws and limitations of French verse ; but, in spite of the predominance of the Norman element in the nation, the English ear was still haunted by memories of the alliterative system which formed the basis of ancient Teutonic poetry. Few Englishmen as yet attempted to write in prose, but among those who did so, such as Mandeville and Wycliffe, we observe that French influence has so far prevailed that the order of words in a sentence follows the logical order of the thought ; while, as to the vocabulary, the prose-writers have no more hesitation than the poets in importing words from abroad. In course of time the invasion of foreign elements becomes more and more noticeable ; and as in France, at the dawn of the Renaissance, the coinage of words struck from a Latin mint is equally ugly and undiscriminating. The Scottish poets especially distinguished themselves by the barbarous ardour of their Latinising. Here, for example, is a typical couplet taken from Gavin Douglas's *Palace of Honour :*—

> The ladyis sang in voices dulcorate
> Facund epistillis quilk quhylum Ovid wrait.[1]

Nor was Lyndsay behindhand in developing the style of his predecessors :—

> Prepotent prince, peirles of pulchritude,
> Glore, honour, laud, triumph, and victorie,
> Be to thy heich excellent celsitude,

---

[1] G. Douglas, *Palace of Honour*, part ii. 12, 13.

> With martiall deedis digne of memorie,
> Sen Atropos consumed hath my glorie,
> And dolent death, allace ! mon us depart,
> I leif to thee my trew unfenzeit hart.[1]

The same tendency is visible in a certain school of English prose-writers. Wilson, author of *The Art of Rhetoric* (1562), gives a specimen—which he declares to be no caricature—of this Latinised English, in " A Letter devised by a Lincolnshire man for a void Benefice to a Gentleman that waited upon the Lord Chancellor for the time being ":—

Pondering, expending, and revoluting with myself, your urgent affability and ingenious capacity for mundane affairs, I cannot but celebrate and extol your magnifical dexterity above all other. For how could you have adapted such illustrious prerogative and domestical superiority, if the fecundity of your ingenia had not been so fertile and wonderful pregnant. Now therefore, being accessited to such splendent renoune and dignity splendidious, I doubt not but you will adjuvate such poor adnihilate orphans as Whilome were condisciples with you, and of antique familiarity in Lincolnshire. Among whom I, being a scholastical panion, obtestate your sublimity to extol mine infirmity. There is a sacerdotal dignity in my native country contiguate to me, where I now contemplate, which your worshipful benignity could soon impetrate for me, if it would like you to extend your sedules, and collaude me in them to the right honourable lord Chancellor, or rather Archigrammacin of England. You know my literature, you know the pastoral promotion. I obtestate your clemency to invigilate thus much for me according to my confidence, and as you know my condign merits for such a compendious living. But now a [2] relinquish to fatigate your intelligence with any more frivolous verbosity, and therefore he that holds the climates be ever more your beautreux, your fortress, and your bulwark—*Amen.*

Dated at my Dome, or rather Mansion Place in Lincolnshire, the penult of the month Sextile.[3]

---

[1] *Complaint of the Papingo*, Sir D. Lyndsay's *Works* (Chalmers), vol. i. p. 297.

[2] *i.e.* " I," showing that the worthy parson probably *spoke* at home with a broad dialect.

[3] Wilson's *Art of Rhetoric* (1562), Fol. 83.

The rapidly spreading influence of classical studies, and the concurrent advance of good sense and criticism, soon put an end to these barbarous experiments. In verse composition Surrey, following instinctively the same line as Marot in France, showed his taste and judgment by taking as the basis of his own improvements the literary practice of Chaucer and Wyatt, which he refined by the usage of current conversation. Satisfied with rejecting what was obsolete in a rich and musical vocabulary, he made no attempt to construct new words or invent new metres, nor did his successors for many years seek to better his example. The task of the English prose-writer was less simple, inasmuch as he wanted the guidance of early masters. Fortunately the right way was shown by those who undertook the translation of the Bible and the Book of Common Prayer into English. Of these, Coverdale and Cranmer were both men of fine intelligence. The nature of their labours taught them the necessity of modulating with flowing and harmonious periods the movement of the sentence. But other and less benignant influences soon began to seduce the imagination of the Englishmen who aimed at the construction of an illustrious vulgar tongue. The modern reader experiences a feeling of surprise in finding the source from which these were derived.

A writer of Spain, Antonio Guevara, Bishop of Guadix (1490-1545), had attempted to write in what he called the *alto estilo*, by deliberately imitating, in his *El Relox de Principes*, the balanced periods and verbal antithesis employed by the Latin orators and historians. As the political influence of Spain was then paramount in Europe, a book composed by an ecclesiastic so distinguished as the Confessor of Charles V. was much in vogue. It was translated into every continental language, and gradually found its way, through French versions, to this country, where it was turned into English first by Lord Berners (whose translation was published in 1539, after his death), and afterwards by Sir Thomas North in 1557. Berners was content with rendering his author's sense, but North attempted also to reproduce the peculiarities of his style, and thus laid the foundations of the Euphuistic manner, afterwards fully developed by John Lyly. A few specimens of early English prose, taken from the successive authors named above, will show how gradual were the steps by which the prose-writers of this country sought to give richness and variety to the instrument they inherited from Wycliffe. The first example is furnished by Lord Berners' preface to Froissart (1523):—

And albeit that those men are right worthy of great laud and praise, who by their writings show and lead us the way to virtue; yet nevertheless the poems, laws, and other acts, that they found, devised, and writ, be mixed with some damage: and sometimes for the truth they ensigne a man to lie: but only history truly with words the acts, gests, and deeds done, completeth all profit; it moveth, stirreth, and compelleth to honesty; detesteth, irketh, and abhorreth vices: it extolleth, enhaunceth, and lifteth up such as be noble and virtuous; depresseth, poistereth, and thrusteth down, such as be wicked, evil, and reprovable.[1]

Here we see that the main aim of the writer is to produce an effect of richness by the copiousness of his vocabulary. He combines, though clumsily,—in the manner afterwards adopted with so much art by Cranmer in the Book of Common Prayer,—words of Saxon and Latin origin identical in sense; he perceives also the value of antithesis in the association of words and ideas: but he shows little taste in selecting his individual phrases, and less art in modulating the cadence of the whole period. Coverdale, in his *Prologue* to the Translation of the Bible (1535), makes a great advance:—

To help me herein I have had sundry translations, not only in Latin, but also of the Dutch interpreters, whom, because of their singular gifts and special diligence in the Bible, I have been the more glad to follow for the most part, according as I was required. But to say the truth before God, it was neither my labour nor desire to have this work put in my hand; nevertheless

---

[1] *English Prose Selections* (H. Craik), vol. i. p. 127.

it grieved me that other nations should be more plenteously provided for with the Scripture in their mother tongue than we; therefore, when I was instantly required, though I could not do so well as I would, I thought it my duty to do my best, and that with a good will.[1]

These are sentences of chaste and dignified harmony ; and there is beauty of the same kind, heightened and diversified by the richness of metaphor, in Cranmer's Preface to his *Defence of the True and Catholic Doctrine of the Sacrament* (1550) :—

I know in what office God hath placed me and to what purpose ; that is to say, to set forth his word truly into his people to the utttermost of my power, without respect of person or regard of thing in the world, but of him alone. I know what account I shall make to him hereof at the last day when every man shall answer for his vocation, and receive for the same good or ill, according as he hath done. I know how Antichrist hath obscured the glory of God, and the true knowledge of his word, overcasting the same with mists and clouds of error and ignorance through false glosses and interpretations. It pitieth me to see the simple and hungry flock of Christ led into corrupt pastures to be carried blindfold they know not whither, and to be fed with poison instead of wholesome meats. And moved by the duty, office, and place, whereunto it hath pleased God to call me, I give warning in his name unto all that profess Christ, that they flee far from Babylon if they will save their souls, and to beware of that great harlot, that is to say the pestiferous see of Rome, that she may make you not drunk with her pleasant wine.[2]

Such were the characteristics of English prose composition before the appearance of North's translation of Guevara. It will be seen that, in all the authors cited, the style is determined by the natural movement of the mind, even in Berners elevation is sought because the writer feels real enthusiasm ; the musical flow of Cranmer's and Coverdale's diction proceeds from an inward fountain of harmonious thought. The *alto estilo* of Guevara, on the other hand, was the product of literary affectation.

---

[1] *English Prose Selections* (H. Craik), vol. i. p. 205.
[2] *Ibid.* vol. i. p. 220.

His nominal subject — the life and sayings of Marcus Aurelius—was selected by him as ground convenient for the display of florid conceits and rhetorical artifices, which he employed with great profusion to disguise the poverty of his thought. From the Latin authors he learned the use of antithesis ; the long-established practice of allegorical interpretation suggested to him the mechanical capacities of metaphor. Aiming at a constant variety of verbal tricks, he introduced them not only into his own narrative but into many fictitious speeches and letters which he asserted to be translations from the genuine compositions of Marcus Aurelius. The English writers were caught with the marked features of his style, and did their best to reproduce them. Here, for example, is North's rendering of what the reader will easily perceive to be a caricature by Guevara of the verbal antithesis used in moderation by Cicero :—

And afterwards all well considered, all examined, and all proved, I find that the more I eat, the more I die for hunger ; the more I drink, the greater thirst I have ; the more I rest, the more I am broken ; the more I sleep, the drowsier I am ; the more I have, the more I covet ; the more I desire, the more I am tormented ; the more I procure, the less I attain.[1]

The practice of elaborating a single metaphor, common among the poets of the Middle Ages, and illustrated in Petrarch's sonnet beginning *Passa la nave mia*, is seen from such a passage as the following to be now affected by the writers of modern European prose :—

Truly the young man is but a new knife, the which in process of time cankereth in the edge: for on one day he breaketh the point of understanding, another he loseth the edge of cutting, and to-morrow the rust of diseases taketh him, and afterwards by adversity he is writhen, and by infirmities he is diseased, by riches he is whetted, by poverty he is dulled again : finally oftentimes it chanceth that the more sharp he is whetted, so much the more the life is put in hasard.[2]

---

[1] North's *Dial of Princes* (1558), Fol. 269.
[2] *Ibid.* Fol. 97.

Again the scholastic habit of arguing from physical to moral phenomena reveals itself in imagery like this :—

What need is it to blase our virtues and deny our naturalities? Certainly there is not so old a horse but if he see a mare will neigh once or twice : there is no man so young nor old but let him see fair young damosels, either he will give a sigh or a wish. In all voluntary things I deny not that one may be virtuous : but in natural things I confess every man to be weak. When you take the wood from the fire it leaveth burning : when summer cometh the cold winter ceaseth : when the sea is calm the waves leave their vehement motions : when the sun is set it lighteneth not the world.

Introduced into England at a time when men's minds were distracted with conflicts of opinion, when the critical sense was just awakening, the question as to the best mode of refining the vulgar tongue being in every one's thoughts, a book like the *Dial of Princes*, however wanting in weight and substance — and the value of its reflections may be fairly judged from the extracts given above—failed not to exert a powerful influence upon the style of writers both in verse and prose. Those who had been educated in an admiration for the manner of Seneca, admired the sententious balance of its rhetorical commonplaces ; it was welcomed with enthusiasm by all who, while desirous of attracting attention by their writing, were conscious of having nothing particular to say. The tricks of Guevara were presently diversfied in his English imitators, by the trick of alliteration, encouraged by the reviving popularity of the writings of Langland ; and both were largely practised by the poet Churchyard. In the abundance of proverbs and illustrations with which he colours his platitudes, we see the effects of *The Dial of Princes ;* his *Davy Dycar* is a direct imitation of *Piers the Plowman ;* while the titles of his books — *Churchyard's Charge, Churchyard's Chips, Churchyard's Challenge* — and the versification of all his later poems are monuments of his plodding persistency in letter-hunting.

Gascoigne, a far better writer, did not escape the

corruptions of the time. His verse indeed is comparatively free from mechanical alliteration, for which in his
critical writings he declares a contempt inherited from
Chaucer, and expressed in Chaucer's phrase; but his
prose, whenever he seeks to be witty and agreeable,
anticipates the chief mannerisms of Lyly. In an Address
to the Queen prefixed to his *Hermit's Tale*, we find the
following sample of the " lofty style " :—

These things (liege Lady) I am bold thus rudely to draw in
sequence before the skilful eyes of your learned Majesty, finding
my youth mispent, my substance impaired, my credit accused, my
talent hidden, my follies laughed at, my ruin unpitied, my truth
unemployed. All which extremities as they have of long time
astonied my understanding, so have they of late openly called me
to God's gates. And your Majesty, being of God godly, and on
our earth our God, by God appointed, I presume likewise to
knock at the gates of your gracious Goodness, hoping that your
Highness will set me on work, though it were noon and past before
I sought service; for, most gracious Lady, though I have over-
long loitered, though I have garishly gadded, and though I tilled
the soil of fancy, and reaped the fruit of folly, I may not yet
always wander wildly, nor finally conclude to despair cowardly,
I may not, like a babe, for one trifle taken from me, throw away
the rest which might have been my contentation; I may not so
much marvel at other men's good haps, that in the meanwhile I
forget mine own defects: for, as fencers, before they be made
masters, must challenge and abide all comers, so Magnanimity
and true Fortitude must be content to abide all frowns of
Fortune before they attain to the height of her wheel; and more
commendable is he which in poverty striveth that no man excel
him for virtues, than he which in prosperity grudgeth at another
man's advancement.[1]

The new mannerism in prose composition reached
its climax in *Euphues*, which was first published two years
after the death of Gascoigne. John Lyly, the author of
this famous book, was born in the Weald of Kent in
1553 or 1554. He was educated at Magdalen College,
Oxford, where he matriculated in 1571, with the entry
against his name *plebeii filius*, and proceeded to his B.A.
degree in 1573. In 1574 he petitioned Lord Burghley,

---

[1] Gascoigne's *Complete Poems* (Hazlitt), vol. ii. p. 138.

but without success, for letters from the Queen to procure him admission as Fellow of the College. He became M.A. in 1575. *Euphues*, or *The Anatomy of Wit*, after being licensed for publication in December 1578, was published in the spring of the following year, and the author was shortly afterwards incorporated as M.A. in the University of Cambridge. His book at once attracted attention in the highest quarters, and hopes, as it appears, were held out to him that on the next vacancy he would be appointed Master of the Revels.[1] No such advancement, however, came to him, though he seems to have been employed as an official writer of " Court Comedies," nine of which he produced before 1589, seven being written in prose, one in rhyme, and one in blank verse.[2] These will have to be noticed in a future chapter. In 1589 a book called *Pappe with an Hatchet* was published in the " Martin Marprelate Controversy," and in defence of the Bishops. Lyly was charged by his literary enemies with being the author.[3] As he never denied the imputation, it is likely enough that he joined in the fray with the hope of preferment ; if so his pamphleteering was not more successful than his plays. The latter seem to have ceased after 1589, perhaps in consequence of the suppression of the Comedies in St. Paul's, where all his dramas had been previously presented by the " Children of Her Majesty's Chapel," and " The Children of Paul's." Nothing more is recorded of his literary performances or of his life ; but we know that he lived in the parish of St. Bartholomew, where three children were born to him, and where he himself was buried on November 30, 1606.

Euphues is a didactic novel in which the moral prevails enormously over the action, and the rhetoric bears a similar proportion to the moral. The title is derived

---

[1] " I was entertained your Majesty's servant by your own gracious favour, strengthened with conditions that I should aim all my courses at the Revels (I dare not say with the promise but a hopeful Item of the Reversion) for which these ten years I have attended with an unwearied patience."—A Petition of John Lillie to the Queen's Majesty, 1590.

[2] Arber's edition of *Euphues*, p. 6.

[3] Gabriel Harvey's *Pierces Supererogation*.

from a passage in Ascham's *Schoolmaster*, which defines
the qualities required in a well-educated man :—

> Εὐφυής is he that is apt by wit and appliable by readiness
> of will to learning, having all other qualities of the mind and
> parts of the body that must serve learning, not troubled, mangled,
> and halfed, but sound, whole, full, and liable to do their office :
> as a tongue, not stammering, or over hardly drawing forth words,
> but plain and ready to deliver the meaning of the mind : a voice,
> not soft, weak, piping, womanish, but audible, strong, and man-
> like : a countenance, not werish and crabbed, but fair and
> comely : a personage, not wretched and deformed, but tall and
> goodly : for surely a comely countenance with a goodly stature
> giveth credit to learning and authority to the person : otherwise
> commonly either open contempt or privy disfavour doth hurt or
> hinder both person and learning.[1]

From this hint Lyly constructed his leading character, a young gentleman of Athens of great wealth and
extraordinary parts, who, wishing to see the world, estab-
lishes himself at Naples, where, falling in with another
young gentleman, named Philautus, of nearly equal accomplishments, he proposes that they shall be to each other as
Damon to Pythias, Pylades to Orestes, Titus to Gysippus,
etc. Unfortunately his virtue proves unequal to these
heroic examples. Philautus is betrothed to a certain fair
but fickle Lucilla, who, in the absence of her father, Don
Ferardo, invites her lover and his friend to supper with
her, maiden propriety being guarded by the presence of a
respectable chaperone, Livia. When the meal is ended,
Lucilla, who has received Euphues with reasonable coldness, proposes that the gentlemen, after the Neapolitan
fashion, shall treat them to "some discourse either concerning love or learning," whereupon Euphues, while
choosing the former subject, contrives, with much art, and
with a view to securing the good graces of Lucilla, to
illustrate it with a vast amount of erudition. Logic,
Rhetoric, Natural History, and Moral Philosophy are all
pressed into his service, but, as becomes a scientific
student in the Courts of Love, he breaks off in the midst

---

[1] *Schoolmaster* (Mayor's edition), book i. p. 21.

of an eloquent period, alleging that he feels in himself "such an alteration that he can scarce utter one word." This judicious display of emotion has the effect of causing Lucilla " to fry in the flames of love," and both she and Euphues retire to their chambers, where—though there is nobody to hear them but the reader—they deliver themselves of more discourses equally long, learned, and logical. Don Ferardo, on his return to Naples, requires his daughter to fulfil her contract with Philautus, but finds that she will have nobody but Euphues. This makes him exceedingly angry, while the jilted Orestes not unreasonably addresses to his Pylades a letter full of bitter reproaches and classical allusions. With all this Euphues remains unmoved, but, in just reward of his perfidy, Lucilla, not long afterwards, transfers her affections to "one Curio, a gentleman of Naples, of little wealth and less wit," leaving her learned lover to moralise on all the circumstances of his misfortune. His reflections inspire him with a wish to benefit his neighbours ; accordingly he sits down to compose "a certain pamphlet," which he chooses to call "a cooling card for Philautus"—for with Philautus he is now reconciled ; and from this he is led on to an Educational Treatise, entitled "Euphues and his Ephoebus." *Vires acquirit eundo.* His discourse obtains him great credit, and he becomes public Reader in the University, "with such commendation as never any had before him " ; but finally, having printed his secular lectures in three volumes, he takes to the study of Divinity, and publishes, as a specimen of his powers, a Dialogue with Atheos : he is also moved to write various moral letters to different friends, one of them containing an instructive narrative of the subsequent fortunes and unhappy end of Lucilla, and another addressed to his old acquaintance, Livia.

In continuation of his novel Lyly wrote a second "romance" called *Euphues and his England*, the plot of which need not be described, as in all essential features the construction resembles the first part, though it has perhaps rather more action in proportion to the discourses.

What has been already said will suffice to give the reader an idea of the character of the whole composition, and will probably cause him to wonder that such a book should have so powerfully influenced the taste of the times. Viewed as a novel, *Euphues* is utterly devoid of constructive ingenuity, human interest, dramatic situation, just eloquence, and it deserves the neglect to which the judgment of posterity has condemned it. But in contemporary opinion and long afterwards it held a very different place. Writing in 1586 of the recent improvements in the English language, William Webbe, author of the *Discourse of English Poetry*, says :—

A manifest example thereof may be the great good grace and sweet vein which eloquence hath attained in our speech, because it hath had the help of such rare and singular wits as from time to time might still add some amendment to the same. Among whom I think there is none that will gainsay but Master John Lilly hath deserved most high commendations, as he hath stepped one step further than any either before or since he first began the witty discourse of his *Euphues*. Whose works surely in respect of his singular eloquence and brave composition of apt words and sentences, let the learned examine and make trial thereof through all the parts of Rhetoric in fit phrases, in pithy sentences, in gallant tropes, in flowing speech, in plain sense, and surely, in my judgment, I think he will yield him that verdict which Quintilian giveth of both the best orators, Demosthenes and Tully, that from the one nothing may be taken away, to the other nothing may be added.[1]

Euphues was as much esteemed by polite society as by the critics. It was accepted with the *Arcadia* as fixing the standard of eloquence at Court.

Hoard up (advises Dekker, in his *Gull's Horn Book*) the finest play-scraps you can get, upon which your lean wit may most savoury feed for want of other stuff, when the Arcadian and Euphuesed gentlewomen have their tongues sharpened to set upon you.[2]

How readily this advice was followed may be inferred from the ridicule poured upon the fashionable style by

---

[1] Haslewood's *Ancient Critical Essays*, vol. ii. p. 46.
[2] *Gull's Horn Book*, chap. vi. p. 36. (Reprinted for W. M'Mullen, 1862.)

the dramatists, notably by Shakespeare in his *Love's Labour's Lost*, and by Ben Jonson in *Every Man out of his Humour*.

Lyly's manner long continued to excite admiration. Edward Blount, a bookseller, in 1632 republished an edition of his plays, of which, addressing the reader in a preface, he says :—

> Our nation are in his debt for a new English which he taught them. *Euphues and his England* began first that language : all our ladies were then his scholars : and that Beauty in Court which could not parley Euphuism was as little regarded as she which now there speaks not French.[1]

The English aristocracy, even in the latter part of the seventeenth century, appreciated the Euphuistic style, and the dedications to Dryden's plays are all composed in a modification of this manner, contrasting strongly with the style adopted by the poet in his critical prefaces, where, addressing the public at large, he discards affectation and trusts entirely to the natural resources of the language and to his own vigorous imagination and tuneful ear. The causes of this very remarkable revolution of taste are well worthy of consideration by the historian and the critic. For it will be observed that in all the critical passages just cited the quality for which *Euphues* is chiefly valued is *eloquence*. This is indeed the leading characteristic of the book ; it is an example of rhetoric in the language of Love composed to suit the taste of the Court. The subject of the story is Love ; not the physical love which is treated of in Ovid's *De Arte Amatoria*, but the metaphysical Love of the first part of the *Roman de la Rose*. Treatises on the rhetoric and casuistry of this art began, as we have already seen, to appear in Europe at a very early date, and the practice of chivalric love-poetry was modified according to the circumstances of each society in which it flourished. The lyrics of the Troubadours developed in Italy into the love-poetry of Petrarch and his successors ; in France and England, into the chivalric Love allegory which grew out of the Romance

[1] Cited in Arber, *Euphues*, p. 18.

of the Rose.   Both styles, but particularly the latter,
commended themselves to the feudal nobility of the
castles, who aimed at forming a standard of language and
manners distinct from that of the vulgar.   When chivalry
decayed, and the quintessence of the institution was concentrated in the Court, the old allegorical artifices of
chivalric poetry dropped out of fashion.   Men and women
no longer cared to regulate their mutual intercourse by
references to Danger, and Pity, and Wicked-Tongue ;
and though Wyatt and Surrey introduced into the Court
the traditions of Petrarch, the attempt was only an ex-
piring flash of the spirit of chivalry.   It was generally
felt that in some way the science of aristocratic love-
making must accommodate itself to the requirements of
the New Learning.   This was the demand of courtly
taste which Lyly deliberately set himself to supply.

Everything in *Euphues* shows that the author knew
very well what he was about.   " In these days," says
Fidus, a retired courtier in *Euphues and his England*, " it
[Love] is thought the signs of a good wit, and the only
virtue peculiar to a courtier, for love they say is in young
gentlemen, in clowns it is lust, in old men dotage, when
it is in all men madness."   Though it was a scholar of
the Universities who was pointing out a new path to the
Gay Science, he knew that he must adapt his pedantry to
the taste of his audience.   "*Euphues,*" says Lyly, in an
address to the Ladies and Gentlewomen of England, " had
rather lie shut in a Lady's Casket, than open in a
Scholar's study ; "[1] and all the efforts of the writer were
directed to form a style, the mechanism of which could
be readily mastered and universally applied at Court.

The first duty of a good courtier of the new style was
of course flattery, and in this art the author of *Euphues*
showed himself an adept.   Here is his description of
Queen Elizabeth, which may be compared with that of
Ascham :—

In questioning not inferior to Nicaulia the Queen of Saba,
that did put so many hard doubts to Solomon ; equal to Nico-

---

[1] *Euphues* (Arber), p. 220.

strata in the Greek tongue, who was thought to give precepts for the better perfection; more learned in the Latin than Amalasunta; passing Aspasia in philosophy, who taught Pericles; exceeding in judgment Themistoclea, who instructed Pythagoras; add to these qualities those that none of these had, the French tongue, the Spanish, the Italian, not mean in every one, but excellent in all; readier to correct mistakes in those languages than to be controlled; fitter to teach others than to learn of any; more able to add new rules than to err in the old : insomuch that there is no Embassadour that cometh into her Court, but she is willing and able to understand his message, and utter her mind, not like unto the kings of Assyria who answer Embassadors by messengers, while they themselves either dally in sin or snort in sleep. Her godly zeal to learning, with her great skill, hath been so manifestly approved, that I cannot tell whether she deserve more honour for her knowledge, or admiration for her courtesy, who in great pomp hath twice directed her progress into the Universities, with no less joy to the students than glory to her state. Where after long and solemn disputations in Law, Physics, and Divinity, not as one wearied with scholars' arguments, but wedded to their orations, when every one feared to offend in length, she in her own person with no less praise to her Majesty, than delight to her subjects, with a wise and learned conclusion, both gave them thanks and put self to pains. . . . Her wit so sharp that if I could repeat the apt answers, the subtle questions, the fine speeches, the pithy sentences, which on the sudden she hath uttered, they would rather breed admiration than credit. But such are the gifts that the living God hath endowed her withal, that look in what art or language, wit or learning, virtue or beauty, any one hath excelled most, she only hath generally exceeded every one in all, insomuch that there is nothing to be added that either man could wish in a woman, or God doth give to a creature.[1]

It was fitting that the " Ladies and Gentlewomen " of England should imitate at a humble distance the accomplishments of their learned Sovereign. Accordingly, in devising the rhetoric of the new Art of Court Love, the ingenious author of *Euphues* was careful to give prominence to those features in the Code of Chivalric Love on which the Sovereign would set the highest value. The Queen was fond of logic and disputation; the Court ladies must therefore learn to analyse their emotions in the scholastic fashion, as indeed their grandmothers had

---

[1] *Euphues and his England* (Arber), p. 459.   Compare pp. 129, 130.

been accustomed to do for ten generations ; but they
must do so in the rhetorical manner suggested by the
study of classical authors.   Thus when Lucilla is reflecting
by herself on her perfidy to Philautus, Lyly makes her
speak thus :—

> But can Euphues convince me of fleeting, seeing for his
> sake I break my fidelity ?   Can he condemn me of disloyalty
> when he is the only cause of my disliking ?   May he justly
> condemn me of treachery who hath this testimony as trial of my
> good will ?   Doth he not remember that the broken bone once
> set together is stronger than ever it was ?   That the greatest blot
> is taken off with the pumice ?   That though the spider poison the
> fly, she cannot infect the bee ?   That though I have been light to
> Philautus, I may be lovely to Euphues ? [1]

But while the new rhetoric was thus based on the old
logical foundation of the schools, it derived its real popularity from the great variety of its illustration.   The
following sonnet of Sidney, who headed the school
opposed to the Euphuists, throws a vivid light on the
objects aimed at by the latter :—

> Let dainty wits cry on the Sisters nine,
> That, bravely masked, their fancies may be told
> Or, Pindar's apes flaunt they in phrases fine,
> Enam'ling with pied flowers their thoughts of gold ;
> Or else let them in statelier glory shine,
> Ennobling new found tropes with problems old ;
> Or with strange similes enrich each line,
> Of herbs or beasts which Ind or Affrike hold.
> For me in sooth no Muse but one I know ;
> Phrases and problems from my reach do grow
> And strange things cost too dear for my poor sprites !
> How then ? even thus,—in Stella's face I read
> What Love and Beauty be ; then all my deed
> But copying is what, in her, Nature writes. [2]

The metaphorical style in the love-poetry of the
Euphuists is a natural growth of the Classical Renaissance ;
it marks the decay of the allegorical interpretation of
Nature which itself largely accounts for the abundant
use of metaphor in the poetry of the Middle Ages.   In

[1] *Euphues* (Arber), p. 58.
[2] Sidney's *Poems* (Grosart), vol. i. p. 45.

Dante and Petrarch sensible objects are used as the symbols of spiritual ideas; and, contrarily, in the allegorical love-poets of England and France, abstract ideas are personified as living agents; but in Lyly's time the study of the classics had discredited the old scholastic style, while the new ideas of Nature, which were beginning to prevail, tended to turn the imagination from the paths of allegory.   The author of *Euphues* was finely sensitive to the tendencies of his age.   His tastes, his training, his learning, were all mediæval, and he goes beyond all his predecessors in his profuse employment of metaphor. Metaphor is, indeed, the mainstay of his manner, but he uses it for merely decorative purposes, or for the display of an erudition which he knew would be acceptable to the Queen.   The *Physiologi*, long established as text-books in the schools, had helped to circulate through society a large amount of mythology about the habits of animals, and Lyly accordingly impressed into the service of his art the great parent source of all these "vulgar errors," the *Historia Naturalis* of Pliny.   When he wishes to prove to the ladies and gentlewomen of England that there is a " medicine for every malady" but love, he proceeds as follows :—

The filthy sow when she is sick eateth the sea-crab and is immediately recured : the tortoise having tasted the viper sucketh origanum, and is quickly revived : the bear, ready to pine, licketh up the ants, and is recovered : the hart, being pierced with the dart, runneth out of hand to the herb dictanum, and is healed.   And can men by no herb, by no art, by no way, procure a remedy for the impatient disease of love ?   Ah, well I perceive that Love is not unlike the fig tree whose fruit is sweet, whose root is more bitter than the claw of a bittern : or like the apple in Persia, whose blossom savoureth like honey, whose bud is more sour than gall.[1]

All this casuistical analysis of the passion of love, illustrated by an inexhaustible fund of metaphorical allusion, was embodied by the author of the new rhetoric in sentences framed on the principles of antithesis and

[1] *Euphues* (Arber's edition), p. 61.

alliteration which, as we have seen, had, since the translation of Guevara's *Dial of Princes*, been making their
way gradually into the texture of English prose composition.

As to antithesis, the structure of Lyly's sentences is
framed upon well-defined principles. His aim is to arrest
attention by a comparison, or rather a contrast, between
different objects and different actions ; and he effects it by
means of a number of clauses, linked to each other by
corresponding conjunctions, and containing each the same
number of substantives, adjectives, and verbs. To avoid
monotony he makes his subordinate clauses of unequal
length, and varies the manner of sequence, comparison,
and conjunction, by such alternative forms as "so—
that," "so—as," "rather—than," "more or less—than,"
"neither—nor," "either—or," "not only—but also." His
sentences are always characterised by a great show of
logic and descriptive rhetoric, these effects being produced
either by the balance of alternative clauses, or by an
accumulation of contrasted words. Here is an example
of the former manner :—

Gentlemen, if I should ask you whether, in the making of a
good sword, iron were more to be required or steel, sure I am
you would answer that both were necessary. Or if I should be
so curious to demand whether, in a tale told to your Lady, disposition or invention be most convenient, I cannot but think
that you would find them both expedient ; for as one metal is to
be tempered with another in fashioning a good blade, lest either,
being all of steel it quickly break, or all of iron it never cut, so
fareth it in speech which, if it be not seasoned as well with wit
to move delight, as with art to manifest cunning, there is no
eloquence ; and in no other manner standeth it with love, for to
be secret and not constant, or constant and not secret, were to
build a house of mortar without stones, or a wall of stones without mortar.[1]

The ladies of England, on the other hand, are thus
described—

There did I behold them of pure complexion exceeding the

---

[1] *Euphues* (Arber's edition), p. 417.

lily and the rose, of favour (wherein the chiefest beauty con-
sisteth) surpassing the pictures that were feigned, or the Magician
that could feign, their eyes piercing like the sunbeams, yet chaste,
their speech pleasant and sweet, yet modest and courteous, their
gait comely, their bodies straight, their hands white, all things
that men could wish, or women would have, which how much it
is none can set down, when as the one desireth as much as may
be, the other more.[1]

Alliteration, which in Gascoigne is mainly used to
produce a cumulative effect of sound, is employed by
Lyly for the same purpose, and also to punctuate the
antithetical form of the sentence.

Were it not, Gentlewomen, that your lust stands for law, I
would borrow so much leave as to resign my office to one of
you, whose experience in love hath made you learned, and whose
learning hath made you so lovely ; for me to intreat of the one
being a novice, or to discourse of the other being a truant, I may
well make you weary, but never the wiser, and give you occasion
rather to laugh at my rashness than to like my reasons.   Yet I
care the less to excuse my boldness to you who were the cause
of my blindness.   And since I am at my own choice, either to
talk of love or of learning, I had rather for this time be deemed
an unthrift in rejecting profit, than a Stoic in renouncing
pleasure.[2]

A style of this kind was, of course, easy to imitate, and
was fitted in every respect to meet the demands of
fashionable taste.   Euphuism established itself as the dialect
of the Court, and thence radiated into every department
of literature over which the Court exercised an influence.
When Lyly had once pointed out the way, it became
necessary for writers of all kinds to show their " wit."
Wit of the kind exhibited in *Euphues* was looked for in
the dialogue of the drama ; in the narrative style of
fiction ; in the dedications of books to noble patrons.
Wit was the main motive in the compositions of the
Metaphysical School of Poetry which flourished so widely
in England through the first half of the seventeenth

---

[1] *Euphues*, p. 444.   [2] *Ibid.* p. 53.

century.   All who in the higher grade of society sought
to show their superiority by the outward signs of dress,
behaviour, and language, went to John Lyly's school to
study the first principles of affectation.

With the downfall of the old hereditary dynasty, and
the disappearance of the scholastic system, after 1688,
the Euphuistic manner soon vanished.   *The Tatler* and
The Spectator, addressing themselves to the task of forming a public opinion in the nation at large, dealt with
themes of common interest and human experience.   For
the expression of natural truth, Lyly's metaphorical
style, drawn from fabulous stories about " Stones, Stars,
Plants, Fishes, Flies," was as little qualified, as was his
antithesis and alliteration to produce lasting pleasure,
when the trick of its mechanism was once understood.
His reputation shared the fate which must ultimately
overtake all those who think of style before substance,
and whose art is produced by means contrary to the
course of nature.   Euphuism was an ingenious attempt to
give an appearance of organic life to a structure formed
out of a medley of exhausted systems—Scholasticism,
Feudalism, Ciceronianism, Petrarchism ; and, like the
parallel movement of the " Précieuses " in France, it failed
to stand the analysis of reason and good sense.

Nevertheless Lyly had made a discovery which was
of permanent value, and for which he ought to receive full
credit.   While the language of philosophy and criticism
was still in a fluid state, he had perceived the advantage
of clearness, correctness, and precision, in the arrangement
of words.   It was not altogether his fault if his age was
more favourable to the development of language than to
the expression of thought.   He at least showed the
nation the possibilities of balance and harmony in English
prose composition ; and the form which he established in
the structure of the English sentence has never been
entirely lost sight of by his successors.   Addison and
Steele, while they aimed at something much beyond the
" fit phrases, pithy sentences, and gallant tropes," which
gratified the taste of Webbe, learned from Lyly how to

present genuine thoughts in an artistic form ; and Burke,
Johnson, and Macaulay, avoiding the petty particularity
of his contrasted words, followed his example in working
up sentences and periods to the climax required for the
just and forcible presentation of the argument.

CHAPTER VIII

COURT ROMANCE: SIR PHILIP SIDNEY

WHILE one section of Elizabeth's Court occupied itself with forming out of the memories of chivalry a dialect and code of manners fitted to distinguish it as a caste, the more generous spirits endeavoured to preserve an ideal of knighthood which should have a practical bearing on the circumstances of their own life. The task was one of singular difficulty. All round them they saw a revolution in the ancient system of things. The conditions of warfare were changing; the old feudal militia and knightly exercises were being superseded by the use of mercenary troops and gunpowder. Education was changing. Arms were no longer, as in the days of Surrey, the groundwork of instruction; but the boy of gentle birth took his place side by side with the son of the farmer or the tradesman at one of the schools which the liberality of men, filled with the spirit of the great classical revival, was founding in every part of England. Here all alike were taught to speak Latin and to study geography and history, and the children of the ruling order became aware of the growing importance of the middle classes in the constitution of society. When the young nobleman or gentleman, having completed his education at the University, was sent to acquire the accomplishments of life on the Continent, he had an opportunity of seeing that the intercourse of monarchs was no longer conducted by means of heralds, but by the arts of scholars and diplomatists; and he might gain an

insight into the new and strange windings which rival
ambitions and religious discord were introducing into the
labyrinth of European politics.   It was only when he
entered upon his life as a courtier, that he seemed to pass
into the atmosphere of the Middle Ages.   At the Court
the image of knighthood, with all its Catholic and Feudal
associations, was constantly before his mind, in the
tournament, the chase, the tennis court, the masque, the
pageant, and other kinds of diversion transmitted from
the ancient life of the castle.   But the old days of adventure had vanished, and in the mere routine of courtly
etiquette there seemed to be no outlet through which the
man of imagination could express his great conceptions in
action.   This harsh contrast between mediæval memories
and modern realities produced in many high - spirited
English gentlemen a state of feeling which is vividly
represented in the life and writings of Sir Philip Sidney.

Born in 1554, Philip Sidney, through both parents,
derived his lineage from the noble and knightly
families of England.   His father, Sir Henry Sidney, the
owner of Penshurst Place in Kent, had been the companion in boyhood of Edward VI., and continued in the
reigns of Mary and Elizabeth to be employed in places
of trust at Court.   He married Lady Mary Dudley,
daughter of the Duke of Northumberland, executed in
the reign of Mary for his conspiracy on behalf of Lady
Jane Grey ; and he thus became the brother-in-law of Lord
Robert Dudley, afterwards Earl of Leicester, so long the
prime favourite of Elizabeth.   After serving meritoriously
as Viceroy in Ireland, Henry Sidney, in 1562, was made
Lord President of Wales ; and, while making his abode
in those parts, not unnaturally sent his eldest son Philip
to the school at Shrewsbury which had been founded in
1551, and—being at that time, according to Camden, the
largest school in England—was taught by Thomas Ashton
as headmaster.[1]   Here Philip remained till, at the age of
fourteen, he was sent to Christ Church, Oxford, where
the extreme Protestant party was then in the ascendant.

[1] Fox Bourne's *Sir Philip Sidney* (1891), p. 26.

His tutor at Christ Church was Dr. Thomas Thornton, a man of mark ; and among his fellow-students were Hakluyt, author of the well-known book of travels, Camden, the antiquary, and Fulke Greville, afterwards Lord Brooke. From his early boyhood the character of Philip Sidney seems to have been remarkably grave and reflective, and this point must be remembered in estimating the autobiographical value of some of his poetry that will be hereafter referred to.[1]

Having finished his University studies he went, in 1572, in attendance on the Earl of Lincoln, ambassador to Charles IX., and was in Paris during the massacre of St. Bartholomew, at the house of Francis Walsingham, his future father-in-law. The same year he started on a course of foreign travel with the view of completing his education, and he remained abroad till 1575. His first experiences were in Germany, where he made the acquaintance of all the Protestant princes, and of the man who exercised a life-long influence over his thought and character. Hubert Languet (1518-81) was a Protestant Humanist, that is, one of a large class which took up an intellectual position not far removed from, but somewhat in advance of, the opinions of Erasmus, and midway between Catholicism and the Protestantism of the more extreme followers of Luther. Bred to a life of diplomacy, he had embraced the opinions of Melanchthon, and endeavoured to form a practical guide of conduct from the blended light of Reason and Scripture. Sidney has drawn his character in the *Arcadia :—*

> The song I sang old Languet had me taught,
>   Languet the shepherd best swift Ister knew
> For clerkly rede and hating what is naught,
>   For faithful heart, clean hands, and mouth as true ;
>   With his sweet skill my skill-less youth he drew
> To have a feeling taste of Him that sits
> Beyond the Heaven, far more beyond our wits.

---

[1] "I will report no other wonder than this," says Fulke Greville, "that though I lived with him and knew him from a child, yet I never knew him other than a man" (the *Life of the Renowned Sir Philip Sidney*, by Sir Fulk Grevil (1652), p. 6). The same quality is noted in many passages of Languet's letters to him. And his father styled him *Lumen familiæ suæ* (Grevil's *Life,* p. 7).

He said the music best thilk powers pleased
  Was jump concord between our wit and will,
Where highest notes to Godliness are raised,
  And lowest sink not down to jot of ill :
  With old true tales he wont mine ears to fill,
How shepherds did of yore, how now they thrive,
Spoiling their flock, or while 'twixt them they strive.[1]

The correspondence between Languet and Sidney furnishes an invaluable clue to the intellectual development of the latter. Delighted with the freshness and enthusiasm of his new friend, the elder man encouraged him to open his heart on every subject, and Sidney was not slow to avail himself of the experience and advice of the diplomatist. Passing on from Frankfort to Vienna, and thence to Venice, he lets Languet see in a letter that he is smitten with the passion of learning for learning's sake : " he is studying astronomy," he says, " and getting a notion of music." [2] Languet, referring to the subject in a later letter, gives him little encouragement in this course. " You must consider," he observes, " what are your prospects, and how quickly you will have to abandon this literary use ; and consequently you ought to give to those matters that are absolutely needful all the little time you have. I call those things needful of which it is discreditable for a man of high rank to be ignorant, and which by and by will perhaps serve you for ornament and resource." [3] Such was in effect also the advice of Castiglione in his *Courtier*, and Sidney, feeling its good sense, made the most of his opportunities. At Venice he became acquainted with Tintoretto and Paul Veronese, who painted a portrait of him, and he attended the entertainments of the magnificoes ; at Vienna, whither he returned in 1575, he acted on the counsels of Castiglione in the *Courtier*, and perfected himself in horsemanship. The account which he gives of his teacher, John Peter Pugliano, in the *Apology for Poetry*, furnishes a vivid illustration of the chivalrous ideal of the age :—

[1] *Complete Poems of Sir Philip Sidney* (Grosart), vol. iii. p. 34.
[2] Letter of 19th December 1573, Fox Bourne's *Life*, p. 73
[3] Letter of 22nd January 1574, Fox Bourne's *Life*, p. 74.

He according to the fertileness of the Italian wit did not only afford us the demonstration of his practice, but sought to enrich our minds with the contemplations therein which he thought most precious.   But with none I remember mine ears were at any time more laden than when, either angered with slow payment or moved with our learner-like admiration, he exercised his speech in praise of his faculty.   He said soldiers were the noblest estate of mankind, and horsemen the noblest of soldiers. He said they were the masters of war and ornaments of peace, speedy goers and strong abiders, triumphers both in camps and courts.   Nay to so unbelieved a point he proceeded, as that no earthly being bred such wonder to a prince as to be a good horseman ; skill of government was but pedantry in comparison. Then he would add certain praises by telling what a peerless beast a horse was, the only serviceable courtier without flattery, the beast of most beauty, faithfulness, courage, and such more that, if I had not been a piece of a logician before I came to him, I think he would have persuaded me to have wished myself a horse.[1]

Returning to England in 1575 with all the external accomplishments of a courtier, he accompanied the Queen in her progress to Kenilworth, and afterwards to Chartley, the seat of the Earl of Essex, one of the recognised models of Elizabethan chivalry.   Here he made the acquaintance of the Earl's daughter, Lady Penelope Devereux, then a girl of about fifteen years old, afterwards the heroine of his *Astrophel and Stella.*   With Essex he formed a strong friendship, and accompanied him to Ireland when he was made Earl Marshal of that country in July 1576 ; only, however, to be witness of the Earl's death within a month of his arrival in Dublin.   One of the last wishes expressed by Essex was the hope that Sidney would marry his daughter. Indeed the young man's popularity at Court seems to have been general ; his beauty and intellectual power were so much admired, that Languet feared he might sink to the level of a mere fashionable dilettante.   " You see," he writes to him, in November 1576, " how unkindly I am answering your letter so full of kindness.   I do thank you for it, though I cannot suffer you to run the risk of squandering your powers in idleness.   I never doubted that you

---

[1] *Apologie for Poetrie* (Arber's Reprint), p. 18.

would at once secure the admiration of all your friends, and of all the noblest men about you." [1]

In 1577 it seemed for a moment as if Sidney were to have an opportunity of finding a channel of action for the large conceptions he had formed of national life and policy. He was sent by the Queen to congratulate Rudolph, son of Maximilian II., on his succession to the Empire, and he seized the opportunity to endeavour to unite the Princes of Germany in a league against Rome and Spain. To Rudolph at Prague he pointed out the dangers threatening national independence from the joint aggression of these powers ; while at Neustadt, and afterwards at Lauterburg, he sought to compose the conflicts that had broken out in the Palatinate between the Lutherans and Calvinists. On his way home he laid the foundation of a firm friendship with William of Orange. Walsingham, now Secretary of State, expressed to Sir Henry Sidney his high approval of his son's conduct during the embassy : "There hath not been any gentleman, I am sure, these many years that hath gone through an honourable charge with so great commendations as he." [2]

But in England all these dreams of great action seemed to melt away amid the petty realities of Court life. There Sidney's energies were mainly absorbed in defending his father, who since 1575 had been Lord-Deputy of Ireland, against the intrigues of the Earl of Ormond. His courtly duties were confined to making costly presents, which his straitened means could ill afford, to the Queen on New Year's Day, or to flattering her in poetical masques, such as " The Lady of the May," which he composed for her entertainment at Theobalds. To Languet he wrote at this period : " The use of the pen has plainly gone from me, and my mind if it ever was active about anything is now, by reason of indolent sloth, beginning imperceptibly to lose its strength, and to lose it without any reluctance. For with what end should our thoughts be directed to various kinds of knowledge, unless the knowledge is put to use for the public good." [3]

[1] *Life* (Fox Bourne, 1891), p. 98.   [2] *Ibid.* p. 128.   [3] *Ibid.* p. 141.

Under these circumstances his imagination, craving for adventure, turned in the direction of exploration and commercial enterprise. He subscribed £25 towards Frobisher's second expedition into the Arctic regions, and asked Languet's opinion about it. But projects of this sort were not to the mind of the Protestant Humanist, who replied (September 1577) that indeed he admired Frobisher's spirit of adventure :—

I am thinking of you, for you seem to rejoice in the circumstance as if it was the best thing possible for your country, especially as I noticed in you last spring a certain longing to undertake this kind of enterprise ; and if Frobisher's foolish hope of finding a North-West passage had power then to fascinate you, what will not these golden mountains do, or rather these islands of gold, as I daresay they shape themselves day and night in your mind? Beware, I do beseech you, and never let "the cursed hunger after gold," whereof the poet speaks, creep over that spirit of yours, into which nothing has hitherto been admitted, save the love of goodness, and the desire of earning the goodwill of all men.[1]

Nor was Languet, who like other Humanists had clear views of International Law, more indulgent to Sidney's chivalrous desire to serve with John Casimir in his expedition in aid of William of Orange.

If your Queen (he writes, 28th November 1577) had been bound by treaty to send troops to the Low Countries and had ordered you to go with them then it would have been your duty to regard the enemies of the Netherlanders as your own foes. But from a mere desire for praise and glory, and that you might give public proof of your courage, you determined to treat as your personal enemies those who seem to you to be taking the wrong side in the war. It is not your business ; it is not for any private person to pass judgment on a question of this kind.[2]

And again he comments on Sidney's state of mind :—

I am much grieved to hear you say that you are weary of the life to which I doubt not God has called you, and that you wish to flee from the glitter of your Court, and betake yourself to some secluded place, where you may avoid the troubles that hamper

---

[1] Fox Bourne's *Life*, p. 159.   [2] *Ibid.* p. 165.

and engross all that live within the circle of Government. I know
that in the splendour of a Court there are so many temptations
to vice, that it is very hard for a man to hold himself clean among
them and to stand upright on such slippery ground. But you
must struggle boldly and virtuously against these difficulties,
remembering that the glory of victory is always in proportion to
the peril undergone.[1]

Yet Languet himself was soon forced to acknowledge
that there was little scope for the energy of manly virtue
in the sphere to which Sidney's circumstances confined
him. Later in the year (1578) he came to England as
an attendant on John Casimir, and some time afterwards
he writes to his friend :—

To tell the truth, the ways of your Court seem to me less
manly than I could have wished. Most of the courtiers sought
to win applause rather by an affected courtesy than by those
virtues which are healthy to the state, and which are the chief
ornaments of generous minds, of high-born men. I was much
grieved, and so were your other friends with me, because you
seemed to be wasting the flower of your youth upon such things.
I fear lest your nature should be warped, lest by habit you should
be brought to find satisfaction in pursuits that only weaken the
mind.[2]

It was not long before the general condition of things
at Court, joined to Sidney's own dislike of the life there,
brought about complications which led to his temporary
retirement. Owing to the caprices of the Queen's favour,
factions prevailed among her attendants. The Earl of
Leicester, Sidney's uncle, had long been all-powerful, but
of late his influence had declined, in consequence of an
entanglement with the Countess of Essex. Sir Christopher
Hatton was the head of another party, and both sets had
also their representative leaders in matters of taste, letters,
and fashion. Philip Sidney and Edward Dyer, the recognised literary chiefs of the Leicester coterie, were at
this time amusing themselves with a proposed reform of
English versification, based on the principles advocated at

---

[1] Letter of 22nd October 1578, Fox Bourne's *Life*, p. 166.
[2] Letter of 14th November 1579, Fox Bourne's *Life*, p. 174.

Cambridge by Gabriel Harvey. The poet Spenser, who had been admitted to their intimacy, writes to his friend at Cambridge respecting their proceedings :—

As for the two worthy gentlemen Master Sidney and Master Dyer, they have me, I thank them, in some use of familiarity ; of whom and to whom what speech passeth for your credit and estimation I leave yourself to conceive, having always so well conceived of my unfeigned affection and zeal towards you. And now they have proclaimed in the ἀρειωπάγῳ a general surceasing and silence of bald rhymers, and also of the very best too ; instead whereof they have by authority of their whole senate prescribed certain laws and rules of quantities of English syllables for English verse ; having had thereof already great practice and drawn me to their faction.[1]

At the head of the other literary party was Edward, Earl of Oxford, a great favourer of the Euphuists, and himself a poet of some merit in the courtly Italian vein. Some of Gabriel Harvey's most grotesque and conceited hexameters were, in later years, said by Thomas Nash to contain a portrait of the Earl, which is certainly characteristic :—

A little apish flat, couched fast to the pate, like an oyster,
French camarick ruffs, deep with a witness, starched to the
    purpose.
Every one A per se A, his terms and braveries in print.
Delicate in speech, quaint in array : conceited in all points :
In courtly guiles a passing singular odd man,
For gallants a brave mirror, a primrose of honour,
A diamond for nonce, a fellow peerless in England.[2]

Between the rival leaders there was a strong antipathy, which ended in September 1579 with a quarrel. Oxford, coming one day into a tennis court, while Sidney was engaged in a game, called him " a puppy " ; to which Sidney answered that the Earl lied. A duel was arranged, but was prevented by the intervention of authority. Languet, writing to Sidney, acquits his friend of all blame in the matter. " I am aware," he says, " that by

---

[1] Gabriel Harvey's *Works* (Grosart), vol. i. pp. 7, 8.
[2] *Ibid.* vol. i. p. 84.

a habit inveterate in all Christendom a gentleman is dis-
graced if he does not resent such an insult.   I think you
were unfortunate to be drawn into this contention, but I
see that no blame can be attached to you for your share
in it." [1]   Sidney's prospects were, nevertheless, prejudiced
by the affair, and were soon damaged, to all appearance
hopelessly, by the boldness with which he wrote to the
Queen protesting against her marriage with the Duke of
Anjou.   In consequence of Elizabeth's displeasure, he
was obliged to leave the Court.   Languet, rather incon-
sistently, advised him to take service under William of
Orange ; but Sidney himself preferred to go into retirement at Wilton, the home of his sister Mary, who had
recently been married to the Earl of Pembroke.   Here
during the year 1580 he busied himself with writing the
Arcadia.

In October 1580 he returned to Court.   Languet
writes to congratulate him on the event, but anticipates
difficulties.   " I think," says he, " there are not many men
among you who would prefer the welfare of the State to
their own interests.   I foresee many troubles, a future
when your nobles will be separated into factions, and at
strife with one another, when the neighbouring nations
will throw fuel on the fire which is to be kindled among
you.   Believe me there are storms brewing, which are not
to be dispelled by the fallacies that have well-nigh driven
all noble-mindedness and simplicity out of the Christian
world." [2]   Happily there was more patriotism and soundness under the surface of English life than Languet
perceived, as appeared eight years later when all sects and
parties in the country combined to repel the invasion of
the Spanish Armada.   But this brighter prospect was
hidden from men's eyes.   Sidney was forced to return to
all the wearisome routine of Court etiquette, New Year's
presents to the Queen, allegorical pageants, tournaments
in which the victory had been pre-arranged.   In the
spring of 1581 the Duke of Anjou came over to England
to press his suit for the Queen's hand, and the occasion

[1] Fox Bourne's *Life*, pp. 181, 182.   [2] *Ibid.* pp. 222, 223.

was celebrated by a tourney at Whitehall, in which
Sidney with three others, the four Foster Children of
Desire, appeared as Challengers to the Defenders of the
Fortress of Perfect Beauty, and were of course hopelessly
defeated. An element of reality was, however, introduced
into his public life by his election as member for Kent to
the Parliament of this year, in which he acted energetically
with the Reforming party, sitting on a Committee for
restraining the practices of the Papists, and helping to
pass an act that made it treasonable to apostatise to the
Church of Rome ; inflicted fine and imprisonment on those
who attended Mass ; and fined those who stayed away
from Church.

Languet died in September 1581, and with his letters
ceases our knowledge of Sidney's inner life. Outwardly
his career continued to be as uneventful and purposeless
as before ; but in 1583 his promotion began. In January
he was knighted, as proxy for John Casimir, who was
then installed as Knight of the Garter, and in the spring
he was made Master of the Ordnance jointly with the
Earl of Warwick. On the 20th of September in this
year he married Frances Walsingham, daughter of the
Secretary of State. After the death of Languet many of
his old tastes and aspirations seem to have revived. In
February 1584 he met Giordano Bruno in the house of
Fulke Greville " to discuss moral, metaphysical, mathe-
matical, and natural speculations " ; and the philosopher
dedicated to him his *Spaccio de la Bestia Trionfante*,
and afterwards his *Gli Eroici Furori*. His thoughts also
turned again to voyages and adventures. Writing to
Sir Edward Stafford in July 1583 he says : " We are here
al solito, Her Majesty seems affected to deal in Low
Country matters ; but I think nothing will come of it.
We are half persuaded to enter into the journey of
Sir Humphrey Gilbert very eagerly ; whereunto your Mr.
Hakluyt hath served for a very good trumpeter." [1]
Hakluyt had, in fact, dedicated his *Voyages* to Sidney in
1582, and, had the latter yielded to the enthusiasm the

---

[1] Fox Bourne's *Life*, p. 295.

narrative roused in his mind, he might have perished
with Sir Humphrey in his famous voyage to Newfoundland.   He was equally interested in Western exploration.
Early in 1583 he obtained a Charter for the conquest and
colonisation of America ; and in December 1584 he was
one of a Committee for defining the limits of Raleigh's
new colony in Virginia.   While the unknown West doubtless excited his fancy, his views were determined by the
practical consideration that English enterprise in America
might be made a counter check to Philip II.'s encroachments in Europe.   In his opinion, says Fulke Greville,
" There were but two ways left to frustrate this ambitious
monarch's designs ; the one, that which diverted Hannibal,
and by setting fire on his own house made him draw in his
spirits to comfort his heart ; the other that of Jason, by fetch-
ing away his golden fleece, and not suffering any one man
quietly to enjoy that which every man so much affected." [1]

So constantly was Sidney haunted by this latter idea,
that he tried secretly to join Drake in his expedition to
America in 1585 to colonise the country and convert the
natives.   Drake, however, who did not wish to have a
partner in his fame, sent notice to the Queen of her
courtier's movements, and she forbade Sidney to sail ;
but, seeing that it was necessary to find active employment for so ardent a spirit, she made him Governor of
Flushing—for the Low Countries had been placed under
her protection—in November of the same year.   Even
in this larger sphere little scope was given for the exercise
of his genius.   The garrison of Flushing was weak, and
the troops ill-paid.   Leicester, who was commander-in-
chief of the Protestant forces, was no match for Philip's
general, the Duke of Parma.   Indolent and selfish, he
wasted his time with players and musicians, and it was
in vain that Sidney appealed to him for energy in action,
and to the Queen and Burghley for money.   Having,
however, obtained leave from his uncle to act on his own
account, he surprised Axel by a feat of arms so brilliant
that it roused Leicester to storm Doesburg, and, by

[1] Fulke Grevil, *Life of the Renowned Sir Philip Sidney* (1652), p. 105.

Sidney's advice, to invest Zutphen.   A strong Spanish
convoy, sent to the relief of this town, was attacked by the
English cavalry under Sidney and Essex on 22nd September.   Though the latter were very inferior in numbers, the
fiery courage with which the charge was made obtained
them some success ; but Sidney, who, from a feeling of
chivalrous punctilio, had put off his armour, was shot
through the thigh.   Carried into Arnheim, he lingered
there in great suffering for nearly a month, and died on
the 15th of October 1586.

The character of Sidney, as displayed in his life, his
letters, and his end, is even more noble and pathetic than
that of Surrey, and is vividly illustrated by the genius of
his writings.   Inheriting from his race on both sides all
the instincts of chivalry, he was placed by circumstances
in a position that constantly forced him to contemplate
the image of a knight-errantry which had vanished for
ever, and to listen to tales of modern adventure in
which he was forbidden to share.   The influence of
older men, the vacillations of his sovereign, and the
necessities of the State, prevented his country from
following that active foreign policy which he ardently
desired to see her adopt.   Enthusiastic and generous in
all his impulses, he had formed for himself the ideal of
a noble life at Court, which was always coming into
antagonism with the petty meanness and servility of his
surroundings.   In all directions some natural obstacle
seemed to hinder him from translating his ideas into
action ; no boon of fortune was granted to him but a
heroic death.   It is just and appropriate that a spirit of
this kind should have been the inventor of Romance in the
modern sense of the word, that is to say, of fiction, in
which the representation of life is recognised as being
contrary to the order of experience, and in which the
imaginary creations of the mind are confessedly removed
from the harsh reality of things.

For it must not be forgotten that Romance originally
bore a meaning quite different from this.   The *Roman*
was at the outset only a history in verse, written in the

vulgar tongue, and opposed to history written in Latin prose. The deeds of Charlemagne or Arthur which it recorded were believed to have been actually performed. If the narrative was full of magic and supernatural incidents, there was nothing in these which the superstitious imagination of the age hesitated to accept as probable, while, in all descriptions of manners and sentiment, the stories reflected vividly the genius of feudal institutions. But as these were gradually replaced by a civil order of things, a new style of romance began to make its appearance. The heroes held up to the admiration of the reader became more abstract, and were regarded as types of knightly virtue in a bygone Age of Gold. By degrees the scene of chivalrous exploit passed into a kind of geographical fairyland : the ancient paladins, Arthur and Charlemagne, were succeeded by Amadis of Gaul, Palmerin of England, Lisuarte of Greece ; champions unknown to history. At the same time, though the knowledge of physical matters had become much more exact, the element of magic and marvel was brought into greater prominence in the new romances, so that the separation between the fictions of the story and the facts of life grew increasingly sharp. Sidney carried the movement one step farther into the region of unreality, by localising the chivalrous action of romance in the mythical land of Arcadia.

Arcadia itself was idealised only by degrees. It is scarcely mentioned as consecrated to poetry in the idylls of Theocritus. By Virgil's time the inhabitants of the country had acquired a reputation for music and singing, which, taken in connection with the legend that Mount Mænalus was a favourite haunt of the god Pan, caused Arcadia to be associated, like Sicily, with the idea of pastoral poetry. The great fame of Virgil's *Fourth Eclogue*, especially in Christian times, further connected Arcadia with the tradition of the Golden Age, and the idea of pastoral innocence and simplicity became predominant with the mediæval poets, who still wrote in Latin and in the bucolic style of Virgil.

In the fifteenth century Baptista Mantuanus, a country-man of Virgil, who had been to some extent anticipated by Petrarch in the fourteenth century, began to use the pastoral dialogue allegorically, as a vehicle for satire on the religious and social corruptions of his time.   Mantuan's *Eclogues* obtained an established place as a text-book of rhetoric in the schools : we have seen him imitated in English by Barclay and Googe, and also translated by Turbervile.   This branch of the stream of pastoralism in the sixteenth century widened into the pastoral drama, represented by such works as Tasso's *Aminta* and Guarini's *Pastor Fido*, and provided materials for the early Italian operas.

But in the fifteenth century it was joined by another river of Arcadian origin which, after assimilating some of the characteristics of the Eclogue, diverged into an outlet of its own.   Many centuries earlier, in the decaying ages of Greek literature, the sophist Longus had treated the idea of pastoral simplicity, as represented in the Eclogue, in the form of a novel.   His *Daphnis and Chloe*, strange to say, found no imitators ; but Boccaccio revived the narrative form of pastoralism in his *Ameto*, an early and crude performance, wherein he represents nymphs telling stories to a hunter, somewhat on the plan afterwards worked out with so much skill in the *Decameron.*   A hundred and fifty years later Jacopo Sanazzaro, a gentle-man of Naples, taking up the idea, sounded the first note of that modern pastoralism which culminated in Rousseau's theory of the superiority of the State of Nature to the State of Civil Society.   Sanazzaro avows in the intro-duction to his *Arcadia* that his motive is to please the jaded imagination of dwellers in cities with the ideas of simple peace and beauty associated with rural life.[1]   With these he combines the sentiment of ideal love, presented

---

[1] Sogliono il più delle volte gli alti e spaziosi alberi negli orride monti dalla natura prodotti, più che le coltivate piante, da dotte mani espurgate negli adorni giardini, a' riguardanti aggradare ; e molto più per li soli boschi i salvatichi uccelli sovra i verdi rami cantando, a chi gli ascolta piacere, che per le piene cittadi dentro le vezzose ed ornate gabbie non piacciono gli ammaestrati (Sanazzaro, *Arcadia*, Proemio, p. 1, *Classici Italiani*, Milano, 1806).

amidst the landscape of the poetical Arcadia, and in
the persons of shepherds, who discourse on their different
experiences, in Eclogues divided from each other by
passages of narrative prose.[1]   Sanazzaro's story has
little action and almost less human interest ; but both
these elements were added by his imitator, George de
Montemayor, a Portuguese, who, in his *Diana Enamorada*,
mixed with conventional Arcadianism pathetic adventures
from real life, such as had already been introduced by
Boccaccio into the *Decameron*, in stories like that of the
patient Griselda.   The *Diana Enamorada* is distinguished
by the undertone of melancholy which characterises all
that is best in Spanish literature, and which proceeds from
the imagination of a people conscious that their greatness
lies in the past.   If I am not mistaken, it is the first work
of European fiction that treats of the subject of hopeless
love and female self-sacrifice, afterwards so fully developed
by the Elizabethan dramatists.   It blends something of the
ideal atmosphere of romances like *Amadis de Gaul* with
the manners of modern life, and anticipates that taste for
complication and intrigue which afterwards gave rise to
the plots of the Spanish playwrights.

Sidney in the *Arcadia* unites the ideal character-
drawing of the late chivalrous romances, with the poetical
landscape of Sanazzaro and the complicated love-plots of
Montemayor.   Briefly told, the plot of the romance is
as follows.   Musidorus, prince of Thessaly, and Pyrocles,
prince of Macedon, travelling together are parted from
each other by shipwreck on the coast of Laconia.   The
former, being rescued by two shepherds of the country,
Claius and Strephon, is conducted to Arcadia, where he is
entertained in the house of one Kalander, from whom he in
time learns the strange situation of affairs in the country.
It seems that Basilius, king of Arcadia, an elderly and
somewhat doting sovereign, has married late in life the

[1] Sanazzaro's Eclogues are mostly written with *sdrucciolo* rhymes.   By
inadvertence I attributed to Dante—in vol. i. p. 73—some verses in this metre
which should have been credited to Sanazzaro.   They occur in his eighth
Eclogue, vv. 11-13.

youthful Gynecia, by whom he has two daughters, Pamela and Philoclea, who, when the story begins, are growing into womanhood.   By an unexplained caprice Basilius, leaving the task of administration to Philanax, a nobleman of the country, has retired into a forest solitude, with the intention of keeping his daughters away from unworthy suitors. The elder, Pamela, he places with a clownish guardian called Dametas, who lives in a lodge with his equally disagreeable wife, Miso, and his daughter Mopsa, while Basilius himself, with Gynecia and Philoclea, occupies another house in the neighbourhood.   From Kalander's narrative it further appears that his own son Clitophon has been taken prisoner by the Helots, who are in revolt against the noblemen of Laconia.   This moves Musidorus —or, as he calls himself, Palladius—out of gratitude to his host and benefactor, to go with a party of Arcadians to attempt the young man's rescue.   In a single combat with the leader of the Helots he recognises his lost friend Pyrocles, who, after deliverance from shipwreck, has fallen into the hands of the Helots, and has been chosen as their captain.   The friends, thus brought together again, are, however, soon parted, for Pyrocles, whose assumed name is Daïphantus, sees the portrait of Philoclea, and goes in search of the original.   Musidorus, following on his track, finds him at last living, in the disguise of an Amazon, and under the name of Zelmane, in the house of Basilius, many amorous complications having been occasioned by mistakes about his sex.   His friend falls in love with Pamela, and, taking the garb of a shepherd, becomes the servant of the clown Dametas.   Both princes make themselves known to the respective ladies of their love ; but when affairs have reached this happy point, Pamela, Philoclea, and Zelmane are carried off by the wicked Cecropia, sister of Basilius, who thinks thereby to do a service to her son, Amphialus, that prince, reputed the best knight in the world, being desperately in love with his cousin Philoclea.   The remainder of the story—which was never finished—is occupied with the fortunes of the prisoners in the castle, and with numerous combats

between knights belonging to the besieging party of
Basilius, who comes to the rescue of his daughters, and
Amphialus who heads the defence.   The thread of the
narrative is infinitely complicated by stories within stories,
related by the numerous persons introduced, in order to
explain their own presence, or the sequence of events
which have led up to the existing situation ; the martial
feats of arms performed by the knights are relieved by
the pastoral sports and poetry of the shepherds.

Viewed as a work of literary art the defects of the
Arcadia are many and obvious.   The action is wanting
in human interest, the characters are conventional, the
structure of the story is confused and irregular.   The
extraordinary medley of elements, out of which the fiction
is composed, helps to produce that incongruous ideal effect
against which Horace warns the inventor of fiction at the
opening of his *Ars Poetica*.   A story, in which Helots
and Pages appear together, in a country combining the
features both of the historic and the poetical Arcadia,
and in which mediæval knights with classical names discourse with each other in a dialect, not exactly like
Euphuism, but equally remote from nature and the true
genius of the English language, necessarily fails to produce in the imagination the illusion required by poetic
probability.   The style of the narrative shows that
the mind of the author was occupied less with the
matter of his conception than with the manner of its
expression.   Nothing is said plainly ; common-place is
disguised by metaphor ; style is mechanically elevated
by tricky arrangement of words.   Here, for example, is a
typical passage :—

There was he received with loving joy of Kalander, with
joyful love of Palladius, with humble though doleful demeanour
of Argalus, whom specially both he and Palladius regarded, with
grateful serviceableness of Clitophon, and honourable admiration
of all.   For being now well viewed to have no hair on his face
to witness him a man, who had done acts beyond the degree of
a man, and to look with a certain bashful kind of modesty, as if
he feared the eyes of men, who was unmoved with the sight of
the most horrible countenances of death, and as if Nature had

mistaken her work to have a Mars's heart in a Cupid's body,—all that beheld him, and all that might behold him did behold him, made their eyes quick messengers to their minds, that there they had seen the uttermost that in mankind might be seen.[1]

When Sidney wishes to describe certain persons thinking how to make the time pass quickly, he writes :—

And so as they sate devising how to give more feathers to the wings of time, there came to the lodge door six maids, all in one livery of scarlet petticoats.[2]

He delights in antithesis and paradox of this kind :—

She was half-ashamed she did love so well, and more than half sorry she could love no better.[3]

And the form of antithesis which he particularly favours is inversion, whether of the sense or of the words. Thus of a river it is said :—

It ran upon so fine and delicate a ground as one could not easily judge whether the river did more wash the gravel or the gravel did purify the river.[4]

And of women's hair twined with garlands :—

Upon their hair they ware garlands of roses and gilliflowers, and the hair was so dressed as that came again above the garlands, interchanging a mutual covering; so as it was doubtful whether the hair dressed the garlands or the garlands dressed the hair.[5]

And :—

Musidorus, as cheerfully going towards, as Pyrocles went frowardly fromward, his death, was delivered to the King, who could not be enough sure of him without he fed his own eyes upon one whom he had begun to fear as soon as the other began to be.[6]

---

[1] *Arcadia* (Sampson Low, Marston, 1893), p. 41.
[2] *Ibid,* p. 247.   [3] *Ibid.* p. 145.   [4] *Ibid.* p. 166.
[5] *Ibid.* p. 247.   [6] *Ibid.* p. 155.

Regarded historically, on the other hand, as a mirror of the feelings of Sidney and the best of his contemporaries, and as a work of fiction contributing to the development of the English drama, the *Arcadia* is a most interesting monument. When we examine it on its lyrical side, as reflecting simply the ideas of its author, we see how strongly the imagination of the time was affected by the opposite elements of which Court Romance was composed. Granted that the representation of chivalry in the *Arcadia* is abstract and superhuman, that is precisely the form it might be expected to assume, in the minds of men haunted by ideas of adventurous action, which they could find no means of putting into practice. The admirers of the *Arcadia* were for the most part characters of the stamp of the " Noble Courtier " sketched by Spenser in *Mother Hubberd's Tale.* To them Sidney's descriptions of men and things seemed natural ; even his affectations of style were valuable to all who, conscious of the great movement of civilisation, were anxious to see dignity and refinement added to their native language. For readers of this kind the *Mort d'Arthure*, with its picture of feudal manners and institutions, was out of date ; on the other hand, Sidney's romance presented to them ideal personages, in a variety of imaginary situations which their minds could readily conceive. Musidorus and Pyrocles, Amphialus and Argalus, expressed to them various types of knightly conduct and character, not less distinct than the different chivalrous " virtues " afterwards allegorically described by Spenser in the *Faery Queen.*

The pastoral element in the *Arcadia* gave equal satisfaction to another mood in the imagination of the same class of reader. It has something of the love of rural objects for their own sake which, as we have seen, was the motive of Sanazzaro's composition. The charming description of Arcadia itself is mainly ideal, but some of its features,—for example

As for the houses of the country—for many houses came

under their eye—they were all scattered, no two being one by the other, and yet not so far off as that it barred mutual succour [1]

—were doubtless suggested to Sidney by the landscape in the neighbourhood of Wilton ; and the beautiful image of the " shepherd boy piping as though he should never be old " [2] breathes the spirit of immortal freshness inherent in the Arcadian tradition, and exquisitely rendered in Keats's *Ode on a Grecian Urn.*

But in the main the idea of pastoralism, expressed in the *Arcadia*, is the antithesis of all that is implied in the idea of a Court. It is an amplification of the feeling Sidney had himself avowed in one of his letters to Languet, and which the latter had warned him not to indulge : " I am much grieved to hear you say that you are weary of the life to which, I doubt not, God has called you, and that you wish to flee from the glitter of your Court and betake yourself to some secluded place, where you may avoid the troubles that hamper and engross all that live within the circle of government." Circumstances had forced Sidney into the retirement which he once contemplated only in imagination, and during his absence from Court he gave utterance to this side of his genius under the cloak of pastoral imagery. A strong personal vein runs through all the poetry in the *Arcadia*, modelled though it was on the example of Sanazzaro. Sidney threw into this remote and abstract form all his ideas about philosophy and religion ; he spoke in pastoral imagery of his associa-tion with Languet ; he introduced himself into the story under the name of the shepherd Philisides ; and all his own ideas on the subject of romantic love found expression through the mouth of Musidorus when, under the disguise of the shepherd Dorus, he won the heart of the Princess Pamela. The same feeling inspires the verses written " In Dispraise of the Court " while Sidney was living at Wilton :—

> Well was I while under shade
> Oaten reeds me music made,

---

[1] *Arcadia*, p. 12.   [2] *Ibid.* p. 12.

Striving with my mates in song;
Mixing mirth our songs among.
Greater was the shepherd's treasure,
Than this false, fine, courtly, pleasure.

Where how many creatures be,
So many puffed in mind I see;
Like to Juno's birds of pride,
Scarce each other can abide:
Friends like to black swans appearing,
Sooner these than those in hearing.[1]

The reader will readily perceive that many elements of Sidney's pastoral sentiment are reproduced by Spenser in the sixth book of the *Faery Queen*.

But, after all, the element in the *Arcadia* which produced the greatest effect upon contemporary taste, on account of the dramatic tendencies of the age, was the one which Sidney derived from his study of Montemayor. Perhaps the most noticeable feature in the story is the complete elimination of the magical and supernatural machinery which formed so important a part of the older romances. In imitation of Montemayor, Sidney now concentrated the main interest of his narrative in the complications of the love-plots. The consequence of this device was to bring the exhibition of female character into great prominence. In the old chivalric poetry and fiction no more than three types of women are represented, the insipid idol of male worship who shows " mercy " and " pity " to her lover according to the regulation pattern of the Cours d'Amour; the fickle mistress, like Cressida, who is inconstant to one lover, and so violates the code of chivalry; and the unfaithful wife of the class of Guinevere or Iseult. The *Arcadia*, on the other hand, is full of feminine heroines, martyrs, and monsters, each of whom plays her own distinct part in the development of the action. There is the ideal maiden, Pamela or Philoclea, type of lofty virtue, forerunner of the heroines of Richardson; the vicious Queen Cecropia recalling the Phædras and Sthenobœas

---

[1] *Poetical Rhapsody*, vol. i. p. 34.

of Greek legend ; Gynecia, the passion-stricken wife with
a respectable elderly husband, a favourite figure in the
modern French novel ; the clownish Mopsa, the original,
perhaps, of Shakespeare's Audrey ; and, above all, the
representative of adventurous, unhappy, self-sacrificing
love in its various aspects ; Helen, Queen of Corinth,
and Parthenia, predecessors of Shakespeare's Viola,
Helena, and Imogen.

The idealism of the *Arcadia*, both in its pastoral and
chivalrous aspect, gave an immense stimulus to the
invention of the dramatist, illustrating the truth of
Horace's observation :

> Segnius irritant animos demissa per aurem
> Quam quæ sunt oculis subjecta fidelibus, et quæ
> Ipse sibi tradit spectator.

The pale and almost bodiless phantoms which floated
vaguely before the imagination in the romance, touched
by the magic wand of Shakespeare and his contemporaries,
acquired colour, beauty, poetry, life.   The gentle pastoral
landscape of a non-existent country reappeared in the
ideal forest of Arden, in the enchanted island of Prospero,
in a Bohemia bordered by the sea.   Basilius, the half-
witted king, his two daughters, and their clownish
attendants, passed into the immortal forms of the exiled
Duke, the melancholy Jaques, Rosalind, and Celia.
Chivalrous sentiments, which in the romance seem only
fantastic or affected, were brought within the range of
probability when declaimed by some well-graced actor ;
and the remoteness of the names Leontes, Antigonus,
Cleomenes, Archidamus, served, like the Greek buskin,
to raise the personages and situations of the romantic
drama above the petty realities of common life.

Nor was it only in sentiment and landscape that the
dramatists were indebted to the *Arcadia* : the story itself
furnished them with innumerable hints for the development of action and character.   I have little doubt, as I
have already said, that the main situation in the story
suggested to Lodge some leading ideas for his *Euphues'*

Golden Legacy; and thus indirectly inspired Shakespeare with the idea of *As You Like It;* and in the *Arcadia*, too, Shakespeare found the suggestion for the episode of Gloster and his sons in *King Lear*, and the combat of cowards in *Twelfth Night*. Beaumont and Fletcher developed, from an incident in the story of Sidney's Queen Erona, the plot of *Cupid's Revenge*. The *Arcadia* was also, I believe, the original source of those numerous complications which in the Elizabethan drama arise from the disguise of sex. Sidney himself borrowed this feature in his romance from Spain ; and the common original of his female page Daïphantus and of Shakespeare's Viola is the Felismena of Montemayor.

Another mood of Sidney's romantic idealism is embodied in the series of Sonnets entitled *Astrophel and Stella*. It is true that these compositions have been subjected to a quite different standard of interpretation. Eminent critics have supposed them to be the product of a genuine and irresistible impulse ; that they record actual feelings, real incidents, and may, therefore, be treated as materials for biography. Thus, says Charles Lamb, " They are not rich in words only, in vague and unlocalised feelings, the failing too much of some poetry of the present day ; they are full, material, and circumstantiated. Time and place appropriates every one of them. It is not a fever of passion wasting itself upon a thin diet of dainty words, but a transcendent passion, words pervading and illuminating actions, pursuits, studies, feats of arms, the opinions of contemporaries, and his judgment of them. An historical thread runs through them, which almost affixes a date to them ; marks the *when* and *where* they were written." [1] Archbishop Trench says of them rather gravely : " They are addressed to one who, if the course of true love had run smooth, should have been his wife. When, however, through the misunderstanding of parents, or through some other cause, she had become the wife of another, Platonic as they are, they would far better have remained un-

---

[1] Charles Lamb, *Some Sonnets of Sir Philip Sidney* (*Essays of Elia*, 1867, p. 283).

written."[1]   The late Mr. J. A. Symonds thought he could detect from the Sonnets exactly how and when Sidney's passion for Stella originated ;[2] and another ingenious commentator believes that the Sonnets record "a tragedy of Conflict, and that the Love went down to the very roots of both in their deepest."[3]

This theory of a profound and all-pervading passion is contradicted by the facts of the case, by the character of Sidney, by the character of the Sonnets themselves.

(1) It is opposed to the facts of the case.   Penelope, Lady Rich, was the daughter of Walter Devereux, Earl of Essex.   She made Sidney's acquaintance in 1576, when he was between twenty-one and twenty-two, and she herself less than fifteen.   Her father was fond of him, and was desirous to bring about between him and his daughter one of those *mariages de convenance* which were common at the time ; but there is nothing to show that the affections of either party were engaged ; while, two years later, a letter written to Languet proves that Sidney had no inclination whatever to be fettered by matrimony.[4]   In 1581 Penelope was constrained to marry the second Lord Rich, who is said to have treated her with neglect and even harshness ; with whom she, however, lived till 1592; after which they lived apart till 1604, when Lord Rich obtained a divorce, while Penelope married the Earl of Devonshire, by whom she had already had several illegitimate children. Beyond, therefore, what is said in the Sonnets, there is nothing to indicate that Sidney was ever really in love with Lady Rich, or she with him ; on the other hand, her later history is not of a kind to lead one to conclude that, had there been genuine passion on both sides, the lover's advances would have been repelled with that severe regard for virtue which one enthusiastic biographer is disposed to set to the credit of the lady.[5]

(2) The theory of a romantic and boyish passion on

---

1 *Household Book of English Poetry*, pp. 390, 391.
2 *Sidney* (Men of Letters Series), p. 121.
3 Grosart. *Complete Poems of Sir Philip Sidney*, vol. i. p. lxvii.
* Letter of Sidney to Languet of 1st March 1578.
5 Grosart, Preface to the *Complete Poems of Sir Philip Sidney*.

Sidney's side is inconsistent with what we know of his character. All testimony proves that from his earliest days he was distinguished by a certain gravity and seriousness of temper. By Languet, a religiously-minded Humanist, he had been taught to control his desires according to the half-Stoic doctrines favoured by that sect. The bent of his imagination caused him to interest himself deeply in public affairs, whether it were the cause of the Reformed Religion in Europe, the independence of England, or the great discoveries of travel and science, which seemed to open out boundless prospects to the active mind. To suppose that such a man, after having been seasoned in all the fashions of society, should suddenly have been carried away by an irresistible passion for a woman, with whom he had long been accustomed to associate without any feelings beyond those of simple friendship, and who had just become the wife of another, is as injurious to his intellect, as his readiness to blazon abroad his illicit relations with Stella, assuming that his passion was sincere, would be to his delicacy and sense of honour.

(3) But in truth the Sonnets themselves are the best proof of the fictitious character of his feelings. They number 110, and so far from having been casual expressions of emotion, as the moment prompted, it is plain enough to the careful reader that the whole series form a regular design, the object being to exercise the imagination on a set theme according to the traditional rules of a particular poetical convention, which required, above all things, a display of " wit " by the poet, partly in placing a single thought in a great number of different lights, partly in decorating it with a vast variety of far-fetched metaphors. Throughout these Sonnets the poet will be found to conform to all the Petrarcan rules ; his style differs from that of his master only in this, that while Petrarch seems often really to be moved by a genuine feeling of tenderness, Sidney's love analysis never once penetrates beyond the bounds of fancy. Let the reader examine one or two characteristic Sonnets, and then decide for himself whether

the man who composed them was speaking the real
language of the heart. The following Sonnet embodies
the conceit common to the numberless poets of this
school, that Love lies in ambush in the eye ; the only
addition made by Sidney to the usual convention is
taken from the particular colour of Stella's eyes :—

> Fly, fly, my friends ; I have my death's wound, fly ;
> See there that boy, that murthring boy, I say,
> Who like a thief hid in dark bush doth lie
> Till bloody bullet get him wrongful prey.
> So, tyran, he, no fitter place could spy ;
> Nor so fair level in so secret stay,
> As that sweet black which veils the heavenly eye ;
> There himself with his shot he close doth lay.
> Poor passenger, pass now thereby I did,
> And stayed, pleased with the prospect of the place,
> While that black hue from me the bad guest hid :
> But straight I saw motions of lightning grace ;
> And then descried the glistenings of his dart :
> But ere I could fly thence it pierced my heart.[1]

Here is a Sonnet which, based on a different image,
is evidently modelled on Petrarch's *Passa la nave mia :*—

> I on my horse, and Love on me doth try
> Our horsemanships, while by strange work I prove
> A horseman to my horse, a horse to Love,
> And now man's wrongs in me, poor beast ! descry.
> The reins wherewith my rider doth me tie
> Are humbled thoughts, which bit of reverence move,
> Curbed in with fear, but with guilt boss above
> Of hope, which makes it seem fair to the eye :
> The wand is will ; thou, Fancy, saddle art,
> Girt fast by Memory ; and while I spur
> My horse he spurs with sharp desire my heart ;
> He sits me fast, however I do stir,
> And now hath made me to his hand so right,
> That in the manage myself take delight.[2]

In other Sonnets words themselves cause excruciating
efforts of metaphysical thought :—

> What may words say, or what may words not say,
> When Truth it self must speak like Flattery ?
> Within what bounds can one his liking stay,

---

[1] Sir P. Sidney's *Complete Poems* (Grosart), vol. i. p. 30.
[2] *Ibid.* vol. i. p. 68.

When Nature doth with infinite agree?
What Nestor's counsel can my flames allay
Since Reason's self doth blow the coal in me?
And, ah, what hope that Hope should once see day,
When Cupid is sworn page to Chastity?
Honour is honoured that thou dost possess
Him as thy slave, and now long-needy Fame
Doth even grow rich, meaning my Stella's name.
Wit learns in thee perfection to express,
Not thou by praise but praise in thee is raised:
It is a praise to praise when thou art praised.[1]

The true inference to be drawn from sonnets, of which those that have been cited are only characteristic examples, is that such compositions are the work of a poet, and not of a historian or an autobiographer. In other words, they must not be read in a matter-of-fact spirit; at the same time, the facts and feelings recorded in them may be regarded as resting on a certain substratum of reality. The nearest analogy to *Astrophel and Stella*, is perhaps Pope's *Elegy on an Unfortunate Lady*, which, until an accident revealed the circumstances of its composition, was believed to be a faithful record of actual facts. Viewed in the light of this example it is not difficult to divine the proportions of fact and fiction out of which *Astrophel and Stella* is constituted. We know that Penelope's father was anxious for her marriage with Sidney; that Sidney himself found something not unattractive in the idea; but that, as he wrote to Languet, there were considerations—whatever they may have been—that stood in the way of the union. When he heard that she was to be married against her will to Lord Rich, he was indignant and disgusted; and it is probable enough that he may have believed his old feeling for her to have been warmer than was actually the case. It was, at any rate, strong enough at the moment to enable his imagination to conceive of their relations as resembling those of hundreds of lovers from the days of the Troubadours downwards; for I think it is hardly doubtful that the whole series of sonnets was designed

---

[1] Sir P. Sidney's *Complete Poems* (Grosart), vol. i. p. 51.

after the marriage had been accomplished, or at least after it was arranged.[1] All the superstructure raised upon this groundwork of reality is, I imagine, purely poetical. It conforms at every point to the requirements of this kind of composition. Stella, of course, embodies in herself the manifold perfections which always inspire the lover; like Laura she is severely chaste, and even repellent; and the numerous situations which give rise to sonnets, such as the lover's sleeplessness, his feelings on hearing that Stella is sick, his despair at seeing her coach pass by without being able to obtain a look, and the kiss which he supposes himself to have stolen from her while she was asleep, are only ideal inventions necessary for the elaboration of the "concetti" which the Petrarcan tradition demands.

He was also inspired by another motive, which he reveals in the sonnet beginning "Let dainty wits cry on the Sisters nine,"[2] namely artistic opposition to the Euphuists. As against the party at Court which treated love as a subject to be developed with all the pedantry of the New Learning, he wished to assert the ancient and chivalrous tradition of Petrarch. Sonnet after sonnet sounds the note that love alone is an adequate source of inspiration, without the artificial supplement of science and learning. And, ideally speaking, there was undoubtedly something striking and pathetic in the situation of a lover who, when happiness was in his power, refrained from availing himself of his opportunities till it was too late. Whenever Sidney in imagination throws himself into this position, and leaves the purely conventional celebration of Stella's perfections, his sonnets reach a very high degree of poetical excellence; for example :—

---

[1] This inference is based on Sonnet ii. v. 5, "I saw and liked; I liked, but loved not," which explains the nature of Sidney's feelings before the marriage : on Sonnet xxxiii. beginning :

> I might !—unhappy word—O me, I might,
> And then would not, or could not, see my bliss;

and on Sonnet xxxvii. when he says that Stella "hath no misfortune but that Rich she is"; showing that when this was written she was actually married.

[2] See *ante*, p. 197.

With how sad steps, O Moon, thou climbst the skies !
How silently and with how wan a face !
What, may it be that even in heavenly place
That busy archer his sharp arrows tries !
Sure, if that long-with-love-acquainted eyes
Can judge of love, thou feelst a lover's case ;
I read it in thy looks ; thy languisht grace
To me, that feel the like, thy state descries.
Then ev'n of fellowship, O Moon, tell me,
Is constant love deemed there but want of wit ?
Are beauties there as proud as here they be ?
Do they above love to be loved, and yet
Those lovers scorn whom that love doth possess ?
Do they call virtue there ungratefulness ? [1]

Or

Come, Sleep ! O Sleep, the certain knot of peace,
The baiting place of wit, the balm of woe,
The poor man's wealth, the prisoner's release,
The indifferent judge between the high and low ;
With shield of proof shield me from out the prease
Of those fierce darts Despair at me doth throw :
O make in me those civil wars to cease,
I will good tribute pay if thou do so.
Take thou of me smooth pillows, sweetest bed,
A chamber deaf of noise and blind of light,
A rosy garland and a weary head :
And if these things, as being thine in right,
Move not thy heavy grace, thou shalt in me
Livelier than elsewhere Stella's image see. [2]

In short, *Arcadia* and *Astrophel and Stella* are equally
to be regarded as the outpourings of an ardent and
chivalrous nature, long pent in the midst of uncongenial
surroundings, and at length permitted to find utterance
during a period of enforced leisure. Both are evidently
conceived in the spirit encouraged during the year 1580,
while Sidney was an exile from the Court, and was under
the inspiration of a sister's tender sympathies and the
solitude of Salisbury Plain. In the various characters of
the romance and the poem he found mouthpieces for his
different feelings. Philisides, the shepherd, provides an

---

[1] Sir P. Sidney's *Complete Poems* (Grosart), vol. i. p. 45.
[2] *Ibid.* vol. i. p. 57.

outlet for his dislike of Court Conventionalism ; Musidorus expresses his loftier aspirations ; Pyrocles and the various champions of the *Arcadia*, his dreams of knightly adventure ; while in the sorrowful history of *Astrophel and Stella*, composed while the poetical mood was still strong in him, he gives utterance alike to the amorous traditions of chivalry and to the ardours of his own imagination.   After his return to Court the literary and romantic impulse seems to have gradually exhausted itself. He takes up the old round of duty and amusement, marries a wife, enters Parliament, engages in the work of administration, occupies himself with designs for thwarting the power of Philip of Spain, fights on behalf of freedom in the Low Countries, and at last meets with the reward of all his repressed chivalry in brilliant victory and glorious death.[1]

[1] For the biographical facts on which the estimate of Sidney given in this chapter is based, I am largely indebted to the *Life* of the poet, written by Mr. Fox Bourne for the *Heroes of the Nations* Series, 1891, a book equally admirable for industry in research and soundness of judgment.

CHAPTER IX

COURT ALLEGORY: EDMUND SPENSER

THE genius of Spenser was by far the most comprehensive that had illuminated the sphere of English poetry since the time of Chaucer. It covered at once the movement developed by the Euphuists for the refinement of the national language, and the ideals of those who aimed at adapting the institution of chivalry to the requirements of the Court. But Spenser surpassed Lyly in intellectual power, as far as he excelled Sidney in the range of his reading and philosophy. His imagination received an impulse from every one of the great sources of thought which in the sixteenth century were agitating the mind of Europe. Catholic Theology, Mediæval Romance, the Philosophy of the Renaissance, the Morality of the Reformation, all contributed elements to the formation of his poetical conceptions. He wanted no quality required to place him in the same class with Homer, Virgil, Dante, Shakespeare, Milton, and, perhaps, I may add Chaucer, but that supreme gift of insight and invention which enables the poet to blend conflicting ideas into an organic form. It must be added that to produce such a form out of the materials at his disposal was probably impossible, so that —apart from a certain defect of judgment implied in the selection of subject—the lack of unity that characterises Spenser's creations is the result not so much of his own artistic incapacity as of the circumstances of his time.

Edmund Spenser was born in Smithfield in 1552 or 1553. He is supposed to have been the son of John

Spenser, a cloth-maker of London, and claims to have belonged to the same family as the Spencers of Althorpe.[1] He was first educated at the Merchant Taylors' School, whence he was sent as a sizar to Pembroke College, Cambridge, in 1569 ; and in the same year it is supposed that he made his first appearance as an author in some translations of Petrarch and Joachim du Bellay, inserted in a volume published by a Dutchman, John Vander Noodt. Both the English Universities were at this time feeling the influence of a wave of the Calvinism which on the Continent had grown out of the milder doctrines of the early Reformers, and at Cambridge these opinions were represented in an extreme form by Cartwright, the Margaret Professor of Divinity, who was deprived of his Chair in 1570. Puritanism of a slightly more moderate colour was also professed by Grindal, Bishop of London, who had been Master of Spenser's college, and is celebrated by him as "Algrind" in *The Shepherd's Calendar ;* while it is conjectured, not without probability, that the " Ruffin," who is mentioned in that poem, was Young, then Bishop of Rochester, but formerly Master of Pembroke Hall. These circumstances are sufficient to account for the vein of Puritanism that runs through the poetry of Spenser, a man evidently of quick perceptions and warm sensibilities, and likely to have formed his religious opinions in the mould of his immediate surroundings.

At Cambridge he came also under an influence of a quite different kind. When he entered Pembroke Hall the College was divided into sets, formed by the supporters and opponents of Gabriel Harvey, of whom I shall have to say more in another chapter. Spenser enlisted himself with all the ardour of his temperament on the side of Harvey, and the latter, a man of considerable learning and force of character, obtained over him an ascendency which, under other circumstances, would have been surprising. Spenser formed with him a lasting friendship, constantly deferred to his very bad taste, and addressed to him the finest of his sonnets. From Harvey he prob-

[1] *Colin Clout's Come Home Again,* 536.

ably derived his predilection for Platonism; but, though, after he had taken his degree, he corresponded frequently with his friend, there are unfortunately no letters between them throwing light on the early career of the poet at the University, of which we know little more than that he took his B.A. degree in 1572-3, and proceeded to his M.A. degree in 1576.

In the latter year he seems to have left Cambridge to live in Lancashire, where he met with the lady, indispensable for all poets of the school of Petrarch, " Rosalynd, the widow's daughter of the glen." This shepherdess possessed all the " cruelty " required by the rules of love and poetry, and, after devoting himself to her service for two years, Spenser, at the suggestion of Gabriel Harvey, again came southwards, and became a member of the household of the Earl of Leicester. In the Earl's service, and very likely with the encouragement of Philip Sidney, he occupied himself with poetical composition. His *Hymns of Love and Beauty* had perhaps been written before this date, while, from the correspondence with Gabriel Harvey, it appears that he had also produced several works that have been lost,—*Dreams, Epithalamion Thamesis, The Dying Pelican, Slumber, Stemmata Dudleiana,* together with *Nine Comedies,*—and that he endeavoured (with signal want of success) to conform to the prevailing fashion of composing English verse in metrical quantity.[1] He was presented at Court, and his view of the life there, doubtless coloured by the opinions of Sidney, was embodied in the first version of *Mother Hubberd's Tale.* This would have, of course, contained the lines describing the Perfect Courtier, a portrait of Sidney; but it may be conjectured that the famous verses on the miseries of Court Suitors were not inserted in the poem till after Spenser's later experiences at Court in 1589.

It was, doubtless, owing to the influence of Leicester and Sidney with Lord Grey, that, when that nobleman was made Lord-Deputy of Ireland in the summer of 1580, he took Spenser with him as his secretary. In Ireland

---

[1] Gabriel Harvey's *Works* (Grosart), vol. i. p. 6.

the poet spent the next nine years of his life, sometimes following the fortunes of the Lord-Deputy in the field, sometimes engaged in official work at Dublin, where, in March 1581, he was made Clerk of Decrees and Recognisances, a post which is said by Fuller to have been lucrative. In the same year he received the lease of the Abbey and Manor of Enniscorthy. He also acted as the deputy of his friend, Lodovick Briskett, who, in 1583, obtained the office of clerk to the Irish Council, but apparently relinquished it in Spenser's favour. When Munster was planted Spenser received the grant of the Castle of Kilcolman, a house formerly belonging to the Desmonds, with about 3000 acres, under the Galtee Hills, on the stream now called Awbeg, and so often celebrated in Spenser's poems under the name of the Mulla. Here, in 1589, he was visited by Raleigh—also an " Undertaker for the planting of Munster "—to whom he read those books of the *Faery Queen* which he had found time to compose in his intervals of leisure. Raleigh, delighted with the poem, carried Spenser with him to the Court of Elizabeth, where the Queen listened with complacency to the flattery lavished upon her by the poet in a thousand dexterous allusions. As a reward for his labour and loyalty she awarded him a pension of £50; but it is said that, through the reluctance of Burleigh, Spenser found great difficulty in obtaining any payment. The first three books of the *Faery Queen* were entered in the Stationers' Register on 1st December 1589. After staying in England for about a year and a half, Spenser returned to Ireland, and amused himself and his friends with a pastoral and poetical account of his experiences at Court in *Colin Clout's Come Home Again*. In 1591 he published a volume of " Complaints," containing *The Visions of Bellay and Petrarch, The Ruins of Rome, Mother Hubberd's Tale, The Ruins of Time, Muiopotmos, The Tears of the Muses.* In 1594 he married a lady whom, in one of the most beautiful of his poems, his *Epithalamion*, he calls " a country lass," but who appears to have been in fact a kinswoman of the Earl of Cork, Elizabeth Boyle. By her, the mistress of his *Amoretti*, he had several children, of whom two sons, called character-istically Peregrine and Sylvanus, survived him. The second portion of the *Faery Queen* was entered in the Stationers' Register in January 1596; in this year the poet also published *Four Hymns on Love and Beauty, Earthly and Heavenly ; Daphnaida*, a dirge on the death of the wife of his friend, Arthur Gorges ; and *Prothalamion*, a poem on the marriage of the two daughters of the Earl of Wor-cester. In April 1598, at the instigation of Tyrone, Munster rose in rebellion. Spenser was appointed, in the following September, Sheriff of Cork, being accounted "a man endowed with good knowledge and learning, and not unskilful or without experience in war ; " but in October the rebels overwhelmed the settlers, and, among other feats, sacked and burned Kilcolman Castle. Ben Jonson relates that a child of Spenser's perished in the flames. The poet, returning to England, with health and heart broken, only survived his misfortunes for a few months. " He died " (16th January 1599-1600), says Jonson, " for lack of bread in King Street (Westminster), and refused twenty pieces sent to him by my Lord of Essex, saying he had no time to spend them." [1]

This is the record of a life full of vicissitude, adventure, and suffering, and such as we might suppose would have drawn from a poet strong and direct utterance of personal feeling. But with the exception of the famous lines in *Mother Hubberds Tale*, and a casual mention of his disappointments in the *Prothalamion*, there is scarcely a passage in Spenser's poetry which can be regarded as an immediate revelation of his inward life. Everything in his poems is concealed under a cloak of allegory. Allegory not only provides the form of his compositions ; it is of the very essence of his thought. It is, therefore, mainly by reference to his character as a poetical

[1] Whatever is known about Spenser's life has been collected with the most indefatigable and praiseworthy industry by Mr. Grosart in his edition of the poet's works published in 1882-84. He questions the truth of the story about Spenser dying in want ; but it does not appear to me that his reasoning, which is of a somewhat abstract nature, invalidates the direct testimony of Spenser's contemporary, Ben Jonson.

allegorist that his place in the history of English poetry
must be determined.   But here a difficulty at once arises.
In judging of his poetical qualities are we to look
primarily to the matter of his allegory, or to the form of
his poetry?   To this question two entirely opposite
answers have been furnished by two schools of critics.
One school, taking him at his own valuation, regards him
primarily as a poetical *philosopher*.   Milton, for example,
observes that he is a better teacher than Scotus or
Aquinas.[1]   Mr. Ruskin has given his own explanation of
the moral teaching conveyed in the first book of the
Faery Queen ; [2] and his example has been followed, though
on lines of their own, by Professors Morley, Dowden, and
Percival.   "' A better teacher than Scotus or Aquinas,'"
says Professor Dowden, referring to Milton's opinion,
'he strove in his own way to make the national life of
England a great unity—spiritual yet not disdaining earth
or the things of earth.   He strove as far as in him lay to
breed a race of high-souled English gentlemen, who should
have none of the meanness of the libertine, none of the
meanness of the precisian." [3]   On the other hand, Hume
and others utterly refuse to attach any value to the
spiritual sense of the *Faery Queen*, and maintain that to
apply this method of interpretation not only deprives the
poem of its most essential beauties, but the reader of the
power of enjoying them.   Thus, says Mr. Lowell—

The true use of Spenser is as a gallery of pictures which we
visit as the mood takes us, and where we spend an hour or two
at a time, long enough to sweeten our perceptions, not so long
as to cloy them. . . . Whenever, in the *Fairy Queen*, you come
suddenly·on the moral, it gives you a shock of unpleasant surprise,
a kind of grit as when one's teeth close on a bit of gravel in a
dish of strawberries and cream.[4]

I cannot agree with either of these extreme opinions.

[1] Milton, *Areopagitica*.   [2] *Stones of Venice*.
[3] Professor Dowden, Essay on Spenser in Grosart's edition of Spenser's
Works, vol. i. p. 337.
[4] J. R. Lowell, cited by Professor Dowden in Grosart's edition of
Spenser's *Works*, vol. i. p. 306.   Compare Hume, *History of England*, chap.
xlvii. Appendix iii.

It seems to me impossible to hold with Mr. Lowell that the moral of Spenser's poems counts for nothing : the sense, no less than the form of his allegory, is an essential and characteristic part of his work.   But I dissent still more decidedly from those who consider that he is to be primarily regarded as a moral teacher.   Spenser does not allegorise like Dante, because he believes all sensible objects to be mirrors of hidden truths ; nor like Langland, because this method of writing is useful for the moral instruction he wishes to convey: Allegory is to him mainly interesting in so far as it serves the purposes of poetry.   From the first glimpse we obtain of him, in his correspondence with Gabriel Harvey, down to his last experiences at Court, recorded in *Colin Clout's Come Home Again*, the requirements of his art are always in his mind ; and the motive of every one of his greater compositions, when detached from the cloudy words with which he chooses to cover it, is found to be primarily poetical.

His earliest poems are an attempt to give a metrical form to the philosophical doctrines in which he had been educated.   At Cambridge he had moved in an atmosphere of Platonism.   Plato's philosophy mixed with the current of theology in the Latin Church through the channel of Boethius, and elements of his doctrine embodied themselves in the poetry of the Troubadours, of Dante, and of Petrarch. In later times opposition to the scholastic interpretation of Aristotle naturally favoured the teaching of his rival, whose system, expounded in Italy by men like Ficino and Pico della Mirandola, was afterwards advocated by the Huguenot Ramus in the University of Paris, and passed into the German Universities ; so that a Platonic cult gradually associated itself all over the Continent with the cause of the religious reformers.   Cheke and Ascham lectured on the Socratic dialogues in Cambridge in the first half of the sixteenth century ; and when Spenser came into residence all that was intellectual in the University was Platonist.   The poet imbibed the humanistic teaching, as Sidney imbibed the doctrines of Languet.   Writing from Leicester House, in later years, he seems to have confided

to Gabriel Harvey his hopes of propagating the Platonic
gospel with the help of Sidney's following at Court, an
aspiration to which his friend replied somewhat sarcasti-
cally by a picture of the actual state of opinion in
Cambridge.[1]   Spenser's two *Hymns to Love and Beauty*
were the poetical fruits of his University education.   These
contain little that is original, but show a remarkable power
of rendering the current philosophical ideas into clear and
flowing verse.   Visible things, the poet taught, following the
main axiom of his master, are patterns of things invisible.

> What time the world's great workmaster did cast
> To make all things such as we now behold,
> It seems that he before his eyes had plast
> A goodly pattern, to whose perfect mould
> He fashioned them as comely as he could,
> Just now so fair and seemly they appear,
> As nought may be amended anywhere.

Beauty is not only an image of the Divine Mind but
an informing power in the soul—

> Thereof it comes that those fair souls, which have
> The most resemblance of that heavenly light,
> Frame to themselves most beautiful and brave
> Their fleshly bower, most fit for their delight,
> And the gross matter by a sovrain might
> Temper so trim, that it may well be seen
> A palace fit for such a Virgin Queen.

The ideal action of the soul in Love is thus described—

> Love is not so light
> As straight to burn at first beholder's sight:

> But they which love indeed look otherwise,
> With pure regard and spotless true intent,
> Drawing out of the object of their eyes
> A more refined form, which they present
> Unto their mind, void of all blemishment ;
> Which it reducing to her first perfection
> Beholdeth free from fleshes frail infection.

In 1596 Spenser, at the instigation of two noble ladies,
the Countess of Warwick and the Countess of Cumberland, modified what was held to be the too pagan

---

[1] Gabriel Harvey's *Works*, vol. i. pp 146-150.

tendency of these poems in two supplementary hymns, one to Heavenly Love, the other to Heavenly Beauty. It was easy for him to extend the idea of the Platonic Eros—as Bonaventura and others had done before him—into the conception of the perfect love of God through Christ ; but he evidently felt a difficulty in expanding his description of intellectual beauty into a more definitely theological form. Words failed him to paint the Wisdom that dwells in the bosom of God, and his description of the Beatific Vision is pale and cold by the side of the blaze of imagery in which Dante paints the glories of the Heaven of Heavens.

Trained in the Platonic system of interpreting life and nature, Spenser, with the natural impulse of a poet, next turned his thoughts to the invention of forms in which he could most appropriately express his ideas. Two principal modes of personification at once suggested themselves, the figures of the Shepherd and the Knight, and it appears that he began to work on both of these at the same time, for his correspondence with Gabriel Harvey shows that in 1580 not only *The Shepherd's Calendar*, but some portion of the *Faery Queen*, had been submitted to his friend's judgment. The former work was completed in 1579. It was published anonymously with a dedication to Philip Sidney, "the President of nobleness and chivalry," signed with the self-depreciating name *Immerito* (Spenser's pseudonym in his correspondence with Gabriel Harvey), and accompanied by a commentary, the work of one E. K., who has been with much probability identified as Edward Kirke, Spenser's friend and fellow-student at Pembroke Hall. E. K., evidently possessing an intimate acquaintance with all the author's intentions, describes his purpose as follows :—

Now as touching the general drift and purpose of his Æglogues I mind not to say much, himself labouring to conceal it. Only this appeareth that his unstayed youth had long wandered in the Common Labyrinth of Love, in which time to mitigate and allay the heat of his passion, or else to warn (as he saith) the young shepherds, his equals and companions of his unfortunate folly, he compiled these xii. Æglogues, which for that they be proportioned to the state of the xii. months he termeth the *Shepherd's Calendar*, applying an old word to a new work.

The name of the poem was borrowed from the French *Kalendrier des Bergers*, an almanac which since the beginning of the sixteenth century had been popularised in England by many translations. The "labyrinth of love" referred to by E. K. is an allusion to Colin Clout's professed passion for Rosalynd, "the widow's daughter of the glen," which the poet celebrated at a later date in *Colin Clout's Come Home Again*. But it must be plain to every reader of *The Shepherd's Calendar* that the suffering occasioned by the insensibility of this shepherdess accounts but very partially for the character of the composition. The shepherd Colin, who is the martyr, appears but in three of the "Æglogues," viz. January, June, December ; and reference to his unhappy state and his poetical genius is made in two more, viz. April and August. But of the remaining seven months five—May, July, September, October, November—are devoted to dialogues on religious questions ; another, February, to a moralisation on the characters of Youth and Age ; while in March the subject of love is treated in a light and fanciful vein, and without any reference to Colin's misfortunes.

If we look below the surface of *The Shepherd's Calendar*, we can hardly doubt that the "drift and purpose" of the composition was not "to warn young shepherds of the folly of Love," but to give a new poetical development to the traditional character of the Eclogue. Spenser observed the various purposes to which the pastoral style had been put by poets differing from each other so widely as Bion, Mantuan, and Marot, and he endeavoured to give unity to their opposite experiments, partly by allegorising the *Kalendrier des Bergers*, partly by assimilating the emotions of his shepherds to the vicissitudes of the seasons. In almost every "Æglogue" we find an attempt to give a new turn to the practice of some pastoral predecessor. For example, from the earliest days the Eclogue had been used as a vehicle for the complaints of lovers, and in Colin's laments over the cruelty of Rosalynd the poet was merely following the example set him by Theocritus and Virgil. In his reflections on the faults of the Roman Catholic and Anglican clergy he had been anticipated by Mantuan, on the one hand, and by Googe, on the other ; while Barclay, by his praises of Archbishop Morton in the character of a shepherd, had furnished him with the suggestion of a compliment to his old patron Grindal, and with the idea of giving the rustic names Morell and Ruffin to the contemporary bishops, Elmore and Young (Rochester). From Marot he borrowed the motive of the dirge in the eleventh Æglogue, and the Elegy or Complaint of the twelfth. Thus, without departing from the convention of pastoral poetry, Spenser modified it for his own purposes with such admirable delicacy and artistic instinct, that he appears as in a certain sense, an inventor, even on well-trodden ground. E. K., when *The Shepherd's Calendar* first appeared, could say, with something like an appeal to authority—

It moved him rather in Æglogues than otherwise to write, doubting perhaps his hability, which he little needed, or minding to furnish our tongue with this kind, wherein it faulteth ; or following the example of the best and most ancient Poets which devised this kind of writing, being both so base for the matter, and homely for the manner, at first to try their habilities ; and as young birds that be newly crept out of the nest, by little first to try their tender wings, before they make a greater flight.

Besides giving a picturesque utterance in pastoral images to the commonplaces of contemporary thought, Spenser had another, and more purely artistic, purpose ; he was making experiments, like Ronsard, though on very different principles, in poetical diction. His design in this direction is thus defended by E. K. :—

And first of the words to speak, I grant they be something hard, and of most men unused, yet both English, and also used of most excellent Authors and most famous Poets. In whom, whenas this our Poet hath been much travailed and throughly read, how could it be (as that worthy Orator said) but that walking in the sun, although for other cause he walked, yet needs he mought be sunburnt ; and having the sound of those ancient Poets still ringing in his ears, he mought needs in singing hit out some of their tunes. . . . But if any will rashly blame such his purpose in choice of old and unwonted words, him may I more justly blame and condemn, or of witless headiness in judging or of heedless hardiness in condemning ; for not marking the compass of his bent, he will judge of the length of his cast ; for in my opinion, it is one special praise of many which are due to this Poet, that he hath laboured to restore, as to their rightful heritage, such good and natural English words, as have been long time out of use, and almost clean disherited. Which is the only cause that our Mother Tongue, which truly of it self is both full enough for prose, and stately enough for verse, hath long time been accounted most bare and barren of both. Which default whenas some endeavoured to salve and recure, they patched up the holes with pieces and rags of other languages, borrowing here of the French, there of the Italian, everywhere of the Latin, not weighing how ill those tongues accord with themselves, but much worse with ours : So now they have made our English tongue a gallimaufray, or hodge-podge of all other speeches.

Let us now turn to the design of the *Faery Queen*. It should be remembered that Spenser's account of his motives in this poem is an after-thought, due to the suggestion of Raleigh, to whom the poet addressed the following letter on January 23, 1589-90 :—

"SIR—Knowing how doubtfully all allegories may be construed, and this book of mine, which I have entitled the *Faery Queen*, being a continued allegory or dark conceit, I have thought good, as well for avoiding of jealous opinions and misconstructions, as also for your better light in reading thereof (being so by you commanded) to discover unto you the general intention and meaning which in the whole course thereof I have fashioned, without expressing of any particular purposes, or by-accidents, therein occasioned. The general end therefore of all the book is to fashion a gentleman or noble person in virtuous and gentle discipline. Which for that I conceived should be most plausible and pleasing, being covered with an historical fiction, the which the most part of men delight to read, rather for variety of matter than for profit of the ensample : I chose the history of King Arthur as most fit for the excellency of his person, being made famous by many men's former works, and also furthest from the danger of envy and suspicion of present time. In which I have followed all the antique poets historical : first Homer, who in the persons of Agamemnon and Ulysses hath ensampled a good governor and a virtuous man, the one in his *Ilias*, the other in his *Odysseis :* then Virgil, whose like intention was to doe in the person of Æneas : after him Ariosto comprised them both in his *Orlando :* and lately Tasso dissevered them again, and formed both parts in two persons, namely, that part which they in philosophy call *Ethice*, or virtues of a private man, coloured in his *Rinaldo :* the other, named *Politice*, in his *Godfredo*. By ensample of which excellent Poets, I labour to portray in Arthur, before he was king, the image of a brave knight, perfected in the twelve private moral virtues, as Aristotle hath devised ; the which is the purpose of these first twelve books : which if I find to be well accepted, I may perhaps be encouraged to frame the other part of politic virtues, in his person, after he came to be king.

To some I know this method will seem displeasant, which would rather have good discipline delivered plainly by way of precepts, or sermoned at large, as they use, than thus cloudily enwrapt in allegorical devices. But such, me seem, should be satisfied with the use of these days, seeing all things accounted by their shows, and nothing esteemed of that is not delightful and pleasing to common sense. For this cause is Xenophon preferred before Plato, for that the one, in the exquisite sense of his judgment, formed a commonwealth such as it should be ; but the other, in the person of Cyrus and the Persians, fashioned a government, such as might best be : So much more profitable and gracious is doctrine by ensample than by rule. So have I laboured to do in the person of Arthur : whom I conceive, after his long education by Timon (to whom he was by Merlin delivered to be brought up, so soon as he was born, by the Lady Igrayne) to have seen in a dream or vision the Faery Queen, with whose excellent beauty ravished, he awaking resolved to seek her out : and so, being by Merlin armed, and by Timon thoroughly instructed, he went to seek her forth in Faery Land. In that Faery Queen I mean Glory in my general intention : but in my particular I conceive the most excellent and gracious person of our Sovereign the Queen, and her kingdom in Faery Land. And yet in some places else I do otherwise shadow her. For considering she beareth two persons, the one of a most royal Queen or Empress, the other of a most virtuous and beautiful lady, this latter part in some places I do express in Belphœbe, fashioning her name according to your own excellent conceit of Cynthia (Phœbe and Cynthia being both names of Diana). So in the person of Prince Arthur I set forth Magnificence in particular, which virtue for that (according to Aristotle and all the rest) it is the perfection of all the rest, and containeth in it them all, therefore in the whole course I mention the deeds of Arthur appliable to that virtue which I write of in that book. But of the twelve other virtues I make xii. other knights the patrons, for the more variety of this history : of which these books contain three.   The first of the Knight of the Red Cross in whom I express Holiness : the second of Sir Guyon, in whom I set forth Temperance : the third of Britomartis, a Lady Knight, in whom I picture Chastity.   But because the beginning of the whole work seemeth abrupt and as depending upon other antecedents, it needs that ye know the occasion of these three knights' several adventures.   For the method of a Poet historical is not such as of an Historiographer.   For an Historiographer discourseth of affairs orderly as they were done, accounting as well the times as the actions ; but a Poet thrusteth into the middest, even where it most concerneth him, and there recoursing to the things forepast, and divining of things to come, maketh a pleasing analysis of all.   The beginning therefore of my History, if it were to be told by an Historiographer, should be the twelfth book, which is the last; where I devise that the Faery Queen kept her annual feast twelve days ; upon which twelve several days the occasions of the twelve several adventures happened, which being undertaken by twelve several knights, are in these twelve books severally handled and discoursed.

The first was this.   In the beginning of the feast, there presented himself a tall clownish young man, who, falling before the Queen of the Fairies desired a boon (as the manner then was) which during that feast she might not refuse ; which was that he might have the achievement of any adventure which during that feast should happen ; that being granted, he seated himself on the floor, unfit through his rusticity for a better place.   Soon after entered a fair Lady in mourning weeds, riding on a white ass, with a dwarf behind her leading a warlike steed, that bore the arms of a knight, and his spear in the dwarf's hand.   She falling before the Queen of Fairies complained that her Father and Mother, an ancient King and Queen, had been by an huge dragon many years shut up in a brazen castle, who thence suffered them not to issue ; and therefore besought the Faery Queen to assign her some one of her knights to take on him that exploit. Presently that clownish person upstarting desired that adventure ; whereat the Queen much wondering, and the Lady much gain-saying, yet he earnestly importuned his desire.   In the end the Lady told him that unless that armour which she brought would serve him (that is, the armour of a Christian man specified by St. Paul v. Ephes.) that he could not succeed in that enterprise ; which being forthwith put upon him with due furnitures there-unto, he seemed the goodliest man in all that company, and was well liked of the Lady. And eftsoons taking on him knighthood, and mounting on that strange courser, he went forth with her on that adventure; where beginneth the first book, viz. :—

A gentle knight was pricking on the plain, etc.

The second day there came in a Palmer bearing an Infant with bloody hands, whose Parents he complained to have been slain by an enchantress called Acrasia; and therefore craved of the Faery Queen to appoint him some knight to perform that adventure, which being assigned to Sir Guyon he presently went forth with that same Palmer, which is the beginning of the Second Book and the whole subject thereof. The third day there came in a groom who complained before the Faery Queen that a vile enchanter called Busirane had in hand a most fair Lady called Amoretta, whom he kept in most grievous torment. Whereupon Sir Scudamoor, the lover of that Lady, took on him that adventure. But being unable to perform it by reason of the hard enchantments, after long sorrow, in the end met with Britomartis, who succoured him and rescued his Love.

But by occasion hereof many other adventures are intermeddled, but rather as accidents than intendments. As the love of Britomart, the overthrow of Marinell, the misery of Florimell, the virtuousness of Belphœbe, and many the like.

Thus much, sir, I have briefly overrun to direct your understanding to the well-head of this History, that from thence gathering the whole intention of the conceit, ye may as in a handfull, gripe all the discourse, which otherwise may happily seem tedious and confused. So humbly craving the continuance of your honourable favour towards me, and the eternal establishment of your happiness, I humbly take leave.—Yours most humbly affectionate.   EDMUND SPENSER.

The reader will observe that the poet does not really fulfil the promise with which he opens his letter, of discovering " the general intention and meaning of his work." He is concerned rather to explain the artistic structure of the poem, than the moral of the allegory. A single sentence in the letter is devoted to declaring the " general end " of the *Faery Queen*, viz. " to fashion a gentleman or noble person in virtuous and gentle discipline." All the rest of the letter is given up to an elucidation of the conduct and machinery of the story itself. And if we look at actual facts, instead of the poet's own account of the facts, we see that it is perfectly natural that this should be so.   Spenser's object was in reality a literary one.   As he sought in *The Shepherd's Calendar* to treat the Eclogue in a new style, so in the *Faery Queen* he aimed at producing a variety of the Romantic Epic of the Italians. As early as 1580 we find from Gabriel Harvey's correspondence with him that he cherished the ambition of " overgoing Ariosto." [1]   He doubtless hoped to achieve this aim by combining with Ariosto's romantic manner the moral style of English allegory.   How far his design was just I shall consider presently.   Meantime we may infer with some confidence that Raleigh, finding the conception of the whole poem somewhat " tedious and confused," " commanded " the poet to bring himself into touch with the general reader by writing an explanatory preface in the form of a letter to himself.

If these considerations are just it follows that, in estimating Spenser's place in English poetry, he is to be regarded in the first place as a poet, and only secondarily as a moralist or philosopher.   The nature of his allegory, pastoral or chivalrous, has to be taken into account, but only so far as it helped to determine the form and character of his compositions.   We have now to decide how far his conceptions were formed in harmony with the laws of his art, and how far his execution did justice to his subjects as he conceived them.

Does Spenser's work satisfy the test of Unity which must be applied to every great creation of art?   Does it conform to the rule of Horace, *Denique sit quidvis simplex duntaxat et unum?*   In other words, does it possess that inward power (whatever it may be and whencesoever it may arise) of so vitalising words, ideas, and images, that they may never fail to produce pleasure for the imagination of capable judges of poetical art?   Looking first to *The Shepherd's Calendar*, there is, I think, undoubtedly poetical unity in the general conception of the work.   As E. K. says, the poet bases his design on the popular almanac in use among country folk, "applying an old name to

[1] Gabriel Harvey's *Works* (Grosart), vol. i. p. 95.

a new work"; the matter of his poem is distributed according to the natural divisions of a period of time determined by a law of nature. Moreover, in intention, at all events, there is unity in the *allegory* of the poem since the various " Æglogues " are " proportioned to the state of the xii. months." It is true that this element in the design is only imperfectly developed ; indeed it would have been obviously impossible to distinguish the treatment of each eclogue by imagining a shade of feeling peculiar to the time of year ; and we find without surprise that from June to October inclusive there is no reference to the character of the season. But, on the whole, the highly poetical idea, that the changes of the successive months may be likened to the progress and decline of human life, is well sustained, and leaves the mind with a sense of completeness and congruity. As to the allegory in the matter of each Æglogue, there is, of course, an inconsistency between the persons of the speakers and the character of their discourse ; but this is a defect which is, to a certain extent, justified by the traditions of pastoral poetry. From Virgil's time these had been unreal and conventional, so that it had become a recognised feature in the eclogue that it should express sentiments and ideas foreign to the life of actual shepherds.[1] Spenser, however, was so daring in his treatment of the pastoral, that he made the unreality more emphatic by imitating, or appearing to imitate, in his style the rudeness of rustic speech, while he caused his persons at the same time to discuss high points of religion and theology. How far he showed good judgment in his practice, is a question which will probably be answered differently according to the view which each reader forms of the main motive of *The Shepherd's Calendar.* Those who, like Sir Philip Sidney, judge it by the established standards of pastoral poetry, will perhaps be inclined to confirm the censure pronounced on it in the *Apologie for Poetry :—*

---

[1] Thus Petrarch says of pastoral poetry : " It is the nature of this class of literature that if the author does not provide a commentary, its meaning may perhaps be guessed, but can never be fully understood " (cited in Herford's *Shepherd's Calendar,* p. 30).

The Shepherds Kalender hath much Poetrie in his Eglogues, indeed worthy the reading, if I be not deceived. That same framing of his stile to an old rustic language I dare not alowe, sith neyther Theocritus in Greek, Virgill in Latin, nor Sannazar in Italian, did affect it.

For my own part, I think that Sidney's censure is too grave and serious for the occasion. Spenser's treatment of the pastoral style is, above all things, allegorical. He must have been perfectly well aware that his shepherds had no counterpart in Nature ; they were to him merely symbolical forms and disguises for the expression of his poetical ideas. Moreover, as we see from the Commentary of E. K., Spenser selected the Eclogue as ground on which he could most conveniently conduct those experiments in metrical composition with which his imagination had been long occupied. In taking this line he was only yielding to influences that were in the air. Wyatt and Surrey had set on foot a new movement in English versification, but had carried it only a little way. The one had begun to refine the rudeness of English conception by acclimatising the methods of Petrarch ; the other had harmonised the roughness of the language so as to make it a fitting instrument for the expression of new ideas. The principle on which Surrey proceeded was sound and just. He based the essential character of his poetical diction on the elder English poets, and adapted it to the conversational usage of the best contemporary society. But as the range of his imagination was limited, the standard of diction which he established, though pure and unaffected, was not equal to the requirements of poetical inventors on a large scale. His reforms, which were in fact closely analogous to those accomplished by Marot in France, did not satisfy the ambition either of scholars who, like Ascham, were enthusiastic admirers of classical antiquity, or of those who, like the Euphuists, aimed at making experiments on their own language for the satisfaction of courtly taste.

As we have seen, these linguistic tendencies had each their champions and directors, the Classicists finding their headquarters at the Universities, the Euphuists at Court. Spenser came under the influence of both parties. Closely connected both with Gabriel Harvey and with Philip Sidney, he made certain experiments in applying the principle of syllabic " quantity " to English verse, of which it need only be said that they were not less uncouth and barbarous than those of his master at Cambridge. Soon, however, perceiving that he was on the wrong road, he gave up the grotesque attempt as hopeless. No less decisive was his rejection of the principle of alliteration, at least in the exaggerated form affected by the contributors to *The Gorgeous Gallery of Gallant Inventions.* " I scorne and spue out " (says his commentator E. K. in his quaint vein, doubtless expressing the poet's own opinions) " the rakehelly rout of our ragged rymers (for so themselves use to hunt the letter) which without learning boast, without judgment jangle, without reason rage and foam, as if some instinct of poetical spirit had newly ravished them above the meaning of common capacity."

Spenser, genuine poet as he was, saw that the metrical experiments both of the Classical Revivalists and of the Letter-Hunters were rendered nugatory by lack of matter, and that, if he was to give his art the extension and refinement which he contemplated, he must appear at least to have something particular to say. Sufficient matter he thought could be provided by the traditional subjects of pastoral poetry ; and accordingly E. K., summarising the merits of his Ægloges, lays stress on the excellence of their thought as follows : " No less, I think, deserveth his wittiness in devising, his pithiness in uttering, his complaints of love so lovely, his discourses of pleasure so pleasantly, his pastoral rudeness, his moral wiseness, his due observing of decorum everywhere in personages, in seasons, in matter, in speech ; and generally in all seemly simplicity of handling his matter and framing his words." Looking on *The Shepherd's Calendar* in the modern spirit, we must decide of course that all this supposed matter is utterly unsubstantial ; but, in estimating Spenser's performance, it is fair to remember that, owing

to the long tradition of pastoral poetry, the question bore
a different aspect to the men of the sixteenth century.

At any rate the poet's object was to rehandle the conventional matter of the Eclogue in a novel form. To
accomplish this design he endeavoured to frame a new
style of poetical diction by blending the archaism of
Chaucer and the provincialism of the Northern English
with the idioms of the language used by refined society.
Like Surrey, he kept his eye always on Chaucer, but, unlike him, he sought to revive the old poet's manner, just
because it was obsolete, and to that extent convenient for
making a sharp division between the language of poetry
and the language of prose. Not understanding the extraordinary science and refinement of Chaucer's style, Spenser
regarded him as the first rude inventor of our tongue.
He spoke of him as "old Tityrus"; praised him for his
homely fables and moralisings; and, generally speaking,
looked back to him with a certain sentimental regret, as a
model of lost simplicity and "the well of English undefiled." The metres of several of his Eclogues are founded
on what he erroneously believed to be the metre of
Chaucer's *Canterbury Tales*. The change in the pronun-
ciation of the language prevented him from perceiving
that his master's treatment of that metre was determined
by the use of the final *e*, the symbol of former inflection;
and he thought that each line contained four accents
instead of five, and was to be measured by the triple
movement employed in the northern dialect by old poets
like Minot. He doubtless read the opening lines of
the Prologue to the *Canterbury Tales* with the following
accentuation :—

> Whánne that A | príle with his | shóures | sóte |
> The dróught | of Márch | had pérc'd | to the róte |
> And báth'd | everie véine | in swíche | licoúr |
> Of which vír | tu engénd | red ís | the flóur, etc.

This irregular movement he thought expressive of the
rusticity of the shepherds in his Eclogues, and he accordingly employs it in February, May, and September,

emphasising its supposed ruggedness, and introducing many varieties of his own.   The following speech furnishes a good example of the composite style resulting from his experiments :—

THENOT

The soveraigne of seas he blames in vain,
That once sea-beat will to sea again :
So loitering live you little herdgrooms,
Keeping your beasts in the budded brooms ;
And when the shining sun laugheth once,
You deemen the spring is come attonce ;
Tho gin you fond flies ! the cold to scorn,
And, crowing in pipes made of green corn,
You thinken to be lords of the year :
But eft, when ye count you freed from fear,
Comes the breme winter with chamfred brows,
Full of wrinkles and frosty furróws,
Drerily shooting his stormy dart,
Which cruddles the blood, and pricks the heart ;
Then is your careless courage accoyed,
Your careful herds with cold bene annoyed ;
Then pay you the price of your surquedry,
With weeping and wailing and misery.

Spenser here departs from the established standard of contemporary diction in using (1) obsolete inflections such as " deemen," " thinken " ; (2) obsolete English words such as " breme " (furious), " accoyed " (daunted) ; (3) old literary French words, such as " surquedry " (pride), and (4) coinages of his own such as " chamfred," an adjective formed from the architectural word " chamfer," meaning a channel cut in stone.[1]   It will probably be generally felt that, though Ben Jonson's criticism, " Spenser writ no language," is, strictly speaking, justified, the effect of this linguistic and metrical experiment in pastoral poetry is very quaint, pretty, and tuneful.

Nor was Spenser less successful in his adaptation of the iambic movement to the nature of his subject, as may be judged from the following very beautiful stanza, quaintly

---

[1] The reader should consult the very excellent edition of *The Shepherd's Calendar*, by Professor Herford, 1895.

put into the mouth of a shepherd distinguished by the clownish name of Hobbinol :—

> Colin, to hear thy rhymes and roundelays,
> Which thou wert wont on wasteful hills to sing,
> I more delight than lark in summer days,
> Whose echo made the neighbour groves to ring,
> And taught the birds, which in the lower spring
> Did shroud in shady leaves from sunny rays,
> Frame to thy song their cheerful cheriping,
> Or hold their peace for shame of thy sweet lays.

A stanza so melodious shows how fully the poet had attained the musical object for which E. K. gives him credit : " Now for the knitting of sentences, which they call the joints and members thereof, and for all the compass of the speech, it is round without roughness, and learned without hardness, such indeed as may be perceived of the least, understood of the most, but judged only of the learned." It also shows the admirable instinct with which Spenser turned to the purposes of metrical music the principle of alliteration, so prodigally wasted by the " rakehelly rout of ragged rhymers " who had preceded him.

Lastly, *The Shepherd's Calendar* afforded Spenser a ground for practising himself in flights of lyrical verse, which preluded the beautiful stanzas of the *Prothalamion* and *Epithalamion*, the work of his later years. Hobbinol in April recites the lay which Colin had made in honour of " Fair Elisa, Queen of Shepherds all," and from which the following stanza may be selected as a specimen :—

> Tell me, have ye seen her angelic face,
>   Like Phoebe fair ?
> Her heavenly havëour, her princely grace,
>   Can you well compare ?
> The Red Rose medled with the white yfere,
> In either cheek depincten lively cheer :
>   Her modest eye,
>   Her Majesty,
> Where have you seen the like but there ?

And in November Colin himself, bewailing Dido " the

great shepherd's daughter" in a dirge, possibly furnished
Milton with the suggestion of a passage in *Lycidas* :—

> Why wail we then ? why weary we the Gods with plaints
> As if some evil were to her betight ?
> She reigns a goddess now among the saints
> That whilome was the saint of shepherd's light,
> And is installed now in heaven's height.
> I see thee, blessed soul, I see,
> Walk in Elysian fields so free.
> O happy hearse !
> Might I once come to thee (O that I might !)
> O joyful verse !
>
> Unwise and wretched men, to weet what's good or ill,
> We dream of death as doom of ill desert ;
> But knew we, fools, what it us brings until,
> Die would we daily, once it to expert !
> No danger there the shepherd can astert ;
> Fair fields and pleasant lays there bene ;
> The fields ay fresh, the grass ay green.
> O happy hearse !
> Make haste, ye shepherds, thither to revert :
> O joyful verse !

On the whole *The Shepherd's Calendar* must be pronounced a truly beautiful and graceful, if somewhat
artificial, composition. The poet had selected in external
nature a real groundwork for his conception, and on
this he built an edifice exquisite and imaginative in
its design, not following the lines of any known style
of poetical architecture, or conforming his diction to any
established standard, but committing himself to the free
exercise of certain faculties of his own, in which he has
had few equals among poets ancient or modern. For the
charming flights of its fancy, for its fine touches of pathos,
and, above all, for the rare melody of its numbers, Spenser's
chief pastoral allegory must be assigned a high place
among the best productions of English poetry.

A more doubtful verdict must be passed on the
execution of the *Faery Queen.* There is undoubtedly a
noble, indeed a sublime, foundation for the poem in its
central design " to fashion a gentleman or noble person in

virtuous and gentle discipline." There is also something eminently poetical in the intention of embodying this image in the ideal knight — a figure consecrated like that of the shepherd, by ancient literary tradition—and in the person of " Arthur before he was a king." Moreover, as the subject was to be treated allegorically, it was open to Spenser to endow his knight with the " twelve private moral virtues, as Aristotle hath devised " ; and in this manner to enrich the poem with all kinds of philosophical and theological learning, as indeed is done in the first and second books of the *Faery Queen*. The general allegorical design was easily expanded so as to include the painting of Classical Mythology, such as the descriptions of Hell and of the Fauns and Satyrs, in the first book ; of the Garden of Proserpine, the Palmer's Wand, and the Wandering Islands, in the second book ; of the Gardens of Adonis and the History of Hellenore, in the third book ; of the Temple of Venus and the Power of Love, in the fourth book. Italian Romance furnished the poet with numberless suggestions, such as the character of Archimago borrowed from Ariosto's Atlante ;[1] the tale of the Squire of Dames adapted from the Host's tale in Ariosto ;[2] the description of Nepenthe founded on Boiardo's and Ariosto's descriptions of the Fountain of Ardenne ;[3] the song of Phædria, and the various imagery in the Bower of Bliss, modelled on the enchanted Gardens of Armida in the *Jerusalem* of Tasso.[4] In the versatility of his invention Spenser imitated, emulated, and even surpassed, the great master of the romantic epic whose example he kept always in sight. No poem in existence can compare with the *Faery Queen* in the richness of its materials. But the question recurs, In what way is all this " variety of matter " fused with the central image of the " brave knight, perfected in all the twelve private moral virtues " ?

---

[1] *Faerie Queen*, book i. *passim*, and *Orlando Furioso*, canto iv.

[2] *Ibid.* book iii. canto vii. 53, and *Orlando Furioso*, canto xxviii.

[3] *Ibid.* book iv. canto iii. 43 ; *Orlando Innamorato*, canto iii. 35-42 ; and *Orlando Furioso*, canto i. 78.

[4] *Ibid.* book ii. canto vi. 14, and book xii., and Tasso's *Jerusalem*, books xiv. xv.

For this, we must always remember, was Spenser's professed and primary motive ; he chose to convey his moral in a form of allegorical narrative, because he thought it would be " most plausible and pleasing, being covered with an historical fiction." If Spenser could illustrate this declared theme with all the branches of learning at his disposal, his object was achieved ; if he failed to work his material into his organic system, as far as his main design was concerned they profited him nothing. The most enthusiastic of Spenser's critical admirers have perceived that this was the ground on which they would be called upon to uphold the reputation of his great work ; but they are by no means agreed as to the line of advocacy which ought to be adopted on his behalf. Upton, his earliest commentator in the eighteenth century, was bold enough to maintain that the *Faery Queen* is constructed on a principle of classical unity. He says :—

In every poem there ought to be simplicity and unity. . . This essential rule Spenser seems to me strictly to have followed : for what story can well be shorter or more simple than the subject of his poem ? A British Prince sees in a Vision the Faerie Queen, falls in love, and goes in secret after the unknown fair ; and at length finds her. The fable has a beginning, a middle, and an end. The beginning is, the British prince saw in a vision the Faerie Queen and fell in love with her : the middle his search after her with the adventures he underwent : the end his finding whom he sought.[1]

Bishop Hurd, on the contrary, rejecting Upton's line of defence, argues that the *Faery Queen* possesses only a " Gothic unity " :—

If (says he), it be asked what is the unity of Spenser's poem ? I say it consists in the relation of its several adventures to one common original, the appointment of the Faerie Queen, and to one common end, the completion of the Faerie Queen's injunction.[2]

Of these two theories, Upton's may be dismissed with the remark that any reader who turns to the *Faery Queen* in the hope of finding the beginning, middle, and end which the commentator speaks of will search in vain. Hurd's

[1] Todd's *Spenser*, vol. ii. p. cxliii.   [2] *Ibid.* p. clviii.

view is more rational. It is supported by Spenser's own
account of his design, and to some extent by the fact that
in each book of the poem there is a reference to the *Faery
Queen* as the great original of the various adventures. But
to produce poetic unity it is not enough to form an idea
in the mind ; it is also necessary that in the execution of
the design this central idea should be felt to communicate
life and being to each constituent part of the poetical
organism. Now it is certain that, if all mention of
Gloriana were excised from the *Faery Queen*, the framework of the poem, as we have it, would be hardly disturbed, a fact which proves conclusively that the central
idea, as described by Spenser, viz., "the image of a brave
knight perfected in the twelve private moral virtues,"
though it may have been in the poet's mind before he
began to write, was not the actual inspiring motive of the
whole work. It does not account for the appearance in
the poem of such irrelevant episodes as the Genealogies
of the British Kings ; the story of Cambell and Canace ;
the histories of Belphœbe and Timias, of Burbon and
Belge ; the Marriage of the Thames and the Medway,
and many others. Hurd's idea of irregular or "Gothic"
unity is no more adequate as an apology for the structure
of the *Faery Queen* than Upton's : it is more profitable
to endeavour to trace the actual genesis of the poem in
Spenser's imagination, and to determine what are the
qualities which have given it the undoubtedly permanent
position it holds in English poetry.

The plain truth of the matter is that Spenser was
inspired to write the *Faery Queen* by reading the *Orlando
Furioso*. The structure of the former poem shows that,
at every stage of the composition, the author was influenced by the manner and method of his Italian predecessor. Like every man of taste and imagination, he
was filled with admiration for the infinite variety, movement, energy, and vivacity, of the *Furioso;* but owing to the
vital difference in their circumstances, he failed to penetrate
the means by which Ariosto gave life and unity to that
astonishing poem. He believed that, like himself, the

poet of Ferrara had conceived the idea of chivalry in a perfectly serious vein, and that his Orlando was intended to set forth the history and example of "a good governor and a virtuous man"; his perplexity must therefore certainly have been great when he asked himself on what principle his master could have thought that his purpose was advanced by the following stanzas, describing Orlando's prowess in the midst of a troop of Dutchmen. Let it be remembered that the exploit is performed before the hero's madness :—

> Il cavalier d' Anglante, ove più spesse
> Vide le genti e l' arme abbassò l' asta ;
> Ed uno in quella e poscia un altro messe,
> E un altro e un altro, che sembrar di pasta :
> E fin a sei n' infilzò ; e li resse
> Tutti una lancia : e perch' ella non basta
> A più capir, lasciò il settimo fuore
> Ferito sì, che di quel colpo muore.
>
> Non altrimente nell' estrema arena
> Veggian le rane di canali e fosse
> Dal cauto arcier nei fianchi e nella schiena.
> L' una vicina all' altra, esser percosse ;
> Ne dalla freccia, finchè tutta piena
> Non sia da un capo all' altro, esser rimosse.
> La grave lancia Orlando da sè scaglia,
> E con la spada entrò nella battaglia.[1]

Nor could he have been greatly edified by the description of one of the feats performed by the hero after he has gone mad :—

> Orlando non responde altro a quel detto,
> Se non che con furor tira d' un piede,
> E giunge a punto l' asino nel petto
> Con quella forza che tutte altre eccede ;

---

[1] *O. F.* canto ix. 68, 69 : " The knight of Anglante, where he saw men and arms to be thickest, couched his lance, and ran one and then another through with it, and then another, and another, as though they had been paste ; he threaded as many as six on it : one lance bore them all : and because it was not long enough to hold more, he left the seventh outside, but so hard hit that he died of his wound. Not otherwise on the edge of the sand are the frogs of the canals and dykes pierced by the wary archer in side and back, one after the other, nor does he remove them from the arrow until it is full from end to end. Orlando, flinging away the heavy lance, entered the battle with his sword."

> Ed alto il leva sì, ch' uno augelletto
> Che voli in aria, sembra a chi lo vede.
> Quel va a cadere alla cima d' un colle
> Ch' un miglio oltre la valle il giogo estolle.[1]

Ariosto, in conceiving the *Orlando Furioso*, had no such grave design as Spenser ascribes to him. He was the child of his time, and his time was one from which the spirit of action and liberty had departed. He had grown up in the midst of Italian cities embellished with all that was beautiful in the arts of sculpture and painting ; in the court of a petty Italian prince, where all motives of high ambition were repressed, even if tyranny was not paramount ; under the shadow of a Papacy, which was the nominal guardian of the Christian religion, but which seemed to have bent all its energies on cultivating the pleasures of the world of sense. He saw himself surrounded at once by the monuments of past greatness,—the civic memories of imperial Rome, the decayed splendour of Teutonic chivalry,—and by all the meanness and servility of an actual world, in which the side of liberty was defended by the cynicism of Machiavelli, as the side of authority was befouled by the cynicism of Aretino. Greatness, even seriousness, of poetical conception, could no more grow out of the thoughts of such a society, than figs could grow on thistles.

Yet the *Orlando Furioso* is not the work of a mere cynic. Never really sublime—for sublimity, at least in the art of poetry, is beyond the reach of those in whom the spirit of liberty is extinct—it is still full of tenderness and pathos ; it shows a knowledge of almost every variety of human character ; a sympathy with nearly every kind of human weakness ; it has proved a source of equal inspiration to poets so essentially unlike each other as Spenser, Shakespeare, and Byron. It is, in fact, the production of a spectator of human action rather than of one who feels

---

[1] "Orlando made no reply to that speech saving to draw back his foot and bring it full upon the chest of the ass with his unequalled strength, sending him up so high that he looked to him who saw him as a little bird flying in the air. The ass falls at last on the top of a hill that rises a mile above the valley."—*O. F.* canto xxix. 53.

himself to be an actor in a national society ; of a poet who deals critically with the marvellous and the supernatural —the main elements of romantic poetry—not without sympathy, but at the same time in the vein of the sceptic and the humourist.

The materials of the *Orlando Furioso* were not invented by Ariosto, they were not even brought together by him for the first time, he merely put the coping stone on a poetical building that had been long in course of erection. The foundations of Italian Romance were provided by the marvellous chronicle imputed to Turpin ; the history called *Reali di Francia ;* the *roman* of the French trouvères called *Les Quatre-Filz-Aymon.* All these related to the supposed historical doings of Charlemagne and his peers. In course of time the municipal civic spirit of the Italians took hold of the archaic materials, and, pretending to revise the historical narrative, used it as a vehicle for modern ideas and feelings. For some reason the paladin they selected as the centre of their narrative was Rotolandus or Roland, whom, under the name of Orlando, Pulci, the chief poet in the court of Lorenzo de' Medici, took as the hero of his *Morgante Maggiore*, representing him, in a conversational style, as a theological warrior, bent on the conversion of the giant from whom the poem derives its name. The spirit in which Pulci writes may be inferred from the reason he gives for writing his *Morgante :*—

> E del mio Carlo imperador m' increbbe ;
> È stata questa istoria, a quel ch' io veggio,
> Di Carlo male intesa, e scritta peggio.[1]

From Pulci the character of Orlando was taken over by Boiardo, who gave it a new turn by representing the hero in love. His *Orlando Innamorato* is a poetical fiction, invented in the spirit of the late romances, like *Amadis de Gaul,* but still preserving the supposed historical foundations of Turpin, joined with the *Pomarium* of Ricobaldo. The *Innamorato* is full of every kind of life,

---

[1] " I was sorry for my Emperor Charlemagne, seeing that his history has been ill conceived and worse written."—*Morgante Maggiore*, canto i. 4.

action, and character, and is seriously romantic ; a slight
vein of humour, however, is blended with the narrative,
and finds expression in the reason which Boiardo, in
the opening of his poem, gives for Turpin's silence on
the subject of Orlando's passion :—

> Questa novella è nota a poca gente,
> Perchè Turpino istesso la nascose,
> Credendo forse a quel conte valente
> Esser le sue scritte dispettose,
> Poichè contra ad amor pur fu perdente
> Colui chi vinse tutte l' altre cose,
> Dico d' Orlando il cavalier ad atto :
> Non più parole omai, veniamo al fatto.[1]

Ariosto, coming the last, resolved to relate the
madness of Orlando which was the consequence of his
love.   Adhering, like his two predecessors, to the authority
of Turpin, he combines the irony of Pulci with the
romance of Boiardo.   While he professes to make Orlando's
misfortunes the main subject of his poem, that paladin is
not nearly so prominent in his story as some of the other
characters ; and indeed, as far as the poem has any external unity, this consists in the adventures of Ruggiero
and Bradamante, which furnish Ariosto with materials
for the execution of his main avowed purpose, namely the
celebration of the House of Este, his patrons.   But, in
fact, the real intention of Ariosto is declared in the first
two lines of his poem—

> Le donne, i cavalier, l' arme, gli amori,
> Le cortesie, l' audaci impresi io canto.[2]

What struck his imagination was the extraordinary
contrast presented by the vast idea of chivalry as it had
accumulated for ages in the hands of superstitious chroniclers, professional trouvères, and literary poets, when compared with the experience of the actual world, as it passed

---

[1] " This story is known to few people because Turpin himself concealed it,
thinking, perhaps, that his history would be disrespectful to that valiant
count, since he who conquered everything else, fell a victim to love ; Orlando
I mean, that accomplished knight.   Now no more words : let us come to
deeds."—*Orlando Innamorato*, canto i. 2.

[2] " I sing of ladies, knights, arms, loves, courtly deeds, bold adventures,"
—*O. F.* canto i. 1.

before his own eyes.　His design in his *Furioso* was to
unite the spirit of the *roman* with the spirit of the *fabliau*,
the chivalrous element of the *Chanson de Roland* with the
bourgeois element in the *Decameron*.　He achieved his object
by narrating with the gravity of an ingenuous historian, and
in a style of studied purity and simplicity, the marvellous
adventures of Charlemagne and his peers, handed down
to him on the authority of Turpin and with all the em-
bellishments of Boiardo.　At the same time he hints to
the reader the extent of his own faith in his narrative by
a sustained commentary on the wonders he records, by
sly epithets and phrases which neutralise the effect of
his extravagant fancies, and by abrupt transitions from
the world of magic to the atmosphere of real life.　In
the quasi-historical part of his narrative propriety required him to be serious ; and, in such passages, his style
becomes lifeless and mechanical ; he vainly seeks for
elevation and sublimity by the introduction of allegorical
personages.[1]　But where his materials allow him to pass
into the region of romance, his fancy regains its liberty,
and he delights the reader with a thousand varying moods
of pathos, humour, and reflection.　Sometimes it pleases
him to write as the sceptical man of the world.　Thus
Angelica, a type of that womanhood which is dwelt upon
in the second part of the *Romance of the Rose*, deceives
Sacripante, an Oriental king, who has come for the love
of her from his distant dominions, and meets her, quite
by accident, in a forest unheard of out of the pages of
romance.　On Angelica's profession of love Ariosto
moralises as follows :—

> Forse era ver, ma non però credibile
> A chi del senso suo fosse signore ;
> Ma parve facilmente a lui possibile,
> Ch' era perduto in vie più grave errore.
> Quel che l' uom vide, Amor gli fa invisibile,
> E l' invisibil fa vedere Amore.

---

[1] This opinion is contrary to that of W. S. Rose, who praises Ariosto's
allegorical personages.　See notes to his translation of *Orlando Furioso, passim*.
The reader can judge for himself by referring to *Orlando Furioso*, cantos vi.
x. xlii.

> Questo creduto fu, chè 'l miser suole
> Dar facil credenza a quel che vuole.[1]

On the other hand, he sometimes lets us see that he has an imaginative sympathy with the greatness of romantic conception. The extravagant courtesy of chivalry pleased his humour, and he delighted in carrying it to absurd extremes. When, for example, Rinaldo and Ferraù are fighting about the aforesaid Angelica, they suddenly become aware that the cunning damsel has stolen away. Immediately they leave off fighting, and, mounting together on Baiardo, Rinaldo's enchanted horse, ride off in pursuit of her. The poet makes this a text for commenting, with an air of amused admiration, on the chivalry of the good old times :—

> Oh gran bontà de' cavalieri antiqui !
> Eran rivali, eran di fe' diversi,
> E si sentian degli aspri colpi iniqui
> Per tutta la persona anco dolersi ;
> Eppur per selve oscure e calli obliqui
> Insieme van, senza sospetto aversi.[2]

Magic and commonplace go hand in hand through Ariosto's story. Bradamante, one of the masculine heroines of the *Orlando Furioso*, having to obtain a magic ring from a certain Brunello, comes in quest of him to a country inn, which is charmingly painted from the ordinary Italian *osteria*, and a canto is closed very characteristically with a scene of bustle and confusion, the cause of which, says Ariosto, shall be related in the next canto. In the next canto, accordingly, after the usual moral reflections of the poet, we see Bradamante hurrying out with the servants of the inn,—just as English rustics turn off an

[1] "Perchance 'twas true, but it would not have been credible to him who was master of his senses ; to him, however, it appeared easily possible, because he was lost in the most grievous of all error. Love makes invisible what a man sees. Love makes man see the invisible. What she said was believed, because poor human nature is wont to give easy belief to what it desires."—*O. F.* canto i. 56.

[2] "O the excellence of the knights of old ! They were rivals ; they were of different faiths ; they felt all their bodies aching with the hard blows they had given each other ; nevertheless, they go off together through dark woods and devious paths, without feeling any suspicion of each other."—*O. F.* canto i. 22.

ale-bench to stare at a balloon,—and fortunate enough to behold the following remarkable spectacle :—

> Vede passar un gran destriero alato,
> Che porta in aria un cavaliero armato.
>
> Grandi eran l' ale e di solor diverso,
> E vi sedea nel mezzo un cavaliero,
> Di ferro armato luminoso e terso,
> E vêr ponente avea dritto il sentiero ;
> Calossi, e fu tra le montagne immerso ;
> E come dicea l' oste (e dicea il vero),
> Quello era un necromante, e facea spesso
> Quel varco, or più da lungi, or più di presso.[1]

Not only does Ariosto heighten the sense of irony in his romance by importing into it the spirit of the *fabliau ;* but he gives an appearance of reality to his supernatural incidents by describing them with the genius of a painter. Bradamante having, after some exciting adventures, succeeded in mastering the wizard, tries to catch his magic horse. But this is not so easy :—

> La donna va per prenderlo nel freno ;
> E quel l' aspetta finchè se gli accosta :
> Poi spiega l' ale per l' aer sereno,
> E si ripon non lungi a mezza costa ;
> Ella lo segue ; e quel nè più nè meno
> Si leva in aria, e non troppo si scosta ;
> Come fa la cornacchia in secca arena
> Che dietro il cane or qua or la si mena.[2]

Such was the admirable skill with which Ariosto fused his heterogeneous materials into a beautiful and harmonious whole. Considered simply as a work of art the *Orlando Furioso* must excite in the mind of every capable critic enthusiastic admiration. In it we see a reflection

[1] "She saw pass a great winged charger which carries in the air an armed rider. Large were his wings and of different colour, and between them sat a knight in iron armour luminous and polished, directing his flight westward. He descended and was lost to sight among the mountains ; and as the host said (and said truly), he was a wizard, and often made that passage sometimes in the distance, sometimes close at hand."—*O. F.* canto iv. 4, 5.

[2] "The lady tries to catch him by the rein, and he waits till she comes up to him, then spreads his wings in the serene air, and alights at a little distance alongside of her. She follows him, and he as before, rises into the air without going too far away, just as a raven does on dry sand when a dog is following him behind."—*O. F.* canto iv. 43.

of the conflict of all the great forces that produced the
Italian Renaissance ; mediæval memories of the Troubadours and the Trouvères, of the Provençal lyric and the
Romantic Gests on the one hand, of John de Meung and
the satiric *fabliau* on the other ; memories mixed with the
mythology of Greece and Rome ; joined to the Court life
of modern Italy; coloured and vivified by imagery derived
from the painting, sculpture, architecture, and classical
learning of the Italian cities. The elements contributed
from all these sources to the narrative, are combined in a
style so pure, so idiomatic, and so flowing, that each
stanza seems to have taken shape, *currente calamo*, instead
of having been fashioned, as we know was the case, with
long and laborious art.

But it was not to be expected that to the English
reader of the seventeenth century the *Orlando Furioso*
would present itself under the same aspect as to ourselves.
To Spenser—the serious Cambridge Platonist, the Protestant Humanist, the friend of Sidney, the courtier for
whom the ideals of chivalry had still some meaning, the
citizen of a nation beginning to be conscious of the greatness
of its destinies—the irony of Ariosto's conception was
imperceptible. He felt only the beauty of the artistic result. He observed the " variety of matter " in the *Furioso*,
and when he considered that he might add to it all
the philosophical and theological resources furnished by
Allegory, it is not surprising that in this respect he should
have hoped to " overgo " Ariosto. He perceived that, as
the Italian poet had taken for his subject the deeds of
Charlemagne and his peers, it was open to himself, as an
Englishman, to base his narrative on the history of King
Arthur. Admiring the great diversity of action and
character in his master's work, he thought that he might
conduct the plan of his own poem on similar lines by
means of his allegorical personages. But he was far
removed from that spirit of contemplative scepticism and
irony which enabled Ariosto to combine his conflicting
materials into one harmonious organism.

When we examine how far Spenser was able to carry

his design of conveying moral truth by means of Ariosto's romantic methods, we see that his allegory carried him safely through the first two books of the *Faery Queen.* The adventures assigned respectively to the Knights of Holiness and Temperance are well conceived ; the various incidents in their career give interest to the narrative ; their failure to achieve their purpose unaided is a happy stroke of invention, as it gives an opportunity for the introduction of Prince Arthur, whose figure is necessary to the organism of the poem. But in the third and fourth books the allegorical machinery breaks down. Though the adventure of Chastity is assigned to Sir Scudamour, the interest of the third book centres almost entirely in the person of Britomart, while Prince Arthur has nothing to do with the advancement of the action. Equally insignificant is the part assigned to the British prince in the fourth book, in which also the idea of the virtue of Friendship, which ought to be prominent, is lost in a multitude of irrelevant episodes. The subject of the fifth book is Justice ; but this, so far from being the "private virtue" promised by the poet, is almost entirely *political ;* relating either to the government of Lord Grey in Ireland, the attacks of Philip II. on the Low Countries, or the religious backslidings of Henry IV. of France. In the sixth book the allegory, which relates to the virtue of Courtesy, is chiefly remarkable for its covert reference to the amour of Sir Walter Raleigh, which brought on him the displeasure of the Queen.

The execution of the design equally breaks down on the purely epical side ; the poem lacks human interest. We cannot believe in the reality, or consequently concern ourselves with the fortunes of beings who are felt to be mere abstractions. Spenser himself did not care about his personages, and his indifference makes him a languid story-teller. In this respect his style presents an extraordinary contrast with that of his master. I cannot give the reader a better illustration of the difference between the two poets than by comparing Ariosto's description of the battle between Orlando and the Ork (a sea-monster of

the same voracious tendencies as the Minotaur), and
Spenser's description of the fight between St. George and
the Dragon at the end of the first book of the *Faery Queen*.

Ariosto's narrative is so concise that it will be as easy
to give it in the poet's own words as in abstract.   Orlando
has set out in a boat with a cable and anchor to attack
the Ork, and sees a lady chained to the rock : [1]—

> Perchè gli è ancor lontana, e perchè china
> La faccia tien, non ben chi sia discerne ;
> Tira in fretta ambi i remi, e s' avvicina
> Con gran disio di più notizia averne.
> Ma mugghiar sente in questo la marina,
> E rimbombar le selve, e le caverne :
> Gonfiansi l' onde ; ed ecco il mostro appare,
> Che sotto il petto ha quasi ascoso il mare.

> Come d' oscura valle umida ascende
> Nube di pioggia e di tempesta pregna,
> Che più che cieca notte si distende
> Per tutto 'l mondo, e par che 'l giorno spegna
> Cosi nuota la fera, e del mar prende
> Tanto che si può dir che tutto il tegna :
> Fremono l' onde.   Orlando, in sè raccolto,
> La mira altier, nè cangia cor nè volto.

> E come quel ch' avea il pensier ben fermo,
> Di quanto volea far, si mosse ratto ;
> E perchè alla donzella essere schermo,
> E la fera assalir potesse a un tratto,
> Entrò fra l' orca e lei col palischermo,
> Nel fodero lasciando il brando piatto ;
> L' ancora con la gomona in man prese,
> Poi con gran cor l' orribil mostro attese.

---

[1] " As she is still afar off, and keeps her face downwards, he sees not
clearly who she is.   In haste he plies both oars and approaches with great
desire to have more knowledge of her.   But now he hears the sea roar, and
the woods and caves rebellow.   The waves swell ; and see ! the monster
appears, who has almost hidden the sea under his breast.   As from a dark
valley ascends in moisture a cloud pregnant with rain and tempest, which
spreads blacker than black night through all the world, and seems to blot out
the day ; so swims the beast and takes of the sea so much that one may say
he holds it all.   The waves boil.   Orlando, collected in spirit, regards him
loftily and changes neither heart nor countenance.   And as one who had his
thoughts well determined on all that he would do, he moved quickly, and, in
order at once to be a defence to the damsel and to assault the beast, he entered

Tosto che l' orca s' accostò, e scoperse
Nel schifo Orlando con poco intervallo,
Per inghiottirlo tanta bocca aperse
Ch' entrato un uomo vi saria a cavallo.
Si spinse Orlando innanzi, e se gl' immerse
Con quella áncora in gola, e, s' io non fallo,
Col battello anco ; e l' áncora attaccolle
E nel palato e nella lingua molle :

Sì che nè più si puon calar di sopra,
Ne alzar di sotto le mascelle orrende.
Così chi nelle mine il ferro adopra,
La terra, ovunque si fa via, suspende,
Chè subita ruina non lo cuopra,
Mentre mal cauto al suo lavoro intende.
Da un amo all' altro l' ancora è tanto alta,
Che non v' arriva Orlando, se non salta.

Messo il puntello, e fattosi sicuro,
Che il mostro più serrar non può la bocca,
Stringe la spada, e per quell' antro oscuro,
Di qua e di là con tagli e punte tocca
Come si può, poi che son dentro al muro
Giunti i nemici, ben difender rocca ;
Così difender l' orca si potea
Dal paladin che nella gola avea.

Dal dolor vinta or sopra il mar si lancia,
E mostra i fianchi e le scagliose schiene ;
Or dentro vi s' attuffa, e con la pancia
Muove dal fondo e fa salir l' arene.
Sentendo l' acqua il cavalier di Francia,
Che troppo abbonda, a nuoto fuor ne viene :
Lascia l' ancora fitta, e in mano prende
La fune che dall' ancora depende.

---

in his boat between the Ork and her, leaving his sword flat in its scabbard.
The anchor with its cable he took in hand ; then with great heart he awaited
the horrible monster.   Soon as the Ork approached and discovered Orlando
close by in the skiff, he opened so wide a mouth to swallow him that a man on
horseback might have entered in.   Orlando darted forward, and dived with his
anchor into the throat, and, if I am not mistaken, with the boat as well ; he
fixed the anchor in his palate and soft tongue ; so that he can no longer lower
from above nor raise from below his horrid jaws.   So one who works the iron
in the mine suspends the earth wherever he makes way, lest a sudden fall
should bury him, while without heeding he minds his labour.   From one fluke
to the other the anchor is so high that Orlando cannot reach up without
leaping.   Having fixed the point, and made himself secure against the monster
closing his mouth, he draws his sword and through that dark cave plies him on
this side and on that with cuts and thrusts.   As well may one defend a hold
when the enemy are now within the wall, as the Ork defend himself from the

E con quella ne vien nuotando in fretta
Verso lo scoglio, ove, fermato il piede,
Tira l' ancora a sè, che in bocca stretta
Con le due punte il brutto mostro fiede.
L' orca a seguire il canape è costretta
Da quella forza ch' ogni forza eccede ;
Da quella forza che più in una scossa
Tira, ch' in dieci un argano far possa.

Come toro salvatico, ch' al corno
Gittar si senta un improviso laccio,
Salta di qua di là, s' aggira intorno,
Si colca e lieva, e non può uscir d' impaccio :
Così fuor del suo antico almo soggiorno
L' orca, tratta per forza di quel braccio,
Con mille guizzi e mille strane ruote,
Segue la fune e scior non se ne puote.

Di bocca il sangue in tanta copia fonde,
Che questo oggi il Mar Rosso si può dire,
Dove in tal guisa ella percuote l' onde,
Ch' insino al fondo le vedreste aprire :
Ed or ne bagna il cielo, e il lume asconde
Del chiaro sol ; tanto le fa salire.
Rimbombano al rumor, ch' intorno s' ode,
Le selve, i monti, e le lontane prode.

In this wonderful description we admire the gravity of
the narrator, and the vividness of his strokes, which seem
to bring a most marvellous adventure within the domain

paladin whom he has within his throat. Vanquished by his pain, now he
bounds out of the sea and discovers his flanks and scaly back ; now he dives
down, stirs up with his belly the sands at the bottom, and makes them fly.
The knight of France, perceiving that the water flows in too fast, comes
swimming out ; he leaves the anchor fixed, and takes in his hand the rope
that is fastened to the anchor. And with that he goes swiftly swimming towards
the rock, where, having steadied his foot, he draws the anchor towards him,
which, fast in its mouth, grapples the hideous monster with its two flukes.
The Ork is constrained to follow the cable by that unequalled force, which
draws further with one jerk than a windlass could draw with ten. As a wild
bull, who feels on a sudden the lasso round his horn, leaps to this side and to
that, wheels round, lies down, and rises up, yet cannot get free from the noose ;
so, drawn by the might of that arm from his ancient peaceful haunts, the
Ork, with a thousand jerks and a thousand strange twists follows the cable and
cannot get loose. From his mouth the blood pours in such abundance that
to this day while the sea might be called Red, while in such wise he lashes the waves
that you might have seen them open to the bottom. And now he bathes the
sky and hides the clear light of the sun ; so high he makes them leap. The
woods, the hills, the distant shores rebellow with a universal roar."—*Orlando
Furioso,* canto xi. 34-43.

of reality ; the brevity of the style which prevents all feeling of languor ; the approximation to prose idiom so judiciously combined with the musical ring of the disyllabic rhymes, and the skill with which the active narrative is accentuated by simile.

Spenser's manner is different enough. He first of all gives us a description of the dragon, extending over seven stanzas—a splendid painting. This is a sample of the manner in which the monster impresses his form on the poet's brilliant imagination :—

> His flaggy wings when forth he did display
> Were lyke two sayles, in which the hollow wind
> Is gathered full and worketh speedy way ;
> And eke the pennes that did his pinions bind
> Were lyke mayne yards with flying canvass lynd,
> With which whenas him list the ayre to beat,
> And there by force unwonted passage fynd,
> The clouds before him fledd for terror great,
> And all the heavens stood still amazed at his threat.

Now, remembering that Ariosto's description of the Ork was given in a simile of four lines, we expect something tremendous from an animal whose properties require sixty-three, and the impetus of whose body can stop the revolution of the spheres. The monster, however, is far from making the most of his advantages. His first movement is to upset horse and man with a brush of his tail. He then carries them both up into the air

> So far as ewen bow a shaft may send,

but it never occurs to him to drop them. The Ork was a better general, as we have seen him force Orlando to leave his throat by the manœuvre of diving. The dragon is wounded under the wing, at which he roars like an angry sea, and tears out the spear with his claws. These three actions occupy three stanzas. Winding his tail round the horse, he compels him to throw his rider, who attacks the dragon on foot but is unable to penetrate his brazen scales. The dragon, impatient of the combat, and endeavouring to fly off, is prevented by his wounded wing ; whereat filled with fury, and remembering

his tail, he again fells the knight to the ground.   These
incidents carry us forward fifty-four lines.   Fortunately
the champion falls backwards into a well of remarkable
virtue :—

> Both Silo this and Jordan did excel,
> And the English Bath, and eke the German Spau,
> Ne can Cephise nor Hebrus match this well.

It is the Well of Life.   The golden Phœbus now begins
to steep his fiery face in the western billows, and St.
George spends the night in the well, while his lady
betakes herself to prayer.   The fortunes of the second
day's fight are much the same as the first, except that
the dragon leaves off in worse case, having his head
cloven, five joints of his tail cut off, and one of his paws
hewn in sunder.   He pours blasts of fire out of his mouth,
and the knight, being forced to retire, stumbles and falls,
this time under a tree whence flows a stream of balm.
The dragon dares not approach the holy place, so that
his enemy refreshes himself all night, Una being still in
prayer.

> The joyous daye gan early to appeare,
> And fayre Aurora from the deawy bed
> Of aged Tithone gan herself to reare,
> With rosy cheeks for shame as blushing red ;

and the knight, arising at the same time, defies his enemy
who comes open-mouthed to make away with him at a
rush.   His impetuosity proves his destruction.   A thrust
of the sword into his throat puts an end to his abominable
existence, and he falls to the ground with the shock of an
earthquake.

The battle thus lasts through three days and fifty-five
stanzas, or nearly five hundred lines.   It is evident that
the small number of incidents in proportion to the length
of the story must prevent all rapidity of movement.   The
dilettante manner in which Spenser treats the whole
affair is illustrated by the four lines of description, cited
above, that open the third day's combat.   There is also

a want of realistic imagination about the narrative which prevents belief. The stupidity of the dragon in not making better use of his wings has already been condemned. In the description we hear the clashing of his brazen scales, and feel his fiery eyes, which blaze like two great beacons ; but during the fight these picturesque circumstances are not brought to our memory. Ariosto would have given life to this part of the story by striking terror into St. George's horse. We see no reason why, when the dragon has once carried horse and man off their feet, he should not grind them to pieces in his three ranks of iron teeth,

> In which yet trickling blood and gobbets raw
> Of late devoured bodies did appeare.

If, however, it be urged that Spenser had no need of such realistic minuteness as the fight is an allegory, then it must be remembered that, except the Well and the Tree of Life, there is nothing in the adventure to recall the allegory to our mind. The dragon is the best described dragon in romance, but he has no diabolical symbols. St. George loses the shield of Faith, and scarcely feels the want of it ; and when the monster is killed by a thrust of the knight's sword in his throat, we forget that this weapon is the Sword of the Spirit. If Spenser is not to be compared with Ariosto, he must be compared with Bunyan, and the necessary inference can be drawn from the parallel battle between Christian and Apollyon.

It must be decided then that, in the poetical qualities required to sustain the interest of the reader through a poem so vast in its scope and in its actual length as the *Faery Queen*, Spenser was far inferior to the master whom he imitated. His poem is deficient alike in unity of action and in clearness of moral. But it must be at once added that, if we are content with Lowell to set aside the design of the work, to regard the *Faery Queen* as a great picture gallery, and to fix our attention on the detached ideas and conceptions that it embodies, the imagination of Spenser is frequently found mounting to heights of poetry which are beyond the reach of Ariosto. The Italian poet was incapable of conceiving the sublime image of Chivalric Honour which is enshrined by Spenser in the following most noble stanza :—

> In woods, in waves, in warres, she wonts to dwell,
> And shall be found with perill and with paine ;
> Ne can the man that moulds in idle cell
> Unto her happy mansions attaine :
> Before her gate high God did sweat ordaine,
> And wakeful watches ever to abide ;
> But easy is the way and passage plaine
> That leads to pleasure : it may soon be spied ;
> And day and night to all her gates stand open wide.

Ariosto's representation of character again,—especially female character,—though full of human interest, wants fineness and delicacy. Spenser's female portraits are coloured with a purity and refinement of feeling worthy of Homer in his character of Nausicaa. His " maidenliness " of feeling, as Coleridge well calls it, is brilliantly exemplified in the episode of Britomart, one of the few actors in the *Faery Queen* who awake living interest. Several of the situations in which this heroine is involved, arising out of the mistakes caused by her masculine attire, are devised and treated with great beauty of imagination. Her " maidenliness," with its freedom from prudery, in the episode of Malecasta, makes a fine contrast to the effrontery of Ariosto in the parallel story of Ricciardetto and Fiordispina ; and there is much charm in her assumption of bravado to conceal her womanly softness, and in Amoret's mixed feelings of gratitude and reserve towards her supposed male preserver. In such passages we feel the influence of Sidney's knightly ideal, a standard which was practically unknown in Italy, as we see from Ariosto's treatment of the story of Bradamante. Not less admirable is the description of Una's adventures in the first book, and of the temptations of Sir Guyon in the second, episodes in which Spenser reaches the highest level of poetical invention.

Ariosto occasionally introduces allegorical personages

---

[1] *Faerie Queene*, book ii. canto iii. 41.

unto his *Orlando*, but always with very ill success ; indeed these conceptions of his want sublimity as much as Spenser's abstract knights want human interest. Compare his description of the monster, who attacks Rinaldo in the Forest of Ardennes, and who is apparently the impersonation of jealousy, with any of Spenser's Seven Deadly Sins :—

> Tutto in tratto vide il ciel turbato,
> Sparito il sol tra nuvoli nascoso,
> Ed uscir fuor d' una caverna oscura
> Un strano mostro in femminil figura.
>
> Mill' occhi in capo avea senza palpebre ;
> Non può serrarli, e non credo che dorma.
> Non men che gli occhi avea l' orecchie crebre ;
> Avea, in loco di crin, serpi a gran torma.
> Fuor delle diaboliche tenebre
> Nel mondo usci la spaventevold forma.
> Un fiero e maggior serpe ha per la coda
> Che pel petto si gira, e che l' annoda.[1]

Here, on the other hand, is the figure of Avarice in the procession in the House of Pride :—

> Next greedy Avarice by him did ride
> Upon a camel loaden all with gold :
> Two iron coffers hong on either side,
> With precious metall full as they might hold ;
> And in his lap an heape of coine he told,
> For of his wicked pelfe his God he made,
> And unto hell himself for money sold ;
> Accursed usury was all his trade,
> And right and wrong y-like in equall balance waide.
>
> His life was nigh unto deth's dore y-plaste,
> And thredbare cote and cobled shoes he ware,
> Ne scarse good morsell all his life did taste,
> But both from backe and belly still did spare,
> To fill his bags and richesse to compare :

---

[1] "Suddenly he saw the heaven darkened, and the sun hidden in clouds, and issuing from a dark cavern a strange monster in female form. In her head she had a thousand eyes without eyelashes : she cannot close them and I believe she never sleeps : her ears are as numerous as her eyes : in place of hair she has a host of serpents. Forth from the darkness of hell issued the frightful shape into the world, holding by the tail a fierce serpent huger than all the rest, which winds round her breast in a knot."—*O. F.* canto xlii. 46, 47.

> Yet childe ne kinsman living had he none
> To leave them to ; but thorough daily care
> To get, and nightly feare to lose his owne,
> He led a wretched life unto himself unknowne.
>
> Most greedie wight, whom nothing might suffice ;
> Whose greedie lust did lacke in greatest store ;
> Whose need had end but no end covetise ;
> Whose welth was want, whose plenty made him pore ;
> Who had enough, yet wished ever more ;
> A vile disese ; and eke in foot and hand
> A grievous gout tormented him full sore,
> That well he could not touch, nor go, nor stand ;
> Such one was Avarice, the fourth of this faire band.[1]

Of the same class are the descriptions of Despair, of Sleep, and, above all, of the Titaness, Mutability, as given in the unfinished cantos of that name, a fragment which I think on the whole, both in conception and execution, the most sublime part of the *Faery Queen.*

Ariosto's word-painting is unequalled for brilliancy and distinctness of colour, but Spenser surpasses him in depth of imagination.   The metal wall under the tapestry in the House of Busirane is likened to

> A discoloured snake, whose hidden snares
> Through the greene grass his long bright burnished back declares.[2]

Prince Arthur, sleeping armed in the dusk, is thus described :—

> His lord in silver slumber lay,
> Like to the Evening Star adorned with deawy ray.[3]

Of a sensual imagination the poet says—

> He like an adder, lurking in the weeds,
> His wandering thoughts in deepe desire does steepe.[4]

Horror is added to the idea of Despair by the character of the landscape round the cave supposed to be the dwelling of the Abstraction :—

[1] *Faerie Queene,* book i. canto iv. 20.   [2] *Ibid.* book iii. canto xi. 28.
[3] *Ibid.* book vi. canto vii. 19.   [4] *Ibid.* book ii. canto v. 34.

> All about old stocks and stubs of trees,
> Whereon nor fruit nor leafe was ever seen,
> Did hang upon the ragged rocky knees.[1]

But the same hand can with equal propriety paint by means of allegory the bright surface and perpetual movement of a river, as in the following exquisite stanza from the episode describing the Marriage of the Thames and the Medway :—

> Then came the Bride, the lovely Medua came,
> Clad in a vesture of unknown geare,
> And uncouthe fashion, that her well became,
> That seemed like silver sprinkled here and theare
> With glittering spangs yet did like stars appeare,
> And waved upon like water chamelot,
> To hide the metal, which yet everywhere
> Bewrayed itself, to let men plainly wot
> It was no mortall worke, which seemed and yet was not.[2]

Nor does Spenser excel merely in passages of external pictorial fancy. His imagination is as subtle as it is vivid. Witness the simile employed to express Britomart's joy at first hearing the praises of Artegall, her unacknowledged lover :—

> The loving mother, that nine months doth beare
> In the deare closett of her painfull side
> Her tender babe, it seeing safe appeare,
> Doth not so much rejoice as she rejoiced there.[3]

And the image of Satan driving the Seven Deadly Sins is one of extraordinary strength and sublimity :—

> And after all upon the waggon beame
> Rode Sathan, with a smarting whip in hand,
> With which he forward lasht the laesy teme,
> So oft as Slowth still in the mire did stand :
> Huge routs of people did about them band,
> Shouting for joy ; and still, before their way,
> A foggy mist had covered all the land ;
> And underneath their feet all scattered lay
> Dead skulls, and bones of men, whose lives had gone astray.[4]

---

[1] *Faerie Queene*, book i. canto ix. 34.
[2] *Ibid.* book iv. canto xi. 45.
[3] *Ibid.* book iii. canto ii. 11.   [4] *Ibid.* book i. canto iv. 36.

The *Faery Queen* is not only to be regarded as a
great picture gallery. It is also a vast experiment in
English metrical composition. The passages I have cited
above show the greatness of Spenser's genius as a painter
in words and images, but they furnish equally remarkable
proofs of his powers as a poetical musician. We saw
from *The Shepherd's Calendar* how much he was preoccupied with inventing a form of diction proper to the
peculiar cast of his pastoral conceptions, and how
successful his experiments proved. In the same way,
when he engaged in the composition of a long narrative
poem his first care was to devise a new metrical vehicle ;
and such was the art with which he constructed it, that
his invention has established itself as one of the standard
measures of the English language. The Spenser stanza
is plainly a development of the eight - lined ballad
strophe first introduced by Chaucer from France. This
consisted of two quatrains with three sets of rhymes, the
quatrains being connected with each other by a common
rhyme in the fourth and fifth lines, thus, a b a b b c b c.
To this measure Spenser gave a new movement by
adding an Alexandrine, rhyming with the sixth and
eighth lines, thus, a b a b b c b c c. He thus approximated
the character of the stanza to the *ottava rima* of the
Italians, in which the last two lines rhyme together and
mark definitely the close of each strophe. Warton blames
Spenser for the long-drawn languor of his stanza,[1] and
indeed, if the object of the poet had been merely to
invent a new vehicle for a metrical narrative, he could
not have devised a more improper instrument ; since the
number of the rhymes and the complexity of their
arrangement necessarily prevent rapidity of movement.
But, as we have seen, the story in the *Faery Queen*
formed only a part of Spenser's design, and his prime
motive was to invent a style which should correspond
with the allegorical nature of his subject. " Spenser
himself *affects* the obsolete," says Pope, in his very just

---

[1] " Remarks on Spenser's Stanza, Versification, and Language," Todd's
Spenser, vol. ii. p. cxxvi.

criticism.[1]   And Daniel in his *Delia* alludes to the archaism of Spenser's chivalric poem, written

In aged accents and untimely words.[2]

But though it be true, as Ben Jonson says, that Spenser "in affecting the ancients writ no language," this is not necessarily a condemnation of his style, because his diction required to be adapted to an action laid in the non-existent region of Fairy Land.

Judged from this point of view I consider Spenser's treatment of his stanza to be a triumph of art. His style exactly suits the unreal nature of his subject; it is an excellent vehicle for the manner in which he himself excelled,—lofty ideal sentiment, brilliant allegorical fancy, flights of abstract morality and melodious combinations of metrical harmony. He was the first to show what could be effected in English poetry by the command of lofty style. Having in *The Shepherd's Calendar* made his first experiment in what E. K. calls "the knitting of sentences whych they call the joints and members thereof," he now invented a new instrument which he applied with a beautiful ease and mastery to the various materials on which he worked. Effects of metre, which had been foreshadowed by Surrey in one or two fine sonnets, were now extended to suit all kinds of moods and feelings. The general effect of the union between Chaucer's archaic style and the terseness of Latin poetry may be judged from a stanza like the following :—

> "Love of yourselfe," she saide, "and *dear constrainte*
> Lets me not sleepe, but waste the *wearie night*
> In *secret anguish* and *unpitied plaint*,
> While you in *carelesse sleepe* are drowned quight ;"
> Her doubtful words made that redoubted knight
> Suspect her truth ; yet since no' untruth he knew
> Her fawning love with foule disdainful spight
> He would not shend, but said, "Deare Dame, I rew
> That for my sake unknowne such griefe unto you grew." [3]

But Spenser when he pleases, can drop his archaism

---

[1] *Epistle to Augustus*, v. 97.   [2] *Sonnets to Delia*, lv.
[3] *Faerie Queene*, book i. canto i. 53.

and rise to the noble directness required by a lofty
theme, as thus :—

> Then woe, and woe, and everlasting woe,
> Be to the Briton babe that shall be borne,
> To live in thraldome of his father's foe ;
> Late king, now captive ; late lord, now forlorne ;
> The world's reproach, the cruel victor's scorne ;
> Banisht from princely bowre to wastfull wood !
> O ! who shall helpe me to lament and mourne
> The royal seed, the antique Trojan blood,
> Whose empire longer here than ever any stood ? [1]

In the following stanza there is a fine simplicity which
is like Homer :—

> But these conditions doe to him propound,
> That if I vanquish him he shall obey
> My law, and ever to my lore be bound ;
> And so will I if he me vanquish may,
> Whatever he shall like to doe or say :
> Goe straight, and take with thee to witness it,
> Six of thy fellows of the best array ;
> And beare with you both wine and juncates fit,
> And bid him eate : henceforth he oft shall hungry sit. [2]

Occasionally he breaks up his stanza in dialogue like
the "stichomythia" of the Greek drama ; not always
with a happy effect. But his power of adapting his metre
to the purposes of dialectic may be judged from the
following stanza, taken from a philosophical debate
between Artegall, the knight of Justice, and a metaphysical giant, who maintains that all things may be
weighed and measured in human scales :—

> For take thy balaunce, if thou art so wise,
> And weigh the wind that under heaven doth blow ;
> Or weigh the light that in the east doth rise ;
> Or weigh the thought that from man's mind doth flow ;
> But if the weight of these thou canst not show,
> Weigh but one word that from thy lips doth fall ;
> For how canst thou those greater secrets know,
> That dost not know the least thing of them all ?
> Ill can he rule the great, that cannot reach the small. [3]

---

[1] *Faerie Queene*, book iii. canto iii. 42.
[2] *Ibid.* book v. canto iv. 49.   [3] *Ibid.* book v. canto ii. 43.

Beautiful metrical effects are produced by various devices. The Spenser stanza gives great scope for the use of reduplication, whether of ideas or words, *e.g.*—

> Born of one mother, in one happie mold,
> Born at one burden, in one happie morn.

> He, in the first flower of my freshest age,
> Betrothéd me unto the onely haire
> Of a most mighty king, most rich and sage ;
> Was never prince so faithful and so faire,
> Was never prince so meek and debonaire.[1]

> But O vaine judgments and conditions vaine,
> The which the prisoner points unto the free !
> The whiles I him condemn, and deem his paine,
> He where he lists goes loose and laughs at me :
> So ever loose so ever happie be,
> But whereso loose and happie that thou art,
> Know, Marinell, that this is all for thee.[2]

Another effect is produced by combination and permutation :—

> Behind him was Reproch, Repentaunce, Shame ;
> Reproch the first, Shame next, Repent behind ;
> Repentaunce feeble, sorrowful, and lame,
> Reproch despiteful, careless, and unkind ;
> Shame most ill-favoured, bestiall, and blind ;
> Shame lowered, Repentaunce sighed, Reproch did scold ;
> Reproch sharp stings, Repentaunce whips entwined,
> Shame burning brond irons in her hand did hold ;
> All three to each unlike, yet made all in one mold.[3]

Experiments are also made in the metrical combinations of proper names, thus preparing the way for those splendid effects of verbal harmony which Milton produces in *Paradise Lost* and *Paradise Regained* :—

> Let Scaldis tell and let tell Hania,
> And let the marsh of Esthambruges tell,
> What colour were their waters that same day,
> And all the moor 'twixt Elvesham and Dell,
> With blood of Henalois that therein fell.[4]

---

[1] *Faerie Queene,* book i. canto ii. 23.
[2] *Ibid.* book iv. canto xii. 11.   [3] *Ibid.* book iii. canto xii. 24.
[4] *Ibid.* book ii. canto x. 24.

From what has been said it will be seen that the place of Spenser in the History of Poetry is a very peculiar one. He cannot be ranked with the great poets whose universal ideas, applicable to human nature in all times and places, raised them to the empyrean of imagination—with Homer and Dante and Shakespeare. He cannot be ranked with that great, though secondary, order of inventors whose penetrating insight pierces through the outward shows surrounding them in their own age to the ideal truth of things—with Chaucer, Ariosto, and Cervantes. In most respects his position in the world of imagination is analogous to the position of Sidney in the world of action. Both were inspired by ideals springing out of a decaying order of society ; and the same environment of circumstance which prevented Sidney from putting his theories of knighthood into practice gave an appearance of unreality to Spenser's epical conceptions.

Spenser was the poet of chivalry. But the times had confined the practice of chivalry within the area of the Court, and all that it was possible for him to portray in verse was the image either of the " brave knight " presented under the " cloudy allegory " of the *Faery Queen*, or of the " perfect courtier," as he saw it in the character of Sidney, and idealised it in *Mother Hubberd's Tale*. Fair and noble is the possibility that he paints for the imagination.

> Yet the brave Courtier, in whose beauteous thought
> Regard of honour harbours more than ought,
> Doth loath such base condition, to backbite
> Anie's good name for envie or despite.
> He stands on tearmes of honourable minde
> Ne will be carriéd with common winde
> Of courts' inconstant mutabilitie,
> Ne after everie tattling fable flie ;
> But heares and sees the follies of the rest,
> And thereof gathers for himselfe the best,
> He will not creepe, nor crouche with fained face,
> But walks upright with comely steadfast pace,
> And unto all doth yeeld due curtesie ;
> But not with kissed hand below the knee,
> As that same Apish crew is wont to doo ;
> For he disdaines himself t' embase theretoo.

He hates fowle leasings, and vile flatterie,
Two filthy blots in noble genterie ;
And lotheful idleness he doth detest,
The canker worm of everie gentle brest.

Or lastly when the bodie list to pause,
His minde unto the Muses he withdrawes :
Sweete Ladie Muses, Ladies of delight,
Delights of life, and ornaments of light !
With whom he close confers with wise discourse
Of Nature's workes, of heavens continuall course,
Of forreine lands, of people different,
Of kingdome's change, of divers gouvernment,
Of dreadfull battales, of renowned Knights ;
With which he kindleth his ambitious sprights
To like desire and praise of noble fame,
The onely upshot whereto he doth ayme ;
For all his minde on honour fixed is,
To which he levels all his purposis,
And in his Prince's service spends his dayes,
Not so much for to gaine, or for to raise
Himself to high degree, as for his grace,
And in his liking to win worthie place,
Through due deserts and comelie carriage.

But for all this picture of noble independence to what shifts of flattery is he not himself reduced ? " In that Faery Queen I mean glory in my general intention : but in my particular I conceive the most excellent and gracious person of our Sovereign the Queen, and her kingdom in Faery Land. And yet in some places I do otherwise shadow her. For considering she beareth two persons the one of a most royal Queen or Empress, the other of a most virtuous and beautiful lady, this latter part in some places I do express in Belphœbe, fashioning her according to your own excellent conceit of Cynthia." Gloriana, Tanaquil, Belphœbe, everything noble is Elizabeth ; everything that is opposed to Elizabeth—Duessa, the false Florimel, Mary Queen of Scots—is false and wicked. Nevertheless the man who could exalt his Sovereign with such resplendent imagery was forced sometimes to tell the truth out of the bitterness of his heart :—

So pitifull a thing is Suter's state !
Most miserable man whom wicked fate

Hath brought to Court, to sue for *had-ywist*,
That few have found, and manie one hath mist !
Full little knowest thou that hast not tried
What hell it is in suing long to bide :
To loose good dayes, that might be better spent ;
To wast long nights in pensive discontent ;
To speed to-day, to be put back to-morrow ;
To feed on hope, to pine with feare and sorrow ;
To have thy Prince's grace, yet want her Peeres ;
To have thy asking, yet waite manie yeeres ;
To fret thy soule with crossés and with cares ;
To eat thy heart through comfortless dispaires ;
To fawne, to crowche, to waite, to ride, to ronne,
To spend, to give, to want, to be undonne.
Unhappie wight, born to disastrous end,
That doth his life in so long tendance spend !
Who ever leaves sweete home, where meane estate
In safe assurance, without strife or hate,
Findes all things needfull for contentment meeke,
And will to Court for shadows vaine to seeke,
Or hope to gaine, himself will a daw trie :
That curse God send unto mine enemie !

Again, Spenser was the poet of Mediæval Allegory. He is treading the same poetical path that Dante and Langland had trodden long before him. All that is learned, and much that is beautiful, in the *Faery Queen* —the idea of Holy Church, the loathsomeness of Error, the excellence of the Cardinal and Christian Virtues, the Seven Deadly Sins, the Temptations of the Flesh, and many images of the same kind—is drawn from the rich treasure-house of Scholastic Theology. But, mixed up as these things are with the action of a romantic fable, they have lost that spirit of universal truth which animates them in the verse of the older poets. The ancient simple sincerity of Catholic feeling evaporates in the abstractions of Protestant Platonism, or strikes hard and harsh notes in the bitterness of religious party spirit ; in the satirical picture of " Corceca and Abessa slow " ; in the mutual recriminations of Piers and Palinode. The Reformation has brought into England a new mode of scriptural interpretation, and with its arrival the old genius of allegorical interpretation has departed.

In truth, whatever virtue there is in the subject-matter of Spenser's poetry proceeds not from the ideas themselves so much as from the mind of the poet. At whatever point the reader penetrates Spenser's artistic motives— whether he has regard to the exquisite sweetness of his lyric verse, as shown in his *Prothalamion* and *Epithalamion ;* or to the graceful dignity of his personal compliments, as illustrated in his pastoral episodes ; or to the moral grandeur of his sentiments in the second book of the *Faery Queen*, and in the two cantos of Mutability— there he will find the working of an almost incomparable poetical intelligence. Spenser composed his poems in the spirit of a great painter, a great musician. He "writ no language," because he wrote about things that had no longer any existence except in his imagination. Yet so beautiful was his imagination that he has secured for the offspring of his fancy an enduring life, illustrating the truth of his own doctrine that

> Wise words taught in numbers for to run,
> Recorded by the Muses, live for ay.

His ideas dwell in a kind of Limbo between the mediæval and the modern world, invested with a mild, harmonious atmosphere, which imparts a certain effect of unity to the most incongruous objects. A sense of beauty, rarely equalled, enabled him to reconcile, as far as mere form is concerned, Catholic doctrine with Pagan philosophy, mediæval romance with classical mythology. What can be more beautiful than the abrupt opening of the eighth canto of the second book after the fall of Sir Guyon, the Knight of Temperance ?—

> And is there care in heaven ? And is there love
> In heavenly spirits to these creatures bace,
> That may compassion of their spirits move ?
> There is :—else much more wretched were the cace
> Of men than beasts : But O ! the exceeding grace,
> Of Highest God that loves his creatures so,
> And all his workes with mercy doth embrace,
> That blessed Angels he sends to and fro,
> To serve to wicked man, to serve his wicked foe !

And yet observe the description of the guardian angel
sent to Guyon :—

> Like as Cupido on Idæan hill,
> When having laid his cruell bow away
> And mortall arrowes, wherewith he doth fill
> The world with murderous spoiles and bloody prey,
> With his faire mother he him dights to play,
> And with his goodly sisters, Graces three ;
> The Goddesse, pleased with his wanton play,
> Suffers herself through sleepe beguild to bee,
> The whiles the other ladies mind theyr mery glee.

If Spenser were to be regarded, in the first place, as
a moral and religious teacher, this description would be a
mistake ; for who could believe in the reality of such an
angel ? But, on the other hand, who, having regard to
Spenser's style, could wish anything to be altered ? Poetry
can never take the place of religion. But it can soothe
and elevate the mind, as nothing else in the world can do,
by depicting the idea of beauty, whether it be derived
from the doctrines of Dionysius the Areopagite, or from
a painting of Titian. " A thing of beauty is a joy for
ever ; " and that is the secret of the enduring life of the
Faery Queen.

CHAPTER X

THE GROWTH OF CRITICISM AND ITS EFFECT ON
POETRY: THE POETICAL EUPHUISTS

I HAVE said that the Miscellanies which appeared from time to time during the latter half of the sixteenth century furnish a series of landmarks by which we may accurately measure the advance of the national taste. The earlier of these collections—Tottel's *Miscellany, The Paradise of Dainty Devices, The Gorgeous Gallery of Gallant Inventions* —show the gradual stages through which the language passed after it had received its first refinement from the hands of Surrey, up to the point at which poets like Gascoigne and Churchyard began to anticipate the movement of Lyly. During the whole of that period the chief aim of the poets was purity of idiom and smoothness and harmony in versification. But in the Miscellanies published towards the close of Elizabeth's reign—*The Phœnix Nest, England's Helicon, England's Parnassus,* and *The Poetical Rhapsody*—it is evident that style is being affected by influences of a more complex and artificial kind.

The Phœnix Nest, published in 1593, is described as being "set forth by R. S. of the Inner Temple, Gent.," and contains a number of compositions signed with initials, such as T. W. (Thomas Watson), N. B. (Nicholas Breton), T. L. (Thomas Lodge), of the nature of sonnets, elegies, epigrams, etc., all indicating a tendency to make metrical experiments in thought and language, sometimes in rhyming stanzas, sometimes in measures determined by the classical principle of quantity. *England's Helicon,* on the contrary, which appeared in 1600, under the editorship of John Bodenham, is almost entirely filled with poems written in the pastoral vein. *England's Parnassus*, edited, in the same year, by R. A., is an Anthology, selected from the works of all English poets from the time of Surrey. *The Poetical Rhapsody*, a collection made by Francis, son of William Davison, Secretary of State, was published in 1602, and is chiefly made up of contributions from men occupying high positions at Court, such as Sidney, Dyer, Raleigh, and Wotton.

In all these Miscellanies we see clearly that the writers are no longer content with the harmonious simplicity of Surrey's diction, which had been the accepted standard for poets of Turbervile's generation. They aim at curious and novel effects of language. The editors have definite ideas of what is to be admired in poetry ; they let us see whom they think the admirable poets of the age. The age itself, in short, is becoming critical as well as poetical, and, in order to understand the aims and motives of its poets, we ought to read the Miscellanies in connection with the various critical treatises which, beginning to appear about the middle of the century, show how much the minds of men were occupied with the difficulties of composing in a newly-formed language, and to what an extent their imaginations were overpowered by the technical excellences of classical and Italian literature.

The first critical treatise in English is Sir Thomas Wilson's *Art of Rhetoric*, published in 1553. The instruction given in this work is in no way original, but it is judicious, and sometimes humorous ; as, however, it does not discuss the art of poetry, it requires no detailed notice. In 1575, George Gascoigne, at the request, as he tells us, of "Master Edward Donati," published his *Notes of Instruction concerning the making of Verse*, describing the practice of metrical composition in his time. Several of his observations are interesting. He points out, with some regret, that no foot is now recognised in England but the iambus.[1]

---

[1] Haslewood's *Ancient Critical Essays*, vol. ii. p. 6. It is to be remembered, however, that Tusser's *Five Hundred Points of Good Husbandry*

So entirely had the principle of Chaucer's versification been lost that Gascoigne describes it as "riding rhyme" (*i.e.* verse not measured by the regular beat of the iambus), and thinks that it is determined solely by the accent. He recommends the use of monosyllables in view of the character of the language ; and—what is of great importance—notes the use of the cæsura, and the different places in which it falls in verses of various length.

Gascoigne made no suggestions of reform in his *Notes ;* but, a few years later, we find, from the correspondence between Spenser and Gabriel Harvey, that a deliberate attempt is being made to base the standard of English metres on quantity instead of on accent and rhyme. This movement is encouraged by Sidney and Dyer, who are at the head of a literary party at Court, and rules of prosody have been actually laid down by one Drant (Fellow of St. John's College, Cambridge), a scholar patronised by these courtiers. Spenser himself has made some experiments in the new style, and sends Harvey his remarks on the result :—

I like your late English hexameters so exceedingly well that I also enure my pen something in that kind, which I find, indeed, as I have heard you so often defend in word, neither so hard nor so harsh but that it will easily and fairly yield itself to our mother tongue. For the only or chiefest hardness which seemeth is in the accent, which sometimes gapeth, and, as it were, yawneth, ill-favouredly, coming short of that it should, and sometimes exceeding the measure of the number, as in *carpenter*, the middle syllable being used short in speech, when it shall be read long in verse, seemeth like a lame gosling that draweth one leg after her ; and *Heaven* being used short as one syllable, when it is in verse stretched out with a *diastole*, like a lame dog that holds up one leg. But it is to be won with custom, and rough words must be subdued with use. For why a God's name may not we, as well as the Greeks, have the kingdom of our own language, and measure our accents by the sound, reserving the quantity to the verse ?[1]

To this Harvey, who would seldom agree with the

---

was composed in an anapæstic rhythm, and that an irregular movement of the same kind was employed in the Moralities.

[1] Gabriel Harvey's *Works* (Grosart), vol. i. p. 35.

ideas of any other man, sent a letter of reply, written in his usual conceited style ; in the course of which he said :—

But ho ! I pray you, gentle sirra, a word with you more. In good sooth, and by the faith I bear to the Muses, you shall never have my subscription or consent (though you should charge me with the authority of five hundred Master 'Drants) to make your carpĕnter our carpĕnter an inch longer or bigger than God and his English people have made him.   Is there no other policy to pull down rhyming and set up versifying, but must needs correct *Magnificat*, and against all order of law, and, in despite of custom, forcibly usurp and tyrannise upon a quiet company of words that, so far beyond the memory of man, have so peaceably enjoyed their several privileges and liberties without any disturbance or the least controlment.[1]

With a faint suspicion, apparently, that this line of argument gave away the whole principle of reform he was himself advocating, he added :—

Nevertheless I grant, after long advice and diligent observation of particulars, a certain uniform analogy and concordance being in process of time espied out.[2]

Some years later Thomas Campion, the author of a short treatise called *Observations on the Art of English Poesy* (1602), reversed this decision by insisting on the necessity of observing strictly the classical rule of quantity. "Neither," says he, "can I remember any impediment, except position, that can alter the accent of any syllable in our English verse.   For though we accent the second syllable of Trumpington short, yet it is naturally long, and so of necessity must be held of every composer." [3]

William Webbe was a labourer in the same cause as Harvey, Sidney, and Drant.   His *Discourse of English Poetry* was published in 1586.   In it he urges, like Spenser, that the character and standard of the language could be determined by the will of those who wrote in it:—

Likewise, for the tenor of the verse might we not (as Horace did in the Latin) alter their proportions to what sorts we listed,

---

[1] Gabriel Harvey's *Works*, vol. i. p. 99.   [2] *Ibid.* vol. i. p. 105.
[3] Haslewood's *Ancient Critical Essays*, vol. ii. p. 186.

and to what we saw would best become the nature of the thing handled or the quality of the words? Surely it is to be thought that if any one of sound judgment and learning should put forth some famous work containing divers forms of true verses, fitting the measures according to the matter, it would of itself be a sufficient authority, without any prescription of rules, to the most part of poets for them to follow and by custom to ratify. For sure it is that the rules and principles of poetry were not precisely followed and observed by the first beginners and writers of poetry, but were selected and gathered severally out of their works for the direction and behoof of their followers. And indeed he, that shall with heedful judgment make trial of the English words, shall not find them so gross or unapt, but they will become any one of the most accustomed sorts of Latin or Greek verses meetly, and run thereon somewhat currently.[1]

By way of illustrating his theories he tried his own hand on the making of English hexameters, and gave as a specimen the following translation of the first line of Virgil's *Bucolics* :—

Tītȳrŭs, hăppĭlȳ thōū līēst tūmblīng ūndĕr ă bēēch trēē![2]

His treatise deals with other matters besides the reform of versification ; but, as may be supposed, he does not show many signs of judgment and good taste. He praises Spenser as " our late famous English poet " (he is referring to *The Shepherd's Calendar*, published in 1579), but he has an equal admiration for Gabriel Harvey ; he exalts Lyly as an almost unrivalled genius, and has a very high opinion of Phaër's translation of Virgil.

George Puttenham, whose *Art of English Poesy* appeared in 1589, is a critic of far higher ability. He was himself a poet, and, according to his own account of himself, had written verses as early as the reign of Edward VI. He was also a courtier, and, having got rid of some of the rust of learning by mixing with polite society, he escaped the fallacies which for a time deluded even a genius so great as Spenser.

True, he acquiesced theoretically in the reasoning of

---

[1] Haslewood's *Ancient Critical Essays*, vol. ii. p. 66.   [2] *Ibid.* vol. ii. p. 69.

Ascham and his followers, and showed "how if all manner of sudden innovations were not very scandalous, specially in the laws of any language or art, the use of the Greek or Latin feet,might be brought into our vulgar poesy, and with good grace enough." [1]   But he sees clearly with Castiglione what must be the true standard of diction in poetry :—

This part in our maker or poet must be heedfully looked into, that it be natural, pure, and the most usual of all his country; and for the same purpose rather that which is spoken in the King's Court, or in the good towns and cities within the land, than in the marches or frontiers, or post towns, where strangers haunt for traffic's sake, or yet in the Universities where scholars use such peevish affectation of words out of the primitive languages, or finally in any uplandish village or corner of a realm ; neither shall he follow the speech of a craftsman or carter or other of the inferior sort, though he be inhabitant or bred in the best town or city in this realm, for such persons do abuse good speeches by strange accents or ill-shapen sounds and false ortho-graphy.   But he shall follow generally the better brought-up sort, such as the Greeks call *charientes*—men civil and graciously behavioured and bred.   Our maker therefore at these days shall not follow Piers Plowman, nor Gower, nor Lydgate, nor yet Chaucer, for their language is now out of use with us ; neither shall he take the terms of Northern men, such as they use in daily talk, whether they be noblemen, or gentlemen, or best clerks, is all of no matter ; nor in effect any speech used beyond the river of Trent, though no man can deny but theirs is the purer English Saxon at this day, yet it is not so courtly nor so curious as our Southern English is, no more is the far Western man's speech ; ye shall therefore take the usual speech of the Court, and that of London, and of the shires lying about London within sixty miles, and not much above. [2]

Puttenham divided his treatise into three parts—(1) On Poets and Poesy ; (2) On Proportion ; (3) On Orna-ment.   The second of these books shows a very remark-able power of observation, thought, and arrangement. He considers Poetical Proportion under the heads of Staff, Measure, Situation, Concord, and Figure, and almost

---

[1] Haslewood's *Ancient Critical Essays*, vol. i. p. 85.   [2] *Ibid.* p. 120.

everything that he says is well worth consideration. Especially interesting are his remarks on the cæsura in English verse, showing as they do that he, like Gascoigne, and indeed Spenser, was quite unaware of the metrical principle on which Chaucer wrote. He says :—

Our ancient rhymers, as Chaucer, Lydgate, and others, used those cæsuras either very seldom or not at all, or else very licentiously, and many times made their metres (they called them riding rhyme) of such unshapely words as would allow no convenient cæsura, and therefore did let their rhymes run out at length, and never stayed but they came to the end, which manner though it were not to be misliked in some sort of metre, yet in every long verse the cæsura ought to be kept precisely, if it were but to serve as a law to correct the licentiousness of rhymers ; besides that it pleaseth the ear better, and showeth more cunning in the maker by following the rule of his restraint.[1]

Puttenham makes it a hard-and-fast rule to place the cæsura " in a verse of ten upon the fourth, leaving six to follow " ;[2] but if he had studied Surrey more carefully he would have seen that the fine ear of that poet had taught him that the place of the cæsura should be varied, and move mainly between the fourth syllable and the seventh.[3]

Sir Philip Sidney's *Defence of Poetry* (1581) is not so much a treatise on Prosody as an Apology for the Art as a whole, having been written mainly in consequence of Stephen Gosson's attack on the stage. He proves that the purpose of poetry is moral and didactic ; shows the high estimation in which poets have always been held ; defines the various orders of poetry ; points out the distinction between Poetry, on the one hand, and Divinity, Philosophy, and History on the other ; after which he passes on to the subdivisions of poetry, and then examines the objections brought against the art. The concluding portion of his treatise, devoted to an examination of the contemporary state of English poetry, and of the language in general, contains some very interesting observations, and especially a criticism on the style of the Euphuists :—

[1] Haslewood's *Ancient Critical Essays*, vol. i. p. 62.
[2] *Ibid.* p. 62.   [3] *Ibid.* See *ante*, pp. 93, 94.

Now for similitudes in certain printed discourses, I think all herbarists, all stories of beasts, fowls, and fishes are rifled up, that they may come in multitudes to wait upon any of our conceits, which certainly is as absurd a surfeit to the ears as is possible.   For the force of a similitude not being to prove anything to a contrary disputer, but only to explain to a willing hearer ; when that is done the rest is a most tedious prattling, rather overswaying the memory from the purpose whereto they were applied, than any whit improving the judgment, already either satisfied, or by similitudes not to be satisfied.[1]

These extracts will indicate sufficiently the nature of the critical questions which were occupying men's thoughts at this period.   Had their minds been more definitely made up about the ends of life and art, as we shall presently see that Marlowe's mind was made up about the principles of dramatic action, there would have been no need to discuss refinements about the true modes of expression.   As it was, in default of obvious subjects of poetry, invention was chiefly occupied in discovering novelties of form to disguise the lack of matter.   Groups and schools of metrical composers, making experiments in the art of poetry, sprang up in all directions, from the doctor of Oxford or Cambridge who lectured his common room on the rules of prosody, down to the manufacturer of love-pamphlets who sought to gain a living in London by studying the caprices of the public taste.   But four main groups stand out clearly in the midst of these varieties : (1) The university scholars who attempted to reform the national poetry on classical lines ; (2) The imitators of Petrarch and of the Italian *Concetti* makers ; (3) The Courtiers who expressed the feelings of chivalrous society in Euphuistic forms ; (4) The men of letters who embodied the spirit of the Renaissance in pastoral romance or classical mythology.

1. The first of these groups was headed by Gabriel Harvey.   The eldest of the four sons of a rope-maker of Saffron Walden, he was born about 1547, and was educated at Christ's College, Cambridge, passing to Pem-

[1] *Apologie for Poetrie* (Arber), p. 68.

broke Hall, where he became tutor. His character was of a kind not infrequently found in societies where men are accustomed " to measure themselves by themselves," and where the only measure recognised is the abstract one of learning. His vanity and pushing arrogance were so extreme, that many members of his College combined to prevent him from proceeding to his degree of Master ; but he had a strong following among the younger men, of whom none was more ardent in his behalf than Spenser.

Harvey was an effective lecturer on rhetoric in his University. He tells us himself that he was of the school of Bembo, whose *Ciceronianism* he enthusiastically admired though in time he had the good sense to perceive the superiority of the principles of Erasmus.[1] Carried away by his love for the classics, and not understanding the true genius of his own language, he set himself to work out an idea of linguistic reform, which had first been started by Ascham. "This matter," the latter had said in his *Schoolmaster*, "maketh me gladly remember my sweet time spent at Cambridge, and the pleasant talk which I oft had with M. Cheke and M. Watson of this fault, not only in the old Latin poets, but also in our new English rhymers at this day. They wished, as Virgil and Horace were not wedded to follow the faults of former fathers (a shrewd marriage in greater matters), but, by right imitation of the perfit Grecians, had brought poetry also to perfitness in the Latin tongue, that we Englishmen likewise would acknowledge and understand rightfully our rude beggarly rhyming, brought first into Italy by Goths and Huns, when all good verses and all good learning were destroyed by them : and after carried into France and Germany : and last received into England by men of excellent wit indeed, but of small learning and less judgment in that behalf.[2]

Ascham argued that, though hexameters might not be suitable to the genius of English, the trimeter iambic, if properly treated, could readily be naturalised in the language. These ideas Harvey did his best to reduce to

---

[1] Gabriel Harvey's *Works* (Grosart), vol. i. p. xxiii.
[2] *The Schoolmaster* (Mayor's edition), p. 176.

practice ; he even went beyond them. We have already had his account of the rules by which he was guided ; and it is amusing to see the gravity with which he applied them. Spenser, for example, having submitted for his approval the following atrocious verses :—

> See ye the blindfolded prety God, that feathered archer,
>   Of lovers miseries which maketh his bloody game ?
> Wote ye why his Moother with a veil hath covered his face ?
>   Trust me, lest he my love happily chance to behold—[1]

Harvey asks, not unreasonably, why " thĕ in the first, yĕ in the first and third, and mў in the last being short, Mē alone should be made long in the very same." [2] Of his own hexameters the following specimen will suffice :—

ENCOMIUM LAURI

> What might I call this tree ? A laurel ? O bonny Laurel !
> Needs to thy boughs will I bow this knee, and veil my bonetto.
> Who but thou the renown of Prince and princely Poeta ?
> Th' one for Crown, for Garland th' other, thanketh Apollo.[3]

This " peevish affectation of words," which Puttenham notes as the besetting sin of University scholars, clung to Harvey to the last. He carried his vicious style even into his quarrels, and poured out his venom with many rhetorical grimaces on the memory of Robert Greene, who had wounded his vanity by a personal allusion. He was himself attacked in return by Greene's friend, Thomas Nash, who in a boisterous and bitter satire heaped ridicule on his family, his person, his pedantry, and his hexameters. Harvey replied to Nash, and the war of pamphlets between the two continued till 1597, when it was stopped by the intervention of the authorities. He died in 1630.

Harvey's practice was followed by Sidney in the *Arcadia*, where are to be found many specimens of English hexameters, sapphics, and other classical metres, in which, as Pope says, the verse " halts ill on Roman feet." The ways of the Cambridge School of poetical

---

[1] Gabriel Harvey's *Works*, vol. i. p. 36.   [2] *Ibid.* vol. i. p. 81.
[3] *Ibid.* vol. i. p. 82.

reform were discredited by Stanyhurst's wretched translation of Virgil (1582); and the only example of the style
possessing the slightest pretensions to elegance is a rendering of Thomas Watson's Latin poem *Amyntas*, by Abraham
Fraunce, Fellow of St. John's College, Cambridge (1591).
Although the reader will at once perceive that Fraunce, in
his attempt to observe the foreign rules of quantity, more
than once does violence to the native rules of accent, yet,
if allowance be made for the wrong principles on which
the writer proceeded, it cannot be denied that the following passage shows a sense of grace and beauty :—

AMYNTAS

Hollow caves, ragg'd rocks, waste hills, green watery fountains,
For pity sweetly reply, and answers make to my mourning.
Strong oak, tall pine-tree, green laurel, beautiful ivy,
For pity sweetly reply, and answers make to my mourning,
Shake their leaves for grief, and bend their boughs to my groaning
Only that one, in whom my joys are only reposed,
Yields no lovely reply, no answer makes to my mourning,
Phillis, fair and fierce ; Phillis, more fierce to Amyntas,
Than strong oak, tall pine, green laurel, beautiful ivy,
Hollow caves, ragg'd rocks, waste hills, green watery fountains.[1]

(2) Not many degrees removed from Harvey's Pole of
icy pedantry, a tribe of metrical Euphuists sought means
of poetical subsistence by working the exhausted mines
of the Italian Petrarchists.   No variety of versifier,
whose work the historian is compelled to examine,
moves in him more bitter indignation than the uninspired
Elizabethan sonneteer.   Surrey had used the sonnet as
an instrument for refining the language of poetry ; in the
hands of Sidney it was animated with fire and invention :
through it Shakespeare gave personal utterance to his
philosophical and tragical view of human nature.   But
men who, without passion, use the sacred theme of love,
merely—so they themselves acknowledge—as a means of
displaying their " wit " ; who blot with their ink the path
consecrated by the feet of Beatrice ; who " torture one
poor word a thousand ways," in order to make it yield

---

[1] The *Countess of Pembroke's Yvychurch*, Act i. Sc. 2 (1591).

some mode of expression which no poet has thought of
before—these men are what Pope calls "the Muses'
hypocrites."

One of the worst offenders in this class, and perhaps the
one who was in his own age most admired, was Thomas
Watson, who must not be confounded with the friend of
Cheke and Ascham. He was born about 1557, and was
educated at Oxford, where he translated first Petrarch's
sonnets into English, and afterwards Sophocles' *Antigone*
into Latin. Among his friends were Secretary Walsingham, the Countess of Pembroke, and the Earl of Oxford,
to the last-named of whom he dedicated in 1583 his
Ἑκατομπαθία, or Passionate Century of Love, a collection
of a hundred sonnets, divided into two parts of which the
first part—to use Watson's own words—"expresseth the
author's sufferance in Love: the latter his long Farewell
to Love and all his tyranny." These torments, it seems,
were not unendurable, for, in the appeal to the reader at
the beginning of the volume, the poet says: "For this
once I hope that thou wilt, in respect of my travail in
penning these love-passions, or for pity of my pains in
suffering them (*although but supposed*), so survey the
faults herein escaped, as either to wink at them as an
oversight of a blind lover, or excuse them as idle toys,
proceeding from a youngling frenzy." [1]

In truth there was no "frenzy," but much method, in
Watson's poetical compositions. A man of wide and
diligent culture, he was acquainted with a great number
of writers, ancient and modern, and was in the habit of
noting in his memory any thoughts that pleased him as
he read. His favourite authors seem to have been the
late Italian poets—especially Serafino—and the French
"Pleiad," with whose reforming aspirations he had much
sympathy. The matter of at least nine of his sonnets is
derived from Serafino's Sonnets or from his *Strambotti ;*
three more owe their being to Ronsard ; while Horace,
Petrarch, Agnolo Fiorenzuola, Girolamo Parabosco, and
Hercules Strozza are all made to contribute from their

[1] Watson's *Poems* (Arber), p. 27.

resources to this Passionate Century of Love.[1]   The
result of this careful economy in Watson's hands may be
appreciated from the poet's account of the manufacture
of his 89th Sonnet called "My Love is Past":—

The two first staffs of this Sonnet are altogether sentential,
and every one verse of them is grounded upon a diverse reason
and authority from the rest.   I have thought good for brevity
sake only to set down here the authorities with figures whereby
to apply every one of them to his due line in order as they stand.
1. Hieronimus: *In deliciis difficile est servare castitatem.*   2.
Ausonius: *Dispulit inconsultus amor,* etc.   3. Seneca: *Amor est
otiosæ causa sollicitudinis.*   4. Propertius: *Errat qui finem versari
quærit amorem.*   5. Horatius: *Semper ardentes acuens sagittas.*
6. Xenophon: *Scribit Amorem esse igne et flamma flagrantiorem,
quod ignis urat tangentes, et proxima tantum cremet, amor ex
longinquo spectantem terreat.*   7. Calenti: *Plurima zelotypo sunt
in amore mala.*   8. Ovidius: *Inferet arma tibi sæpe rebellis amor.*
9. Pontanus: *Si vacuum siniat perfidiosus amor.*   10. Marcellus:
Quid lacrimis meis proterve insultas puer?   11. Tibullus: *At
lascivus amor rixæ mala verba ministrat,* and   12. Virgilius:
Bellum sæpe petit ferus exitiale Cupido.

> Love hath delight in sweet delicious fare;[1]
> Love never takes good counsel for his friend;[2]
> Love author is and cause of idle care;[3]
> Love is distraught of wit, and hath no end;[4]
>   Love shooteth shafts of burning hot desire;[5]
>   Love burneth more than either flame or fire;[6]
> Love doth much harm through jealousy assault;[7]
> Love once embraced will hardly part again;[8]
> Love thinks in breach of faith there is no fault;[9]
> Love makes a sport of other's deadly pain;[10]
>   Love is a wanton child, and loves to brawl;[11]
>   Love with his war brings many souls to thrall.
> These are the smallest faults that lurk in love;
> These are the hurts which I have cause to curse;
> These are those truths that no man can disprove;
> These are such harms as none can suffer worse.
>   All this I write that others may beware
>   Though now myself twice free from all such care.[2]

We find from Puttenham's *Art of Poetry* that at this

---

[1] Watson is very honest in acknowledging his obligations; but his age
was one in which credit was specially given to learning.
[2] Watson's *Poems*, p. 125.

period a bad practice had been revived from decadent periods of literature of writing poems in the form of geometrical figures, such as rhombuses, triangles, and the like.[1] Happily few relics of these metrical monstrosities have found even a tomb in English poetry ; but the reader who is curious to see what they were like, will find that one of Watson's " passions " embodied itself in such a form in his 71st Sonnet, which he describes as " A Pasquine Pillar erected in despite of Love."[2] It is to be observed that Watson's so-called sonnets in Ἑκατομπαθία are not written within the orthodox fourteen lines. He tries to show originality by extending the limit to eighteen lines, but there is no unity in the structure, which is merely a sequence of three stanzas of six lines each.

More tolerable than Watson, in so far as he is less affected and pretentious, Henry Constable may be taken as the type of a large class of sonneteers, who imitated directly the manner of the later Italian Petrarchists. He was the son of Sir Robert Constable of Newark, and was born in 1562. Educated at St. John's College, Cambridge, he took his B.A. degree in January 1579-80. He became a Roman Catholic, and after leaving Cambridge lived for some time in Paris, where he at first acted as a spy in the service of the English Government. He seems, however, to have been suspected of disloyalty, for when he sought employment in 1595, he protested that he had no wish to see Roman Catholicism violently restored in England. Not long afterwards he conspired to make the Queen a Roman Catholic, and became a pensioner of the King of France about 1600. He returned to England in 1603, and in 1604 was sent to the Tower ; from which, however, he was soon released, and seems to have remained in obscurity till his death in 1613.

Like all the Petrarchists, his aim was to discover some new metaphysical idea about love, to embody it in a sensible image, and to wind up the sonnet with an

---

[1] Haslewood, *Ancient Critical Essays*, vol. i. pp. 75-85.
[2] Watson's *Poems*, p. 117.

epigram. It is needless to say that, as the " metaphysics " of the subject had been long since exhausted, all that he was really in quest of was images and epigrams. He writes, for example, " Of the Birth of his Love," advising his " love," remembering that he is mortal, to " fly low," lest he should burn his wings in the flames of the Sun that he worships ; the conclusion of the sonnet is as follows :—

> A Muse's words caused thee with Hope to fly ;
> An angel's face Desire hath begot ;
> Thyself engendered of a goddess eye :
> Yet for all this immortal thou art not.
> Of heavenly eye though thou begotten art,
> Yet thou art born but of a mortal heart.[1]

Among other ancient commonplaces of the subject he paints " Love's Seven Deadly Sins " ; he devotes one sonnet to his " Lady's going over early to bed, thus depriving him too soon of her sight " ; another to his Lady walking in the Garden where every flower reflects a distinct colour from her person.[2] Or again, Love is a beggar at his Mistress's mouth, the door of beauty : he espies two cherries there, which will suffice to keep him from starving : he takes them, and is ready with his answer when the lady asks

> " But beggars can they nought but cherries eat ? "
> " Pardon my Love : he is a goddess son,
> And never feedeth but on dainty meat ;
> Else need he not to pine as he hath done ;
> For only the sweet fruit of this sweet tree
> Can give food to my Love and life to me." [3]

Perhaps the most original, at any rate the most ingenious, of his sonnets is the one in which he illustrates his theme with the imagery of devotion, " To his Lady's hand ; upon occasion of her glove, which in her absence he kissed " :—

> Sweet hand ! the sweet yet cruel bow thou art,
> From whence at me five ivory arrows fly ;
> So with five wounds at once I wounded lie,
> Bearing in breast the print of every dart.

---

[1] *Diana* (Hazlitt's edition, 1859), p. 3.   [2] *Ibid.* pp. 4, 6, 13.
[3] *Ibid.* p. 12.

> Saint Francis hath the like—yet felt no smart,
>   Where I in living torments never die ;
>   His wounds were in his hands and feet, where I
> All these same helpless wounds feel in my heart.
>   Now as Saint Francis (if a saint) am I :
>   The bow that shot these shafts a relique is,
>   I mean the hand—which is the reason why
>   So many for devotion thee would kiss :
> And I thy glove kiss as a thing divine,
> Thy arrows' quiver, and thy relique's shrine.[1]

Constable calls his mistress Diana ; other poets followed in the same vein, each of whom had a Laura. To cite only a few instances, Thomas Lodge celebrated his Phillis ; Giles Fletcher the elder his Licia ; Samuel Daniel his Delia ; and Michael Drayton (more honest than his brethren) his Idea. The compositions of all these sonneteers are only variations of a single principle ; the highest merit they can claim is epigrammatic ingenuity and verbal polish : and their chief value is the historical one of proving how completely the form of the sonnet in Elizabeth's time was the offspring of fashion, and how ill-grounded is the criticism which interprets them literally and uses them for the purposes of biographical narrative.

After the fashion had run its course for some years, nothing seems to have been left for the ambitious Petrarchist to invent but a mixture of nonsense and nastiness, and the distinction of having achieved this combination must be allowed to one Barnabe Barnes, son of Richard Barnes, Bishop of Durham, who in 1593 published a collection of sonnets and lyrics under the title of *Parthenophil and Parthenophe.* As an example of the nonsense by which this affected fool was inspired, the reader will probably be satisfied with his xlvi. Sonnet :

> Ah pierce-eye piercing eye and blazing light
>   Of thunder thunderblazes burning up !
> Oh sun sun-melting, blind, and dazing sight !
>   Ah heart down driving heart, and turning up !
> O matchless beauty beauty's beauty staining !
> Sweet damask rose-bud Venus' rose of roses !

---

[1] *Diana* (Hazlitt), p. 13.

> Ah front imperious duty's duty gaining !
> Yet threatful clouds did still inclose and closes !
> Oh lily leaves, when Juno lillies leaves,
>   In wondering at her colours grain distained !
> Voice which rocks voice and mountains hilly cleaves
>   In sunder at my loves with pain complained !
> Eye, lightning sun, heart beauty's bane unfeigned !
>   Oh damask rose ! proud forehead ! lily ! voice !
>   Ah partial fortune ! sore chance ! silly choice ![1]

As to his other distinguishing quality, his capacity for it may be inferred from the verses of John Marston, who in his satire called *Curio Inamorato* expresses the disgust which every manly taste must feel for the whole tribe to which Barnes belongs.

>   Out on Phrigio,
> That wished he were his mistress puppy cur to go
> And lick his mistress feet ! O pretty grace
> That pretty Phrigio begs but Pretty's place !
> Parthenophil, *thy* wish I will omit ;
> So beastly 'tis I may not utter it,
> But, Punicus, of all I'll bear with thee,
> That fain would be thy mistress " smug monkey.'
> Here's one would be a flea (jest comical) ;
> Another his sweet lady's verdingal.
>   . . . Another he
> Her silver-handed fan would gladly be.
> Here's one would be his Mistress necklace fain,
> To clip her fair, and kiss her azure vein.
> Fond fools, well wished, and pity but should be,
> For beastly shapes to brutish souls agree.[2]

It was indeed time for the tide to turn, as it did. When these lines were written Petrarchism had been exchanged for devotional sentiment ; Barnes of course " repented " with the fashion, and in 1595 published *A Divine Century of Spiritual Sonnets.*[3]

---

[1] Barnes's *Poems* (Grosart), p. 31.

[2] Marston's *Scourge of Villanie.*

[3] It may seem incredible, but the works of this idiot, including *Parthenophil and Parthenophe*, have been reprinted in our own generation by the Rev. Alexander Grosart, who admires him, and considers him "a worthy." I should otherwise not have noticed him ; but it seems necessary to warn the reader that a man may have lived in the age of Elizabeth, and yet have written vile stuff.

(3) Refreshing indeed it is to turn from the tricks of these amorous Schoolmen to the poetry of the great soldiers and statesmen who were the chief ornaments of the Court of Elizabeth. Placed as they were by fortune in a position which raised them above the necessity of achieving distinction by their wit, there was no occasion for such men to call attention to themselves by artifice or affectation. And as the pen was not their natural instrument, they seldom took it up except under some strong external impulse. Much of the prevailing Euphuism of the time mixes itself with the expression of their thoughts, but these are stamped with the personality of their own character, vigour, and purpose ; some of the best lyrics of the age were the work of its leading men of action. Sidney, Dyer, Oxford, Essex, and Raleigh, have all of them left occasional verses, which have secured a place in the memories of their countrymen.

Sidney, indeed, was something more than an occasional poet. As the first author of chivalrous and pastoral romance in England he may claim the glory of poetic invention ; but, as I have shown, romance is with him a vehicle for the expression of personal emotion. A strong vein of Euphuism runs through his style, but this corresponds so closely with the ideal character of his thought, that it produces an effect quite different from the frigid ingenuity of the average Elizabethan sonneteer. There is a sufficient basis of reality in the circumstances under which his sonnets were composed to give verisimilitude to his sentiments, and the ardour and vivacity which animate the imagery of these compositions are also found in such songs as that beginning with the stanza—

> Ring out your bells, let mourning shows be spread,
>   For Love is dead.
> All love is dead, infected
> With plague of deep disdain ;
> Worth, as nought worth, rejected,
> And faith fair scorn doth gain.

> From so ungrateful fancy,
> From such a female franzy,
> From them that use men thus,
> Good Lord, deliver us.[1]

But perhaps his most characteristic mode of lyrical expression is his trochaic verse of four accents, a rhythm which I believe he was the first to employ, and which after him became justly popular. There is much charm in the following verses, the tune of which probably inspired Barnfield with his delightful lines, "As it fell upon a day ":—

> In a grove most rich of shade,
> Where birds wanton music made,
> May, then young, his pied weeds flowing,
> New perfumed with flowers fresh growing,
>
> Astrophel with Stella sweet
> Did for mutual comfort meet,
> Both within themselves oppressèd,
> But each in the other blessèd.
>
> Him great harms had taught much care
> Her fair neck a foul yoke bare ;
> But her sight his cares did banish ;
> In his sight her yoke did vanish.
>
> Wept they had, alas the while !
> But now tears themselves did smile,
> While their eyes, by love directed,
> Interchangeably reflected.
>
> Sigh they did, but now betwixt
> Sighs of woe were glad sighs mixt ;
> With arms crost yet testifying
> Restless rest and living dying.
>
> Their ears hungry of each word
> Which the dear tongue would afford,
> But their tongues refrained from walking,
> Till their hearts had ended talking.
>
> But when their tongues would not speak,
> Love itself did silence break ;
> Love did set his lips asunder,
> Thus to speak in love and wonder.[2]

---

[1] Sir Philip Sidney's *Poems* (Grosart), vol. ii. p. 23.
[2] *Ibid.* vol. i. p. 179.

Sir Edward Dyer is a name always joined with Sidney's, and Gabriel Harvey speaks of them together as " the two very diamonds" of Elizabeth's Court.   The son of Sir Thomas Dyer, he was born (according to Aubrey) at Sharpham Park, Somersetshire,[1] not later, I should suppose, than 1540, and was educated—so says Anthony à Wood —either at Balliol or Broadgates Hall, but left Oxford without taking a degree and travelled on the Continent.[2] He then joined the Court and became a great favourite (at least) of the Queen.   Leicester seems to have thought of setting him up as a rival of Sir Christopher Hatton, and Elizabeth proved her high opinion of him by sending him on diplomatic missions to the Low Countries in 1584 and to Denmark in 1589.   She also employed him to search for manors which had been concealed from her ; but his proceedings in this business did not give her full satisfaction, and he was obliged to appeal to Lord Burghley for protection.   After the accession of James I. he seems to have retired from Court, and to have lived quietly till his death in 1607.

The number of poems which can be confidently ascribed to Dyer is small, but some of them have real merit, and not only justify the reputation which he enjoyed in his day, but are interesting as mirrors of his character and feelings.   Oldys says of him that " he would not stoop to fawn ";[3] and this may well be believed of the writer of the famous lines " My mind to me a kingdom is."   But Dyer's position as Elizabeth's favourite must have been one of extreme difficulty ; he had to satisfy the vanity of the Woman, without offending the pride of the Queen, or forfeiting his own self-respect ; and whether or not the following verses were intended as an offering of flattery, they doubtless truly expressed the poet's sense of his most unenviable lot :—

The touch, the sting, the torment of desire,
To strive beyond the compass of restraint,

---

[1] Aubrey, *Letters by Eminent Persons* (1813), vol. ii. part i. p. 338.
[2] *Athenæ Oxonienses* (Bliss), vol. i. p. 740.
[3] *Choice Notes*, by William Oldys (1862), p. 37.

Kept from the reach whereto it would aspire,
Gives cause (God knows) too just to my complaint.
    Besides the wrong which worketh my distress
    My meaning is with silence to suppress.

Oft with myself I enter in device
To reconcile these weary thoughts to peace ;
I treat for truce, I flatter and entice
My wrangling wits to work for their release :
    But all in vain I seek the means to find
    That might appease the discord of my mind.

For when I force a feignèd mirth to show,
And would forget and so beguile my grief,
I cannot rid myself of sorrow so,
Although I feed upon a false belief :
    For inward touch of discontented mind
    Returns my cares by course unto their kind.

Weaned from my wild, and thus by trial taught
How far to hold all fortune in regard,
Though here I boast of knowledge dearly bought,
Yet this poor gain I reap for my reward :
    I know hereby to harden and prepare
    A ready mind for all assaults of care.

Whereto, as one even from the cradle born,
And not to look for better to ensue,
I yield myself, and wish these times outworn,
That but remain my torments to renew ;
    And leave to those these days of my despite,
    Whose better hap may live to more delight.[1]

Or again :—

        The fere and fellow of thy smart,
            Prometheus, I am indeed,
        Upon whose ever living heart
            The greedy gryphes do daily feed.
            But he that lifts his heart so high,
            Must be content to pine and die.[2]

The contradictoriness of his situation is dwelt on in the following flowing and epigrammatic lines :—

        As rare to hear as seldom to be seen,
        It cannot be, nor never yet hath been,
        That fire should burn with perfect heat and flame,
        Without some matter for to yield the same.

---

[1] *Writings in Verse and Prose of Sir Edward Dyer*, p. 52 (Grosart, Miscellanies of the Fuller Worthies Library).   [2] *Ibid.* p. 55.

> A stranger case, yet true by proof, I know,
> A man in joy that liveth still in woe ;
> A harder hap who hath his love at list,
> Yet lives in love as he all love had mist.
>
> Who hath enough, yet thinks he lives without,
> Lacking no love, yet still he stands in doubt.
> What discontent to live in such desire,
> To have his will, yet ever to require ! [1]

If these verses were meant for the eye of the Queen it must be acknowledged that they show rare tact as well as technical skill.

Another favourite of Elizabeth had, like Dyer, personal experience of the capricious moods of his Sovereign, and his more tragic fate gives a deeper significance to

VERSES MADE BY THE EARL OF ESSEX IN HIS TROUBLE

> The ways on earth have paths and turnings known ;
>   The ways on sea are gone by needle's light ;
> The birds of the air the nearest way have flown,
>   And under earth the moles do cast aright.
> A way more hard than these I needs must take,
>   Where none can teach, nor no man can direct ;
> Where no man's good for me example makes,
>   But all men's faults do teach *her* to suspect.
> *Her* thoughts and mine such disproportion have ;
>   All strength of love is infinite in me ;
> She us'th th' advantage time and fortune gave
>   Of worth and power to get the liberty.
> Earth, sea, heaven, hell are subject unto laws,
> But I, poor I, must suffer and know no cause. [2]

We may well believe, too, that the pastoral note, first struck by Sanazzaro and repeated by Sidney, came home to the heart of Essex, who, in the following beautiful lines, breathes the desire, so often felt by men mixing much in artificial society, for a life of solitude and contemplation :—

---

[1] *Writings in Verse and Prose of Sir Edward Dyer*, p. 50 (Grosart, Miscellanies of the Fuller Worthies Library.

[2] *Poems of Sir Walter Raleigh and other Courtly Poets* (Hannah), 1875, p. 177.

> Happy were he could finish forth his fate
>   In some unhaunted desert most obscure
> From all societies, from love and hate
>   Of worldly folk ; there might he sleep secure,
> Then wake again, and ever give God praise,
>   Content with hips, and haws, and bramble-berry ;
> In contemplation spending all his days,
>   And change of holy thoughts to make him merry :
> Where, when he dies, his tomb may be a bush,
> Where harmless robin dwells with gentle thrush.[1]

Sir Walter Raleigh, on the other hand, when it suited his purpose, made use of Pastoralism, as the recognised vehicle of Court flattery, and his lost poem *Cynthia*, alluded to in Spenser's dedicatory letter prefixed to the *Faery Queen*, was doubtless conceived in this vein. Spenser speaks of Raleigh in *Colin Clout's Come Home Again* as " the Shepherd of the Sea " ; but, when he is writing in a really characteristic manner, Raleigh himself lays aside pastoral affectation. Though his imagery is vivid and metaphorical, it is often homely ; his thought is very plain and direct, and his poetry breathes a spirit of high disdain and fierce indignation, mixed with a strong feeling of religion, evidently the result of personal experience. His most striking lyrics seem to have been composed in great crises, when the prospect of death was close. The following lines, for example, taken from *The Pilgrimage*, were perhaps written when he was sent to the Tower in 1604 :—

> Be Thou, my speaker, taintless pleader,
> Unblotted Lawyer, true proceeder.
> Thou givest Salvation even for alms,
> Not with a bribed lawyer's palms :
> And this is mine eternal plea
> To him that made heaven, earth, and sea,
> That, since my flesh must die so soon,
> And want a head to dine next noon,
> Just at the stroke, when my veins start and spread,
> Set on my soul an everlasting head !
> Then am I ready, like a palmer fit,
> To tread those blest paths that before I writ.
> Of death and judgment, heaven and hell,
> Who oft doth think must needs die well.[2]

---

[1] *Poems of Sir Walter Raleigh and other Courtly Poets* (Hannah), 1875, p. 177.   [2] *Ibid.* p. 28.

" The Lie " (which, though the authorship has been questioned, is certainly Raleigh's) may have been composed at the same period ; the opening is very characteristic of the writer :—

> Go soul, the body's guest,
>   Upon a thankless arrant ;
> Fear not to touch the best ;
>   The soul shall be thy warrant.
> Go, since I needs must die,
> And give the world the lie.[1]

His penetrating and satiric temper shows itself also in his well-known " Reply " to Marlowe's " Come live with me and be my love " ; and the same relentless logic runs through " A Poesy to prove Affection is not Love " :

> Desire attained is not desire,
> But as the cinders of the fire.
>
> As ships in ports desired are drowned,
> As fruit once ripe then falls to ground,
> As flies that seek for flames are brought
> To cinders by the flames they sought ;
> So fond desire when it attains,
> The life expires, the woe remains.
>
> And yet some poets fain would prove
> Affection to be perfect love ;
> And that desire is of that kind,
> No less a passion of the mind ;
> As if wild beasts and men did seek
> To like, to love, to choose alike.[2]

Edward de Vere, 17th Earl of Oxford, is unfortunate in being chiefly known to posterity as the antagonist of Sidney in the quarrel already alluded to ; beyond this little is recorded of him.[3] We see, however, that he was a great patron of literature, and headed the literary party at Court which promoted the Euphuistic movement. His own verses are distinguished for their wit, and in their terse ingenuity reflect something of the coxcombry which seems to have been a leading feature in his character. Doubtless he was proud of his illustrious ancestry, and of

---

[1] *Poems of Sir Walter Raleigh and other Courtly Poets* (Hannah), p. 23.
[2] *Ibid.* p. 23.   [3] See p. 211.

his own office of Great Chamberlain of England, which had been hereditary in his family since the reign of Henry II. ; he was, therefore, careful to conform, in his verse at least, to the external requirements of chivalry, as may be seen in his sonnet, " Love thy Choice," which has something of the old-fashioned air of Surrey, and may have been a youthful composition :—

> Who taught thee first to sigh, alas, my heart ?
> Who taught thy tongue his woeful words of plaint ?
> Who filled thine eyes with tears of bitter smart ?
> Who gave thee grief and made thy joys to faint ?
> Who first did paint with colours pale thy face ?
> Who first did break thy sleeps of quiet rest ?
> Above the rest in court who gave thee grace ?
> Who made thee strive in honour to be best ?
> In constant truth to bide so firm and sure ?
> To scorn the world regarding but thine end ?
> With patient mind each passion to endure ?
> In one desire to settle to thy end ?
>   Love then thy choice, wherein such choice thou bind,
>   As nought but death may ever change thy mind.[1]

But in later years his natural turn for epigram seems to have prevailed over his chivalrous sentiment, as may be seen in the famous lines beginning " If women would be fair and yet not fond." [2]   Oxford was a contributor to *The Paradise of Dainty Devices*, and here his sententiousness takes the shape of devotional poems in Lord Vaux's manner ; but on the whole, the epigram, pure and simple, seems to have been his favourite form of composition, and in this his studied concinnity of style is remarkable, as the following examples will show :—

QUESTIONS AND ANSWERS

> Doth sorrow fret thy soul ? O direful sprite !
> Doth pleasure feed thy heart ? O blessed man !
> Hast thou been happy once ? O heavy plight !
> Are thy mishaps forepast ? O happy than !
> Or hast thou bliss in eld ? O bliss too late !
> But hast thou bliss in youth ? O sweet estate ! [3]

---

[1] *Poems of Thomas, Lord Vaux*, etc. (Grosart, Fuller Worthies Library), p. 65.   [2] Inserted in *The Golden Treasury*.
[3] *Poems of Thomas, Lord Vaux*, etc., p. 69.

GRIEF OF MIND

What plague is greater than the grief of mind ?
The grief of mind that eats in every vein,
In every vein that leaves such clods behind,
Such clods behind as breed much bitter pain ;
So bitter pain that none shall ever find,
What plague is greater than the grief of mind ? [1]

He was not only witty in himself, but the cause of wit
in others. Several of the courtiers set themselves to solve
the problem proposed in his well-known epigram :—

Were I a king, I might command content,
Were I obscure, unknown should be my cares,
And were I dead, no thoughts should me torment,
Nor words, nor wrongs, nor love, nor hate, nor fears.
A doubtful choice—of these three which to crave,
A kingdom, or a cottage or a grave. [2]

Sir Philip Sidney declared that there could be no doubt
as to the answer :—

Wert thou a king, yet not command content,
Sith empire none thy mind could yet suffice.
Wert thou obscure, still cares would thee torment,
But wert thou dead, all care and sorrow dies.
An easy choice—of these three which to crave ;
No kingdom, nor a cottage, but a grave. [3]

(4) Turning from the Court to the People, we find
that the general drift of the national imagination was
determined by the growing influence of the Classical
Renaissance. This is indicated in the middle and end of
Elizabeth's reign by the wide popularity of Pastoralism,
which was affected alike by the professional poets, who
sought to make profit out of the public taste, and by
amateurs, who wrote as the fancy seized them. One set
of poets, following Spenser's lead, treated pastoralism on
its lyrical side, and embodied their thoughts for the most
part in Eclogues, Elegies, or Descriptive and Devotional

[1] *Poems of Thomas, Lord Vaux*, etc., p. 67.
[2] *Poems of Raleigh, Wotton*, etc. (Hannah), p. 147.   [3] *Ibid.* p. 147.

Verses; another, inspired by Sidney's *Arcadia*, wrote Romances in prose, mixed with pastoral lyrics; or found their themes in the classical legends which had been made popular by Golding's translation of Ovid's *Metamorphoses*. All alike sought to attract attention by peculiarities in the titles of their books, the names of their ideal personages, and the conceits of their style.

The eldest of this group, and the one who connected it with the poetry of Gascoigne's and Churchyard's generation, was Nicholas Breton, the son of William Breton, a cadet of an old Essex family, who, like many of the younger sons of gentlemen at that period, had gone into trade and amassed a considerable fortune. Nicholas must have been born about the beginning of the reign of Edward VI. He had grown to manhood when his mother, being left a widow, married the spendthrift George Gascoigne, who evidently exercised a strong influence on the formation of Nicholas's taste. Very little is known of the events of his life. He would seem, from what he says of himself, "to have spent some years at Oxford,"[1] but there is no record of him in Anthony Wood's *Athenæ Oxonienses*. He began to write about 1577, and his last literary work, *Fantastics*, was produced as late as 1626. He tried all styles, satirical, devotional, pastoral, combining the moral and sententious vein of Gascoigne with the new manner which had been brought into popularity by *The Shepherd's Calendar*. The titles of his books —*Breton's Bower of Delights, Pilgrimage to Paradise, Arbour of Amorous Devises* — mark the taste of the generation that produced *The Paradise of Dainty Devices;* but the Miscellanies called *The Phœnix Nest* and *England's Helicon* contain many poems signed with his name or initials; and a few years later he produced his most successful work, *The Passionate Shepherd*, the name of which sufficiently indicates its pastoral character. He also wrote in Spenser's elegiac manner *Amoris Lachrimæ*, a lament for the death of Sir Philip Sidney; and, in common with many poets of the time, he was patronised

---

[1] Breton's *Works* (Grosart), " A Floorish upon Fancie," p. 50.

by Sidney's sister, in whose honour he composed *The Countess of Pembroke's Passion*. In his later days he fell in with the taste that was arising for metaphysical devotional poetry ; the titles of his poems, *The Ravisht Soul, The Blessed Weeper, The Longing of a Blessed Heart, The Soul's Heavenly Exercise*, seem to anticipate the style of Donne and Crashaw, but, unlike the latter poet, who became a member of the Roman Catholic Church, Breton remained attached to the Anglican doctrine.[1]

His merits rarely rise above allegorical ingenuity and smooth versifying. He had much facility and a ready power of imitation. His *Flourish upon Fancy*—which, in the mode of *The Gorgeous Gallery of Gallant Inventions*, he calls " as gallant a gloss upon so trifling a text as ever was written "—is a collection of what, within our own memory, used to be known as album verses. In this he copies his stepfather, Gascoigne, whose manner is also followed in his *Pilgrimage to Paradise*, a narrative poem relating rather obscurely the adventures of five pilgrims on their heavenly journey. The description of the church to which the pilgrims came may be taken as a sample of the style of this composition :—

> The gate is Grace, Contrition is the key,
> The lock is Love, the porter Penitence,
> When humble faith must heavenly favour stay,
> Till pity talk with virtue's patience.
> While angels' sighs the sinner's way devise,
> To have his entrance into Paradise.[2]

A number of moral poems, *Pasquil's Passion of the World's Waywardness, Pasquil's Foolscap, Pasquil's Precession*, and *Pasquil's Prognostication*, glance in the old-fashioned, satirical vein of Barclay, in his *Ship of Fools*, at current manners, borrowing here and there a suggestion from Sir Philip Sidney, as in the burden running through

---

[1] Mr. Grosart, with his usual industry, has collected Breton's works and such facts as are known about his life in an edition published in 1879.

[2] Breton's *Works* (Grosart), vol. i. " The Pilgrimage to Paradise," p. 20.

the dull catalogue of evils enumerated in *Pasquil's Precession,* as—

> A graceless child, and an unquiet wife,
> An idle servant, and a privy thief,
> A long delay, and an ungodly life,
> A helpless care, and a consuming grief,
> And from despair that never finds relief,
> And from the drone that robs the honey bee,
> The lord of heaven and earth deliver me.[1]

After the publication of Sidney's *Arcadia* and *Astrophel and Stella,* Breton, abandoning for a time the proverbial sententiousness of Churchyard and Gascoigne, began to imitate the new pastoral manner, and in his *Passionate Shepherd* came nearer inspiration than in any other of his poems. The following verses are charming in their simplicity:—

> Who can live in heart so glad
> As the merry country lad?
> Who upon a fair green balk
> May at pleasure sit and walk,
> And amid the azure skies
> See the morning sun arise,
> While he hears in every Spring
> How the birds do chirp and sing;
> Or before the hounds in cry
> See the hare go stealing by,
> Or along the shallow brook,
> Angling with a baited hook,
> See the fishes leap and play
> In a blessed sunny day;
> Or to hear the partridge call
> Till she have her covey all;
> Or to see the subtle fox,
> How the villain plies the box,
> After feeding on his prey;
> How he closely sneaks away
> Through the hedge and down the furrow,
> Till he gets into his burrow:
> Then the bee to gather honey,
> And the little black-haired coney

---

[1] Breton's *Works* (Grosart), vol. i. "Pasquil's Passe Precession and Prognostication," p. 7

On a bank for sunny place
With her fore-feet wash her face :
Are not these with thousands moe
Than the courts of kings do know ? [1]

There is something of Milton's *Allegro* in this, and *A Report sung in a Dream between a Shepherd and his Nymph* has in it a graceful air of whim, which would have hardly been expected of Breton, judging by his early poems :—

Say that I should say I love ye ?
   Would you say 'tis but a saying ?
But if Love in prayers move ye,
   Will you not be moved with praying ?

Think I think that Love should know ye ?
   Will you think 'tis but a thinking ?
But if Love the thought do show ye,
   Will ye close your eyes with winking ?

Write that I do write you blessèd,
   Will you write 'tis but a writing ?
But if Truth and Love confess it,
   Will ye doubt the true enditing ?

No, I say, and think, and write it,
   Write, and think, and say your pleasure :
Love and Truth and I endite it
   Ye are blessèd out of measure. [2]

The tune of his best-known verses, *Phillida and Corydon*, is plainly inspired either by Sidney's *Astrophel and Stella*, or by Barnfield's " As it fell upon a day."

A man of far finer genius than Breton, Richard Barnfield may be classed with this pastoral group, though he had in him nothing professional, and only wrote as the fancy seized him. The son of Richard Barnfield, a gentleman of Yorkshire, he was born in 1574, and was matriculated at Brasenose College, Oxford, in 1589, but seems not to have taken his degree. He was a friend of Thomas Watson, author of Ἑκατομπαθία, whose death he laments in his *Affectionate Shepherd*, a poem written in imitation of Virgil's *Alexis*, and published in 1594, when Barnfield was only twenty. In 1595 he published

[1] Breton's *Works* (Grosart), vol. i., " The Passionate Shepherd," p. 6.
[2] Breton's *Works* (Grosart), vol. i., poems from *Phœnix Nest* and *England's Helicon*, p. 9.

Cynthia, a series of sonnets, and in 1598 his *Encomion of Lady Pecunia;* after which he seems to have written no more, though he did not die till 1626.[1]

Like all the literary poets of the age, he lacked the inspiration of a great subject, as he lets us see very plainly in his preface to the *Encomion of Lady Pecunia:* "Being determined to write of something, and yet not resolved of anything, I considered with myself if one should write of love (they will say) why every one writes of Love; if of Virtue, why who regards Virtue? To be short I could think of nothing, but either it was common or not at all in request." There is, nevertheless, something uncommon in everything Barnfield did, and his originality of style is chiefly shown in the beauty of his pastoral descriptions. I cite two examples, and the reader will certainly forgive the length of the second in consideration of the charming humour and delicacy of the conception. In the first passage there is a touch of Spenser's archaic mannerism, but the imagery is all Barnfield's own :—

> Wilt thou set springes in a frosty night
> To catch the long-billed wood-cock and the snipe,
> (By the bright glimmering of the starry night),
> The Partridge, Pheasant, or the greedy Grype?
>   I'll lend thee lime-twigs and fine sparrow-calls,
>   Wherewith the fowler silly birds enthralls,
>
> Or in a misty morning if thou wilt
> Make pitfalls for the Lark and Pheldifare,
> Thy prop and sweak shall be both over-gilt :
> With Cyparissus self thou shalt compare
>   For gins and wiles the ouzel to beguile,
>   Whiles thou under a bush shall sit and smile.
>
> Or with hair-pipes (set in a muset hole),
> Wilt thou deceive the deep-earth-delving coney?
> Or wilt thou in a yellow boxen bole
> Taste in a wooden splent the sweet lythe honey?
>   Clusters of crimson grapes I'll pull thee down,
>   And with vine-leaves make thee a lovely crown.[2]

The following from *The Shepherd's Content* was doubt-

---

[1] His poems have been reprinted by Mr. Arber in *The English Scholars' Library*, 1876; and also by Mr. Grosart.
[2] Barnfield's *Poems* (Grosart), p. 19.

less a composition suggested by the description of the
shepherd boy in Sidney's *Arcadia*,[1] and shows signs of
Spenser's influence, but the application of the pastoral
imagery to the customs of feudal England is original.

> He sits all day loud-piping on a hill,
> The whilst his flock about him dance apace,
> His heart with joy, his ears with music fill ;
> Anon a bleating wether bears the base,
> A lamb the treble ; and to his disgrace
> > Another answers like a middle mean ;
> > Thus every one to bear a part are fain.
>
> Like a great King he rules a little land,
> Still making statutes and ordaining laws,
> Which, if they break, he beats them with his wand ;
> He doth defend them from the greedy jaws
> Of raving wolves, and lion's bloody paws.
> > His field his Realm, his subjects are his Sheep,
> > Which he doth still in due obedience keep.
>
> First he ordains by Act of Parliament,
> (Holden by custom in each country town),
> That if a sheep with any bad intent
> Presume to break the neighbour hedges down,
> Or haunt strange pastures that be not his own :
> > He shall be pounded for his lustiness,
> > Until his master find out some redress.
>
> Also, if any prove a strageller
> From his own fellows in a foreign field,
> He shall be taken for a wanderer,
> And forced himself immediately to yield,
> Or with a wide-mouthed mastiff cur be killed ;
> > And if not claimed within a twelve month's space,
> > He shall remain with Landlord in that place.
>
> Or if one stray to feed far from the rest,
> He shall be pinched by his swift pie-bald cur ;
> If any by his fellows be opprest,
> The wronger (for he doth all wrong abhor)
> Shall be well banged, so long as he can sturre,
> > Because he did annoy his harmless brother,
> > That meant not harm to him or any other.
>
> .   .   .   .   .
>
> Thus doth he frolic it each day by day,
> And when night comes, draws homeward to his cote

---

[1] See p. 222.

Singing a jig or merry roundelay,
(For who sings commonly so merry a note,
As he that cannot chop or change a groat ?)
    And in the winter nights (his chief desire)
    He turns a crab or cracknell in the fire.

He leads his wench a country Horn-Pipe round,
About a Maypole on a Holiday,
Kissing his lovely lass (with garlands crowned),
With whooping heigh-ho singing care away ;
Thus doth he pass the merry month of May,
    And all the year after in delight and joy
    (Scorning a king) he cares for no annoy.[1]

Barnfield was also the author of the well-known and beautiful lines, beginning "As it fell upon a day," and of the fine sonnet, "If Music and sweet Poetry agree"; both of which were once supposed to be the work of Shakespeare.[2]

Another variety of poetical Euphuism was introduced by Robert Greene, of whose personal history I shall speak at large when I consider him in his capacity of dramatist. He was the first to treat subjects of love in the form of the Italian "novella," combining Lyly's narrative mannerism with pastoral lyrics and eclogues after the example set by Sidney in his *Arcadia*. These occasional verses show very often graceful and tender feeling, as well as a delicate artificiality of style, and sometimes rise into a fine rapture of poetry, as in the "Description of his Mistress," given by the shepherd-prince Melicertus in *Menaphon* :—

Tune on, my pipe, the praises of my love,
    And midst thine oaten harmony recount
    How fair is she that makes thy music mount,
And every string of thy heart's harp to move.

Shall I compare her form unto the sphere,
    Whence sun-bright Venus vaunts her silver shine ?
    Ah, more than that by just compare is thine,
Whose crystal locks the cloudy heavens do clear !

---

[1] Barnfield's *Poems* (Grosart), p. 43.
[2] They were published with *The Encomion of Lady Pecunia*, but as a separate section of the volume, in 1598. Barnfield's claim to the authorship is well established by Mr. Grosart's reasoning.

How oft have I descending Titan seen
  His burning locks couch in the sea-queen's lap,
  And beauteous Thetis his red body wrap
In watery robes, as he her lord had been.

Whenas my nymph, impatient of the night,
  Bade bright Astræus with his train give place,
  While she led forth the day with her fair face,
And lent each star a more than Delian light.

Not Jove or Nature, should they both agree
  To make a woman of the firmament,
  Of his mixed purity could not invent
A sky-born form so beautiful as she.[1]

After the rise of Marlowe's influence in the theatre, Greene abandoned his Euphuistic manner, and sought to satisfy the new dramatic taste ; but his style was taken up and elaborately extended by Thomas Lodge, a poet of considerable genius, who for many years tried to support himself by writing. He was the second son of Sir Thomas Lodge, once Lord Mayor of London, and was probably born about 1558. Educated first at the Merchant Taylors' School in 1570, he went to Oxford in 1573 as servitor to Edward Hoby, Gentleman Commoner of Trinity ; took his B.A. degree in 1577, and became M.A. in 1580. His first appearance as a writer was in 1579, when he defended the stage against the attacks of Gosson. He himself wrote for the theatre. His *Wounds of Civil War* is a tragedy in Seneca's style ; but he also helped Greene—when the latter was striving to rival Marlowe's *Tamburlaine*—in the composition of *A Looking-Glass for London*. His earliest attempt at original composition was a narrative tract in the manner of *Euphues—An Alarum against Usurers*, published in 1584. In 1588 he made a voyage to the Canaries, and during his absence his *Glaucus and Scilla*, the first of English mythological poems, was published. This was followed in 1590 by his best-known work, *Euphues' Golden Legacy*—from which Shakespeare took the plot of *As You Like It*—and by *Euphues' Shadow*. In 1591 Lodge accompanied Thomas

---

[1] *Greene and Peele's Dramatic and Poetical Works* (Dyce), p. 287.

Cavendish on his voyage to the Straits of Magellan ; in the same year Spenser alluded to him in *Colin Clout's Come Home Again* as "pleasing Alcon,"[1] while he himself published the first of his prose satires *Catharos*. He appeared in 1593 among the sonneteers with a series of poems addressed to " Phillis," and wrote soon afterwards in the Euphuistic style a romantic history of *The Life and Death of William Longbeard*. Returning to the satiric vein, he published his *Spider's Web* in prose in 1594, and *A Fig for Momus*, a collection of satires and epistles in verse, in 1595. His last work—as far as is known—was his *Margarite of America*, a story published in 1596 ; after which he seems to have abandoned literature for medicine. He became a Roman Catholic, and died in 1625.[2]

Lodge has suffered the fate of all poets who have thought of their style before their subject. He had a graceful fancy, a fine taste, and a tuneful ear, but his mind was not possessed by any idea of universal interest. He was first inspired to write by the atmosphere of prevailing Euphuism ; most of his compositions —plays, novels, histories, sonnets, and satires—are steeped in this fashionable manner. For many of the subjects he attempted he had no turn. His dramas are written with a heavy hand ; his satires are of that general kind which awakens no fear, and therefore no interest. The sonnet had long ceased to yield any fresh store of conceits ; and the only novelties that Lodge could introduce into it for the glorification of his Phillis were double rhymes and fresh mechanical combinations of sound ; for example :—

> I wrote in Mirrha's bark, and as I wrote
> Poor Mirrha wept, because I wrote forsaken,
> 'Twas of thy pride I sung in weeping note,
> When as her leaves great moan for pity maken.
>   The falling fountains, from the mountains falling,
> Cried out alas, so fair and be so ruthless,
> And babbling echoes never ceasèd calling,
> Phillis disdain is fit for none but truthless.

---

[1] *Colin Clout's Come Home Again*, v. 394.
[2] His works have been published by the Hunterian Club, 1887, with an excellent Memoir by Mr. Gosse.

The rising pines, wherein I had engravèd,
Thy memory consulting with the wind,
Are trucemen to thy heart and thoughts depravèd,
And say thy kind should not be so unkind.
But out alas, so fell is Phillis fereless,
That she hath made her Damon well-nigh tearless.[1]

On the other hand, when he leaves the sonnet and strikes a pastoral note, the following charming verses show at once that he is on his own ground :—

My Phillis hath the morning sun
  At first to look upon her,
And Phillis hath morn-waking birds
  Her risings for to honour.
My Phillis hath prime-feathered flowers
  That smile when she treads on them,
And Phillis hath a gallant flock
  That leaps since she doth own them.
But Phillis hath so hard a heart,
  Alas ! that she should have it
As yields no mercy to desart,
  Nor grace to those that crave it.
Sweet sun, when thou lookst on,
Pray her regard my moan,
Sweet birds, when you sing to her,
To yield some pity woo her ;
Sweet flowers, when as she treads on,
Tell her her beauty deads one ;
  And if in life her love she nill agree me,
  Pray her before I die she will come see me.[2]

The themes with which his genius is most in sympathy are mythological or romantic love stories in which his fancy can wander freely, and makes excursions at pleasure into lyric verse. He had something of Ovid's ingenious invention ; and this shines particularly in *Scilla's Metamorphosis*, the first of a long line of subjects suggested to English poets by classical mythology. Here his narrative style is picturesque and flowing :—

---

[1] *Phillis* (1593), sonnet xiv.
[2] These lines are erroneously ascribed by Mr. Grosart to Dyer (Fuller Worthies Miscellanies, Dyer's *Poems*, p. 41). They appear in Lodge's *Phillis* (1593).

He that had seen the sweet Arcadian boy
Wiping the purple from his forcèd wound,
His pretty tears betokening his annoy,
His sighs, his cries, his falling to the ground,
    The echoes ringing from the rocks his fall,
    The trees with tears reporting of his thrall ;

And Venus starting at her love-mate's cry,
Forcing her birds to haste her chariot on
And full of grief, at last with piteous eye
Seen where all pale with death he lay alone ;
    Whose beauty quailed as wont the lilies droop,
    When wasteful winter winds do make them stoop.

Her dainty hand addressed to daw her dear,
Her roseal lips applied to his pale cheek,
Her sighs, and then her looks and heavy cheer,
Her bitter threats, and then her passions meek ;
    How on his senseless corpse she lay a-crying,
    As if the boy were then but new a-dying.

" This " (says Mr. Gosse, justly) " is very close to the
earliest manner of Shakespeare ; and if we turn from
Glaucus and Scilla to *Venus and Adonis*, we shall be
struck by the resemblance in many points.   There can
be no doubt that the young Shakespeare borrowed from
Lodge his tone, the mincing sweetness of his versification,
and the ' precious ' use of such words as ' lily,' ' purple,'
' crystal,' and ' primrose.' " [1]

Lodge may also claim the honour of having inspired
Shakespeare with *As You Like It*.   In *Euphues' Golden
Legacy*, the story is very gracefully told in prose inter-
spersed with lyrics, as in Sidney's *Arcadia* and Greene's
Menaphon.   The songs have much beauty though of an
artificial kind.   Here is Rosader's (Orlando's) description
of Rosalynde, whose name is borrowed from *The Shepherds
Calendar :*—

                Like to the clear in highest sphere,
                Where all imperial glory shines,
                Of self-same colour is her hair,
                Whether unfolded or in twines.
                        Heigh ho, fair Rosalynde !

---

[1] Memoir of Thomas Lodge.   Prefixed to the works of the author.
Printed for the Hunterian Club, 1887.

Her eyes are sapphires set in snow,
Refining heaven by every wink ;
The gods do fear when as they glow,
And I do tremble when I think.
       Heigh ho, would she were mine !

Her cheeks are like the blushing cloud
That beautifies Aurora's face,
Or like the crimson silver shroud,
That Phœbus' smiling looks doth grace
       Heigh ho, fair Rosalynde !

Her lips are like two budded roses,
Whom ranks of lilies neighbour nigh,
Within which bounds she balm encloses
Apt to entice a deity.
       Heigh ho, would she were mine !

And Rosalynde's own madrigal, describing " how many fathom deep she is in love," has all the graceful, though effeminate, fancy characteristic of the epigrammatists of Alexandria :—

Love in my bosom like a bee
    Doth suck his sweet ;
Now with his wings he plays with me,
    Now with his feet :
Within mine eyes he makes his nest,
His bed amidst my tender breast ;
My kisses are his daily feast,
And yet he robs me of my rest.
       Ah wanton, will ye ?

And if I sleep, then percheth he
    With pretty flight,
And makes his pillow of my knee
    The livelong night.
Strike I my lute, he tunes the string ;
He music plays if so I sing ;
He lends me every lovely thing ;
Yet cruel he my heart doth sting :
       Whist wanton, still ye !

Else I with roses every day
    Will whip you hence,
And bind you, when you long to play,
    For your offence.
I'll shut my eyes to keep you in ;
I'll make you fast it for your sin ;
I'll count your power not worth a pin ;
Alas ! what hereby shall I win,
       If he gainsay me ?

> What if I beat the wanton boy
> With many a rod ?
> He will repay me with annoy
> Because a God.
> Then sit thou safely on my knee,
> And let thy bower my bosom be.
> Lurk in mine eyes ; I like of thee:
> Oh, Cupid, so thou pity me,
> Spare not, but play thee.

Lodge, in all his poems, toys with the spirit of the Renaissance in the manner of a Euphuist. But the artificiality of Euphuism is borne down by the powerful genius of Christopher Marlowe, who, following up, in his *Hero and Leander,* the path opened out by Lodge, treats his theme with a more than Pagan freedom. Since Chaucer's *Troilus and Cressida* no poem had appeared giving anything like the same direct and dramatic representation of human passion. Chaucer had depicted female fickleness and levity violating the laws and conventions enforced on chivalrous lovers by the *Cours d'Amour.* Marlowe, in his expansion of the pseudo - Musæus, represents, with all the energy of his genius, the effects of youthful love, portraying with astonishing skill the difference of its manifestation in the heart of either sex. Though his style is coloured with the conceits and mannerism of the period, yet, as compared with the diction of contemporary Euphuistic writers, it has a fiery strength and vigour not to be found in any other man. Take, for example, the description of Leander on his return to his father's house after his first meeting with Hero :—

> Home when he came, he seemed not to be there,
> But, like exilèd air thrust from his sphere,
> Set in a foreign place ; and straight from thence,
> Alcides-like by mighty violence,
> He would have chased away the swelling main,
> That him from her unjustly did detain.
> Like as the sun in a diameter
> Fires and inflames objects removed far,
> And heateth kindly, shining laterally :
> So beauty sweetly quickens when 'tis nigh,

> But, being separated and remov'd,
> Burns where it cherish'd, murders where it lov'd.
> Therefore even as an index to a book,
> So to his mind was young Leander's look.
> O none but gods have power their love to hide !
> Affection by the countenance is descried ;
> The light of hidden fire itself discovers,
> And love that is conceal'd betrays poor lovers.
> His secret flame apparently was seen :
> Leander's father knew where he had been ;
> And for the same mildly rebuked his son,
> Thinking to quench the sparkles new-begun.
> But love, resisted once, grows passionate,
> And nothing more than counsel lovers hate ;
> For as a hot, proud, horse highly disdains
> To have his head controll'd, but breaks the reins,
> Spits forth the ringled bit, and with his hoves
> Checks the submissive ground ; so he that loves
> The more he is restrain'd the worse he fares :
> What is it now but mad Leander dares ?
> " O Hero, Hero ! " thus he cried full oft ;
> And then he got him to a rock aloft,
> Where having spied her tower, long stared he on't,
> And pray'd the narrow toiling Hellespont
> To part in twain, that he might come and go ;
> But still the rising billows answered, " No."
> With that he stripp'd him to the ivory skin,
> And crying, " Love, I come," leap'd lively in.[1]

Marlowe died before he had completed the poem ; it was finished by George Chapman, and no stronger proof of the greatness of Marlowe's genius can be furnished than the contrast between the work of the two men. Chapman did not write without inspiration ; but whereas Marlowe's style—as the above splendid passage shows— is all flame, his successor's, even in his most brilliant moments, is half smoke. He is smothered by his Euphuism ; witness the following powerful and characteristic lines, describing the apparition of the angry Venus :—

> All were in heaven, now they with Hero were :
> But Venus' looks brought wrath and urgèd fear.
> Her robe was scarlet ; black her head's attire ;
> And through her naked breast shin'd streams of fire,

---

[1] Marlowe's *Works* (Dyce), p. 286.

As when the rarefièd air is driven
In flashing streams, and opes the darken'd heaven.
In her white hands a wreath of yew she bore ;
And breaking th' icy wreath sweet Hero wore,
She forc'd about her brows her wreath of yew,
And said, " Now, minion, to thy fate be true,
Though not to me ; endure what this portends :
Begin where lightness will, in shame it ends.
Love makes thee cunning ; thou art current now,
By being counterfeit : thy broken vow
Deceit with her pied garters must rejoin,
And with her stamp thou countenances must coin :
Coyness and pure deceits, for purities ;
And still a maid wilt seem in cozened eyes,
And have an antic face to laugh within,
While thy smooth looks make men digest thy sin.
But since thy lips (least thought forsworn) forswore,
Be never virgin's vow worth trusting more." [1]

In these two passages the reader will observe with
what magnificent ease Marlowe masters thought, while
Chapman seems to struggle with it ; the consequence is
that the verse of the former is harmonious and flowing,
but that of the latter often labours heavily.   Conceit itself
—and he has plenty of it—seems to sit lightly on
Marlowe ; for example :—

So lovely-fair was Hero, Venus nun,
As Nature wept, thinking she was undone,
Because she took more from her than she left,
And of such wondrous beauty her bereft :
Therefore in sign her treasure suffered wrack,
Since Hero's time hath half the world been black. [2]

A touch of humour redeems this extravagance ; but when
a conceit of Chapman's gets hold of the bit there is no
holding it.   Witness the passage describing Leander after
swimming back from Sestos :—

His most kind sister all his secrets knew,
And to her, singing like a shower, he flew,
Sprinkling the earth that to their tombs took in,
Streams dead for love to leave his ivory skin ;
Which yet a snowy foam did leave above,
As soul to the dead water that did love.

---

[1] Marlowe's *Works* (Dyce), p. 297.   [2] *Ibid.* p. 280.

> And from thence did the first white roses spring,
> (For love is sweet and fair in everything),
> And all the sweeten'd shore as he did go,
> Was crown'd with odorous roses white as snow.[1]

Even in the reflective passages, which are congenial to Chapman's style, Marlowe maintains his superiority :—

> It lies not in our power to love or hate,
> For will in us is overrul'd by fate.
> When two are stript, long ere the course begin,
> We wish that one should lose the other win,
> And one especially do we affect,
> Of two gold ingots, like in each respect :
> The reason no man knows ; let it suffice,
> What we behold is censur'd by our eyes.
> When both deliberate, the love is slight :
> Who ever lov'd that lov'd not at first sight ?[2]

The following is the opening of the Third Sestiad, where Chapman takes up his predecessor's tale :—

> New light gives new directions, fortunes new,
> To fashion our endeavours that ensue.
> More harsh, at least more hard, more grave and high,
> Our subject runs, and our stern Muse must fly.
> Love's edge is taken off, and that light flame,
> Those thoughts, joys, longings, that before became
> High inexperienc'd blood, and maid's sharp plights,
> Must now grow staid, and censure the delights,
> That, being enjoy'd, ask judgment ; now we praise,
> As having parted : evenings crown the days.[3]

What distinguishes Marlowe from all other narrative or dramatic poets of his time, is a certain elemental simplicity and greatness of conception. He rises equally above the affectations of archaism and of novel conceit. Some of his contemporaries are distracted in their endeavour to conceive ideal action by means of the images of an extinct chivalry ; others are perplexed by the intrusion into their religious creed of the images of an extinct polytheism. Marlowe fixes his imagination steadily on those elements of human nature which remain the same in all places and all ages. He ignores the traditions of

---

[1] Marlowe's *Works* (Dyce), p. 290.
[2] *Ibid.* p. 281.   [3] *Ibid.* p. 289.

chivalry and the moral restraints of religion.   By so doing
he gains energy for his ideas of human nature, but he at
the same time renders them narrow and contracted, because
the ethical principles of chivalry and Christianity have
become part of the human conscience.   Want of moral
instinct and of Catholic sympathy prevents Marlowe from
attaining, either as a dramatic or an epic poet, the supreme
position which might have been his, had the force of his
genius been tempered by those qualities.   Compared with
Troilus and Criseyde, his *Hero and Leander* lacks dramatic
interest, variety, and relief.   It never reaches the depths
of pathos which Virgil sounds in the Fourth *Æneid*, nor
the heights of spiritual feeling of which Spenser has given
us examples in the *Faery Queen*.   Fortune favoured him
in obliging him to leave his poem a splendid fragment ;
and Chapman's comparative failure did him a further
service, by suggesting what might have been accomplished had *Hero and Leander* been completed by the
same hand that began it.   In truth, however, there is
little to lead us to suppose that Marlowe would have
done much better than his successor.   His poetic impulse
had exhausted itself in a picture of youthful passion ;
and the poverty of invention, shown in the passage
describing Leander swimming the Hellespont, makes it
probable that the poet would have failed to bring the
story to an adequately tragic conclusion.

CHAPTER XI

THE EVOLUTION OF THE ENGLISH POETICAL DRAMA: THE
TRANSITION FROM PAGEANT TO THEATRE; FROM
INTERLUDE TO TRAGEDY, COMEDY, AND HISTORY

WE are apt to think of the drama under Elizabeth as if it
were the sudden creation of the great poets who began to
write towards the close of the reign of that monarch.
Augustus Schlegel, who may be considered as the father
of modern dramatic criticism, and who was, above all
things, anxious to establish his theory of the essential
contrast between the classic and romantic drama, was
emphatic in his insistence on this doctrine. Shakespeare,
he says, "forms such a singular exception to the whole
history of art that we are compelled to assign a particular place to him. He owed hardly anything to his
predecessors, and he has had the greatest influence on
his successors; but no man has yet learned from him
his secret. For two whole centuries, during which his
countrymen have diligently employed themselves in the
cultivation of every branch of science and art, by their
own confession, he has not only never yet been surpassed,
but he has left every dramatic poet at a great distance
behind him." [1]

While the truth of this last proposition is undeniable,
the genius of Shakespeare is not well served by those who
represent it as miraculous. For not only is injustice thus

[1] Schlegel's *Lectures on Dramatic Literature*, Lecture xiii.

done to the lesser fellow-workers who contributed with him to the development of his art, but the vastness of his own intellect and the grand balance of his judgment are not fully appreciated till they are seen in their relation to his surroundings. To suppose that the single efforts of meditation in any one man could have invented a structure so comprehensive and various as the romantic drama, is the height of critical superstition; on the other hand, a knowledge of the manner in which Shakespeare drew suggestions of dramatic action and character from his predecessors and contemporaries, can only serve to heighten our admiration for the incomparable resources of his genius.

Much has been done to correct the disproportionate ideas propagated by Schlegel and the hero-worshipping school of criticism. The excellent history of the English stage by Collier, the judicious literary criticism of Dr. Ward, and the enthusiastic appreciation of the minor Elizabethan dramatists by the late Mr. J. A. Symonds, and others, have thrown a brilliant light on the state of the English stage before the age of Shakespeare. It can no longer be said with truth that "if in the labours of the contemporaries of Shakespeare, even the older who continued to write at the same time with himself, we can discover the resemblance of his style and traces of his art, still it will always remain doubtful whether we are to consider these as the feeble model or the imperfect imitation." [1] But something still remains to be done, and as the object of this history is in particular to exhibit the general march of poetic thought and imagination among the English people, I shall endeavour in the following pages to trace the slow gradations by which the dramatic art passed out of the rudimentary conditions, peculiar to it in the Middle Ages, into the hands of those who brought the form of the romantic drama to its full perfection.

Two sets of external causes determine the growth of a national drama; changes in the taste of the audience,

[1] Schlegel's *Lectures on Dramatic Literature*, Lecture xiii.

and improvements in the traditions and appliances of the art itself.   With regard to the former, one of the most remarkable features in the English romantic drama, pointing to its unmistakably national origin, is the extent to which its form has been modified to suit the tastes of all ranks and classes of English society.   As we have already seen, the oldest kind of dramatic exhibition in England sprang up as a branch of Church education.   The Miracle Play, originally acted in the interior of churches, for the purpose of familiarising the people with the mysteries of the Christian faith, was presently removed to the church-yard, thence to the village green, and thence again to the streets of towns like York and Coventry ; while, in the course of its migrations, it gradually altered its character from doctrine to imitation, and began to exhibit many of those peculiarities of structure and dialogue which are preserved in the most highly developed examples of the Elizabethan drama.[1]

The Morality, as the name implies, involved a fresh step in the secularisation of the stage.   Its didactic aim, however, still testifies to the influence of the Church, and its frequently learned matter, as well as its allegorical forms, show that it was in the first instance adapted to the satisfaction of the more refined tastes of the nobility. The performers in these pieces were either minstrels in the establishment of great houses,[2] itinerant companies privileged by their noble masters to go about the country with plays,[3] or " children of the chapel," whether of the King's court or one of the castles of the nobility.[4]   As these players supported themselves by " the loving benevo-lence and favours of the people," [5] the tastes of the multitude had to be consulted as well as those of the aristocracy ; and records of companies of players, attached to such populous centres as London, Coventry, Mile End, Kingston,

---

[1] Vol. i. chap. xi.

[2] Warton, *History of English Poetry*, 8vo ed. vol. i. p. 94.

[3] Collier, *History of English Dramatic Poetry*, vol. i. p. 42.

[4] The Duke of Norfolk had his "children of the chapel" (Collier, *History of English Dramatic Poetry*, vol. i. pp. 36-38).

[5] Collier, *History of English Dramatic Poetry*, vol. i. pp. 42, 84.

and the like, prove that the love of the moralities as well as of the miracle plays, was widely spread.[1]

In the reign of Henry VIII. the centre of influence in the drama, as in every other department of social life and art, passes from the Castle to the Court. The word Interlude, now almost universally employed to denote the old Morality, seems to symbolise the dominant influence determining the taste of the age. Performed in the intervals between the courses at banquets, the new Moralities were necessarily made shorter than those of the old style exemplified in *The Castle of Perseverance.* At the same time the Morality still continued to be used for the purposes of instruction, and, when it was exhibited before popular audiences with this aim, the freedom with which opinions were advocated in it soon called for the intervention of the State. In 1543, the first Act of Parliament was passed for the regulation of the stage, and to guard against the propagation of doctrines contrary to those of the Church of Rome. A proclamation issued in 1553 forbade the printing and sale of books, and the playing of interludes, without the Royal License ; while the widespread taste for dramatic performances was indicated in 1572 by the Act to regulate and control itinerant actors and minstrels.[2]

Meantime the growing refinement of the age caused great attention to be paid to the construction of plays exhibited before the Sovereign, and in such learned societies as the Universities and the Inns of Court. As early as 1514 we find the appointment of an officer, called Serjeant-at-Arms and Revels, to superintend the Royal entertainments ; and in 1546 occurs the first definite mention of the Master of the Revels (*magister jocorum*).[3] Elizabeth's accession marked the beginning of a rapid development of dramatic taste among the higher classes. Plays of a more elaborate structure than had hitherto been attempted were acted by the members

[1] Collier, *History of English Dramatic Poetry*, vol. i. p. 47.
[2] *Ibid.* vol. i. pp. 127, 157, 203.
[3] *Ibid.* vol. i. p. 133.

of Gray's Inn and the Inner Temple, and by the scholars
of the two great Universities ; while the children of Paul's,
the children of Windsor, and the servants of Lord Howard
and the Earl of Warwick, are constantly recorded as
performing before the Queen at Richmond, Hampton
Court, Whitehall, and Greenwich.[1]

With audiences of this kind a learned and classical
education naturally determined the form of the drama ;
but the popular tradition was preserved in those pieces in
which the success of the actors depended on the favour of
less sophisticated judges.   In the remoter parts of the
country licenses to act were required from two justices
of the peace, and the players performed in halls in the
chief towns, and supported themselves by such money as
they could collect from the spectators.   Puritanic sentiments, rapidly spreading among the middle classes,
frequently brought these artistic servants of the nobility
into collision with the municipal authorities.   We find,
for example, the servants of the Earl of Worcester
engaged in a dispute with the Corporation of Leicester
as to their right to play in the town ; and the Crown
itself met with opposition when it exercised its prerogative
on behalf of the players against the wishes of the citizens.
In 1574 a Royal Patent to perform plays having been
issued for the first time to the servants of the Earl of
Leicester, the Lord Mayor and Corporation of London
disputed the right of the company to act in their city.[2]
The next year an Act of the Common Council was passed
to regulate the exhibition of plays which was prohibited
unless the performance was first sanctioned by the Lord
Mayor and Aldermen, and a license granted by the Lord
Mayor.   From an order of the city authorities in this
year we find that the gathering of the people to witness
plays was attended with certain evils, among which
are enumerated the infection of the plague ; the
corruption of youth ; the wasting of time by poor
people ; the withdrawing of people from public prayer.

---

[1] Collier, *History of English Dramatic Poetry*, vol. i. pp. 168-212.
[2] *Ibid.* pp. 209-213.

The remedies proposed by the authorities to counteract these mischiefs were the restriction of the right to play in private houses, and the prohibition of all performances on Sunday.   In 1589 this severity was increased by reason of the players having introduced matters of state and religion on the stage.   Some of the playwrights had also joined in the Martin Marprelate Controversy, and the consequence was that all theatrical representations were stopped in the city.[1]

The great opposition which the wandering companies of players met with from the municipal authorities, while pursuing their vocation of amusing the public, drove them to provide a settled home for the practice of their art beyond the reach of civic interference.   In 1575 and 1576 three theatres were built, one at Blackfriars and two at Shoreditch, and before the end of the century several others were added, of which the most famous was the Globe. To these play-houses a medley of traditions, made up of the practice of the itinerant stage, the learning of the Universities and the Inns of Court, the pictorial scenic effects aimed at in the Court Masques and Pageants, was now attracted as to a common centre.   The audiences were composed of all classes, so that the dramatist had to take account of various and often conflicting tastes in the composition of his play.

Such were the external influences which helped to limit and define the conditions of dramatic representation in England before the close of the sixteenth century. But a yet stronger determining influence was exercised on the genius of the individual poet, by the ancient dramatic forms and traditions which he endeavoured to bring into conformity with the requirements of his age. Fortunately, a great number of old English plays have been preserved by the industry of Dodsley and others, and from these it is possible to derive an intelligible idea of the gradual process which culminated in the forms of Shakespearian Tragedy and Comedy.   It is true that our knowledge of the dates at which the surviving

---

[1] Collier, *History of English Dramatic Poetry*, vol. i. pp. 279-282.

Moralities and Interludes were first produced is imperfect, and the historians of the stage, dealing with the more mature work of the dramatist, have not thought it necessary to attempt any classification of these primitive efforts. Dr. Ward, however, says :—"In the English Moralities it is not easy to draw a distinction between particular groups ; and such signs of advance as they show would best be gathered from an attempt to survey them chronologically."[1] I am quite of this opinion, and as for the particular purpose of this history it is necessary to proceed step by step, while the changes in the construction of the English play in the course of its evolution throw much light on the progress of the national imagination, I shall endeavour to discriminate the features of the more characteristic Interludes, and the modifications in them which prepared the way for the later drama.

In dealing with the rise of the drama in England I showed how the form of the first Moralities was derived from the Miracle Plays. In all of them the prevailing idea is one of conflict between Good and Evil, and in the older examples, such as the *Castle of Perseverance*, and the *World and the Child*, the aim is distinctly theological.[2] But just as in the Miracle Plays, the dramatic instinct gradually prevailed over the didactic—as appears from the contrast between the York and Beverley plays—so in the Moralities the desire of amusing the spectators led the dramatist always to make his allegorical personage more real and human ; hence, in plays like *Hick Scorner*, the dialogue between the different abstract characters came to be closely modelled on the language of common life. As the nation advanced in refinement, the dwindling influence of the theological element in the drama manifested itself in the more secular character of the instruction which the dramatist endeavoured to impart.

This is particularly the case in the Morality entitled *The Four Elements*, produced about 1517, in which, though the form is still determined by the idea of conflict between

---

[1] Ward, *History of English Dramatic Literature*, vol. i. p. 60.
[2] Vol. i. chap. xi.

the powers of Good and Evil, these powers are represented by Knowledge and Ignorance. The hero of the Interlude is Humanity, the natural representative of Humanum Genus in the *Castle of Perseverance ;* but the Good Angel of the older play is now replaced by Studious Desire, and his antagonist by Sensual Appetite.[1] The aim of the dramatist is to popularise Science by means of the stage ; he declares by the mouth of the "Messenger" :—

> But because some folk be little disposed
> To sadness, but more to mirth and sport,
> This philosophical work is mixed
> With merry conceits to give them comfort,
> And occasion to cause them to resort
> To hear this matter, whereto if they take heed
> Some learning to them thereof may proceed.[2]

The author also bethinks himself that his audience— particularly if they happen to be at dinner—may prefer to have their instruction in an abbreviated form, and he describes his play as "A new interlude and a merry of the nature of the Four Elements, declaring many proper points of philosophy natural, and of divers strange effects and causes ; which interlude, if the whole matter be played, will contain the space of an hour and a half ; but if ye list ye may leave out much of the sad matter as the Messenger's part, and some of Nature's part, and some of Experience's part, and yet the matter will depend conveniently, and then it will not be past three-quarters of an hour's length." [3]

The plot is as follows : Natura Naturata tells Humanity that he is compounded of the Four Elements, and there- fore must not lead a merely animal life. Humanity humbly asks her to teach him how to live, and she puts him into the hands of Studious Desire, who gives him instruction in astronomy and geography ; but unluckily the hero makes the acquaintance of Sensual Appetite, and is by him introduced to a Taverner and other bad com-

---

[1] See vol. i. p. 418.
[2] Dodsley, *Old English Plays* (1874), vol. i. p. 10.
[3] *Ibid.* vol. i. p. 2.

panions, so much to the injury of his education and
morals, that when Studious Desire, who has gone off to
get the assistance of Experience, returns with that person,
Humanity is found to have quitted the stage. The two
Virtues are accordingly left to discourse with each other
on scientific matters, particularly on geography and the
recent discovery of America; but presently Humanity
returns with Sensual Appetite, and expresses a wish to
have some conversation with Experience. His bad companion leaves him, and Experience gives him instruction,
proving to him by ancient methods the roundness of the
earth. Though delighted with this instructive discourse,
Humanity is not proof against the seductions of Sensual
Appetite, who presently reappears on the stage with
Ignorance, and the two beguile the hero with dances and
songs, till Nature re-enters and reproves the prodigal.
She doubtless converted him, but the play has come
down to us in an imperfect state, so that we can only see
that the form of *The Four Elements*, though not less
didactic, is less morally "tragical," than that of the older
Moralities. Another Interlude of the same period, called
Wyt and Science, reproduces these characteristics, but
seems to be intended for a less educated audience ; its
leading feature is a conversation in rustic dialogue between
Idleness and Ignorance.[1]

In these two Interludes the moralist is mainly influenced by the ideas of the Renaissance ; but, as was to be
expected, the Morality was soon employed to promote the
ends of the Reformation ; and three surviving examples
show the manner in which at different epochs the
dramatist sought to put matter of this kind before the
audience. The first manner is exhibited in *Lusty Juventus*,[2] an interlude written by one Robert Wever, in the
reign of Edward VI. Here the dramatist preserves the
old form representing the conflict between Good and
Evil ; but Human Nature, the conventional hero, is
replaced by Youth ; the object of the writer, as announced

---

[1] Edited for the Shakespeare Society by Mr. Halliwell in 1848.
[2] For this Interlude see Dodsley's *Old Plays* (1874), vol. ii. p. 41.

by the prologue, being to show the necessity of a true religious education :—

> For as much as man is naturally prone
> To evil from his youth, as Scripture doth recite,
> It is necessary that he be speedily withdrawn
> From concupiscence of sin his natural appetite.

The personages introduced are Messenger, Lusty Juventus, Good Counsel, Knowledge, Sathan the Devil, Hypocrisy, Fellowship, Abominable Living, and God's Merciful Promises. Lusty Juventus is, like Human Nature in the older Moralities, represented at the opening as well inclined to good instruction, and the Devil appears lamenting over the decline of his power :—

> I am in sore dread to show my face,
> My auctority and works are so greatly despised,
> My inventions, and all that ever I have devised.
> O, O, full well I know the cause
> That my estimation doth thus decay ;
> The old people would believe still in my laws,
> But the younger sort lead them a contrary way.
> They will not believe, they plainly say,
> In old traditions and made by men,
> But they will live as the Scripture teacheth them.

Hypocrisy, as the minister of Satan, undertakes to seduce Juventus, and with the aid of Fellowship and Abominable Living he is so successful, that Youth slides back into the superstition and the ill living of the old ways. Good Counsel convinces him of his sin, and he falls into a state of despair, from which he is finally recovered by God's Merciful Promises.

New Custom puts forward the same moral as *Lusty Juventus* in a different form.[1] This play can hardly have been written before 1570 ; and the names of the actors indicate much bitterness of feeling against the Roman Catholics, the legacy of the Marian persecutions. They are :—

---

[1] Dodsley's *Old Plays*, vol. iii. p. 1.

The Prologue
Perverse Doctrine, *an old Popish priest.*
Ignorance, *another, but elder.*
New Custom, *a Minister.*
Light of the Gospel, *a Minister.*
Hypocrisy, *an old Woman.*
Cruelty, *a Ruffler.*
Avarice, a *Ruffler.*
Edification, *a Sage.*
Assurance, *a Virtue.*
God's Felicity, *a Sage.*

The object of this Interlude is to show that what is called by many people the *new* custom, is really the primitive doctrine of the Church; the old form of the Morality, the direct conflict between Good and Evil, is now discarded; the play is divided into acts and scenes; and the action, such as it is, consists in the conversion of Perverse Doctrine into Sincere Doctrine by the skilful pleading of Light of the Gospel. As usual this spiritual περιπέτεια is very abruptly effected, Perverse Doctrine being up to the last moment represented as a very thorough scoundrel, who is quite ready to avail himself of the wicked means suggested to him by Cruelty and Avarice. His description of New Custom is characteristic ·—

They have brought in one, a young upstart lad, as it appears;
I am sure he hath not been in the realm very many years,
With a gathered frock, a polled head, and a broad hat,
An unshaved beard, a pale face; and he teacheth that
All our doings are nought, and hath been many a day.
He disalloweth our ceremonies and rites, and teacheth another
    way
To serve God than that which we do use,
And goeth about the people's minds to seduce.
It is a pestilent knave, he will have no priests no corner-cap to
    wear;
Surplices are superstition: beads, paxes, and other gear.
Crosses, bells, candles, oil, bran, salt, spittle, and incense,
With cursing and singing, he accounts not worth three half-
    pence,
And cries out on them all (if to repeat them I wist)
Such holy things wherein our religion doth consist.

But he commands the service in English to be read,
And for the Holy Legend the Bible to put in his stead,
Every man to look thereon at his list and pleasure,
Every man to study divinity at his convenient leisure,
With a thousand new guises more you know as well as I.
And to term him by his right name, if I should not lie,
It is New Custom, for so they do him call,
Both our sister Hypocrisy, Superstition, and Idolatry and all ;
And truly, me-thinketh, they do justly and wisely therein,
Since he is so diverse, and so lately crept in.

The descriptions of the actors in this play, given in
the list, show the inevitable tendency of all allegorical
representations in England from Piers Plowman downwards, to substitute real persons for abstractions.   The
tendency is carried forward another step in the *Conflict of
Conscience*, a Morality probably composed about the same
time as *New Custom*, or a little earlier, and representing the
apostasy, the remorse, and the despair, of Francis Spira, an
Italian lawyer, who abandoned his Protestant convictions,
" for fear of the loss of life and worldly goods," about the
year 1550.[1]   This person appears in the Morality under
a generic name which is thus naïvely accounted for :—

And here our author thought it meet the true name to omit,
And at this time imagine him PHILOLOGUS to be :
First for because a comedy will hardly him permit
The vices of one private man to touch particularly :
Again now shall it stir them more, who shall it hear or see ;
For if this worldling had been named, we would straight deem
        in mind,
That all by him then spoken were, ourselves we would not find.
But sith Philologus is nought else but one that loves to talk,
And common [2] of the Word of God, but hath no further care
According as it teacheth them in God's fear for to walk,
If that we practise this indeed, Philologi we are ;
And so by his deserved fault we may in time beware :
Now if, as author first it meant, you hear it with this gain,
In good behalf he will esteem that he bestowed his pain.

The strange mixture of real and allegorical personages which the moralist's manner of treating his subject

---

[1] Dodsley's *Old Plays* (1874), vol. vi. p. 1.   [2] Commune.

rendered necessary, may be gathered from the list of *dramatis personæ*.

The actors' names, divided into six parts, most convenient for such as be disposed either to show this comedy in private houses or otherwise :—[1]

Prologue.		Avarice.	
Mathetes.	For one.	Suggestion.	For one.
Conscience.		Gisbertus.	
Paphinitius.		Nuntius.	
Satan.		Hypocrisy.	For one.
Tyranny.		Theologus.	
Spirit.	For one.	Cardinal.	For one.
Horror.		Cacon.	
Eusebius.		Philologus.	For one.

It is interesting to observe that in this interlude—an enormously long one—the writer departed from fact for the purpose of preserving the traditional form of the Morality.   Francis Spira committed suicide under the pressure of remorse ; but the conclusion of *The Conflict of Conscience* represents him as having been converted, though in the following very peculiar fashion.

ACT VI. Scene Last

Nuntius

O joyful news which I report, and bring unto your ears !
Philologus, that would have hanged himself with cord,
Is now converted unto God with many bitter tears :
By Godly counsel he was won, all praise be to the Lord.
His errors all he did renounce, his blasphemies he abhorred,

---

[1] The players at this period disguised their faces with masks.   See Puttenham, *Art of English Poesy*, lib. i. xiv. : "Thenceforth fearing none ill-will or enmity at anybody's hands, they left their disguisings and played bare face, till one Roscius Gallus, the most excellent player among the Romans, brought up these vizards which we see at this day used, partly to supply the want of players, when there were more parts than there were persons, or that it was not thought meet to trouble and pester princes' chambers with too many folks.   Now by the change of a vizard one man might play the king and the carter, the old nurse and the young damsel, the merchant and the soldier, or any other part he listed very conveniently."

And being converted left his life, exhorting foe and friend
That do profess the faith of Christ to be constant to the end.
Full thirty weeks in woful wise afflicted he had been,
All which long time he took no food, but forced against his will
Even with a spoon to pour some broth his teeth between :
And though they sought by force this wise to feed him still,
He always strove with all his might the same on ground to
    spill ;
So that no sustenance he received, no sleep could he attain,
And now the Lord in mercy great hath eased him of his pain.

While this group of Interludes reflects the bitter spirit of religious partizanship prevailing in the early part of Elizabeth's reign, another indicates the tendency of the moralist to depart from theological tradition and to look for subjects rather in manners than in doctrine. This movement manifests itself in various shapes in four interludes, *The Nice Wanton*, *The Disobedient Child*, *Like Will to Like*, and *The Three Ladies of London*. The two former of these plays are very commonplace in conception. *The Nice Wanton*,[1] written about 1560, shows the sad consequences of spoiling children. The names of the *dramatis personæ* are—

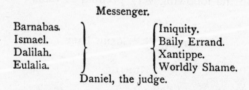

Messenger.

Barnabas.   ⎫   ⎧Iniquity.
Ismael.   ⎪   ⎪Baily Errand.
Dalilah.   ⎬   ⎨Xantippe.
Eulalia.   ⎭   ⎩Worldly Shame.

Daniel, the judge.

Ismael and Dalilah are the two profligates of the piece, whose course of wickedness runs from playing truant at school to the gallows and suicide ; the Vice Iniquity in no way differs from the human actors, and he is finally condemned to death by Daniel the judge ; the only other abstraction in the play, Worldly Shame, is brought in merely to persuade the mother, Xantippe, to make away with herself after the ruin of her children, an act from which she is dissuaded by her pious son, Barnabas, who thus illustrates the propriety of his name.

[1] Dodsley, *Old Plays* (1874), vol. ii. p. 158.

In the *Disobedient Child*,[1] published in 1560, there are no abstract characters ; the names of the players being—

The Prologue Speaker.	The Young Woman.
The Rich Man.	The Serving Man.
The Rich Man's Son.	The Priest.
The Man Cook.	The Devil.
The Woman Cook.	The Perorator.

The plot is of the simplest kind, being simply a representation of the evil consequences of marrying against the will of one's father ; and nothing remains of the structure of the old Moralities but Sathan, the Devil, who might himself have been omitted, as he merely comes on the stage to make a long speech (beginning, " Ho, ho, ho, what a fellow am I "), in which he refers to his secret influence on the Rich Man's Son, and then vanishes without taking any part in the action.

Like Will to Like,[2] written by Ulpian Fulwell in 1568, combines the characteristics of these new Interludes of manners, with some of the features of the older Moralities. The names of the players are—

The Prologue.		Lucifer.	
Tom Tosspot.	For one.	Ralph Roister.	For one.
Haukin Hangman.		Good Fame.	
Tom Collier.		Severity.	
Hance.		Philip Fleming.	For another.
Virtuous Life.	For one.	Pierce Pickpurse.	
God's Promise.		Honour.	
Cuthbert Cutpurse.		Nichol Newfangle, *The Vice*.	

In many respects this Interlude is an extension of the homely motives represented in the old Morality, *Hick Scorner*, the aim of which, as we saw in the last volume, was to blend amusement with instruction by painting the manners of the people under the guise of personified abstractions.[3]   In *Like Will to Like*, however, we have

---

[1] Dodsley's *Old Plays*, vol. ii. p. 265.
[2] *Ibid.* (1874) vol. iii. p. 302.
[3] See vol. i. p. 424.

typical human characters—loafer, thief, and drunkard—
themselves introduced, labelled with appropriate names,
and engaged in a more complicated plot. The course
of the action is developed by the Vice, Nichol Newfangle,
who, by accommodating himself to the inclinations of the
different actors, brings them to trouble in various ways,
and gives significance to the title of the play. He it is
who provides the chief entertainment, from the moment
when he enters in company with his "bottle-nosed god-
father," Lucifer, to the close of the play, when he rides
away to Hell on his patron's back. Not always lucky
in his adventures, he is in one scene roughly handled by
two of his dupes, but the clever devices with which he
deludes those who trust in him were doubtless a source
of infinite delight to the rude spectators of the Morality.
The close imitation of manners is illustrated by the character of the drunken Hance, who is represented as stam-
mering in his cups. Melancholy to relate, the Virtuous
Abstractions are reduced to the level of the Greek
chorus; they do little more than converse among
themselves; and poetical justice has to be satisfied with
the doom awarded to fools and knaves by the judge
Severity and Haukin Hangman. The reader may not be
displeased with the following extract—a soliloquy of the
rustic Mephistopheles—from this vivacious drama :—

[*Here entereth in* NICHOLAS NEWFANGLE, *and bringeth in with
him a bag, a staff, a bottle, and two halters, going about the place,
showing it unto the audience, and singeth thus :*—

Trim mer-chandise, trim, trim : trim mer-chandise, trim, trim.

[He may sing this as oft as he thinketh good.]

Marry, here is merchandise, who so list for to buy any !
Come, see for your love, and buy for your money.
This is land which I must distribute anon,
According to my promise, ere I be gone :

For why Tom Tosspot since he went hence
Hath increased a noble just unto ninepence ;
And Ralph Roister, it may no otherwise be chosen,
Hath brought a pack of wool to a fair pair of hosen.
This is good thrift, sirs, learn it who shall,
And now a couple of fellows are come from Cutpurse Hall ;
And there have they brought many a purse to wrack.
Lo, here is gear that will make their necks for to crack ;
For I promised Tom Tosspot and Ralph Roister a piece of
    land ;
Lo, here it is ready in my right hand :
A wallet and a bottle ; but it is not to be sold.
I told them before that of Beggar's Manor it did hold,
And for Cuthbert Cutpurse and Pierce Pickpurse here is good
    fare :
This is the land of the two-legged mare,
Which I to them promised, and to divide it with discretion ;
Shortly you shall see I will put them in possession.
How like you this merchandise, my masters ?   Is it not trim ?
A wallet, a bottle, a staff, and a string ?
How sayst thou, Wat Waghalter ? [1]   Is not this a trim thing ?
In faith Ralph Roister is in good case as I suppose ;
For he hath lost all that he hath, save his doublet and his hose ;
And Tom Tosspot is even at that same point ;
For he would lose a limb or jeopard a joint ;
But behold, yonder they come both, now all is gone and spent :
I know their errand, and what is their intent.

The somewhat farcical treatment of manners in *Like Will to Like* is exchanged for a more genuinely comic style in *The Three Ladies of London,* a play produced in 1584, in which the genius of the old Morality probably reached the highest level of which it was capable.[2]   The author, Robert Wilson, was himself an actor, and, like the famous Tarlton, was accustomed to amuse his audiences by improvised wit ; but he was also a dramatist of real invention, and thoroughly understood the requirements of the stage.   His purpose in *The Three Ladies of London* was evidently to produce a dramatic satire on the manners of the day by engaging allegorical personages, invested, like Langland's abstractions, with all the attributes of reality, in a regularly contrived action.   The three ladies, Love,

---

[1] It is evident that in this speech the Vice must have been addressing himself to individuals in the audience.
[2] Dodsley's *Old Plays,* vol. vi. p. 244.

Conscience, and Lucre, have estates in London; and the other characters in the piece, when first introduced to us, are on their way to town hoping to get "entertainment" in the household of one or other of them. Usury, Fraud, Simony, and Dissimulation, as is to be expected from their names, are intent upon the service of Lucre; but Simplicity prefers the establishment of Love. The four rogues act as go-betweens in introducing to their mistress different suitors—such as an Italian merchant, an artisan, and a lawyer—and make their own profit out of the business. Simplicity, who has more shrewdness than his name seems to imply, watches their proceedings, and when his cousin, Sincerity, a clergyman, comes to ask for a living, he is able to give him some practical hints as to the course he should adopt. He advises him to get Conscience to use her influence with Lucre for his cousin's preferment; but soon it appears that Love and Conscience have come down in the world, and have been obliged to sell their house to Lucre. Conscience, however, gives Sincerity the recommendation he desires, and is then invited to dinner by Hospitality. Sincerity finds that the interest of Conscience is not very powerful with Lucre, and all that he gets by way of preferment is the parsonage of St. Nihil, which, Dissimulation advises his mistress, may be spared from the pluralities of Simony. Hospitality meanwhile falls into the hands of Usury, and is murdered by him; Love and Conscience, turned out of doors by Lucre, are reduced to such straits that Conscience is obliged to sell brooms; and Lucre reigns supreme. Love and Conscience, under pressure of want, begin to be corrupted by Lucre; Love is married to Dissimulation; while Conscience allows her beautiful face to be spotted by the contents of "the box of all abominations." The gradual degeneration of Conscience is finely represented:—

LUCRE

Usury, carry in these brooms, and give them to the maid,
For I know of such store she will be well afraid.
                    [*Exit* USURY *with the brooms.*

Hold, Conscience; though thy brooms be not worth a quarter so
  much,
Yet to give thee a piece of gold I do it not grutch;
And if thou wouldst follow thy mind, thou shouldst not live in such
  sort
But pass thy days with pleasure, store of every kind of sport.

CONSCIENCE

I think you lead the world in a string, for everybody follows you:
And sith every one doth it, why may not I do it too?
For that I see your free heart and great liberality,
I marvel not that all people are so willing to follow ye.

LUCRE

Then, sweet soul, mark what I would have thee do for me.
That is, to deck up thy poor cottage handsomely;
And for that purpose I have five thousand crowns in store,
And when it is spent, thou shalt have twice as much more.
But only see thy rooms be neat, when I shall hither resort,
With familiar friends to play, and pass the time in sport;
For the deputy, constable, and spiteful neighbours do spy, pry, and
  eye about my house,
That I dare not be once merry within, but still mute like a mouse.

CONSCIENCE

My good Lady Lucre, I will fulfil your mind in every kind of thing,
So that you shall be welcome at all hours, whomsoever you do
  bring:
And all the dogs in the town shall not bark at your doings, I trow;
For your full pretence and intent I do throughly know,
Even so well as if you had opened the very secrets of your heart,
For which I doubt not but to rest in your favour by my desert.

But the end approaches. The judge appears. Lucre is
arrested, and accused of adultery and robbery, and as
being accessory to murder. She is sentenced to be carried
off by Diligence, the constable, and thrown down to the
lowest hell. Love, having given herself over to Lust, is
doomed to the same punishment. Says the stern judge:—

Then judgment I pronounce on thee, because thou followed Lucrè,
Whereby thou hast sold thy soul to feel like torment with her:
Which torments comprehended are in the worm of Conscience,
Who raging still shall ne'er have end, a plague for thine offence.

Care shall be thy comfort, and sorrow thy life sustain ;
Thou shalt be dying, yet never dead, but pining still in endless
　　pain.
Diligence, convey her to Lucre : let that be her reward,
Because unto her cankered coin she gave her whole regard.
But as for Conscience, carry her to prison,
There to remain until the day of the general session.

This striking play may be regarded as a landmark
alike in the development of the English imagination, and
in the history of the English drama. Much of the spirit
and doctrine of the mediæval Church still survives in it,
and we feel how deeply the conscience of the people was
imbued with its stern, uncompromising teaching—" the
love of money is the root of all evil "—and how naturally
this found expression in the allegorical form of poetry
peculiar to the Middle Ages. Many of the actors in the
Vision of Piers the Plowman, Lady Lucre (Lady Mede),
Conscience, and Simony, reappear in *The Three Ladies of
London ;* and Langland's vigorous satire on contemporary
manners, embodied in the Confessions of the Seven Deadly
Sins,[1] is reproduced in the speeches in which Usury
and Simony relate their fortunes and adventures. On
the other hand, we perceive that the structure of the
Morality has been carried to a point beyond which it
would be impossible to develop it. The old doctrinal
principle of the conflict between Good and Evil no longer
furnishes the plan of the action ; though the moral is plain
enough, it is nevertheless evident that the dramatist is
thinking throughout of the taste of his audience, and of
the means by which he can provide them with dramatic
entertainment. The allegorical personages are introduced
in the costume of everyday life, Dissimulation, when we
first see him, " having on a farmer's long coat and a cap,
and his pole and beard painted motley " ; while Simplicity
enters " like a miller, all mealy, with a wand in his hand."
The latter character replaces " the Vice," who, after the
manner of Nichol Newfangle in *Like Will to Like*, had
gradually been transformed into the comic character which

---

[1] See vol. i. p. 219.

the audience now looked for in the Interlude, and who
was destined in time to change again into the Fool or
Clown of the Shakesperian comedy.   Simplicity—the part
was doubtless played by Wilson—appears more frequently
than any of the other persons, at once amusing the
spectators by the mixture of folly and shrewdness in his
remarks, and explaining to them the progress of the
action.   He frequently addresses himself directly to the
audience, as thus, in one scene where he enters " with a
basket on his arm " :—

> You think I am going to market to buy roast meat, do ye
>   not ?
> I thought so ; but you are deceived, for I wot what I wot.
> I am neither going to the butcher's to buy veal, mutton, or beef,
> But I am going to a blood-sucker ; and who is it ? faith, Usury,
>   that thief.
> Why, sirs, 'twas no marcle [miracle] he undid my father that was
>   called Plain-Dealing,
> When he has undone my lady, and Conscience, too, with his
>   usuring.
> I'll tell ye, sirs, trust him not, for he'll flatter *bon facion* [*bon façon*]
>   and sore,
> Till he has gotten the baker vantage ; then he'll turn you out of
>   door.

While changes in public opinion were thus transmuting
the matter of the Interlude, the natural dramatic instincts,
both of the poets and their audience, tended more and
more to modify its allegorical form and to develop the
direct imitation of Nature in character, dialogue, and
scenery.   Henry VIII., with his passion for music and
his love of splendour, encouraged all improvements in the
purely scenic part of the performance.   Masques, modelled
in the Italian fashion, enlivened his banquets, and allegorical impersonations afforded an opportunity for the
display of magnificent costumes.   Morris dances were
introduced into the interlude in the beginning of this
reign, and we find, in a play of so early a date as *The
Four Elements*, the gravity of the action relieved by
occasional songs.   A class of interlude now made its
appearance almost entirely devoid of moral purpose, and

dependent for its effect mainly on the farcical nature of the situation and wit of the dialogue. Of this variety the inventor was John Heywood, the earliest of a race of dramatists who sought to provoke laughter by quips and buffooneries, and whose line was carried on by Tarlton, and by Robert Wilson, author of *The Three Ladies of London*. Heywood was educated at Broadgates Hall, now Pembroke College, Oxford, and afterwards became a member of the King's Chapel choir, obtaining celebrity in that capacity not less for his witty conversation than for his knowledge of music. A steady Roman Catholic, he was in danger of being charged with conspiracy under Edward VI., but enjoyed the favour of Mary, and, after the accession of Elizabeth, left England to settle in Mechlin, where he was alive as late as 1576. He was the father of Jasper Heywood, the translator of Seneca.

In spite of Heywood's attachment to his Church, he did not forbear from satirising her representatives on the stage. Two of his Interludes (which he began to write about 1520) may be described as *fabliaux* in a dramatic form; short pieces with only a few actors, well adapted for what they were probably intended, an entertainment to be presented while the king was at dinner. The earlier of the two, *The Pardoner and the Friar*, represents a dispute in Church between two members of those classes, who come forward in turn and address the audience at length, describing their own characters and the practices of their several professions; after which both begin to preach at once, each contriving to utter a single line, or sometimes a few lines together, at the end of which he is interrupted by his antagonist. This process is continued for a long time till their patience being exhausted they fall to blows, and have at last to be parted by the Parson of the Parish and a certain Neighbour Pratt, who do their best, though with little success, to carry the combatants out of Church. This Interlude must have been written before 1521 as it speaks of Leo X. as the reigning Pope.

The Four P.P., an Interlude, the name of which was probably intended to parody the title of *The Four Elements*, is more elaborate in its construction, but not less farcical in its character. The actors—who are indicated by the title—are a Palmer, a Pardoner, a Pothecary, and a Pedlar, of whom the three former, happening to meet, praise themselves and abuse each other. Unable to settle the question of precedence, they take the Pedlar as a judge, who, finding their claims equally balanced, determines that the place of honour shall be assigned to the most skilful liar of the party :—

> And now I have found one mastery
> That ye can do indifferently ;
> And is nother selling nor buying,
> But even on very lying,
> And all ye three can lie as well
> As can the falsest devil in hell.

The three rivals exercise their inventive powers in the art of lying till at last the Palmer says :—

> Yet I have seen many a mile,
> And many a woman in the while.
> Not one good city, town, or borough
> In Christendom but I have been thorough ;
> And this I would ye should understand,
> I have seen women five hundred thousand,
> And oft with them have long time tarried,
> Yet in all places where I have been,
> Of all the women that I have seen,
> I never saw nor knew in my conscience
> Any one woman out of patience.

After so amazing a statement there can no longer be a doubt as to the award, and the Palmer is, with general assent, proclaimed to be the conqueror. Heywood evidently took great pains to make his dialogue smart and amusing, and also tried to please his audience with verbal jingles in the manner of Skelton, who had found out a metrical trick that the public could readily understand. The following dialogue illustrates this point :—

POTHECARY. Then tell me this are you perfit in drinking ?
PEDLAR.   Perfit in drinking ? as may be wished by thinking.

POTHECARY. Then after your drinking how fall ye to winking?
PEDLAR.   Sir, after drinking, while the shot [1] is tinking,
          Some heads be swynking, but mine will be sinking,
          And upon drinking my eyes will be pinking :
          For winking to drinking is alway linking.

The imitation by Heywood of real persons and actual situations brought the Interlude a step nearer to the comedy of the ancient world ; while, at the same time, an intelligent appreciation of the art of Plautus and Terence, now commonly studied at the Grammar Schools and the Universities, led the dramatist to make further innovations on the form of the Interlude, by introducing from the Roman comedians new features of character and plot. In the Interlude *Thersites*, produced in 1537,[2] the interest is centred in the character from which the play takes its name, and which seems to be suggested by the *Miles Gloriosus* of Plautus. " This Interlude following," says the Advertisement to the first printed edition of the play, " doth declare how that the greatest boasters are not the greatest doers." Only five actors appear, viz. Thersites, his mother, Mulciber (Vulcan), Miles, a knight, and Telemachus. Thersites, having obtained from Vulcan celestial arms, brags enormously of his prowess, and challenges all the heroes and giants, mentioned in history sacred and profane, to meet him in combat. His mother is much disturbed by her son's warlike excitement, but the ardour of the champion is cooled by the appearance of a snail, and it is only by an effort that he can summon up resolution enough to make this monster draw in its horns. His vaunts after his triumph over it pass all bounds, and his opinion of himself is raised still higher by the appearance of Telemachus bearing a letter from Ulysses, in which that former enemy of Thersites humbly begs him to use his influence with his mother to cure Telemachus of an internal complaint. The old

---

[1] *I.e.* reckoning.
[2] Dodsley's *Old Plays*, vol. i. p. 389. The date is ascertained by the lines closing the play—

Beseech ye also that God may save his Queen
Lovely Lady Jane and the Prince that He hath sent them between.

woman—who is something of a witch—and Thersites
dispute as to the expediency of granting Ulysses' request;
at last the former gives way and pronounces the required
charm.   Thersites, thus uniformly successful, announces
that he is about to set out in quest of Miles, a knight
from whom he had previously fled for protection to his
mother; but the knight appearing suddenly on the scene,
the hero runs away, and the Interlude ends with an exhortation to the audience :—

> If you give your minds to the sin of pride,
> Vanish shall your virtue, your honour away will slide :
> For pride is hated of God above,
> And meekness soonest obtaineth his love.

This somewhat trivial moral is almost the only feature of
the old Interlude that survives in the play, the author of
which has spent all his pains in elaborating the farcical
character of Thersites, the Skeltonical jingle of the versification, and the alliterative incantation of the old witch.

The idea of *Jack Juggler* is derived from the *Amphi-
tryo* of Plautus.[1]   The person from whom this Interlude
takes its name, and who, while he is called "the Vice,"
appears to have at once human attributes and superhuman powers, plays the part of the false Amphitryon in
the Latin comedy.   He has a fellow-apprentice, Jenkin
Careaway, whom he dislikes, and, as he says,

> My purpose is
> To make Jenkin believe, if I can,
> That he is not himself but another man.

In this he is successful enough, and though the Interlude
altogether lacks the fine and subtle quality of the Latin
play, it would have enabled the author to provide a not very
critical audience with sufficient mirth in the mishaps of
the genuine Careaway, and the mistakes of his master
and mistress as to his identity.   Considerable invention is
shown in adapting the standing character of the Vice—

---

[1] Dodsley's *Old Plays* (1874), vol. ii. p. 103.

always on terms of close familiarity with the spectators—
to a situation of this kind ; but the dramatist is hard put
to it to discover a moral.　He gets out of his difficulty
by a long address to the audience, the drift of which is
sufficiently indicated in the two first stanzas :—

> Somewhat it was, saith the proverb old,
> That the cat winked when her eye was out,
> That is to say, no tale can be told,
> But that some English may be picked thereof out,
> If so to search the Latin and ground of it men will go about,
> As this trifling Enterlude that before you hath been rehearsed,
> May signify some further meaning if it well be searched.
>
> Such is the fashion of the world nowadays,
> That the simple innocents are deluded,
> And an hundred thousand divers ways,
> By subtle and crafty means shamefully abused,
> And by strength, force, and violence ofttimes compelled
> To believe and say the moon is made of a green cheese,
> Or else have great harm, and percase their life lese.

Step by step, the way had been prepared for the conversion of the Interlude into the regular Comedy, and the
first specimen of this was furnished in *Ralph Roister Doister*,
written about 1550 by Nicholas Udall, headmaster of
Eton.[1]　The ἦθος of the Morality may be still recognised
in the design of the author announced in his Prologue :—

> The wise poets long time heretofore
>   Under merry comedies secrets did declare,
> Wherein was contained very virtuous lore,
>   With mysteries and forewarnings very rare ;
>   Such to write neither Plautus nor Terence did spare,
> Which among the learned at this day bears the bell :
> These with such other therein did excel.
>
> Our comedy or interlude, which we intend to play,
>   Is named *Roister Doister* indeed,
> Which against the vainglorious doth inveigh,
>   Whose humour the roisting sort continually doth feed,
>   Thus by your patience, we intend to proceed
> In this our interlude by God's leave and grace :
> And here I take my leave for a certain space.

---

[1] Dodsley's *Old Plays*, vol. iii. p. 53.

The "vain-glorious, cowardly Blockhead," who gives his name to the play, imagines that all women are in love with him, and is himself enamoured of Dame Christian Custance, a widow, betrothed to Gawin Goodluck, a merchant. The part of the Vice is taken by Matthew Merrygreek, described in the list of *dramatis personæ* as "a needy humourist," and modelled on the character of the Parasite of Latin comedy, whose cue it is to fool the boaster to the top of his bent. In part the comedy depends on the development of character, and in this respect the plot is skilfully contrived, Matthew Merrygreek's object being always to lead Roister Doister on by his boasting disposition into situations where his real cowardice will be discovered. In part the amusement arises out of the broad farce of the incidents. Ralph pushes his suit with the widow by means of a letter which he gets a scrivener to write for him, but, being a poor scholar, he copies it out with such wrong punctuation that the compliments are all turned into insults, and the purport is exactly opposite to what is intended. When his suit is rejected, he threatens to burn Christian's house down, and marches against it with his servants ; but his forces are met by the widow and her maids, who rout them with their distaffs. This scene would seem to have been suggested by an episode in the ancient Miracle Play, *The Murder of the Innocents*, in which Herod's man, the boaster Watkin, is seized and beaten by the bereaved mothers[1] ; and, indeed, throughout the play, the dramatist, though modelling himself on Plautus, and dividing his comedy into the orthodox five acts, never departs far from the English tradition. The names of the actors have the allegorical stamp, and the dialogue, interspersed with songs, is written in the lumbering old-fashioned style, peculiar to the Interludes.

Gammer Gurton's Needle, written (in all probability) by John Still, a Cambridge scholar, afterwards Bishop of Bath and Wells, in 1566, is still more English in character, and considerably less classical in construction, than *Ralph*

[1] Vol. i. p. 415.

Roister Doister.[1] The plot of this comedy is set forth in the Prologue :—

> As Gammer Gurton, with many a wide stitch,
> Sat piecing and patching of Hodge, her man's breech,
> By chance or misfortune as she her gear tossed
> In Hodge leather breeches, her needle she lost.
> When Diccon the bedlam had heard by report
> That good Gammer Gurton was robbed in this sort,
> He quietly persuaded with her in that stound,
> Dame Chat, her dear gossip, this needle had found.
> Yet knew she no more of the matter (alas !)
> Than knoweth Tom, our clerk, what the priest saith at mass.
> Hereof there ensued so fearful a fray,
> Mas Doctor was sent for these gossips to stay ;
> Because he was curate and esteemed full wise ;
> Who found what he sought not by Diccon's device.
> When all things were tumbled and clean out of fashion,
> Whether it were by fortune, or some other constellation,
> Suddenly the needle Hodge found by the pricking,
> And drew it out of his buttock, where he found it sticking.
> Their hearts then at rest with perfect security
> With a pot of good nale they struck up their "plaudity."

Diccon, the Bedlam, whose knavery is the main cause of all this confusion, is an "Abraham man," or a pretended lunatic, like Edgar in *King Lear*, but in reality a very cunning scoundrel. He steals a slip of bacon from Gammer Gurton's house, and then, passing on to her neighbour, Dame Chat, tells her that Tib, Gammer Gurton's maid, has persuaded her mistress that the Dame has stolen one of her cocks. This brings about a personal encounter between the two women, and the loss of the needle gives Diccon an opportunity for still further mischief. Having assured Dr. Rat, the curate, an ally of Gammer Gurton's, that Dame Chat has the needle, he shows him how he may recover it by creeping into her house unawares : he then steals off to let Dame Chat know that Hodge, Gammer Gurton's man, is coming to rob her hen-roost, so that the Dame, standing prepared at the hole, belabours the curate as he creeps in in search of the needle. All this is laughable enough, and shows

[1] Dodsley's *Old Plays*, vol. iii. p. 162.

that the dramatist had studied intelligently the niceties of plot in the Latin comedians, with the view of adapting them to the humours of the English Vice.   Nor is the comedy, though far removed from the didactic character of the primitive interlude, altogether wanting in moral.   This, it is true, is of a very rustic kind, and the dialogue, as is proper in such a piece, abounds in provincialism, after the manner of Plautus.

All the elements in English comedy up to this point had been contributed to it by native tradition and popular taste ; and, as was to be expected, the product, though wholesome, was rude, and while often ingenious, usually vulgar.   A refining influence was now brought to bear upon the stage by the learned lawyers who cultivated the drama in the Inns of Court, and by the Court Wits whose aim it was to frame a dialect of their own, distinct from the idiom of the people.   The first to turn the drama in this direction, was the versatile George Gascoigne, who in 1561 exhibited in Gray's Inn a version of Ariosto's *I Suppositi*, under the name of *The Supposes*. Like all Italian comedies, this play preserved the old Latin character, the plot turning on the mistakes caused by a confusion between the identity of two young men who have exchanged the position of master and servant. Gascoigne translated it into nervous English prose, the style of which perhaps furnished Lyly with some suggestions for his elaborately constructed dialect.   In the following passage the reader will at once recognise all the features of Euphuism, as they have been already described :—

But alas ! I find that only love is unsatiable, for as the fly playeth in the flame, till at last she is cause of her own decay, so the lover, that thinketh with kissing and colling to content his unbridled appetite, is commonly seen the only cause of his own consumption.[1]

Gascoigne was also the author of another play, very different in character from *The Supposes*, but curiously

[1] *Supposes*, Act i. Scene iii.   Gascoigne's *Works* (Hazlitt), vol. i. p. 210.

representative of that double disposition, fluctuating between dissipation and repentance, which manifests itself in this poet, in Greene, and in other writers of the Elizabethan period. It is called *The Glass of Government*, and its intention is thus described by the dramatist :—

> A Comedy I mean for to present,
> No Terence phrase : his rhyme and mine are twain :
> The verse, that pleased a Roman rash intent,
> Might well offend the godly preacher's vein.
> Deformed shows were then esteemed much,
> Reformed speech doth now become me best :
> Men's words must weigh and tried be by touch,
> Of God's own word, wherein the truth doth rest.

As these words indicate, the play is of the nature of a Morality, modelled on more or less classical lines, of some polish, and of mortal dulness. The Argument may be given in Gascoigne's own words :—

> Two rich citizens of Antwerp, being nigh neighbours, and each of them having two sons of like age, do place them together with one godly teacher. The schoolmaster doth briefly instruct them their duty towards God, their Prince, their Parent, their Country, and all Magistrates in the same. The eldest, being young men of quick capacity, do (parrot-like) very quickly learn the rules without book ; the younger, being somewhat more dull of understanding, do yet engrave the same within their memories. The elder, by allurement of parasites and lewd company, begin to incline themselves to concupiscence. The parents, to prevent it, send them together to the University of Douai ; whereas the younger in short space be (by painful study) preferred, that one to be secretary unto the Palsgrave, that other becometh a famous preacher in Geneva. The eldest, turning to their vomit, take their carriage with them, and travel the world. The one is apprehended and executed for a robbery (even in sight of his brother) in the Palsgrave's Court : that other whipped and banished Geneva for fornication, notwithstanding the earnest suit of his brother for his pardon. The whole comedy a figure of the rewards and punishments of virtues and vices.[1]

This "comedy" is written in prose, it is divided into

[1] Gascoigne's *Works* (Hazlitt), vol. ii. pp. 3, 4.

five acts, each of which is closed with a chorus; and
verses are interspersed with the dialogue.

From Lyly's prose comedies, on the other hand,
almost all trace of popular taste and of the old Morality
has disappeared.   They are eight in number: *The
Woman in the Moon, Campaspe, Sapho and Phaon,
Endimion, Gallathea, Midas, Mother Bombie, Love's Metamorphosis*, of which the first named was produced before
1584.   The character of these plays was determined by
the fact that they were all acted before the Queen by the
children of Paul's.   The absence of the people from the
representation left the dramatist at liberty to indulge to
the full the love of learned allusion, the thirst for flattery,
and the craving for curiosities in thought and language,
which distinguished the taste of Elizabeth.   Of the plays
themselves, little need be said, since all that is characteristic in them has already been noticed in the chapter on
Euphues.   They have even less moral than Heywood's
Interludes, of which they may be considered a refined
sequel.   They make scarcely any attempt at the comic
representation of character; the only approach to an
imaginative creation in them being Sir Topas in *Endimion*,
a personage modelled in part on the Thersites of the
Interlude already described, with the addition of a lofty
vein of pedantic eloquence, which furnished Shakespeare
with the suggestion of Don Armado.   Nor do they
depend for their interest on comic situation.   As may be
gathered from their titles, they are all, with the exception
of *Mother Bombie*, written on classical, usually mythological, themes, and the author's aim is to remove the
action out of the ordinary sphere of human interest.
Mother Bombie indeed has a plot of considerable intricacy,
after the manner of the Latin comedians; but its childish
fatuity may be imagined from the description given by
some of the actors engaged in it :—

DROMIO.   *Memphio* had a fool to his son, which *Stellio* knew
not; Stellio had a fool to his daughter, unknown to *Memphio*;
to cosen each other, they dealt with their boys for a match; we
met with *Lucio* and *Halfpenny*, who told the love between *their*

master's children, the youth deeply in love, the fathers unwilling
to consent.

RISCIO. I'll take the tale by the end,—then we four met,
which argued we were no mountains; and in a tavern we met,
which argued we were mortal; and every one in his wine told
his day's work, which was a sign we forgot not our business; and
seeing all our masters troubled with devices, we determined a
little to trouble the water before they drunk; so that in the attire
of *your* children, *our* master's wise children bewrayed their good
natures; and in the garments of *our* master's children *yours*
made a marriage; this all stood upon us poor children, and
your young children, to show that old folks may be overtaken by
children.[1]

It will be readily derived from this that, in Lyly's
plays, everything depends on the "wit" of the dialogue.
Devoid of human nature and human interest, the course
of the action wanders confusedly through a series of
conversations, in which the speakers encounter each other
like fencers with incessant thrusts and parries of words,
turning sense topsy-turvy, striking sparks from the
collision of their quips and conceits, with an activity
which was doubtless highly satisfactory to the audiences of
the time, but which is now unutterably tedious. Lyly
was a man of brilliant talents, without a glimpse of genius.
He has a fine fancy, clear and cold like moonlight, which
never touches the heart; a skilled invention, incapable of
bringing into being the airy creatures of imagination.
And yet, in spite of his frigidity and vapid conceit, we
see that Lyly is conducting true poets to the brink of
great discoveries and unexplored regions of art. His is
the refining influence, by means of which Shakespeare will
learn how to fuse the elements of manners and character,
inherent in the old Interlude, into a new form of comedy.
Comparing the brilliant and balanced periods of Lyly's
sentence with the jolting verse of the Moralities, we find
the original source of the delightful prose dialogue of
Twelfth Night. Cold and unpoetical as is the lunar

---

[1] *Mother Bombie*, Act v. Scene iii. John Lilly's *Dramatic Works* (edited
by Fairholt, 1858), p. 140.

light in *Endimion ;* uninspired as is the vision of fairies which, in this play, flits for a moment across the stage tormenting mortals,[1] it is in these inventions that he who reflects will find an anticipation of the incomparable elf-world, presently to come into being in the *Midsummer Night's Dream.*

Summed up, therefore, the dramatic movement from Interlude to Comedy may be thus described.   The Morality, gradually dropping the didactic purpose and the allegorical form bequeathed to it by its old traditions, passed insensibly to the simple imitation of manners.   In order to provide the amusement required to compensate the audience for the severity of their instruction, it had, at a very early period, been customary to give the representative of Evil in the play a ludicrous appearance ; and from this custom the "Vice" attired in the garb of the fools kept by great men, became an established character in the Interlude.   Employed to embroil the action or to amuse the audience by his wit, the Vice was readily transformed into the Fool or Clown, so familiar to us in the plays of Shakespeare.   Heywood was the first to make the interest of the Interlude depend solely on the action of human personages.   The study of the classics suggested to Udall and Still the manner in which the traditional features of the Morality might be blended with plots of the kind found in Plautus and Terence.   Gascoigne began the refinement of dialogue by his prose translation of Ariosto's comedy, *I Suppositi ;* while Lyly carried this improvement still further by enlivening prose dialogue with his Euphuistic wit.   It remained for Shakespeare to take account of these opposite elements, and by his all-embracing genius to create out of them the poetical Comedy.

The manner in which the form of Tragedy and Tragi-Comedy, as conceived by Shakespeare, grew out of the Interlude is more complex, but in my opinion not less certain.   In his very admirable volume on *Shakespeare's Predecessors,* the late Mr. J. A. Symonds

---

[1] John Lilly's *Dramatic Works* (Fairholt), vol. i. p. 57.

puts forward a theory of the origin of the English Romantic Tragedy, which, though plausible, is also, I think, misleading. He maintains that for many years in the early part of Elizabeth's reign a struggle proceeded on the stage between two types of tragedy, the one modelled on the lines of Seneca, and favoured by the Court; the other, resembling the Italian *farsa*—a species of play which imitated Nature in every shape without distinction —adapted to the tastes of the people. The latter class, he thinks, prevailed, and being fully developed in the hands of Marlowe and Shakespeare, at last drove its rival from the theatre.[1]

No evidence is adduced in support of this opinion, except the description of contemporary plays given by critics like Whetstone and Sidney, and the names of some of the plays preserved in the annals of the stage by Collier. Nor has any example of an English drama answering to the Italian *farsa* come down to us. On the contrary, every ancient romantic play, containing the element of tragedy, before the appearance of Marlowe, is of a type utterly unlike either the tragedies or the tragi-comedies of Shakespeare. Tragedies or tragi-comedies there are of an early date, but all of them have a close affinity with the Interludes, and either contain the character of the Vice, or some other comic personage intended, like the Vice, to amuse the people, without relation to the action as such. For instance, Grim, the collier of Croydon, an established farcical character, is introduced in Edwards' *Damon and Pithias*, where the scene is laid in the Court of Dionysius of Syracuse (1564); in *Appius and Virginia* (1563) there is a vice "Haphazard"; and in *Cambyses* (1561) that part is performed by "Ambidexter," who enters "with an old capcase on his head, an old pail about his hips for harness, a scummer and a pot-lid by his side, and a rake on his shoulders." His character is a variation of the boaster's in *Thersites* which had been rendered popular by that Interlude. Both this tragedy and *Appius and Virginia* include among

[1] *Shakespeare's Predecessors*, chapters vi. vii.

the actors allegorical personages like those of the Moralities.

With such evidence before us we should be wrong to look for the origin of English tragedy in an abstract popular taste for "romance," such as Mr. Symonds imagines to have prevailed : it is equally certain that, so far from there being a conflict between the type of tragedy favoured by the Court, and that dear to the people, both the form of tragedy cultivated by the learned societies, and that exhibited in the popular theatres, sprang, though in different ways, out of an idea which, for many generations, had been consecrated by the authority of Seneca.

Misfortune has of course always been the most essential element in tragedy, and in the highest conception of tragedy the idea of justice has been no less invariably present. In Greek tragedy—at least as represented by Æschylus and Sophocles—this shows itself in the doctrine that sin produces the curse of enduring evil ; and that there is in Nature a law of Necessity exacting the purgation of the offence, even by the sacrifice of comparatively innocent individuals. Out of the stories from which the greater Greek tragedians evolved this moral, Seneca drew examples favourable to the Stoic doctrine of physical Necessity. It was his object to exalt the freedom of man's will as something independent of the overwhelming force of external Nature, to inculcate the advantage of death, and even the expediency of suicide. Accordingly all his plays exaggerate the elements of misfortune, and completely subordinate the idea of eternal justice associated with suffering. On one of its sides the philosophy of Seneca was not opposed to the teaching of the Catholic Church. While Christianity held with the Stoic that death was a release from the evils of the world, and that all earthly things were vanity, it encouraged hopes of which Seneca knew nothing, holding that "to depart and be with Christ was far better." Regarding universal "history," mainly as matter for the promotion of her own doctrines, the Church, in her system of education, dwelt impressively on the downfall of earthly grandeur, and her doctrines on the subject were embodied by Boccaccio in his *De Casibus Illustrium Virorum*, which, as a text-book in the schools, became the fountain-head of the mediæval idea of tragedy.   This is defined by the Monk in Chaucer's *Canterbury Tales* as follows :—

> Tragedie is to sayn a certain storie,
> As olde bookes maken us memorie
> Of him that stood in great prosperitie,
> And is yfallen out of high degree,
> Into miserie, and endeth wretchedly.

Translated by Lydgate in his *Fall of Princes*, Boccaccio's book provided the English reader with a long list of illustrious and unfortunate men taken from universal history, and this, as we have seen, was amplified by the authors of *The Mirror for Magistrates*, with many examples drawn from the annals of their own country. The national conception of tragic misfortune was moreover intensified by the atmosphere of gloom, horror, and blood, which prevails in the tragedies of Seneca, now made familiar to the public by means of translations.

But while men were thus taught to associate the idea of tragedy with the horrible rather than the terrible, they were also recovering for tragedy the sense of justice.   Seneca had dwelt on the freedom of the will, but to the Christian this doctrine carried with it consequences unrecognised by the Stoic.   Man in the Christian scheme was, to a very great extent, the author of his own misfortunes.   Every Miracle Play, exhibited in the streets of Chester or Coventry, taught the people the story of man's Fall and the necessity of his Redemption.   Every one of the older Moralities represented, allegorically, the conflict perpetually proceeding in the mind of man between the principles of Good and Evil ; and as the Reformation took deeper root in the country, the idea of the antagonism between Conscience and the Will became more and more prominent in the Moralities.   Vice must be punished ; virtue must be rewarded ; evil must be converted to good.   By degrees these moral ideas expressed themselves in a tragic form

by means of the Interlude, the framework of which had
been long ago determined by comic influences. Hence in
the oldest English tragedies the line that divides genuine
tragic composition from comedy is very faintly drawn,
and the public regarded what was exhibited to them merely
as a variety of the moral entertainment to which they had
been for generations accustomed. A tragedy was little
more than some true history of misfortune presented to
them in a dramatic form, just as *The Mirror for
Magistrates* was tragedy presented in an epic form. And
as in the Miracle Plays they were not disturbed by any
sense of irreverence, in witnessing scenes of buffoonery
associated with imitations of the most sacred things, so
they perceived no incongruity when they found the drama
of *Cambyses* described to them as follows :—

A lamentable tragedy, mixed full of pleasant mirth, containing the life of Cambyses, king of Persia, from the beginning of
his kingdom unto his death, his one good deed of execution,
after that many wicked deeds, and tyrannous murders, committed
by and through him, and last of all his odious death by God's
justice appointed in such order as followeth.[1]

The " odious death " of the tyrant is accomplished
coram populo, and in the most bloody manner possible, as
may be seen from the stage direction :—

*Enter the King without a gown, a sword thrust up into
his side bleeding.*[2]

This is so far quite in the manner of Seneca, who
(though his tragedies were never acted) delighted in the
representation of horrible physical suffering as enforcing
his doctrine that death is a release from evil : the English
dramatist, however, regards the death of Cambyses as a
punishment for his crimes.

The revived idea of Justice in tragedy is excellently
illustrated in the play of *Appius and Virginia*, which, with
all its anomalies, is not wanting in a certain elemental
pathos and elevation of feeling, and which is thus
described :—

---

[1] Dodsley's *Old Plays*, vol. iv. p. 158.   [2] *Ibid.* vol. iv. p. 244.

" A new tragical comedy of *Appius and Virginia.*
Wherein is lively expressed a rare example of the Virtue of
Chastity by Virginia's constancy in wishing rather to be
slain at her own father's hands, than to be dishonoured by
the wicked judge Appius." [1]   Appius is represented, not as
an unmitigated villain, but as a man torn by an inward
conflict between passion and duty, who is persuaded to the
worse course by the Vice Haphazard.   There is no lack of
dramatic power in the following dialogue :—

APPIUS.   I find it, I mind it, I swear that I will,
                 Though shame or defame may happen, no skill.
                 But out, I am wounded, how am I divided ?
                 Two states of my life from me are now glided :
                 For Conscience he pricketh me contemned,
                 And Justice saith Judgment will have me condemned ;
                 Conscience saith, Cruelty sure will detest me ;
                 And Justice saith, Death in the end will molest me ;
                 And both in one sudden methinks they do cry,
                 That fire eternal my soul shall destroy.

         [*Here let him make as though he went out and let Conscience
         and Justice come out after him, and let Conscience hold
         in his hand a lamp burning, and let Justice have
         a sword and hold it before Appius' breast.*

HAPHAZARD.   Why these are but thoughts, man why, fie for shame,
                 fie !
                 For Conscience was careless, and sailing by seas,
                 Was drowned in a basket, and had a disease,
                 Sore moved for pity, when he would grant none,
                 For being hard-hearted was turned to a stone :
                 And sailing by Sandwich he sank for his sin ;
                 Then care not for Conscience the worth of a pin.
                 And judgment judged Justice to have a reward,
                 For judging still justly, but all is now marred ;
                 For gifts they are given where judgment is none ;
                 Thus judgment and justice a wrong way hath gone.
                 Then care not for Conscience the worth of a fable ;
                 Justice is no more, nor aught to do able. [2]

After Virginia has been killed, Justice and Reward appear
on the stage.   Appius, thrown into prison, commits

[1] Dodsley's *Old Plays*, vol. iv. p. 106.   [2] *Ibid.* p. 128.

suicide, and the news of this is brought to the audience, who are further gratified with the sight of Haphazard being carried off to the gallows.

In the Prologue to Edwards' *Damon and Pithias* we find an illustration at once of the manner in which "history" appealed to the mediæval imagination, as furnishing true examples of conduct ; of the English idea of tragic imitation ; and of the mixed nature of the drama in England, which gave rise to the form of Tragi-Comedy :—

> But now for to be brief, the matter to express,
> Which here we shall present in this ; Damon and Pithias.
> A rare example of friendship true, it is no legend lie,
> But a thing once done indeed, which histories do descry,
> Which done of yore in long time past, yet present shall be here,
> Even as it were in doing now, so lively it shall appear.
> Lo, here in Syracuse, th' ancient town, which once the Romans won.
> Here Dionysius palace, within whose court this thing most strange was done,
> Which matter mixed with mirth and care a just name to apply,
> As seems most fit we have it termed a tragical comedy.[1]

Damon, accused in the Court of Dionysius of being a spy, is condemned to death by the tyrant. He asks leave to return to Greece to settle his affairs, promising to return. The dialogue that thereupon follows is noteworthy as illustrating the decay of the spirit of European chivalry in the atmosphere of Machiavellian cynicism.

DIONYSIUS.   A pleasant request ! as though I could trust him absent,
　　　　　　Whom in no wise I cannot trust being present.
　　　　　　And yet, though I swore the contrary, do that I require,
　　　　　　Give me a pledge for thy return, and have thine own desire.
　　　　　　He is as near now as he was before [*Aside*].
DAMON.　　There is no surer nor greater pledge than the faith of a gentleman.
DIONYSIUS.   It was wont to be ; but otherwise now the world doth stand.[2]

Pithias offers to be hostage for his friend, and he is to be

---

[1] Dodsley's *Old Plays*, vol. iv. p. 12　　　[2] *Ibid*. vol. iv. p. 54.

put to death if the latter fails to present himself on a
stated day. Damon arrives in Syracuse just after the
appointed hour, as Pithias is being led out to execution.
Both contend before Dionysius for the right to die, a
spectacle of heroic friendship, which so moves the king that
he announces his conversion to the paths of virtue, and
banishes all flatterers and parasites from his Court. Thus
the play, like the Shakespearian Tragi-Comedy, ends
happily.

Meantime in the Inns of Court the more strict and
learned conception of Tragedy, as it was understood by
Seneca, maintained its ground. The first example of the
regular Five-Act Tragedy in England is Sackville's *Ferrex
and Porrex* (1562), of which the argument is as follows :—

> Gorboduc, king of Britain, divided his realm in his life-time
> to his sons Ferrex and Porrex. The sons fell to dissension. The
> younger killed the elder. The mother, that more dearly loved
> the elder, for revenge killed the younger. The people moved
> with the cruelty of the fact rose in rebellion, and slew both
> father and mother. The nobility assembled, and most terribly
> destroyed the rebels ; and afterwards for want of issue of the
> Prince, whereby the succession of the Crown became uncertain,
> they fell to civil war, in which both they and many of their
> issues were slain, and the land for a long time almost desolate
> and miserably wasted.[1]

None of these actions is presented on the stage : all
of them are reported by professional messengers or other
persons who have been eye-witnesses of them. The place
of action is filled by a dumb show before each act,
signifying allegorically the nature of the events, to the
accompaniment of music. There is a chorus—as in the
tragedies of Seneca—of four ancient and sage men of
Britain, who—also after Seneca's manner—comment on
the course of events at the close of each act.

In spite of the contemptuous tone in which Schlegel
speaks of it,[2] *Ferrex and Porrex* is a work of great
merit. It follows the practice of Seneca merely in its

---

[1] Sackville's *Works* (edited by Sackville-West, 1895), p. 3.
[2] As cited in Ward's *English Dramatic Literature*, vol. i. p. 107.

form : the conception is original and is worked out in a truly English spirit, preserving the serious purpose of the mediæval drama, and enforcing a lofty and patriotic moral. Throughout this play, as in *The Mirror for Magistrates,* we see how deeply the lessons of the Wars of the Roses had impressed the imagination of Englishmen, and how grave were the dangers they anticipated from a doubtful succession.[1] The ἦθος of the drama resembles that of the Greek tragedians rather than that of Seneca : the misfortunes of the kingdom are represented as the fruits of the curse entailed by the civil war between Morgan and Cunedagius ;[2] but each crime committed by the actors in the play is the product of free will, and is followed by its own retribution ; while at the close of the tragedy the final triumph of justice is confidently anticipated :—

> But now, O happy man, whom speedy death
> Deprives of life, he is enforced to see
> These hugy mischiefs, and these miseries,
> These civil wars, these murders, and these wrongs.
> Of justice yet must God in fine restore
> This noble crown unto the lawful heir :
> For right will always live, and rise at length,
> But wrong can never take deep root to last.[3]

A noble conclusion, and quite unlike the moral of Seneca's plays. There is also great dramatic narrative power and tragic pathos in the description by Marcella, a lady of the Court, of the death of Porrex.

> But hear his ruthful end :
> The noble prince, pierced with the sudden wound,
> Out of his wretched slumber hastily start,
> Whose strength now failing, straight he overthrew,
> When in the full his eyes, even now unclosed,
> Beheld the queen, and cried to her for help.
> We then, alas, the ladies which that time
> Did there attend, seeing that heinous deed,
> And hearing him oft call the wretched name
> Of mother, and to cry to her for aid

---

[1] Dr. Ward has also well pointed out that the dramatists reflect upon the danger of a foreign marriage for the Queen (see *English Dramatic Literature,* vol. i. p. 109).

[2] Chorus at the end of Act iii. Sackville's *Works,* p. 51. [3] *Ibid.* p. 91.

> Whose direful hand gave him the mortal wound,
> Pitying, alas (for nought else could we do),
> His ruthful end, ran to the woeful bed,
> Despoiled straight his breast and, all we might,
> Wiped in vain with napkins next at hand
> The sudden streams of blood that flushed fast
> Out of the gaping wound.   O what a look,
> O what a rueful steadfast eye, methought,
> He fixed upon my face, which to my death
> Will never part from me, when with a braid [1]
> A deep-fetched sigh he gave, and therewithal
> Clasping his hands, to heaven he cast his sight;
> And straight pale death pressing within his face,
> The flying ghost his mortal corpse forsook. [2]

Nothing so fine as this had appeared in English poetry since Surrey had shown the capacity of the English language for poetic diction in blank verse; and it seems strange that, after the revelation of such a vehicle of dramatic expression, the stage should have had to wait nearly thirty years for the "mighty line" of Marlowe. Here is another passage of rare pathos and harmony :—

> Ah, noble prince, how oft have I beheld
> Thee, mounted on thy fierce and trampling steed,
> Shining in armour bright before the tilt,
> And with thy mistress' sleeve tied on thy helm,
> And charge thy staff to please thy lady's eye,
> That bowed the head-piece of thy friendly foe !
> How oft in arms on horse to bind the mace,
> How oft in arms on foot to break the sword,
> Which never now these eyes may see again ! [3]

The defect of Sackville, as a dramatist, is that, with all his great intellectual power, he failed to perceive that the principle of tragic action had altered its sphere.   His mind was essentially political.   Deeply impressed with the evils and horrors of the Civil Wars, which yet lingered in men's memories, he sought, in *Ferrex and Porrex*, as in his *Induction*, to draw from the history of Britain examples to warn his countrymen against conduct likely to occasion the recurrence of these calamities.

---

[1] A start.   [2] Sackville's *Works*, p. 66.   [3] *Ibid.* p. 68.

His imagination therefore naturally dwelt on the Greek stories of hereditary Nemesis. He did not see that the evils he dreaded belonged to a past stage of society, and that what was henceforth to make the greatness of the English stage was the representation of the conflict between Good and Evil *in the soul of Man*. This truth he might have divined from the character of the rudest of the Moralities he must often have witnessed ; but his mind was preoccupied by old tradition. Free will, it is true, plays a certain part in the sequence of tragic events in *Ferrex and Porrex :* Gorboduc's folly in dividing his kingdom is the immediate source of all the ills that flow from it ; but behind this folly there is, as in Greek Tragedy, the moving necessity of the family curse. Compare this motive with the development of the tragic action in *King Lear*, and the contrast between the principles of ancient and modern tragedy springs into vivid light ; the one set of situations in which the will and power of the individual man count for so little ; the other, in which his will and conduct are the cause of almost everything.

What was a serious fault in the conception of *Ferrex and Porrex* becomes a fatal defect in the conception of *The Misfortunes of Arthur*, a play in itself of very great literary merit, written by Thomas Hughes of Gray's Inn, and acted before the Queen at Greenwich in 1587. The argument is as follows :—

At a banquet made by Uther Pendragon for the solemnising of his conquest against the Saxons, he fell enamoured of Igerna, wife to Gorlois, Duke of Cornwall, who perceiving the king's passion, departed with his wife, and prepared war at Cornwall, where also, in a stronghold beyond him, he placed her. Then the king levied an army to suppress him, but waxing impatient of his desire to Igerna, transformed himself by Merlin, his cunning, into the likeness of Gorlois, and after his acceptance with Igerna he returned to his siege, where he slew Gorlois. Igerna was delivered of Arthur and Anne, twins of the same birth. Uther Pendragon, fifteen years after, pursuing the Saxons, was by them poisoned. Arthur delighted in his sister Anne, who made him father of Mordred. Seventeen years after, Lucius Tiberius of

Rome demanded a tribute due by conquest of Cæsar. Arthur gathered his powers of thirteen kings besides his own, and leaving his Queen Guenevera in the tuition of Mordred, to whom likewise he committed the kindgom in his absence, arrived in France, where after nine years' war he sent the slain body of Tiberius unto Rome for the tribute. During his absence Morded grew ambitious, for the effecting whereof he made love to Guenevera, who gave ear unto him. Then by the assistance of Gilla, a British lord, he usurped, and for maintenance entertained with large promises the Saxons, Irish, Picts, and Normans. Guenevera, hearing that Arthur was already embarked for return, through despair purposing diversely, sometimes to kill her husband, sometimes to kill herself, at last resolved to enter into religion. Arthur at his landing was resisted on the Strands of Dover, where he put Mordred to flight. The last field was fought at Cornwall where, after the death of one hundred and twenty thousand, saving on either side twenty, Mordred received his death and Arthur his deadly wound." [1]

The machinery of this tragedy imitates that of *Ferrex and Porrex:* it has dumb shows before each act: the incidents are reported not represented : the chorus comments on the course of events. But the deep moral feeling of Sackville is wanting. Though the subject of the play is carefully selected from legendary history, after the Greek fashion, the only moral the author can extract from it is this :—

> See here the store of great Pendragon's brood,
> The t'one quite dead, the t'other hastening on ;
> As men, the son but green, the sire but ripe,
> Yet both forestalled ere half their race were run !
> As kings, the mightiest monarchs of this age,
> Yet both suppressed and vanquished by themselves.
> Such is the brittle breath of mortal man,
> While human nature works her daily wracks :
> Such be the crazed crests of glorious crowns,
> While worldly powers like sudden puffs do pass. [2]

Vanitas vanitatum : the true Catholic mediæval teaching ! But could this moral be impressed upon the imagination of an English audience by so shadowy a myth as the fable of Arthur, which never really took root in the national

---

[1] Dodsley's *Old Plays*, vol. iv. p. 260. [2] *Ibid.* vol. iv. p. 338.

imagination ?   The coldness of the moral in the play is counterbalanced by strict attention to literary form; Seneca is imitated in the smallest particulars.   Gorlois' ghost rises, like the ghost in *Thyestes*, to set the curse in motion ; the long speeches are full of " sentences " after the manner of the Roman poet: antithesis and " stichomythia," or dialogue by means of single lines, abound : and I suspect that, if any one would take the trouble to examine the composition of the play, it would be found to be very largely a mosaic of ideas suggested by Lucan and Seneca.[1] Its literary workmanship is admirable, and in point of construction it compares very favourably with the dramas of Marlowe : but the life which that remarkable poet put into his work is wanting.   *The Misfortunes of Arthur* shows us unmistakably that in the Elizabethan drama the romantic form prevailed over the classical, not, as Mr. Symonds supposed, merely because the popular taste preferred the one to the other, but because the former was inspired by a living principle of action, and the latter was not.

The fourth class of Shakespearian drama, the Chronicle History, finds its rude prototype in the Interlude of *King Johan*.   John Bale, the author of this play, was a native of Suffolk, who, being converted from Roman Catholicism, became, like many inhabitants of the eastern counties, a most vehement promoter of the reformed doctrine.   He was appointed to the see of Ossory by Edward VI.; fled from England in the reign of Mary ; and returning on the accession of Elizabeth, was made a prebendary of Canterbury in 1560.   He died in 1563.   *King Johan* was probably written during the reign of Edward VI.[2]   It is a Morality composed with the view of discrediting the priesthood, of exalting the civil at the expense of the

---

[1] I had written this before I had the advantage of reading Mr. J. W. Cunliffe's excellent essay on "The Influence of Seneca on Elizabethan Tragedy," in which a vast number of imitations of Seneca are pointed out in this play.   See his Appendix ii. p. 130.

[2] I infer the approximate date from the speech of the Interpreter that follows the play, in which " our late King Henry " is spoken of.   The conclusion of the play points to the reign of Elizabeth, but the usual prayer for the reigning monarch would of course have been adapted to the circumstances of the time.

ecclesiastical power, and of elevating the Monarchy alike above the heads of the native feudal nobility and the foreign clergy. Instead of enforcing his moral, like the author of *Lusty Juventus* or *The New Custom*, by means of an abstract plot, he employs an historic example, intending by the allegory of John's reign to signify the condition of things in the reign of Edward VI. At the end of the first act he introduces an Interpreter, after the manner of the old miracle plays, to explain his view of John's policy and character—a view which is sufficiently remote from historic truth, but which reflects the opinions of the Protestant Moralist.

> In this present acte we have to yow declared,
> As in a myrrour, the begynnynge of Kynge Johan,
> How he was of God a magistrate appoynted,
> To the governaunce of thys same noble regyon,
> To see mayntayned the true faythe and relygyon ;
> But Satan the Devyll, which that time was at large,
> Had so great a swaye that he could it not discharge.
>   .   .   .   .
> In the second acte thys wyll apeare more playne,
> Wherein Pandulphus shall hym excommunycate
> Within thys hys lande and depose him from hys reigne,
> All other princes they shall move hym to hate,
> And to persecute after most cruel rate.
> They wyll hym poysen in their malygnyte,
> And cause yll report of hym alwayes to be.
>
> This noble Kynge Johan, as a faythful Moyses,
> Withstode proude Pharao for hys poore Israel,
> Myndynge to brynge it out of the lande of darkenesse,
> But the Egyptyanes did agaynst hym so rebell,
> That hys poore people did styll in the desert dwell,
> Tyll that duke Josue, which was our late Kynge Henrye,
> Closely brought us into the lande of mylke and honye.
>
> As a strong David, at the voyce of verytie,
> Great Golye, the pope, he strake downe with hys slynge,
> Restorynge agayne to a Christian lybertie
> Hys lande and people, lyke a most victoryous kynge ;
> To his first bewtye intendynge the Church to brynge
> From ceremonies dead to the lyvynge wurde of the Lorde :
> Thys the seconde acte wyll plenteously recorde.

Such being the purpose of the Interlude it may be divined

that it is composed in the spirit not so much of a historical poet as of a religious partisan. For every real personage in the play there are two abstractions, with whom the human characters discourse without any sense of strangeness. There is a Vice, Sedition, but he is not a jester : indeed the whole tone of the Interlude is so serious and didactic that we may reasonably conjecture, with Collier, that it was intended to gratify the ultra-Protestant taste of the Corporation of Ipswich, in whose archives the MS. was long preserved.[1] *King Johan* furnishes an early example of the little importance attached by the English dramatists to mere external unity or probability in comparison with the unity of moral idea. Between the issue of the Interdict in the first act and its removal in the second, seven years have elapsed ; but there is nothing in the machinery of the action to explain this, and it is only signified to the audience by a casual observation of the Pope.[2] One of the *dramatis personæ* is Dissimulation, who conspires with Sedition to poison the king, and the resolute fanaticism of whose character is represented with considerable dramatic force. Suddenly, and without the slightest sense of impropriety, this abstraction changes into the historic person of Simon of Swinsett, who brings the king the poisoned cup :—

> Symon of Swynsett my very name is per de ;
> I am taken of men for monastycall Devocyon ;
> And here have I brought you a marvellouse good pocyon,
> For I harde ye saye that ye were very drye.[3]

After King John's death the author still feels it necessary to continue the action, in order that the audience may be under no misapprehension as to the monarch's real character. Verity enters and, apostrophising the spirit of Leland, enters into a controversy with Clergy and Nobility, who are inclined to defame John's memory. His efforts are supported by Imperial Majesty, who expresses equal loathing for Papists and Anabaptists, and reads all the other personages a lecture on the duties of govern-

---

[1] Collier's Introduction to *Kynge Johan* (Camden Society's Publications), p. 6.

[2] *Kynge Johan*, pp. 42, 43.   [3] *Ibid.* p. 81.

ment. It is noticeable that the ideal which Bale presents is still the old feudal theory of the orders—nearly two centuries before commended by Langland—but that the figure of the Ploughman is now omitted.

> The administracyon of a prince's governaunce
> Is the gift of God and his high ordynaunce,
> Whom with all your power ye three ought to support
> In the lawes of God to all hys people's comfort.
> First yow the Clergye, in preachynge of God's worde,
> Then yow Nobilitye, defendyng with the sworde,
> Yow, Cyvyle Order, in executing justyce.
> Thus, I trust, we shall seclude all manner of vyce,
> And after we have established our kyngdom
> In peace of the Lorde and in hys godly fredome,
> We wyll confirm it with wholesome laws and decrees,
> To the full suppressynge of Antichriste's vanytees.[1]

---

[1] *Kynge Johan*, p. 101.

CHAPTER XII

THE INFANCY OF THE ROMANTIC DRAMA: GREENE, PEELE, MARLOWE, KYD

HITHERTO the art of the dramatist had found expression in forms consecrated by long popular usage or by scholastic tradition, but modified by the inward and spiritual changes which were gradually transforming the life of the English people. Influences alike of the Renaissance and the Reformation had altered without revolutionising these venerable precedents. The Morality, offspring of the Catholic Church in the Middle Ages, had been converted into an instrument for propagating the doctrines of Luther and Calvin. It had allied itself, without any sense of incongruity, with the forms of Latin comedy employed by Plautus and Terence. Tragedy had sought to unite the practice of Seneca, sanctioned by the approval of the mediæval schools, with the allegorical pageants, beloved by the people, in the representation of subjects chosen from the legendary periods of English history. There was so far no antagonism in the national mind between the idea of the drama and the idea of morals and religion. But the time had now come when these great forces in the life of the country were to be torn harshly asunder ; when the movement of the Renaissance was to be opposed to that of the Reformation ; when the stage, once regarded as a seminary of religious education, second only to the pulpit, was to be attacked by the bitterness of sectarian hatred as one of the principal schools of the World, the Flesh, and the Devil.

The beginning of the aggression undoubtedly came from the Puritans. As the rupture with the Papacy had been the result of political rather than of religious causes, the transfer to the Sovereign of the Headship of the National Church had been effected, even in spite of the spoliation of the monasteries, without any immediate convulsion in the religious framework of society. But we see, alike from the sermons of Wycliffe and the poems of Langland, that a very large part of the people of England, as was the case with all the Teutonic races, had for generations been strongly inclined to the Reformation on its spiritual side, and when the persecution arose under Mary, with all its attendant evils of forfeiture, banishment, and death, the suppressed antagonism to authority in Church and State broke into a flame. Many of the Protestant exiles took refuge, and some even received ordination after the Presbyterian fashion, in Geneva, the centre of all that was most extreme in the Reforming movement. Returning to England on the accession of Elizabeth, these men were often instituted in livings by patrons who sympathised with their opinions. They obtained lucrative posts in the Universities, and were sometimes promoted to Bishoprics. Calvinism for the first half of Elizabeth's reign became the strongest organised intellectual force in the country, and as its advocates maintained not only Calvin's metaphysical dogmas, but (in many cases) his theories of church government and his system of moral discipline, they naturally came into collision with every kind of established custom and institution, and more particularly with the stage.

The Puritans objected to the stage much on the same ground as Tertullian had objected to the study of Greek and Latin literature. They held it to be popish and pagan in its origin ; they pointed, with some reason, to the irreverence with which sacred things were exhibited on it for the amusement of the vulgar : but beyond this they were offended at it as a worldly mode of entertainment opposed to the " godly discipline." Political prejudice inflamed their feelings against it still further. The return of the Genevan exiles had spread a leaven of democratic feeling through the middle classes ; and when the players, who were the licensed servants of the nobility, claimed their privileges of acting in the towns, they were opposed by the authorities, professedly on account of the injury they did to the public morals, but quite as often in reality because they were the representatives of some worldly-minded Jeroboam, who was infringing the rights of the godly citizens of Worcester or Norwich.

Between 1570 and 1587 at least six violent attacks were made on the stage in the form of pamphlets.   The first, of which there is a record, was John Northbrooke's *Treatise wherein Dicing, Dancing, Vain Plays or Interludes are reproved*, published in 1577.   Stephen Gosson's *School of Abuse*, dedicated to Sir Philip Sidney, appeared in 1579 ; and in 1583 the famous puritan, Philip Stubbes, wrote his *Anatomy of Abuses*, one division of which was devoted to *Stage Plays and Interludes with their wickedness*. This was followed in 1586 by Whetstone's *Touchstone for the Time*, but as that writer had himself published a play, *Promos and Cassandra*, he confined himself to protesting against the exhibition of plays on Sunday. In 1586 appeared an anonymous but very violent tract, *A Second and Third Blast of Retreat from Plays and Theatres*, while William Rankin's *Mirror of Monsters*, published in 1587, is full of abuse of plays and players. The Martin Mar-Prelate controversy, which began in 1587, and embroiled all estates in the country, drew into the *melée* the pens of Lyly and Nash, who fought on the side opposed to the Puritans.

Bitter and illiberal as was the spirit in which these attacks were made they were not without justification. The Renaissance in England had begun to part company with the Reformation.   As the standard of chivalrous manners decayed, a considerable portion of the higher classes in England strove to imitate the utterly corrupt morals of Italy.   Among them were travelled sons of the nobility, scholars of the University, and the gentlemen of the Inns of Court.   The object of their admiration was the quality called by the Italians *virtù;* their rule of life was *Fais ce que vouldras;* and, as the worst kind of corruption is the corruption of the best, these degenerate representatives of the English aristocracy acquired the name of *Italianate* Englishmen, the definition of which is so vividly given in the famous passage of Ascham's *Schoolmaster.* Many of them indeed, on their return to England, lacked the bravado to sustain a fashion of viciousness which was not natural to them, and which was equally disgusting to the chivalrous Sidney and the Puritanic Stubbes. But the principles of taste which they helped to form advanced, as a matter of course, from an imitation of the manners to the cultivation of the literature of the Italian Renaissance, so that the epoch which introduced the English reader, by the aid of translations, to the thoughts of Virgil and Seneca, made known to him, in the same way, the loose tales of Cinthio and Bandello.

The first to open this path, as so many others in English literature, was George Gascoigne. He was himself led to it by natural inclination. A spendthrift and gambler in his youth, yet accustomed to good society, always shifting his occupations, half soldier and half scholar, equally ready with his sword and his pen, he had seen the world in many parts and under many lights, and he was ready enough to employ his energy in any honourable direction which could bring him profit. His success did not reach the measure of his ambition. Perhaps he lacked concentration of purpose, or his imagination was greater than his capacity for action ; poets are often more distinguished for absence of mind than for readiness of wit ; and Gascoigne, we know, was a poor marksman,[1] a defect which must in those days have interfered with his usefulness in war. However this may have been, he certainly sympathised with the Italian passion for personal adventure, and reflected it in his autobiographical poems, *Don Bartholomew of Bath* and *Dulce Bellum Inexpertis.* We have already seen him translating

---

[1] Gascoigne's *Poems* (Hazlitt), vol. i. p. 377.

Ariosto's comedy, *I Suppositi;* and his first published volume contained an imitation—probably the first which had appeared in England—of the Italian *novella*, under the title of *The Adventures of Don Ferdinando Ieronimi.*[1] Neither this story nor *Don Bartholomew* argues any great moral strictness in the author : both might have been with propriety included in that division of his works which he called "Weeds"; but Gascoigne was at least aware that such "Italianate" compositions were not congenial with the prevailing taste of his countrymen. Conscience, indeed, seems to have been a lively principle in his nature : as his years advanced his style becomes duller, but his moral more edifying ; until at last the dashing soldier of fortune, the narrator of the adventures of Don Ferdinando, develops into the author of *The Glass of Government* and *A Drum of Doomsday for Dainty-mouthed Drunkards.* He was a friend of George Whetstone, the author of *Promos and Cassandra,* who, after his death, undertook the defence of his memory, and put the story of his career before the public in an exceedingly prosy copy of verses, entitled, *The Well-employed Life and Godly End of G. Gascoigne, Esquire.* In this composition Gascoigne is made to address his biographer as follows :—

> Thou seest my death, and long my life didst know,
> My life ?—nay, death : to live I now begin :
> But some will say, *Durus hic est sermo;*
> 'Tis hard indeed for such as feed on sin.
> Yet trust me, friends (though flesh doth hardly bow),
> I am resolved I never lived till now.
>
> And on what cause in order shall ensue ;
> My worldly life (is first) must play his part :
> Whose tale attend, for once the same is true ;
> Yea, Whetstone, thou hast known my hidden heart,
> And therefore I conjure thee to defend
> (When I am dead) my life and godly end.

Whetstone was himself inclined to Puritanism, and, as I have already said, he had joined, though with moderation, in the attack on the abuses of the stage. But he

---

[1] He pretends in this to be translating a story of " Bartello " ; but the tale is obviously a record of his own adventures.

was not without artistic perceptions, as appears from the soundness of his criticism on the contemporary drama :—

"At this day," says he, "the Italian is so lascivious in his comedies, that honest hearers are grieved at his actions : the Frenchman and Spaniard follows the Italian's humour : the German is too holy : for he presents on every common stage what preachers should pronounce in pulpits. The Englishman in this quality is most vain, indiscreet, and out of order : he first grounds his work on improbabilities : then in three hours runs he through the world : marries, gets children, makes children men, men to conquer kingdoms, murder monsters, and bringeth Gods from Heaven and fetcheth Devils from Hell. And, that which is worst, their ground is not so imperfect as their working indiscreet : not weighing, so the people laugh, though they laugh them (for their follies) to scorn. Many times (to make mirth) they make a clown companion with a king : in their grave counsels they allow the advice of fools : yea, they use one order of speech for all persons : a grave indecorum, for a crow will ill counterfeit the nightingale's sweet voice : even so affected speech doth misbecome a clown. For to work a comedy kindly, grave old men should instruct : young men should show the inperfections of youth : strumpets should be lascivious : boys unhappy : and clowns should be disorderly : intermingling all these actions in such sort as the grave matter may instruct ; and the pleasant delight : for without this change the attention would be small and the liking less." [1]

Whetstone's criticisms seem to be directed against historical tragedies of the class of *Cambyses ;* and he deserves credit both for his critical discernment in perceiving that tragi-comedy must at least satisfy the essential conditions of moral unity on which Horace dwells in his *Ars Poetica*, and for the originality of his attempt to found a tragi-comic fable on situations like those of the Italian *novella*. His *Promos and Cassandra* was based on one of the novels of Giraldi Cinthio, and was written in 1578. He did not, however, understand the art of dramatic condensation : his play was divided into two parts, and being obviously unfitted for perform-

[1] Letter to William Fleetwood, Esq., Recorder of London, 29th July 1578.

ance on the stage, was afterwards reduced by him to a
narrative form, in which shape it proved the inspiring
source of Shakespeare's *Measure for Measure.*

Whetstone stood alone in the moderation of his attitude towards the stage and Puritanism ; and the poet who
next calls for our attention furnishes a tragic example of
the results of transplanting the standard of Italian morals
into the society of England.   Robert Greene was known
to his contemporaries as a Euphuistic writer on the subject of love ; as a playwright ; and as a dissolute liver.
I have already spoken of him in his capacity of poetical
Euphuist : of his plays I shall speak presently.   But the
events of his life, illustrating as they do in the most vivid
manner the motives of the men who changed the character
of the English drama, are deserving of careful attention.
In the fluctuations of his temper Greene bears a strong
resemblance to Gascoigne ; but as he went far beyond
his predecessor in lawless defiance of the public conscience,
so did he surpass him in the violence and profuseness
with which he proclaimed to the world his fits of repentance.   Many of his prose tracts, especially towards the
close of his life, are of the nature of confessions, and few
poets have shown less reserve in exposing the depths of
their nature to the scorn or compassion of their fellows.

Robert Greene was born at Norwich some time between
1550 and 1560, probably about nine years after Kett's
insurrection had convulsed the whole region of East
Anglia.   His parents, as he himself tells us, were re-
spected by their fellow-citizens, and it may be surmised
that the early training he received was strongly tinged
with the Calvinistic doctrine which prevailed in Norwich.
He was educated at St. John's College, Cambridge,
where he graduated as B.A. in 1578, taking the degree
of M.A. from Clare Hall in 1583.   Between these two
dates he was persuaded by some of his wilder University
companions to travel in Italy and Spain, " in which
places," he tells us in one of his tracts, " I saw and
practised such villainy as is abominable to declare.   Thus
by their counsel I sought to furnish myself with coin,

which I procured by cunning sleights from my father and my friends ; and my mother pampered me so long, and secretly helped me to the oil of angels, that I grew thereby prone to all mischiefs ; so that, being then conversant with notable braggarts, boon companions, and ordinary spend-thrifts, that practised sundry superficial studies, I became as a stem grafted into the same stock, whereby I did absolutely participate of their nature and qualities."[1]   On his return to England he endeavoured to naturalise his acquired habits, and it is best to let him tell his story in his own words :—

I ruffled out in my silks, in the habit of malcontent, and seemed so discontent, that no place would please me to abide in, nor no vocation cause me to stay myself in : but after I had by degrees proceeded Master of Arts, I left the University and away to London ; where (after I had continued some short time, and driven myself out of credit with sundry of my friends) I became an author of plays, and a penner of love pamphlets, so that I soon grew famous in that quality, that who for that trade grown so ordinary about London as Robin Greene?   Young yet in years, though old in wickedness, I began to resolve that *there was nothing bad that was profitable :* whereupon I grew so rooted in all mischief that I had as great delight in wickedness as sundry hath in goodness, and as much felicity I took in villany as others had in honesty. . . . Yet let me confess a truth that even once, and yet but once, I felt a fear and horror in my conscience, and then the terror of God's judgments did manifestly teach me that my life was bad, that by sin I deserved damnation, and that such was the greatness of my sin that I deserved no redemption.   And this inward motion I received in Saint Andrew's Church in the City of Norwich, at a lecture or sermon there preached by a godly and learned man, whose doctrine, and the manner of whose teach-ing I liked wonderfully well ; yea, in my conscience, such was his singleness of heart and zeal in his doctrine that he might have converted the worst monster in the world.

Well, at that time, whosoever was worst, I knew myself as bad as he ; for being new come from Italy (where I learned all the villainies under the heavens), I was drowned in pride, whore-dom was my daily exercise, and gluttony with drunkenness was my only delight.

At this sermon the terror of God's judgments did manifestly

[1] "The Repentance of Robert Greene," Dyce, *Greene and Peele's Dramatic and Poetical Works,* p. 3.

teach me that my exercises were damnable, and that I should be
wiped out of the book of life, if I did not speedily repent my
looseness of life and reform my misdemeanours.

At this sermon the said learned man (who doubtless was
the child of God) did beat down sin in such pithy and persuasive
manner, that I began to call unto mind the danger of my soul,
and the prejudice that at length would befall for those gross sins
which with greediness I daily committed : in so much as sighing
I said to myself, " Lord have mercy on me and send me grace
to amend and become a new man ! "   But this good motion lasted
not long in me ; for no sooner had I met with my copesmates,
but seeing me in such a solemn humour, they demanded the
cause of my sadness : to whom, when I had discovered that I
sorrowed for my wickedness of life, and that the preacher's words
had taken a deep impression in my conscience, they fell upon me
in jesting manner, calling me Puritan and Precisian, and wished
I might have a pulpit, with other such scoffing terms, that by their
foolish persuasion the good and wholesome lesson I had learned
went quite out of my remembrance ; so that I fell again with the
dog to my old vomit, and put my wicked life in practice, and
that so thoroughly as ever I did before.

Thus although God sent his Holy Spirit to call me, and
though I heard him, yet I regarded it no longer than the present
time, when suddenly forsaking it, I went forward obstinately in
my vices.   Nevertheless soon after I married a gentleman's
daughter of good account, with whom I lived for a while ; but
forasmuch as she would persuade me from my wilful wickedness,
after I had a child by her, I cast her off, having spent up the
marriage-money which I obtained by her.

Then I left her at six or seven, who went into Lincolnshire
and I to London, where in short space I fell into favour with
such as were of honourable and good calling.   But here note
that though I knew how to get a friend, yet I had not the gift or
reason how to keep a friend, for he that was my dearest friend I
would be so sure to behave myself toward him that he should
ever after profess to be my utter enemy, or else vow never after
to come into my company.

Thus my misdemeanours (too many to be recited) caused the
most part of those so much to despise me that in the end I
became friendless, except it were in a few alehouses, who commonly for my inordinate expenses would make much of me, until
I were on the score, far more than ever I meant to pay by twenty
nobles thick.   After I had wholly betaken me to the penning of
plays (which was my continual exercise) I was so far from calling
upon God that I seldom thought on God, but took such delight

in swearing and blaspheming the name of God that none could think otherwise of me than that I was the child of perdition. . . . These vanities and other trifling pamphlets I penned of love and vain phantasies was my chiefest stay of living, and for these my vain discourses I was beloved of the more vainer sort of people, who being my continual companions, came still to my lodging, and there continued quaffing, carousing, and surfeiting with me all the day long.[1]

I see no reason whatever to question the authenticity of this autobiography, or—up to a certain point—the sincerity of the feelings which it professes. The only deduction to be made from it arises from the fact that to the day of his death the author was a professional rhetorician. He was master of a popular style, in which he found a source of profit. Lyly's most brilliant disciple, Greene was ready to avail himself of any subject which offered opportunities of treatment in the Euphuistic manner. When he began to write he naturally turned, like his master, to the theme of Love, and for several years poured forth a succession of amorous pamphlets and romances which were read with eagerness by all sorts and conditions of men, to whose barbarous taste the tricks of Euphuism seemed miracles of art. Thus between the years 1583 and 1589 we find him producing *Mamillia*, 1583 ; *Mirror of Modesty, Morando, Card of Fancy*, 1584 ; *Planetomachia*, 1585 ; *Menaphon, Euphues, his Censure to Philautus*, 1587 ; *Tully's Love*, 1589 ; to which may probably be added *Alcida, Arbasto*, and *Penelope's Web*. Among his patrons were all that section of the Court which, headed by the Earl of Oxford, cultivated the new dialect, including persons of such distinction as the Earls of Leicester, Arundel, Derby, and Essex ; the Countesses of Derby, Cumberland, and Warwick ; Lady Fitzwater, and Lady Mary Talbot.

It is always to be remembered, to Greene's credit, that, whatever were his private excesses, there is little or nothing of a corrupting tendency in his writings ; his style, though soft and effeminate, is distinguished by

---

[1] "The Repentance of Robert Greene," *Greene and Peele's Dramatic and Poetical Works* (Dyce), pp. 23-25.

fineness and delicacy of fancy, a quality which doubtless endeared him to female readers.   After a time his vein was exhausted, or his readers wearied of his sugary sweetness, and it then became necessary for him to find a new range of subjects.   The readiest road to make money was to gratify the public curiosity by a recital of his own varied experience of the world ; and accordingly, from 1590 till his death he continued to supply the book-sellers with tracts or romances of a personal nature, such as *Never too Late, A Groat's-worth of Wit bought with a Million of Repentance*, or with pamphlets which, under the generic title of " Coney-catching," exposed the artifices of the different kinds of sharper in town.   The Euphuistic style is as prominent in these as in *Menaphon* or the *Censure to Philautus*.   Thus *A Notable Discovery of Coosenage* (1591) opens with the following address, " To the young Gentlemen, Merchants, Apprentices, Farmers, and plain Countrymen " :—

Diogenes, gentlemen, from a counterfeit coiner of money became a current corrector of manners, as absolute in the one, as dissolute in the other ; time refineth men's affects, and their humours grow different by the distinction of age.   Poor Ovid, that amorously writ in his youth the art of love, complained in his exile amongst the Getes of his wanton follies.   And Socrates' age was virtuous, though his youth was licentious.   So, gentle-men, my younger years had uncertain thoughts, but now my ripe days call on to repentant deeds, and I sorrow as much to see others wilful, as I delighted once to be wanton.[1]

These are the postures of a rhetorician ; and though we need not conclude that Greene was a hypocrite in his outcries about repentance, he knew that Repentance paid. He was, in fact, a poor creature, without the manliness of Gascoigne or the genius of Marlowe, a rake, who, so far from being able to act up to the standard of Italian *virtù*, which his companions admired, was reduced to making money out of exhibitions of the weakness of his own will. While he preached to his fellow playwrights and the public, he continued to live as before, and he died of the

[1] Halliwell's Edition (1859), p. 3.

effects of a debauch on pickled herrings and Rhenish wine. His last illness was watched by the tender care of a poor woman, the wife of a shoemaker near Dowgate, with whom he lodged, and to whom he was largely in debt ; and he was buried in the New Church near Bedlam on the 4th September 1592.

None of Greene's dramas was published before his death, and the learned editor of his works, Mr. Dyce, considers it impossible to say at how early a date they were produced upon the stage.   While it is with hesitation that I express an opinion at variance with one proceeding from a source so accurate and acute, it seems to me that the evidence, external and internal, points clearly to the conclusion that all Greene's surviving plays were written after the production of Marlowe's *Tamburlaine*, and as this fact, if established, is of vital importance both critically, as throwing light on the genius of Greene, and historically, as illustrating the progress of the drama, I proceed to lay my reasons before the reader.

Mr. Collier believes that *Tamburlaine* was the first play written in blank verse that was acted in a public theatre.[1]   He is probably right, for the author in his prologue shows that he is venturing on an innovation :—

> From jigging veins of rhyming mother wits,
> And such conceits as clownage keeps in pay,
> We'll lead you to the stately tent of war,
> Where you shall hear the Scythian Tamburlaine
> Threatening the world with high astounding terms,
> And scourging kingdoms with his conquering sword.[2]

The effect of this play on the public taste was prodigious ; and followed as it shortly was by *Faustus*, and afterwards by Kyd's *Spanish Tragedy*, it shook the position of Greene and his school, who had hitherto been the most popular purveyors for the stage.   If we may trust the autobiographical novel, *A Groat's-worth of Wit*, Greene, after beginning his literary career as a writer of Euphuistic romance, had taken to play-writing as a means of supporting himself.   This would have been about 1585,

---

[1] *History of English Dramatic Poetry*, vol. iii. p. 112.
[2] Marlowe's *Works* (Dyce), p. 5.

when he had taken his M.A. degree, and left Cambridge.
He tells us in the tale referred to that he was turned to
this course by a player who had made a name by acting
in *Delphrygus* and *King of the Fairies*, names which seem
to point to the fact that a species of drama, founded on
classical fables, like Lyly's prose comedies, was then in
vogue.   Such a style would have been quite congenial
with the facile bent of Greene's fancy, and it is not
unreasonable to conjecture that he produced many plays
on such subjects written in "jigging rhymes," like George
Peele's *Arraignment of Paris*, and mixed perhaps with
passages of prose of the kind found in his own later
dramas, together with "such conceits as clownage keeps
in pay."   These lesser lights paled when Marlowe's genius
in all its splendour rose suddenly above the horizon ;
the public began to express their discontent with the
Euphuistic style ; and Greene was forced to defend his
practice.   Like all monarchs in possession who feel their
power to be on the decline, he affects disdain of the new
comer, and says in his address to the reader prefixed to
his *Perimedes the Blacksmith* (1588) :—

I keep my old course to potter up something in prose, using
mine old poesy (posy) *Omne tulit punctum*, although lately two
gentlemen poets made two madmen of Rome beat it out of their
paper bucklers, and had it in derision that I could not make my
verses jet (strut) upon the stage in tragical buskin, every word
filling the mouth like the faburden of Bo-Bell, daring God out of
heaven with that atheist Tamburlan, or blaspheming with the
mad priest of the sun ; but let me rather openly pocket up the
ass at Diogenes' hand than wantonly set out such impious instances of intolerable poetry, such mad and scoffing poets, that
have prophetical spirits as bred of Merlin's race.   If there be any
in England that set the end of scholarism in English blank-verse,
I think either it is the humour of a novice that tickles them with
self-love, or too much frequenting the hothouse (to use the
German proverb) hath sweat out all the greatest part of their wits.

Here it is plain that the writer reprobates in the first
place those Machiavellian principles on which, as I shall
show, Marlowe founded his drama ; and which Greene
alludes to in his *Repentance ;* and that in the second place

he makes a faint protest against the new-fangled blank
verse as a vehicle of dramatic expression.   It is to Greene's
credit that, to the end of his life, he endeavoured, even
when imitating Marlowe's manner, to carry out his own
principle of mingling instruction with amusement (*utile
dulci*) : all his plays have a faint shadow of a moral in
them.   But in point of style he soon found that he must
surrender to his formidable rival : public taste after the
appearance of *Tamburlaine* insisted on a certain amount
of rant, rodomontade, bloodshed, and villainy, in sounding
blank verse ; and as the following extracts from his dramas
show, Greene did his best to follow in the footsteps of
the reigning favourite.   In his *Orlando Furioso*, Sacripant,
having been mortally wounded by Orlando, makes his
departure with the following not unsuccessful imitation of
Marlowe in his worst moments :—

> Phœbus, put on thy sable-suited wreath,
> Clad all thy spheres in dark and mourning weeds,
> Parched be the earth to drink up every spring :
> Let corn and trees be blasted from above ;
> Heaven turned to brass, and earth to wedge of steel ;
> The world to cinders.   Mars, come thundering down,
> And never sheath thy swift revenging sword,
> Till, like the deluge in Deucalion's days,
> The highest mountains swim in streams of blood.
> Heaven, earth, men, beasts, and every living thing,
> Consume and end with County Sacripant.[1]

In *A Looking Glass for London*, the joint work of
Greene and Lodge, Rasni, King of Nineveh, enters with
an address to his subordinate allies, which it will be at
once perceived is a copy of *Tamburlaine* :—

> So pace on, ye triumphant warriors,
> Make Venus' leman, armed in all his pomp,
> Bash at the brightness of your hardy looks,
> For you, the viceroys, are the cavaliers
> That wait on Rasni's royal mightiness.
> Boast, petty kings, and glory in your fates,
> That stars have made your fortunes climb so high
> To give attend on Rasni's excellence.[2]

---

[1] *Greene and Peele's Dramatic and Poetical Works* (Dyce), p. 108.
[2] *Ibid.* p. 117.

The Machiavellian morality, first introduced on the stage by Marlowe, is embodied in *James IV.*, where Ateukin, the flattering villain of the play, urges the king to murder his wife :—

> Why, prince, it is no murder in a king,
> To end another's life to save his own.
> For you are not as common people be,
> Who die and perish with a few men's tears ;
> But if you fail the state doth whole default,
> The realm is rent in twain in such a loss.
> And Aristotle holdeth this for true,
> Of evil needs [that] we must choose the least :
> Then better were it that a woman died,
> Than all the help of Scotland should be blent.
> 'Tis policy, my liege, in every state,
> To cut off members that disturb the head :
> And by corruption generation grows,
> And contraries maintain the world and state.[1]

The *History of Alphonsus, King of Arragon* (which from internal evidence I should take to be Greene's first play in Marlowe's manner), imitates closely the plan of action in *Tamburlaine*, and sometimes reproduces almost exactly that poet's exaggerated conception of *virtù*. Thus in *Tamburlaine*, the conqueror being about to die, commands his son Amyras to mount his chariot (drawn by vanquished kings) and to receive the crown. The prince resists vehemently, and when he at last obeys his father, he expresses himself as follows :—

> Heavens witness me with what a broken heart,
> And damned spirit I ascend this seat,
> And send my soul, before my father die,
> His anguish and his burning agony.[2]

When Alphonsus, in Greene's play, has conquered his enemies he magnanimously distributes all the crowns to his lieutenants, reserving to himself only the prospect of wider conquests. Albinius, one of his subordinates, professes his reluctance to avail himself of his leader's generosity in exactly the same manner as Marlowe's Amyras :—

[1] *Greene and Peele's Dramatic and Poetical Works* (Dyce), p. 211.
[2] Marlowe's *Works* (Dyce), p. 73.

Thou king of heaven, which by thy power divine,
Dost see the secret of each living heart,
Bear record now with what unwilling mind
I do receive the crown of Arragon.[1]

The play of Greene which bears the least resemblance to Marlowe is *The History of Friar Bacon and Friar Bungay ;* but I doubt not that the feeble episodes of magic, which form one portion of this ill-constructed drama, were the result of the vast popularity of *Faustus.*

While Greene was thus compelled to follow the triumphal march of Marlowe, his genius struggled to assert itself ; and his efforts to blend the violent and rhetorical vein and the loftier spirit of his rival with his own tastes and dramatic traditions, though unhappy enough in their artistic issues, give a certain character and interest to his plays. He was meant by nature for a novelist rather than for a playwright. His fancy, graceful, pastoral, and tender, is most at home when it is dwelling amid sheepfolds, and on the downs of Arcadia, and it is almost pathetic to see how gladly he escapes from the atmosphere of blood and thunder to which the public craving condemns him, to indulge for a moment in idyllic by-play in some retired woodland nook. His softer nature appears in the construction of his plots, which abound in tragic incidents, but invariably end happily. If his kings of Nineveh exalt themselves to heaven like Tamburlaine, it is only that they may afterwards repent in sackcloth and ashes, like the author of the *Groat's-worth of Wit.* He kills his *dramatis personæ* plentifully, but casually. In *Friar Bacon and Friar Bungay*, for example, two Oxford scholars go to consult Friar Bacon, who shows them in his magic glass their fathers engaged in a duel. Though previously friends, the young men at once fall to fighting, and stab each other on the stage. This incident is quite unnecessary to the action of the play. To relieve his scenes of horror or solemn rhetoric, the dramatist takes obvious pleasure in bringing in clowns who chatter together in a semi-Euphuistic dialect, and are soundly belaboured by a madman, or carried away on the back of a devil,

---

[1] *Greene and Peele's Dramatic and Poetical Works* (Dyce), p. 234.

after the manner of the old-fashioned Vice, for the gratification of the spectators. Marlowe disdained these antiquated tricks, which were doubtless surviving relics of Greene's original style.

What is best and most characteristic in the plays of Greene is the poetry of his pastoral landscape, and his representation of the characters of women ; in both of these respects he exercised an unmistakable influence on the genius of Shakespeare. His pastoral vein is displayed rather in his novels than in his dramas : it runs very happily through *Menaphon*, and even more so through *Pandosto*, a story which furnished Shakespeare with the outline of his *Winter's Tale*. But there are touches of the same quality in his *Orlando Furioso*, and the rustic scenes in *Friar Bacon and Friar Bungay* have much charm. Perhaps the best lines Greene ever wrote are those describing Oxford in the latter play :—

EMPEROR. Trust me, Plantagenet, these Oxford schools
Are richly seated near the river side :
The mountains full of fat and fallow deer,
The battling pastures lade with kine and flocks,
The town gorgeous with high-built colleges,
And scholars seemly in their grave attire,
Learnèd in searching principles of art.
What is thy judgment, Jaques Vandemast ?
VANDEMAST. That lordly are the buildings of the town,
Spacious the rooms, and full of pleasant walks ;
But for the doctors, how that they be learnèd,
It may be meanly, for aught I can hear.[1]

Greene was also the first to exhibit on the stage romantic ideals of female character. It is true that he could only represent one type of woman under various aspects,—loving, virtuous, constant, unfortunate, or all at once. So possessed was his imagination of the beauty of this ideal, that he bestowed it on a heroine who would seem least of all to deserve it—the fickle, treacherous, and roving Angelica of Ariosto ; and he even altered the story of the *Orlando Furioso* for the sake of his imaginary character. The type is reproduced in the somewhat insipid

---

[1] *Greene and Peele's Dramatic and Poetical Works* (Dyce), p. 166.

person of Margaret, the fair Maid of Fressingfield, who, wooed by Lord Lacy on behalf of Prince Edward, first falls in love with the deputy-wooer, and braves the displeasure of the Prince ; then, being deceived by a heartless stratagem of her lover to test her constancy, prepares to retire into a convent ; but afterwards, on hearing the explanation of Lacy, returns to his arms without any show of resentment. This unvarying conception is worked out with some care in Greene's romantic history of James IV., which, if we set aside its utter want of historic truth, is perhaps the best constructed of his plays. Virtue is here seen triumphant in Ida resisting the solicitations of the king ; tender fidelity shines in the persecuted Queen Dorothea ; both are developments of the simple character of Isabella in the *Groat's-worth of Wit;* in other words of Greene's own forsaken and deeply injured wife. There is something truly pathetic in the steadiness with which the poet kept this idea of moral beauty before his imagination throughout his dissolute career : the name which he assigned to the heroic Queen of James IV. was apparently that of his wife ; nor did he hesitate in his last moments to trust his wife's generosity for the repayment of the debt incurred to the poor people who had cared for him on his friendless deathbed.[1] Pale and shadowy as Greene's creations appear in comparison with the infinite variety of Shakespeare's heroines, it is honourable to him that he should have introduced on the English stage the prototype of Viola and Imogen.

Passing on to Peele, we find ourselves in company with a man less interesting in his life and character than Greene, but with a finer range of imagination, which gave an impulse of its own to the development of the drama. Like Greene, Peele, in his later plays, *Edward I.,* *The Battle of Alcazar,* and *David and Bethsabe,* felt the influence of Marlowe, but without, like Greene, succumbing to

---

[1] "Doll I charge thee by the love of our youth, and by my soul's rest, that thou wilt see this man paid ; for if he and his wife had not succoured me I had died on the streets."—Greene's last letter to his wife Dyce, *Account of R. Greene and his Writings* (Works), p. 57.

it ; on the other hand, his earlier manner, as exhibited in *The Arraignment of Paris*, evidently helped to inspire the style of Shakespeare in *A Midsummer Night's Dream*, and was afterwards extended by Ben Jonson in his Masques. Peele's *Old Wives' Tale*, in itself a poor performance, contains the germ of Milton's *Comus*.

The son of a silversmith in London, but descended from a gentle family in Devonshire, George Peele was born in 1558. He was entered first at Broadgates Hall —afterwards Pembroke College—Oxford ; but became a student of Christ Church in 1573, where he took his B.A. degree in 1577, and proceeded to his M.A. degree in 1579. At Oxford he wrote his *Tale of Troy*, which he did not publish, however, till 1589, and his fame as a poet seems to have been established in the University, for when Albertus Alasco, the Polish Prince Palatine, visited it in 1583, Peele with others was selected to entertain him with a comedy, entitled *Rivales*, and a tragedy on the subject of Dido. After this year he appears to have lived in London, supporting himself mainly by the devising of pageants or the writing of plays. In 1584 his *Arraignment of Paris* was acted before the Queen by the children of the chapel ; in 1585 he devised the pageant for the Lord Mayor's show. When Essex and his troops in 1589 set sail for Spain, Peele wrote a " Farewell " for them, in blank verse, full of the enthusiasm which had animated the nation since the defeat of the Spanish Armada in the previous year ; and on Essex's return he welcomed him with *An Eclogue Gratulatory* in the semi-archaic pastoral style, which had been made fashionable by Spenser's *Shepherd's Calendar*. He was at this time one of the actors in the Blackfriars Theatre, having a house opposite on the Bank-side, where he lived with his wife and daughter ; and I imagine that during this period most of his surviving plays were written. His *Chronicle of Edward the First* and his *Battle of Alcazar* (if it be his), both probably produced shortly before, or not long after, 1590, show unmistakable traces of the influence of Marlowe ; the *Old Wives' Tale*, though it was not printed till 1595,

might be taken for an earlier production, though a hexameter line in it, quoted in ridicule from Gabriel Harvey,
looks like a reference to the quarrel which began in 1592
between that person and Thomas Nash.[1] *David and Bethsabe*, not printed till 1599, when Peele was dead, was,
I doubt not, written after the appearance of *Tamburlaine*.
Peele was one of the companions of Greene and Marlowe,
and resembled them in the manner of his life. He
appears to have been in his day almost as celebrated as
Theodore Hook for his practical jokes, but the wit in most
of these, if they are truly reported, would in latter times
have found its proper appreciation in a police court. He
died, according to Meres,[2] of disease, towards the close of
the sixteenth century.

Two only of Peele's dramas require detailed notice,
The Arraignment of Paris and *David and Bethsabe*. The
former is of special interest as an example of the classical-
romantic play, composed mainly for the gratification
of the learning and vanity of Elizabeth, after the
Moralities had fallen into their decline, and before
Tamburlaine had given a new stimulus to the public taste.
In respect of its subject it belongs to the school of Lyly,
but it is constructed with great ingenuity out of a variety
of materials. It is divided into five Acts, in the orthodox
manner of Seneca, whose influence is also visible in the
Prologue, spoken by Ate, who announces the curse which
is to fall on Troy from—

> The fatal fruit
> Raught from the golden tree of Proserpine.[3]

But the first Act is full of a charming stream of pastoral
verse, in which Pan, Faunus, Silvanus, Pomona, and
Flora, prepare to welcome the rival goddesses on Mount
Ida. The following beautiful passage shows the spirit
and style of their discourse :—

---

[1] O that I might,—but I may not, woe to my destiny therefore !
From G. Harvey's *Encomium Lauri ;* quoted in ridicule by Huanebango in
Peele's play.

[2] *Palladis Tamia* (1598), *Shakspere Allusion Books*, part i. p. 164.

[3] *Greene and Peele's Dramatic and Poetical Works* (Dyce), p. 351.

> Not Iris in her pride and bravery
> Adorns her arch with such variety ;
> Nor doth the milk-white way, in frosty night,
> Appear so fair and beautiful in sight,
> As done these fields and groves and sweetest bowers,
> Bestrewed and decked with parti-coloured flowers.
> Along the bubbling brooks and silver glide,
> That at the bottom do in silence slide ;
> The water-flowers and lilies on the banks,
> Like blazing comets, burgen [burgeon] all in ranks ;
> Under the hawthorn and the poplar tree,
> Where sacred Phœbe may delight to be,
> The primrose, and the purple hyacinth,
> The dainty violet, and the wholesome minth,
> The double daisy, and the cowslip, queen
> Of summer flowers, do overpeer the green ;
> And round about the valley as ye pass,
> Ye may ne see for peeping flowers the grass :
> That well the mighty Juno, and the rest,
> May boldly think to be a welcome guest
> On Ida hills, when, to approve the thing,
> The Queen of Flowers prepares a second spring.[1]

Paris and Œnone appear as pastoral lovers, and sing a melodious song of "Cupid's curse." In the second Act the goddesses present themselves to Paris for the award, and after a show of pageants, like those in *The Tempest*, the apple is adjudged. The third Act introduces a new element in the discourse of the Spenserian shepherds, Hobbinol, Diggon, and Thenot, who bewail the death of Colin from love, in consequence of the cruelty of the shepherdess Thestylis. Mercury also appears to Œnone, now forsaken by Paris, and tells her that he is sent to summon the faithless shepherd to account for his award before the council of the gods. The council is held in the fourth Act, the scene being Diana's bower on Ida ; Paris makes an oration in blank verse before the assembly, pleading the irresistible power of beauty ; and the gods, considering the original question to be still open, debate it with much heat ; till at last Apollo suggests that the judgment as to woman's worthiness must be given by a woman, and that Diana, to whom the region belongs, shall be appointed arbitress. This proposal, being

---

[1] *Green and Peele's Dramatic and Poetical Works* (Dyce), p. 352

agreed to, opens the way to a splendid compliment to Elizabeth in the fifth Act, in which Diana "describes the Nymph Eliza, a figure of the Queen" :—

It is enough and, goddesses, attend.
There wons within these pleasant shady woods—
Where neither storm nor sun's distemperature
Have power to hurt by cruel heat or cold,
Under the climate of the milder heaven,
Where seldom lights Jove's angry thunderbolt,
For favour of that sovereign earthly peer ;
Where whistling winds make music 'mong the trees,—
Far from disturbance of our country gods,
Amid the cypress-springs, a gracious nymph,
That honours Dian for her chastity,
And likes the labours well of Phœbe's groves ;
The place Elyzium hight, and of the place
Her name that governs there Eliza is ;
A kingdom that may well compare with mine,
An ancient seat of kings, a second Troy,
Y-compassed round with a commodious sea :
Her people are y-clepèd Angeli,
Or, if I miss, a letter is the most :
She giveth laws of justice and of peace ;
And on her head, as fits her fortune best,
She wears a wreath of laurel, gold and palm :
Her robes of purple and of scarlet dye.
Her veil of white as best befits a maid :
Her ancestors live in the House of Fame :
She giveth arms of happy victory,
And flowers to deck her lions crowned with gold.
This peerless nymph whom heaven and earth belove,
In whom do meet so many gifts in one,
On whom our country gods so often gaze,
In honour of whose name the Muses sing ;
In state Queen Juno's peer, for power in arms,
And virtues of the mind, Minerva's mate ;
As fair and lovely as the Queen of Love,
As chaste as Dian in her chaste desires :
The same is she, if Phœbe do no wrong,
To whom this ball in merit doth belong.[1]

Of course the justice of this sentence is at once perceived. Venus, Pallas, and Juno resign their claims, and the three Fates "deliver the ball of gold to the Queen's own hands."

In this admirable piece, fancy, taste, and scholarship

[1] *Greene and Peele's Dramatic and Poetical Works* (Dyce), p. 368.

unite to promote the required end ; and it may safely be
pronounced that a more exquisite tribute of poetical flattery
was never offered upon any stage.   The *Arraignment
of Paris* is a monument of the extent and limitation of
Peele's dramatic powers.   His genius was the product of
the love of pageantry and masquerade, a legacy of the
allegorical tradition of the Middle Ages, which was
deeply rooted in the taste of the English people under
Elizabeth.   He was a master of whatever was pictorial
and external in theatrical art.   As a dramatic rhetorician
he was hardly, if at all, inferior to Marlowe ; in wealth of
poetic diction, warmth of fancy, and richness of invention,
he perhaps excelled all his contemporaries whose names are
usually coupled with his own.   But in the higher creative
powers he was deficient.   His plays contain no character
that rouses the affection ; no imaginative situation that
awakens the interest ; no universal sentiment that touches
the heart.   Whatever can be done by fancy, taste, knowledge
and judgment, Peele does, and his excellences and defects
are nowhere better seen than in his *David and Bethsabe.*

His vast intellectual superiority to Greene is apparent
when we compare this drama with Greene's Scriptural
play, *A Looking Glass for London.*   Both plays are plainly
inspired by Marlowe's *Tamburlaine.*   But whereas Greene
seizes crudely on Marlowe's external characteristics, and,
following the bent of his own nature, introduces vaunting
kings merely in order afterwards to plunge them into
affliction, and purge them with repentance, Peele perceives that, in the representation of lawless will, the
new poet has discovered a dramatic principle capable
of almost limitless extension.   He avails himself of it,
but unlike Marlowe, keeps his imagination within due
bounds, and never loses sight of the old tragic principle
of the consequences of sin.   His admirable judgment is
shown in the selection of his subject, which at once gives him
scope for sounding eloquence in the speeches assigned to
such characters as Absalom, Shimei, and Achitophel, and
enables him to preserve a moral balance in the progress
of the action.   His contrasts are developed with great

dramatic dexterity. All his warmth of fancy is lavished with incomparable splendour of diction on the opening scene, describing the beauty of the bathing Bathsheba, but at the same time the noble simplicity of the Bible narrative is maintained, and the course and connection of events are brought with consummate skill into the compass of the play. The severity of the moral is enforced by the chorus, which makes its appearance twice, first to announce prophetically David's coming woes, and again after the death of Absalom. These two choruses sufficiently emphasise the distinction between the styles of Peele and Marlowe :—

> O proud revolt of a presumptuous man,
> Laying his bridle in the neck of sin,
> Ready to bear him past his grave to hell !
> Like as the fatal raven, that in his voice
> Carries the dreadful summons of our deaths,
> Flies by the fair Arabian spiceries,
> Her pleasant gardens and delightsome parks,
> Seeming to curse them with his hoarse exclaims,
> And yet doth stoop with hungry violence
> Upon a piece of hateful carrion ;
> So wretched man, displeased with those delights
> Would yield a quickening savour to his soul,
> Pursues with eager and unstanched thirst
> The greedy longings of his loathsome flesh.
> If holy David so shook hands with sin,
> What shall our baser spirits glory in ? [1]

The second chorus moralises on the downfall of the arrogant Absalom :—

> O dreadful precedent of his just doom,
> Whose holy heart is never touched with ruth
> Of fickle beauty or of glorious shape,
> But with the virtue of an upright soul,
> Humble and zealous in his inward thoughts,
> Though in his person loathsome and deformed ! [2]

Both morals are worked out with so much simplicity and propriety in the action, that we almost forget how very little of his own imagination Peele has put into the play. He has created no character ; he has added no

---

[1] *Greene and Peele's Dramatic and Poetical Works* (Dyce), p. 469.
[2] *Ibid.* p. 482.

touch of pathos to the materials with which he deals : his merit lies solely in the playwright's craft of having provided a fitting metrical and dramatic form for the historic narrative of the Old Testament.

Christopher Marlowe, on the other hand, the great genius who may be justly called the founder of English poetic drama, kept no measure with the ancient traditions of the stage. Between him and the Puritanic element in the nation the rupture was absolute and complete. Will, or force, or passion, freed from the restraints of Conscience and Law, was the motive of all his dramatic composition, and his work shows at once the strength and weakness which comes from the determined pursuit of a single principle of art.

He was the son of John Marlowe, a shoemaker of Canterbury, where he was born in February 1563-64. Educated first at the King's School in that town, he was removed to Cambridge in March 1580-81, and matriculated as Pensioner of Benet, now Corpus Christi, College. He took his B.A. degree in 1583, and that of M.A. in 1587. From a passage in Greene's *Groat's-worth of Wit*, Marlowe would appear to have come while at Cambridge under the influence of Francis Kett, Fellow of Benet College, who held heretical opinions, for which, eventually, in 1589, he was burned at Norwich. External and internal evidence shows also that Marlowe had closely studied the works of Machiavelli, and had thus settled on a line of thought which he before long found means of expressing in a dramatic form. His first play, *Tamburlaine*, appears to have been acted before 1587 ; and it was soon followed by *Faustus*. *The Jew of Malta* was produced about 1589 or 1590 ; *Edward II.* and *The Massacre at Paris* were probably the last works that came from his hand. While in London he lived much with Greene, Peele, Lodge and Nash, the band of university scholars who supported themselves by writing for, and sometimes acting on, the public stage. Of his personal habits nothing more is known than can be gathered from Greene's " Address " ; and all that seems certain is, that he came to a violent end in 1594, being stabbed in the eye by one Francis Archer, a serving-man, who was his rival in love. His memory, which was peculiarly hateful to the Puritans, has perhaps been blackened to excess by their malignity ; but it is likely enough that a man animated by the spirit which breathes in the dramas of Marlowe endeavoured to embody his opinions in his life.

His plays have of late years been frequently considered mainly on their technical side, and considering the vast effect produced on the English poetical drama by Marlowe's adoption of blank verse, this is not unnatural. As regards his own genius, however, it is not the right way of judging ; for it is plain enough that he made his technical innovation because blank verse was the only vehicle of poetical expression adequate to the character of his thought ; we see from *Tamburlaine* that he regarded eloquence as a means to a practical end ; and the style of his dramas therefore cannot be fully appreciated without a full comprehension of the intellectual and imaginative motive which inspired his composition. What was this ? Mr. Symonds says it may be described by the phrase *L'Amour de l'Impossible*.[1] In one sense, measuring the vastness of Marlowe's conceptions and his exaggerated manner of expression by the limits of actual fact, this is true ; but in another sense, looking to his philosophy, to his ideas of dramatic creation, and to his view of rhetoric, it is the exact opposite of the truth. Marlowe composed on a principle which was simple, direct, and consistent with itself, but which was distinct from every principle which had hitherto inspired tragic conception, though some approach to it had been made in the tragedies of Seneca. In Marlowe's plays there is no trace of the hereditary curse of sin, which elevates the tone of Sophocles and Æschylus ; there is no trace of the doctrine of physical Necessity, which is the ruling thought of Seneca ; there is but seldom any trace of the conflict between good and evil, conscience and passion, which prevails in the Miracle Plays

[1] *Shakspere's Predecessors*, pp. 608-622.

and Moralities.   What we do find in Marlowe is Seneca's
exaltation of the freedom of the human will, dis-
sociated from the idea of Necessity, and joined with
Machiavelli's principle of the excellence of *virtù*.   This
principle is represented under a great variety of aspects ;
sometimes in the energy of a single heroic character, as
in *Tamburlaine ;* sometimes in the pursuit of unlawful
knowledge, as in *Faustus ;* again, in *The Jew of Malta*, in
the boundless hatred and revenge of Barabas ; in Guise
plotting the massacre of the Huguenots out of cold-blooded
policy ; and in Mortimer planning the murder of Edward
II. from purely personal ambition.   Incidentally, no doubt,
in some of these instances, the indulgence of unrestrained
passion brings ruin in its train ; but it is not so much for
the sake of the moral that Marlowe composed his tragedies,
as because his imagination delighted in the exhibition of
the vast and tremendous consequences produced by the
determined exercise of will in pursuit of selfish objects.
So far from loving grandiosity and extravagance for their
own sake, the violence of his conceptions springs from a
belief of what is possible to the resolved and daring soul.

The first play in which he embodied these ideas was
Tamburlaine, the hero of which is evidently meant to be
the incarnation of *virtù*.   The development of his character and fortunes is represented with great splendour of
description and with finely contrasted effects.   Feebleness
and imbecility of purpose are in the opening scene vividly
portrayed in the person of Mycetes, the idiotic King of
Persia, who is very characteristically represented as unable
to express himself with dignity, and who is deposed by
his own brother Cosroe.   Cosroe's vain delight in the
mere external grandeur of royalty brings into relief the
manly simplicity of Tamburlaine, whose person is thus
vividly described :—

> Of stature tall and straightly fashioned,
> Like his desire, lift upwards and divine.
>
> .   .   .   .
>
> Pale of complexion wrought in him with passion,
> Thirsting with sovereignty and love of arms ;

His lofty brows in folds do figure death,
And in their smoothness amity and life ;
About them hangs a knot of amber hair,
Wrapped in curls, as fierce Achilles' was,
On which the breath of heaven delights to play,
Making it dance with wanton majesty ;
His arms and fingers long and sinewy,
Betokening valour and excess of strength ;
In every part proportioned like the man
Should make the world subdued to Tamburlaine.[1]

When Cosroe, by the aid of this Scythian shepherd, has acquired the crown of Persia, he thinks that his simple ally will be satisfied with being made regent of Persia and lieutenant-general of his armies, while he himself departs " to ride in triumph through Persepolis." Hardly has he gone when Tamburlaine appeals to his captains—

TAMBURLAINE.	Why, say, Theridamas, wilt thou be king ?
THERIDAMAS.	Nay, though I praise it, I can live without it.
TAMB.	What say my other friends ? will you be kings ?
TECHELLES.	I, if I could, with all heart my lord.
TAMB.	Why that's well said, Techelles : so would I,
	And so would you, my masters, would you not ?
USUMCASANE.	What then, my lord ?
TAMB.	Why then, Casane, shall we wish for aught
	The world affords in greatest novelty,
	And rest attemptless, faint, and destitute ?
	Methinks we should not. I am strongly moved
	That, if I should desire the Persian crown,
	I could attain it with a wondrous ease.[2]

Thereupon he marches against Cosroe, defeats, and kills him. Nothing is allowed to stand in the way of his will. He has carried off Zenocrate, daughter of the Soldan of Egypt, and she, though betrothed to the prince of Arabia, falls in love with her captor. Agydas, her faithful attendant, upbraids her for her inconstancy, and incurs the resentment of Tamburlaine, who sends him a dagger after the fashion of the Roman emperors. Agydas understands the message, and displays the stoical *virtù* of Seneca's philosophical heroes :—

It says, Agydas, thou shalt surely die,
And of extremities elect the least ;

---

[1] Marlowe's *Works* (Dyce), p. 13.   [2] *Ibid.* p. 17.

> More honour and less pain it may procure,
> To die by this resolved hand of thine,
> Than stay the torments he and heaven have sworn.
> Then haste, Agydas, and prevent the plagues
> Which thy prolonged fates may draw on thee :
> Go, wander free from fear of tyrant's rage,
> Removed from the torments and the hell,
> Wherewith he may excruciate thy soul ;
> And let Agydas by Agydas die,—
> And with this stab slumber eternally.[1]

Another kind of *virtù*, determined resolution, even in
defeat, is represented in the person of Bajazeth, who being
overcome by Tamburlaine is treated by him with horrible
cruelty, being carried about with his wife in a cage, and
offered food like a wild beast. This he refuses, and at
last brains himself against the bars of the cage. Tamburlaine, in spite of his ruthless ferocity when opposed,
can be clement and magnanimous. He is very anxious
to spare the city of Damascus, as being part of the
dominions of Zenocrate's father ; but his terms are refused
by the inhabitants. When too late the virgins of the
place go out to appeal to him for mercy. A fierce
struggle then proceeds in his breast between his inclination and his will. He enters " all in black and very
melancholy." He orders all the inhabitants to be put to
the sword ; and then at once breaks into a passionate
soliloquy, declaring his love for Zenocrate. Even this
must not interfere with his resolves :—

> But how unseemly is it for my sex,
> My discipline of arms and chivalry,
> My nature and the terror of my name,
> To harbour thoughts effeminate and faint ?
> Save only that in beauty's just applause,
> With whose instinct the soul of man is touched ;
> And every warrior that is rapt with love
> Of fame, of valour, and of victory,
> Must needs have beauty beat on his conceits :
> I, thus conceiving and subduing both,
> That which hath stooped the chiefest of the gods,
> Even from the fiery-spangled veil of heaven,
> To feel the lovely warmth of shepherds' flames,

---

[1] Marlowe's *Works* (Dyce), p. 21.

> And mask in cottages of strowéd reeds,
> Shall give the world to note, for all my birth,
> That virtue solely is the sum of glory,
> And fashions men with true nobility.[1]

The character of Zenocrate is admirably conceived as a foil to that of her husband. At first an unwilling captive to Tamburlaine, she is subdued by his all-powerful will, and gives him a boundless love and devotion; but her softer nature is condemned to suffer agonies in the desolation of her native land, the overthrow of her father, the death of her betrothed, the massacre of her country-women, and the tragic end of Bajazeth and his empress, over whose adversity Tamburlaine has forced her to exult; yet the first part of the drama ends with her exaltation as the wife of the universal conqueror.

The second part of *Tamburlaine* is of inferior interest, but it contains some passages of gorgeous rhetoric. Marlowe seems to have felt that he must exhibit the will of his hero, not only triumphant over his enemies, but in opposition to the power of death, nature, and even of God himself. After fresh victories he loses his wife Zenocrate; and as human endeavours can here avail him nothing he finds an issue for his emotions in empty bombast :—

> What is she dead?   Techelles, draw thy sword,
> And wound the earth that it may cleave in twain,
> And we descend into th' infernal vaults
> To hale the fatal sisters by the hair,
> And throw them in the triple moat of hell,
> For taking hence my fair Zenocrate.[2]

One of his sons proves a coward; Tamburlaine kills him. Here, too, his feelings require an outlet in blasphemy, which he hurls against the deity under the name of Jove :—

> By Mahomet, thy mighty friend, I swear,
> In sending to my issue such a soul,
> Created of the many dregs of earth,
> The scum and tartar of the elements,

---

[1] Marlowe's *Works* (Dyce), p. 33.   [2] *Ibid.* p. 52.

> Wherein was neither courage, strength, or wit,
> But folly, sloth, and damnéd idleness,
> Thou hast procured a greater enemy
> Than he that darted mountains at thy head,
> Shaking the burden mighty Atlas bears,
> Whereat thou, trembling, hidd'st thee in the air,
> Clothed with a pitchy cloud for being seen.[1]

To show his contempt for religion he bids his soldiers burn the Koran, and defies Mahomet, in words which the poet probably intended to be understood allegorically :—

> Now, Mahomet, if thou have any power,
> Come down thyself and work a miracle.
> Thou art not worthy to be worshippéd,
> That suffer'st flames of fire to burn the writ
> Wherein the sum of thy religion rests :
> Why send'st thou not a furious whirlwind down'
> To blow thy Alcoran up to the throne
> Where men report thou sitt'st by God himself ?
> Or vengeance on the head of Tamburlaine,
> That shakes his sword against thy majesty,
> And spurns the abstracts of thy foolish laws ?
> Well, soldiers, Mahomet remains in hell ;
> He cannot hear the voice of Tamburlaine.
> Seek out another Godhead to adore ;
> The God that sits in heaven, if any God,
> For he is God alone, and none but he.[2]

In the face of his own coming death he maintains his pride unbendingly, for he feels that his spirit will live in his children.   After the famous scene in which he appears driving the conquered kings in his chariot, he feels his end approaching, and addresses his followers :—

> Give me a map ; then let me see how much
> Is left for me to conquer all the world,
> That these my boys may finish all my wants.[3]

The map being brought, he traces on it the course of his conquests, and concludes with the following splendid exhortation :—

> Look here, my boys ; see what a world of ground
> Lies westward from the midst of Cancer's line.

---

[1] Marlowe's *Works* (Dyce), p. 62.   [2] *Ibid.* p. 69.   [3] *Ibid.* p. 72.

Unto the rising of the earthly globe,
Whereas the sun, declining from our sight,
Begins the day with our antipodes !
And shall I die, and this unconqueréd ?
Lo, here, my sons are all the golden mines
More worth than Asia and the world beside ;
And from the Antarctic Pole, eastward behold
As much more land as never was descried,
Wherein are rocks of pearl that shine as bright
As all the lamps that beautify the sky :
And shall I die, and this unconqueréd ?
No, lovely boys, what death forbids my life,
That let your lives command in spite of death ?[1]

Tamburlaine is the type of resistless force ; Faustus, on the other hand, represents the resolute pursuit of knowledge as an instrument of material power. This is unquestionably Marlowe's greatest play ; it is indeed one of the greatest plays that the world possesses ; for in it the poet has been compelled, by the nature of his story and his own profound imagination, to pass beyond the limits of Machiavellism, and to sound the depths of the human heart, in an exhibition of that conflict between Will and Conscience which was embodied in outline in the old Moralities, and found its highest development in the dramas of Shakespeare. In this tragedy accordingly there are more distinct traces of the primitive traditions of the English theatre than in any other of Marlowe's works. Faustus is described in the prologue as " born of parents base of stock." He has acquired the highest academic fame as a disputant in theology ; but having exhausted the sciences without positive result, he aims at magical power :—

O what a world of profit and delight,
Of power, of honour, and omnipotence,
Is promised to the studious artizan !
All things that move between the quiet poles
Shall be at my command : emperors and kings
Are but obeyéd in their several provinces ;
But his dominion that exceeds in this
Stretcheth as far as doth the mind of man ;
A sound magician is a demigod :
Here tire, my brains, to gain a deity.[2]

---

[1] Marlowe's *Works* (Dyce), p. 72. [2] *Ibid.* p. 80.

He consults the wizards Valdes and Cornelius as to his initiation : Valdes says he can get all the wealth of the world "if learned Faustus be but resolute"; to which Faustus replies :—

> Valdes, as resolute am I in this
> As thou to live : therefore object it not.[1]

In the same temper, when calling up the spirits, he encourages himself: "Then fear not Faustus to be resolute." He summons Mephistophilis from hell, and the interest of the situation lies in the character of this fiend, and in the alternations of Faustus between resolution and repentance. There is a grandeur of conception in the following dialogue beyond anything to be found in Goethe's *Faust*, however superior the latter may be in intellectual subtlety :—

FAUSTUS.   Tell me, what is that Lucifer thy lord.
MEPHISTOPHILIS. Arch-regent and commander of all spirits.
F.   Was not that Lucifer an angel once ?
M.   Yes, Faustus, and most dearly loved of God.
F.   How comes it then that he is prince of devils ?
M.   O, by aspiring pride and insolence,
     For which God threw him from the face of heaven.
F.   And what are you that live with Lucifer ?
M.   Unhappy spirits that fell with Lucifer,
     Conspired against our God with Lucifer,
     And are for ever damned with Lucifer.
F.   Where are you damned ?
M.   In hell.
F.   How comes it then that thou art out of hell ?
M.   Why this is hell, nor am I out of it :
     Thinkst thou that I that saw the face of God,
     And tasted the eternal joys of heaven,
     Am not tormented with ten thousand hells
     In being deprived of everlasting bliss ?
     O Faustus, leave these frivolous demands,
     Which strike a terror to my fainting soul.[2]

Resolute as Faustus is in the face of declarations like these, his spirit wavers after he has despatched Mephistophilis to Lucifer to make promise of his soul.

---

[1] Marlowe's *Works* (Dyce), p. 81.   [2] *Ibid.* p. 83.

FAUSTUS. Now, Faustus,
          Must thou be damned, canst thou not be saved.
          What boots it then to think on God or heaven?
          Away with such vain fancies, and despair ;
          Despair in God, and trust in Belzebub.
          Now go not back, Faustus, be resolute :
          Why waver'st thou?   O something soundeth in mine ear,
          "Abjure this magic, turn to God again."
          Why He loves thee not.
          The God thou serv'st is thine own appetite,
          Wherein is fixed the love of Belzebub.[1]

At this point the Good and Evil Angels, the traditional figures of the ancient Moralities, enter—though it is to be presumed that they are invisible to Faustus—and exhort him in different directions. Faustus makes a contract with Lucifer, sealed with his blood, to give him his soul at the end of twenty-four years, during which period Mephistophilis is to fulfil all his desires. Hardly, however, is the bargain made, when Faustus's resolution once more begins to falter, and so acute is his logic that it seems as if a way were still open to repentance.

FAUSTUS. When I behold the heavens then I repent,
          And curse thee, wicked Mephistophilis,
          Because thou hast deprived me of these joys.
MEPHISTOPHILIS. 'Twas thine own seeking, Faustus, thank thyself.
          But thinkst thou heaven is such a glorious thing?
          I tell thee, Faustus, 'tis not half so fair
          As thou, or any man that breathes on earth.
F. How prov'st thou that?
M. 'Twas made for man ; then he's more excellent.
F. If heaven was made for man, 'twas made for me,
          I will renounce this magic and repent.

          [*Enter Good and Evil Angels.*]

G. A. Faustus, repent ; yet God will pity thee.
E. A. Thou art a spirit ; God cannot pity thee.
F. Who buzzeth in mine ears? I am a spirit?
          Be I a devil, yet God may pity me ;
          Yea, God will pity me, if I repent.
E. A. Ay, but Faustus never shall repent.
F. My heart is hardened, I cannot repent :
          Scarce can I name, salvation, faith, or heaven :
          Swords, poisons, halters, and envenomed steel,

---

[1] Marlowe's *Works* (Dyce), p. 85.

Are laid before me to despatch myself,
And long ere this I should have done the deed,
Had not sweet pleasure conquered deep despair,
Have not I made blind Homer sing to me
Of Alexander's love and Œnon's death ?
And hath not he that built the walls of Thebes,
With ravishing sound of his melodious harp,
Made music with my Mephistophilis ?
Why should I die then, or, basely, despair ?
I am resolved ; Faustus shall not repent.[1]

Yet once more there is a sharp struggle in his heart. Mephistophilis, questioned who made the world, refuses to reply :—

FAUSTUS.   Think, Faustus, upon God who made the world.
MEPHISTOPHILIS. Remember this.   [*Exit.*]
F.   Ay, go, accursed spirit, to ugly hell ;
                 'Tis thou hast damned distresséd Faustus' soul :
                 Is't not too late ?
[*Re-enter Good Angel and Evil Angel.*]
E. A.   Too late.
G. A.   Never too late, if Faustus will repent.
E. A.   If thou repent, devils will tear thee in pieces.
G. A.   Repent, and they shall never raze thy skin.
                                                    [*Exeunt.*]
F.   O Christ, my Saviour, my Saviour,
                 Help to save distresséd Faustus' soul.[2]

But Lucifer and Belzebub, summoned by Mephisto-philis, appear and threaten Faustus with the consequences of his violated contract ; the scholar submits, and his Good Angel vanishes, not to appear again till the close of the drama, when the door of repentance is shut for ever. The course of the action henceforth moves on, through a variety of magical adventures, up to the final soliloquy, which must be known by heart to every lover of English litera-ture, and which, as a representation of mental agony and despair, is only equalled, in the whole range of the world's poetry, by the speech of Satan to the Sun in *Paradise Lost.*

As Tamburlaine, the rude shepherd, is Marlowe's example of physical *virtù,* and Faustus, the base-born scholar, of intellectual *virtù,* so Barabas the Jew, member of a detested, despised, and persecuted nation, is his type

---

[1] Marlowe's *Works* (Dyce), p. 88.   [2] *Ibid.* p. 89.

of steadfast resolution in pursuit of implacable revenge. Possessed of almost boundless wealth, acquired by his own industry and skill, Barabas finds himself suddenly deprived of it by the injustice of the Christian defenders of Malta, who forfeit it to procure the ransom of the island from the Turks. The Jew by his crafty devices recovers a large portion, but, being determined to inflict vengeance on the Governor of the island, he makes use of the love of the Governor's son for Abigail, his own daughter, to embroil the young man in a quarrel with Mathias, another youth upon whom Abigail has bestowed her affections. Henceforth the course of his revenge drives the Jew to a succession of murderous devices to secure his own safety. The rivals kill each other ; Abigail in despair becomes a Christian ; Barabas, to punish her, sends her poison by the hand of Ithamore, a Turkish slave whom he has purchased to be an instrument of his villainies ; she, perceiving herself to be dying, confesses to a friar the nature of the fraud which has brought about the death of the Governor's son ; the friar, though forbidden by his religion to reveal the secrets of the confessional, lets Barabas see that he is aware of his crime, and, to save himself from this danger, the Jew murders the friar with the aid of Ithamore, who in turn, needing money for his own pleasures, extorts it from his master by threatening to denounce him. Barabas poisons him ; as, however, Ithamore has confessed before his death, the Jew is arrested, but, when at the point of execution, escapes by simulating suicide. His body is thrown without the walls ; he betrays the city to the Turks, and is by them made Governor ; but feeling his position to be insecure among the Christians, he arranges with them to betray the Turks into their hands. Having devised an infernal machine to destroy the Turks, he entices them into his trap, and is about to set it in motion, when the Christian Governor, to whom the working of the engine has been explained, makes him the victim of his own contrivance, and earns the gratitude of the Turks by exposing the nature of the plot against their lives.

This is indeed a story of villainy worthy of the

Italian Renaissance; and it is with propriety that the poet introduces Machiavelli as the Prologue, letting his own admiration for the Italian philosopher plainly appear in the speech which he assigns to him :—

> Albeit the world thinks Machiavel is dead,
> Yet was his soul but flown beyond the Alps,
> And now the Guise is dead is come from France,
> To view this land and frolic with his friends.
> To some perhaps my name is odious ;
> But such as love me guard me from their tongues,
> And let them know that I am Machiavel,
> And weigh not men, and therefore not men's words.
> Admired I am of those that hate me most.
> Though some speak openly against my books,
> Yet will they read me, and thereby attain
> To Peter's chair ; and when they cast me off
> Are poisoned by my climbing followers.
> I count religion but a childish toy,
> And hold there is no sin but ignorance.[1]

The sordid villainy of Barabas towards the close of the play deprives him of all claim to sympathy ; but in the opening acts, where he is the victim of injustice, there is, from a human point of view, some excuse for his fierce desire of revenge, and it is interesting to see with what skill Marlowe makes him turn so-called Christian logic against the persecutors of his race. Thus, when he is persuading his daughter to consent to his frauds, we find the following argument :—

> ABIGAIL.   What, shall I be betrothed to Lodowick ?
> BARABAS.   It's no sin to deceive a heretic ;
> For they themselves hold it a principle
> Faith is not to be kept with heretics.
> But all are heretics that are not Jews ;
> This follows well, and therefore, daughter, fear not.[2]

Even when Barabas' crimes recoil upon his own head, it is plain that the poet is not without sympathy for a villain so determined :—

> BARABAS.   And, villains, know you cannot help me now.
> Then, Barabas, breathe forth thy latest fate,
> And in the fury of thy torments strive
> To end thy life with resolution.[3]

---

[1] Marlowe's *Works* (Dyce), p. 145.   [2] *Ibid.* p. 159.   [3] *Ibid.* p. 178.

Of the two remaining plays, the work entirely of
Marlowe's hand, one, *Edward II.*, is historical ; the other,
The Massacre at Paris, represents a contemporary tragedy :
in both the principle of *virtù* is predominant.   The former
exhibits it, chiefly by way of contrast, in the character of
a weak king, who, though mastered by a passion for an
unworthy favourite, has not resolution to sustain him
against his nobility ; and who, when, by a flash of energy,
he has got possession of the persons of his nobles, lacks
determination to put them to death.   The closing scenes
of the play, which exhibit the abdication and murder of
Edward, are only inferior, as representations of despairing
agony, to the last moments of Faustus, and vividly recall
the speech of Satan to Beelzebub in *Paradise Lost ;*—

> Fallen Cherub, to be weak is miserable,
> Doing or suffering.

On the other hand, the virtue of resolution is illustrated
in the character of young Mortimer, whose Machiavellian
self-seeking carries him to the height of power :—

> The prince I rule, the queen do I command,
> And with a lowly congé to the ground,
> The proudest lords salute me as I pass ;
> I seal, I cancel, I do what I will.
> Feared am I more than loved ;—let me be feared,
> And when I frown make all the court look pale.
> I view the prince with Aristarchus' eyes,
> Whose looks were as a breeching to a boy.
> They thrust upon me this protectorship,
> And sue to me for that that I desire ;
> While at the council-table grave enough,
> And not unlike a bashful puritan,
> First I complain of imbecility,
> Saying it is *onus quam gravissimum*,
> Till, being interrupted by my friends,
> *Suscepi* that *provinciam*, as they term it,
> And to conclude, I am Protector now :
> Now is all sure : the Queen and Mortimer
> Shall rule the realm, the King ; and none rule me.
> Mine enemies will I plague, my friends advance ;
> And what I list command who dares control ?
> *Major sum quam cui possit fortuna nocere :*

> And that this be the coronation day,
> It pleaseth me and Isabel the queen.[1]

But the will of Mortimer encounters the stronger will of the young Edward ; he falls, yet in his fall preserves the grandeur of resolution, exclaiming :—

> Base Fortune, now I see that in thy wheel
> There is a point to which when men aspire,
> They tumble headlong down : that point I touched,
> And seeing there was no place to mount up higher,
> Why should I grieve at my declining fall ?
> Farewell, fair Queen ; weep not for Mortimer,
> That scorns the world, and, as a traveller,
> Goes to discover countries yet unknown.[2]

Virtù in *The Massacre at Paris* is represented by Guise who, despising religion and the rest of mankind, makes fanatical passions the instrument of his own towering ambition.   His character, as is usual with Marlowe, is developed in soliloquy :—

> Now, Guise, begin those deep-engendered thoughts
> To burst abroad, those never dying flames,
> Which cannot be extinguished but by blood.
> Oft have I levelled, and at last have learned
> That peril is the chiefest way to happiness,
> And resolution honours' fairest aim.
> What glory is there in a common good,
> That hangs for every peasant to achieve ?
> That like I best that flies beyond my reach.
> Set me to scale the high Pyramides,
> And therein set the diadem of France ;
> I'll either rend it with my nails to naught,
> Or mount the top with my aspiring wing,
> Although my downfall be the deepest hell.
>
> .   .   .   .   .   .
>
> The plot is laid, and things shall come to pass,
> When resolution strives for victory.[3]

These examples, I think, are sufficient to show the predominant character of Marlowe's tragic genius : they prove also that it was an intellectual principle, much more than, as some have supposed, his adoption of blank verse, which wrought the great revolution in the English drama.

---

[1] Marlowe's *Works* (Dyce), p. 218.   [2] *Ibid.* p. 221.   [3] *Ibid.* p. 228.

Marlowe used blank verse, because it was the only possible
vehicle for his thought : of him more than of almost any
other poet is it true that the style is the man.   His diction
shows no trace of considered art, but seems to follow,
with amazing flexibility, every movement of his energetic
imagination.   Sometimes it flows slowly with the solemn
depth of reflection : more often it rushes forward to its
immediate goal with a fiery volubility ; and at times it is
full of throbs and spasms like groans extorted from a
resolute spirit in torment.   Its prevailing character of
swiftness is indicated by the great number of lines which end
trisyllabically, or polysyllabically: unexpected irregularities
of movement produce sublime effects, as in the clashing of
accents, and of iambic and trochaic rhythms, in such a
line as—

> Sée where Christ's blóod stréams in the firmamént,[1]

or in the broken-backed Alexandrine, so suggestive of
mental agony :—

> O Pythagoras metempsychosis ! were that true.[2]

Marlowe mixes Latin lines with English just as it suits his
purpose for the moment, making Faustus, for example,
quote, with true tragic effect, the *O lente lente currite noctis
equi*, of Ovid's *Amores*, in the last moments of his life.
And, generally speaking, the " mightiness," which Ben
Jonson rightly ascribes to his lines, proceeds from a
certain elemental force and simplicity of genius, which
spontaneously finds great words for the expression of
great emotions.   Drayton says of him very finely—

> Next Marlowe, bathed in the Thespian springs,
> Had in him those brave translunary things
> That the first poets had ; his raptures were
> All air and fire, which made his verses clear ;
> For that fine madness still he did retain,
> Which rightly should possess a poet's brain.[3]

Such raptures burst forth spontaneously into splendid
flashes of poetical expression,—

---

[1] Marlowe's *Works* (Dyce), p. 134.   [2] *Ibid.*
[3] Drayton, *To Henry Reynolds Of Poets and Poesie* (1627).

> O thou art fairer than the evening air,
> Clad in the beauty of a thousand stars ! [1]

Marlowe has often been accused, and justly, of violence and exaggeration. He shared the admiration which every man of intelligence must feel for the genius of Lucan, the first book of whose *Pharsalia* he had translated, obviously while still a young man ; and he introduces into his tragedies many of those rhetorical effects which in Lucan are the product of studied declamation. But I doubt whether Marlowe loved bombast for its own sake. The curses and blasphemies in which his *dramatis personæ* indulge, the vastness of their images, and the violence of their metaphors, are rather the result of a boundless conception of the power of the human will, which, as we have seen, was with him the motive of dramatic composition. Eloquence was the means by which he thought the imagination should be roused to the great possibilities of action : he shows how essential is the gift to the kingly character, by exhibiting its defect in the imbecile King Mycetes, and its power, in the mouth of Tamburlaine, to raise above itself the sober and steadfast temper of men like Theridamas.

> Won with thy words and conquered with thy looks,
> I yield myself, my men, and horse to thee,
> To be partaker of thy good and ill,
> As long as life maintains Theridamas. [2]

On this account, too, Theridamas excuses himself for his treason to Cosroe, after he has listened to some of Tamburlaine's most swelling periods :—

> You see, my lord, what working words he hath ;
> But when you see his actions top his speech,
> Your speech will stay, or so extol his worth,
> As I shall be commended and excused
> For turning my poor charge to his direction. [3]

The splendour of Marlowe's genius, however, must not blind us to its limitations. In basing tragedy mainly on

---

[1] Marlowe's *Works* (Dyce), p. 132.   [2] *Ibid.* p. 12.   [3] *Ibid.* p. 15.

the representation of the absolute freedom and energetic exercise of the human will, he cut himself off from representing the true order of Nature and human society, the action of which is determined by a conflict between many opposing wills. Hence his dramas are very ill-constructed. He cares nothing for the development of plot, and concentrates his whole attention on the exhibition of an abstract principle, embodied for the moment in a single character. When he has placed his leading personage in a situation where his ruling purpose—be it desire of conquest, as in Tamburlaine; revenge, as in Barabas; ambition, as in Mortimer or Guise—can have full play, he is satisfied. His invention occupies itself with finding means to remove the obstacles that oppose the achievement of this central purpose, and up to a certain point his method produces interesting dramatic situations: the first two acts, for example, of the *Jew of Malta* are excellent. But after a time the action drags through want of complexity; and then the exhibition of character becomes mechanical and monotonous.

Again, Marlowe's theory of dramatic action is contrary to the constitution of human nature: it eliminates the factor of Conscience. Following Machiavelli in counting " religion but a childish toy," and in holding that there was " no sin but ignorance," he exalted " resolution " as the highest of human virtues. But this is a principle better suited for melodrama than for tragedy. If there is something fascinating in the steady purpose of even a savage like Tamburlaine, or of a villain like Barabas, how infinitely inferior in dramatic interest is such a representation, to the portrayal of that complexity of motives and circumstance which produces the entanglements of human conduct! How ill does it compare, for example, with the situations produced by the *irresolution* of Hamlet and Macbeth, or by the senile folly of Lear? Shakespeare was not less keenly alive than Marlowe to the dramatic value of resolute will as a principle of action: he has represented it in the character of Iago, working on the credulous weakness of Othello; but he has constructed

the complex action of his tragedy in such a way that the
spectators are never left for a moment in doubt as to
the moral judgment they ought to pass on the various
characters.   For the same reason *Faustus* is Marlowe's
greatest and most interesting play, because in that alone
does he give a sustained representation of the state of a
human soul torn between the conflicting principles of good
and evil.

Once more.   The narrowness of Marlowe's conception
of Man and Nature is seen in his representations of female
character.   As his tendency was to make everything in
his plays bow before the march of some supreme, irresistible
will, the weaker feminine element in Nature was necessarily
thrust by him into a subordinate position.   Marlowe, like
Greene, can represent only one type of woman—a being
who becomes the devoted, but almost passive, instrument
of masculine resolution.   Zenocrate, Abigail, Isabel, and
(strange to say) Catherine de Medicis, all of them cast in
this mould, are the only creations he can show against
the endless varieties of female character depicted in the
dramas of Shakespeare.

Considering these features in Marlowe's dramas, we
cannot fail to be struck with the contrast between his
genius and the genius of men like Sidney and Spenser.
The two latter reflect the chivalrous element that was still
strong in English society, the high principle of honour,
the elevation of sentiment, the sense of duty and religion.
From all these restraining principles in the conscience
of the nation Marlowe cut himself off ; and by his exaltation of the Machiavellian principle severed his connection, not only with Puritanism, but with whatever was
most lofty and noble in the history of England.   On the
other hand, his imagination was borne along, as Spenser's
and Sidney's never was, on the full stream of a great
national movement.   His dramas were produced just
before, and just after, the defeat of the Spanish Armada—
that is to say at the moment when the people were
awakening to the full consciousness of greatness in their
dangers and their destinies.   It was no mere coincidence

that made the representation of resolute will the dominant feature in his plays: in so doing he expressed an enthusiastic sentiment, uppermost for the moment in the minds of all classes ; and many characteristics of his style were the unconscious reflection, quite as much of what was passing in the minds of his audience, as of his own tastes and sentiments. He represents the buccaneering spirit, then prevailing in a large portion of the English people, just as Sidney and Spenser represent the knightly traditions handed down from the times of the Crusades ; and when the " groundlings," who formed so large a portion of the spectators in the theatre, listened to Marlowe's thundering declamations and his gorgeous rhetoric, describing the extent of the globe and all its treasures of gold, and pearls, and precious stones, they saw in the ideal representation, not merely the greatness of Tamburlaine, but the possibilities opened to them by the enterprise of their own living heroes, Drake and Hawkins.

The extraordinary mixture of sublimity and vulgarity in Marlowe's plays helped to determine the course of English dramatic taste. To judges like Drayton his excellence lay in the rare qualities of his imagination ; but such critics were the minority, and the bulk of his audience delighted mainly in his faults, his loud declamation, the violence of his conceptions, and the atmosphere of blood that pervaded his tragedies. His superficial characteristics were easily imitated, and the popular applause which they drew forth excited emulation among those who were capable of giving them further extension. *Tamburlaine* and *Faustus* were received with enthusiasm, but the popularity of both paled before that of *The Spanish Tragedy*, a play written in the new style of blank verse, and probably first acted about 1588.[1]

Thomas Kyd, the author of this piece, was the son of a London scrivener, and must have been born about the same time as Greene. He was educated at Merchant Taylors' School, where he obtained some knowledge of Latin ; he was also acquainted with French, Italian,

---

[1] Dodsley's *Old Plays* (1874), vol. v. p. 1.

and Spanish.   Scarcely anything is known of his
life ; he was, however, the author not only of the drama
just mentioned, but of *Cornelia*, a play translated from
the French of Garnier ; while from internal evidence
there would seem to be little doubt that *Soliman and
Perseda*, a tragedy first printed in 1599, but perhaps acted
some years earlier, was also the work of his pen.   He was
an intimate friend of Marlowe, and after the death of
that poet was accused of sharing his irreligious opinions.
Oldys says that he died in poverty in 1595.

The direct testimony of Ben Jonson, as well as the
casual satirical allusions of Shakespeare, indicate the deep
impression which *The Spanish Tragedy* made upon the
public taste.   Jonson in the induction to *Cynthia's Revels*
makes one of his "children" say : "Another whom it
hath pleased Nature to furnish with more beard than
brain, prunes his mustaccio, lisps, and with some score of
affected oaths, swears down all that sit about him : 'That
the old *Hieronimo*, as it was first acted, was the only best
and judiciously penn'd play of Europe.'"   Again he says,
in the induction to *Bartholomew Fair*, acted in 1614:
"He that will swear *Jeronimo* or *Andronicus* are the best
plays yet, shall pass unexcepted at here, as a man whose
judgment shows it is constant, and hath stood still these
five-and-twenty or thirty years."   And there can be very
little doubt that the ardent appreciation of Kyd's pieces
shown by the public provoked the criticism of Thomas
Nash in his preface to Greene's *Menaphon*, published in
1589 : "It is a common practice nowadays amongst a
sort of shifting companions that run through every art
and thrive by none, to learn the trade of *Noverint*,
wherein they were born, and busy themselves with the
endeavours of art, that could scarcely latinise their
neck verse if they should have need ; yet English Seneca
read by candle-light yields many good sentences, as *Blood
is a beggar*, and so forth ; and if you entreat him fair in a
frosty morning he will afford you whole *Hamlets*, I should
say handfuls of tragical speeches.   But O grief ! *tempus
edax rerum ;* what's that will last always?   The sea

exhaled by drops will in continuance be dry, and Seneca, let blood line by line and page by page, at length must needs die to our stage, which makes his famished followers to imitate the *Kid* in Æsop, who, enamoured with the fox's new fangles, forsook all hopes of life to leap into a new occupation ; and these men, renouncing all possi- bilities of credit or estimation, to intermeddle with Italian translations."

Kyd's style in the *Spanish Tragedy* is indeed made up of the more vulgar elements in Seneca's and Marlowe's plays, without the intellectual quality that distinguishes either.   From Seneca he borrows ghosts and " sentences " ; Marlowe provides him with precedents of rant and bloodshed.   By the help of these hints, Kyd managed to put together a tragedy utterly devoid of any true tragic motive, but not wanting in striking scenes and melodramatic effects, and acceptable accordingly to that public taste which is always caught by loud noise and glaring colours.

The *Spanish Tragedy* is, I think, plainly written in emulation of Marlowe's *Jew of Malta*.   Like that tragedy it represents an action of cold-blooded murder followed by a sanguinary revenge.   But whereas Marlowe gives a certain intellectual interest to his play, by making the Jew the victim of injustice, in a situation contrived with great force and probability, Kyd is utterly unable to produce such a complication among his *dramatis personæ* as shall prepare the way for the *denouement* he has imagined. Marlowe's conception of will and resolution is beyond him : he is obliged to work up to his central situation by employing the machinery of Seneca.   The *machinery* only ; for Seneca's idea of Necessity has nothing to do with the evolution of Kyd's plot.   The ghost of a certain Andrea, a young nobleman of Spain, appears in the opening scene, and tells the audience a long story of his adventures in the world below, which have ended in his introduction to Revenge through the clemency of Proser- pine.   Revenge then appears, and promises to exhibit to Andrea a spectacle which shall prove extremely agreeable

to him, and which is in fact the action of the play.   But
when the real play begins, it becomes at once obvious
that the appearance of these two spectral figures is
unnecessary, for Andrea has been killed in battle, and has
no particular reason to complain of his treatment at the
hands of Balthazar, his conqueror and natural enemy.
The latter has been taken prisoner by the joint energy
of Lorenzo, son of the Duke of Castile, and Horatio, son of
Hieronimo, Marshal of Spain ; and when we first see these
personages, Balthazar is committed to the charge of
Lorenzo, with whom he forms a strong friendship.   He
falls in love with Bell 'Imperia, Lorenzo's sister, who has
been betrothed to Andrea.   This lady easily consoles
herself for her lover's death by transferring her affections
to Horatio, but pretends that she does so out of consideration for Andrea, in the following truly ridiculous
speech :—

> Yet what avails to wail Andrea's death,
> From whence Horatio proves my second love ?
> Had he not loved Andrea as he did,
> He could not sit in Bell 'Imperia's thoughts.
> But how can love find harbour in my breast,
> Till I revenge the death of my belov'd ?
> Yes, second love shall further my revenge :
> I'll love Horatio, my Andrea's friend,
> The more to spite the Prince that wrought his end.

Horatio and Bell 'Imperia appoint to meet in the
orchard of Hieronimo's garden, where there is a love-scene
worthy of the *Rehearsal*.   Lorenzo and Balthazar are,
however, aware of the assignation : they disguise themselves, and—though in the opening scenes they have been
presented as chivalrous young princes—kill Horatio,
just as if they had been first and second murderers in
a play of Shakespeare.   Roused by the noise, Hieronimo
comes running into the orchard " in his shirt," exclaiming,
in words which Kyd's contemporaries were never tired of
ridiculing, " What outcries pluck me from my naked bed ? "
He finds the body of his son hanging on a tree.   His
reason totters from the shock, but he recovers himself,

and bends all his energies to discover the murderers. Bell 'Imperia, who knows, in some way not explained, that her brother and Balthazar are guilty of the crime, sends word of this to Hieronimo ; and Lorenzo, fearing that the latter suspects the truth, resolves, just like Barabas in the *Jew of Malta*, to remove the sole witnesses of the deed, his own man and Balthazar's, who had helped in the assassination. He sets one of them to murder the other, and in the following speech we have the *Jew of Malta* pure and simple :—

LORENZO

Now to confirm the complot thou hast cast,
Of all these practices I'll spread the watch,
Upon precise commandment from the king,
Strongly to guard the place, where Pedringano
This night shall murder hapless Serberine.
Thus must we work that will avoid distrust :
Thus must we practice to prevent mishap :
And thus one ill another must expulse.
This sly enquiry of Hieronimo
For Bell 'Imperia breeds suspicion ;
And this suspicion bodes a further ill.
As for myself, I know my secret fault,
And so do they ; but I have dealt for them.
They that for coin their souls endangered
To save my life, for coin shall venture theirs :
And better 'tis that base companions die,
Than by their life to hazard our good haps ;
Nor shall they live, for me to fear their faith :
I'll trust myself, myself shall be my friend,
For die they shall, slaves are ordained to no other end.

Henceforth the play runs its bloody course of murder mixed with madness. Pedringano is hanged for the murder of Serberine, but Bell 'Imperia, between whom and Balthazar a marriage has been arranged, on political grounds, by Spain and Portugal, plots with Hieronimo, and the pair contrive a resolute plan of revenge. Under plea of presenting an entertainment at Balthazar's marriage, Hieronimo devises a play in which Lorenzo, Balthazar, Bell 'Imperia and himself are all to take parts. Isabella, Hieronimo's wife and Horatio's mother, who has gone mad for the loss of her son, stabs herself on the stage, an incident that proves no obstacle to the entertainment, in which, Hieronimo kills Lorenzo, and Bell 'Imperia kills Balthazar and afterwards herself. Hieronimo is arrested, but after explaining his conduct, he manages in the first place to stab the Duke of Castile, Lorenzo's father, who is quite innocent of his son's misdeeds, and then plunges the knife into his own heart. Balthazar's father, the Viceroy of Portugal, and the King of Spain, who have been spectators of the play, are left like Moonshine and Lion in Bottom's drama " to bury the dead," which they do with much composure ; the Viceroy, however, gives his attendants the following remarkable instructions :—

> And thou, Don Pedro, do the like for us ;
> Take up our hapless son, untimely slain ;
> Set me with him, and him with woeful me
> Upon the main-mast of a ship unmanned ;
> And let the wind and tide hale me along
> To Scylla's barking and untamed gulph ;
> Or to the loathsome pool of Acheron,
> To weep my want for my sweet Balthazar.

The Ghost and Revenge, who have throughout been commenting upon the various acts in this human tragedy, now enter, and the former, though he has hitherto expressed himself as somewhat dissatisfied with the progress of events, acknowledges that he has no fault to find with the conclusion :—

> Ay, now my hopes have end in their effects,
> When blood and sorrow finish my desires :
> Horatio murdered in his father's bower ;
> Vile Serberine by Pedringano slain ;
> False Pedringano hanged by quaint device ;
> Fair Isabella by herself misdone ;
> Prince Balthazar by Bell 'Imperia stabbed ;
> The Duke of Castile and his wicked son
> Both done to death by old Hieronimo ;
> My Bell 'Imperia fallen, as Dido fell,
> And good Hieronimo slain by himself.
> Ay, these were spectacles to please my soul.

And no doubt the spectators were as much pleased

as the Ghost. In truth the whole play shows that the average taste of Elizabethan audiences was not far raised above that of the Spanish populace at a bull-fight. By the vehemence and vigour of their craving for striking stage effects and strong emotions, they compelled even the greatest dramatists to make their tragic action bloody, and though Shakespeare, by the grandeur of his genius, kept this dramatic tendency on the whole within bounds, it cannot be denied that even in him there are scenes, which it is difficult reasonably to defend from Voltaire's reproach of " barbarism."

Marlowe and his school must therefore submit to a mixed verdict. By the vehemence of their imagination they undoubtedly prepared the way for a new conception of tragic action. Even in the work of Marlowe's vulgar-souled disciple, Kyd, there are some great strokes of nature. The whole of his energy was thrown into the conception of the half mad character of Hieronimo, and though he was incapable of working out his idea completely, the situation in his play lent itself to additions by finer hands ; one scene in particular, inserted probably by Ben Jonson, between a painter and Hieronimo, in which the latter describes how he desires to have himself depicted in the act of discovering his son's body, is among the masterpieces of English tragedy.[1] Appropriated by the invention of Shakespeare, deprived of its stupid and savage ideas of revenge, reunited with ideas of conscience, religion, and philosophy, the character of the half-mad old Marshal served as the ground-work for the character of Hamlet ; while the whole situation devised by Kyd, including the contrivance of the play within the play, was made to contribute to the immortal representation of tragic irresolution, afforded by the story of the Prince of Denmark. But judged on its own merits, the *Spanish Tragedy* is an index of the low level to which the English drama must have sunk, had the poets continued to gratify the uneducated tastes which for the moment prevailed in the theatre. Kyd's genius—as far as he had

[1] Dodsley's *Old Plays*, vol. v. pp. 117-124.

any—represented the appetites of the Saxon portion of the nation, divorced alike from the religious instincts of the Teutonic race, illustrated generations before in the writings of Wycliffe and Langland; from the spirit of Norman chivalry, embodied in the creations of Sidney; from the learning of the Latin Church, preserved in the allegory of Spenser; in a word, from all those historic influences which had continued to soften and elevate the character of the entire nation. Severed from its great traditions, the English temper then, as often since, tended to concentrate itself on the pursuit of material ends, and might even have embraced the malign ideals recommended to it by the Italian Renaissance. It is not the smallest part of Shakespeare's glory, that he should have saved the popular imagination from itself, and, by restoring to tragedy the elements of conscience, religion, and chivalry, which Marlowe had expelled from it, should have convinced his countrymen of " the purpose of playing "; namely, " to show virtue her own feature, scorn her own image, and the very age and body of the time his form and pressure."

END OF VOL. II.